FIFTH EDITION
PRINCIPLES OF
Macro-Monetary ECONOMICS

Kishore G. Kulkarni

Professor of Economics, CB77
Metropolitan State College of Denver
P.O. Box 173362
Denver, Colorado 80217-3362

Adjunct Professor
University of Colorado—Boulder
Colorado School of Mines
Josef Korbel School of International Studies (JKSIS)
University of Denver

KENDALL/HUNT PUBLISHING COMPANY
4050 Westmark Drive   Dubuque, Iowa 52002

Cover images:
Dollar bills © JupiterImages Corporation, Inc.
Euro image © JupiterImages Corporation, Inc.
Yen image © JupiterImages Corporation, Inc.

Copyright © 1986, 1992, 1997, 2003, 2009 by Kendall/Hunt Publishing Company

ISBN 978-0-7575-5914-3

All rights reserved. No part of this publication may be reproduced, stored in a retrieval system, or transmitted, in any form or by any means, electronic, mechanical, photocopying, recording, or otherwise, without the prior written permission of the copyright owner.

Printed in the United States of America
10 9 8 7 6 5 4 3 2

To the three beautiful girls in my life:

Jayashree, Lina, and Aditi,

who insisted that they be named!

Contents

List of Illustrations vii
Preface ix

Chapter 1   **Introduction and a Few Definitions** 1

Chapter 2   **Laws of Demand and Supply** 15

Chapter 3   **National Income Accounting and GDP Calculation** 33

Chapter 4   **Gold Standard Mechanism and Empirical Evidence** 45

Chapter 5   **Essence of Classical Economics: Pre-1930s Era** 63

Chapter 6   **The Keynesian Macroeconomics: Commodity or Product Market** 75

Chapter 7   **Money, Money Supply, and Banking Business in the United States, and the Money Creation Process of Banks** 103

Chapter 8   **Federal Reserve Banking and Monetary Policy Making in the U.S.** 127

Chapter 9   **The Old Quantity Theory by Irving Fisher and Monetary Theory of Classical Economists** 141

Chapter 10   **The Keynesian Macro-Monetary Theory and the Keynesian Chain** 153

Chapter 11   **Revised Quantity Theory of Money, the Optimum Monetary Policy, and Monetarism** 169

Chapter 12   **Inflation: Causes, Consequences, and Cures** 187

Chapter 13   **Business Fluctuations, Business Cycles, and Their Theoretical Explanations** 199

Chapter 14	**Phillips Curve Hypothesis: Old and New and Effectiveness of Macro Policies**	.211
Chapter 15	**Expectations Hypotheses and Time Lags Involved in Policy Effectiveness**	.223
Chapter 16	**Macro-Monetary Theory in Open Economy Setting: IS-LM and BB Curve Derivations and Mundell-Fleming Model**	.235
Chapter 17	**Recent Developments in Macro-Monetary Theory: A Short Review**	.265
Chapter 18	**Aggregate Demand and Aggregate Supply Analysis**	.277
Chapter 19	**Survey of International Monetary System: Past, Present, and Future**	.295
Chapter 20	**Fiscal and Monetary Policy-Making in the United States: A Historical Review**	.307
	Index	.323

List of Illustrations

Figure 1.1	Circular Flow: Real and Money Flows	7
Figure 1.2	Production Possibilities Curve (PPC)	8
Figure 1.3	Graphing Variables from Table 1.1	11
Figure 1.4	Slope of a Linear Relationship	11
Figure 1.5	Slope of a Non-linear Relationship	12
Figure 2.1	Demand Curve and Inverse Relationship	19
Figure 2.2	Shifts of Demand Curve	20
Figure 2.3	Consumer Surplus: Area under the Demand Curve	23
Figure 2.4	Supply Curve: Price and Quantity Supplied	25
Figure 2.5	Producer Surplus	26
Figure 2.6	Market Demand Curve from Individual Demand Curves	27
Figure 2.7	Market Equilibrium	28
Figure 2.8	Economic Consequences of Price Ceiling Policy	30
Figure 2.9	Economic Consequences of Price Floor Policy	32
Figure 4.1	Quantity Supplied of Gold and Quantity Demanded of Gold for Non-Monetary Purposes	49
Figure 4.2	Demand for Gold for Non-Monetary Purposes and Supply of Gold	50
Figure 4.3	Supply for Gold and Demand for Gold for Non-Monetary Purposes	51
Figure 5.1	Wage Rate vs. Quantity of Labor	68
Figure 5.2	Supply and Demand for Loanable Funds	70
Figure 5.3	Demand for Supply of Loanable Funds	71
Figure 5.4	Product Market Equilibrium	72
Figure 6.1	Consumption Function	79
Figure 6.2	Saving Function Derived from Consumption Function	83
Figure 6.3	Optimum Investment Determination	85
Figure 6.4	Total Expenditure Curve	86
Figure 6.5	Equilibrium Income Determination	88
Figure 6.6	Aggregate Demand with Active Government	92
Figure 7.1	Year-on-Year Change in the Components of the U.S. Money Supply: 1960–2007	123
Figure 7.2	Currency Component of the U.S. Money Supply: 1959–2007	124
Figure 7.3	The Euro Money Supply: 1998–2007	126
Figure 10.1	Transactions Demand for Money	156
Figure 10.2	Liquidity Preference Curve	159
Figure 10.3	Equilibrium of Money Market	161
Figure 10.4	Effectiveness of Monetary Policy: Keynesian View	162

Figure 10.5	Investment Determination	163
Figure 10.6	Liquidity Trap and Monetary Policy	165
Figure 11.1	Demand for Money: Two Interpretations	176
Figure 11.2	Money-Market Equilibrium	177
Figure 13.1	Business Fluctuations	202
Figure 14.1	The Original Phillips Curve	214
Figure 14.2	Modern Times Phillips Curve	216
Figure 14.3	Accelerationists' Phillips Curve	219
Figure 14.4	Clockwise Movement: Non-Accelerationist's Hypothesis	220
Figure 15.1	Effectiveness of the Policy	225
Figure 15.2	Expectation Hypothesis and Policy Effectiveness	229
Figure 15.3	Time Lags in Policy Action	232
Figure 16.1	Derivation of IS Curve	239
Figure 16.2	Money Market Equilibrium	241
Figure 16.3	LM Curve	242
Figure 16.4	General Equilibrium and IS-LM	244
Figure 16.5	Monetary Policy and IS-LM	246
Figure 16.6	Effectiveness of Fiscal Policy and IS-LM	247
Figure 16.7	Liquidity Trap and Demand for Monetary Curve	248
Figure 16.8	Liquidity Trap and LM Curve	249
Figure 16.9	Classical Model and IS-LM	250
Figure 16.10	Demand for and Supply of Foreign Exchange	255
Figure 16.11	BB Curve	256
Figure 16.12	General Equilibrium Using the BB Curve	257
Figure 16.13	Expansionary Monetary Policy in Open Economy Setting	258
Figure 17.1	Aggregate Demand-Aggregate Supply Model: Classical Economists' and Keynesian View	268
Figure 17.2	Monetarist World and Aggregate Demand-Aggregate Supply Model	270
Figure 17.3	Stagflation and Aggregate Demand-Aggregate Supply Model	271
Figure 17.4	The Magic of Laffer Curve	272
Figure 18.1	Money Market Equilibrium and the Price Changes	280
Figure 18.2	IS-LM Framework and the Price Level Change	281
Figure 18.3	Derivation of the Aggregate Demand Schedule	282
Figure 18.4	Labor Market Analysis and the Optimum Employment	284
Figure 18.5	Equilibrium of the Labor Market	285
Figure 18.6	Total Product Curve	286
Figure 18.7	Aggregate Demand and Aggregate Supply Curves	287
Figure 18.8	Classical Beliefs in the Labor Market	289
Figure 18.9	Classical Beliefs and the Aggregate Demand and Supply Curves	290
Figure 18.10	Keynesian Analysis and the Labor Market Equilibrium	291
Figure 18.11	Keynesian Analysis and the Aggregate Supply Curve	292
Figure 20.1	The Laffer Curve	312

Preface

It is a great pleasure to present this new edition; it reflects many substantial changes from the fourth edition of *Principles of Macro-monetary Theory*, which was published by Kendall/Hunt Publishing Company in 2003. (The first edition of this book was published in 1986.) Over the years we have sold numerous copies and have received many valuable comments from thousands of students who read these chapters. In the fifth edition, while we have revised all chapters to infuse modern literature, ideas, theories, and updated data, we have also developed a very useful study guide that includes lists of important concepts, definitions, and practice problems. This book, therefore, includes the most simplified explanations of macroeconomic concepts and theories taught in any introductory macroeconomics class. In describing the theories, we have assumed that students have no prior background in economics, and that this is their first class in economic theory.

Hence, this edition begins with simple demand and supply arguments that govern the market mechanism, then builds on this subject with monetary developments such as money supply making in the United States and the gold standard system. The main macroeconomic theories are presented in a historical perspective starting with classical economics (Chapter 5) and Keynesian economics (Chapter 6). The functioning of institutions such as U.S. commercial banks (financial institutions) and the Federal Reserve System are discussed in Chapters 7 and 8, respectively. The essence of monetary theories of classical economics (à la old quantity theory of money) is presented in Chapter 9, while Keynesian arguments are summarized in Chapter 10. Even if a Keynesian bias is visible up through Chapter 10, the next chapter (Chapter 11) is completely "anti-Keynes" in terms of development of monetarism. Using the work of Friedman, we evaluate a number of problems with traditional Keynesian thinking.

In later chapters, we visit such important problems as inflation (Chapter 12), business cycles (Chapter 13), and the Phillips Curve Hypothesis (Chapter 14). Our analysis of the Phillips curve trade off brings in policy analysis with a major contribution from the Expectation Hypotheses summarized in Chapter 15. The last five chapters include somewhat modern developments in macro theory, including aggregate demand-aggregate supply framework (Chapter 16), a summary of new developments in macro monetary theory (Chapter 17), and macro theory in an open economy setting (Chapter 18). Open economy analysis requires some knowledge of the international monetary system, which is covered in Chapter 19. Chapter 20 integrates the theories with practice and evidence from the U.S. economy. It shows that contemporary theories had a major impact on policy making and that studying economics is, in fact, a fruitful, applicable, and relevant venture.

I am quite sure that students will find the new edition interesting, stimulating, and rewarding. Instructors can choose to focus on certain chapters, but in general a typical one-semester macro class would cover all of this information.

In completing this revision, I have incurred an enormous debt to numerous individuals. Mr. Stace Nicholson, one of my brightest graduate students, served as an invaluable research assistant. Without his many hours of hard work this revision could not have been finished on time. He was aptly supported by Ms. Sadie Cox and together they have made my work much easier. Mr. Michael Shanley and Ms. Camila Martins-Bekat took time from their busy schedules to read the proofs quickly and efficiently. Several faculty colleagues have supported this venture, either by their presence around me or by many useful discussions that have led to refining my thoughts in presenting this material. I inadvertently may miss some names in the following list, but the prominent inspiring individuals are:

- John P. Cochran, Dean, School of Business, Metropolitan State College of Denver
- Erick L. Erickson, Metropolitan State College of Denver
- Kamal Upadhyaya, University of New Haven
- Vani Kocherlakota, University of Nebraska-Kearney
- Debasri Mukherjee, Western Michigan University
- Vijaya Sharma, University of Colorado-Boulder
- Rod Eggert, Colorado School of Mines
- Ilene Grabel, University of Denver
- Tom Farer, University of Denver
- Lauren Davis, Colorado School of Mines
- Daniel Jerrett, Colorado School of Mines
- Robert McNown, University of Colorado-Boulder
- Jesus Valencia, Slippery Rock University
- Geetha Rajaram, Whittier College
- Bansi Sawhney, University of Baltimore
- Chaitram Talele, Columbia State College
- Varkey Titus, Macon State University

The thousands of students I teach at different institutions have provided unlimited energy and zeal and inspired me to complete this book. I was absolutely amazed to run into one exceptional student (Mr. Christopher Dratz) who, after reading my entire textbook in less than three days, scored high enough points on the Test of Understanding College Economics (TUCE) to receive credit for the macro class! Students such as Chris and many others, make teaching a very worthwhile profession. I owe a huge debt of gratitude to the curious young minds who give me compliments by their words or through their actions by attending my classes.

Completing this book also meant spending many hours away from family obligations. The understanding of my family members—my wife Jayashree, and our daughters Dr. Lina Kulkarni, DDS, and Aditi Kulkarni—to whom I dedicate this edition, is deeply appreciated. Editors and designers at Kendall/Hunt Publishing Company, Dubuque, Iowa, have been extremely cheerful and friendly. Ms. Ashley Blum, Jade Sprecher, and Ms. Karen Hoffmann spent long hours working on this project, provided guidance, and finished the book in time for early adoption. Their invaluable support and friendly attitude definitely made the revisions in this edition go very smoothly. I sincerely hope that readers like the exposition in this edition, and feel free to comment about its contents by sending an e-mail to my address: kulkarnk@mscd.edu.

Kishore G. Kulkarni
Denver, Colorado

Chapter 1

Introduction and a Few Definitions

SUMMARY

Economics is a field of study which, due to its broad scope, has often frustrated efforts to define it correctly and completely. The most widely accepted definition of economics comes from Lionel Robbins of Cambridge University: "Economics is a science that studies human behavior as a relationship between ends and scarce means that have alternate uses." In order to clarify this definition, this chapter presents a short explanation of collective versus individual ends or wants, as well as resources or means to attain them.

While economics in general is difficult to define, it is necessary to know the definitions of some specific key concepts in order to understand the subject. These concepts are presented in this chapter in turn with short explanations. *Microeconomics* and *macroeconomics,* or the study of small and large economic principles, respectively, are each briefly explained. Also, factors of production—*land, labor, capital,* and *enterprise*—are presented, as well as the returns to each. The concept of *opportunity cost* is explained, shedding light on the saying "there is no such thing as a free lunch."

To understand the concept of production, three questions must be answered: what to produce, how to produce, and for whom to produce? Each is integral for decision making, and this chapter presents the concept of *economic system* as a means for finding the appropriate answers and mobilizing the necessary resources. It is further noted that decision making in an economic system can either be dominated by government (communism) or by individuals (capitalism). In a capitalist system, consumers and producers make exchanges in what is termed as a *circular flow,* in either *real* or *money* terms (to explicate, a circular flow diagram is provided). Also, it is explained that economic decision making can fall into two categories: *positive economics* considers facts without value judgment, while *normative* economics is not based on absolute certainty and therefore tends to be more subjective. This chapter then shows the usefulness of a *production possibilities curve* in assessing graphically how effectively an economy employs resources in the production process.

Finally, the chapter uses graphs to illustrate fundamental concepts of economics, such as *independent* and *dependent variables* (representing either a positive or negative relationship), *quadrants*, and *slope*. Secondly, it explains in detail the graphing process and its ability to represent the relationship between dependent and independent variables as related to the slope. The graphs derive economic hypotheses, which are then used to construct the economic models integral to understanding the concepts used throughout this book.

Introduction 1.1

This textbook will begin by defining a few key concepts that are used extensively in economic literature. Many students will also realize that some of the economic concepts are so specific that they require more extensive explanation. Also, there is the philosophical question of whether economics is an art or a science. This is a very important and practical issue, as many schools include the economics department in the College of Arts, while others put it in the College of Business.

Another point of lively debate comes from attempts to define completely and correctly the term "economics." Some have called economics a science of supply and demand, others have referred to it as the art of understanding trade-off, and still others have defined it as the science of managing money! Jacob Viner of Harvard University defined economics "as something that the economists do." While this is of course a useless definition, it does serve to demonstrate the frustrations of attempting to accurately define what economics is. John Maynard Keynes, one of the greatest economists of the twentieth century, has elaborately described economics as "an easy subject, at which few excel." Keynes' extended definition, while describing economics as it existed in 1924, still presents an accurate characterization of economics today.

Keynes wrote, "The study of economics does not seem to require any specialized gifts of an unusual order. Is it not, intellectually regarded, a very easy subject compared with the higher branches of philosophy and pure science? Yet good or even competent economists are rarest of birds. An easy subject, at which few excel! The paradox finds its explanation, perhaps, in that the master economist must possess a rare combination of gifts. He must be a mathematician, historian, statesman, philosopher—in some degree. He must understand symbol and speak in words. He must contemplate the particular in terms of the general, and touch abstract and concrete in the same flight of thought. He must study the present in the light of the past for the purposes of the future." Perhaps, when Prof. Viner defined, "economics is what economists do," he had this broader definition of an "economist" in his mind.

Nonetheless, the most acceptable definition of economics, and the one that comes closest to correctly and completely defining economics, is given by Prof. Lionel Robbins of Cambridge University. His definition is as follows: Economics is a science that studies human behavior as a relationship between ends and scarce means that have alternate uses.

This definition, of course, brings to mind several questions: What are "ends"? What are the means to satisfy these ends? People's ends are called "wants" and there are two types of wants: (a) individual wants and (b) collective wants.

Individual wants are those that have to be satisfied by every individual, depending of course upon given circumstances. Examples of individual wants are water, shelter, clothes, and food. These are, by definition, wants that have to be satisfied individually. Collective or social wants are those that have to be satisfied in a group. Several examples of collective wants are education, health care, public parks, transportation, and defense.

The means to satisfy wants are the resources owned by the people. For individual wants, these resources include such things as personal income. As you can imagine, for many people this resource is scarce. Even some millionaires will complain about not having enough resources to satisfy all their wants. Moreover, this resource of personal income has several (what Prof. Robbins called alternate) uses. One can use the income to buy groceries, medicine, automobiles, or any number of other things. Now, according to Robbins's definition, when means are scarce, and when there is an abundance of wants to satisfy, how people behave is studied by a science called "economics." Hence, it is resolved that economics is a science and it studies human behavior under special conditions. Therefore, economic behavior primarily involves understanding trade-offs, making priorities, realizing costs and benefits of a decision, and making choices. There are numerous occasions when this behavior is relevant and important for a person and for a community.

There are two major branches of general economics: microeconomics and macroeconomics. "Micro," the Latin term, means something small, tiny, or little. Hence economics of small things like the behavior of only one firm rather than a whole economy is studied under microeconomics. In fact, the theory of (one) firm forms a big segment in microeconomics. Similarly, the decisions of only one consumer about what quantity of good(s) to consume are studied under microeconomics. That topic is popularly called consumer choice theory.

On the other hand, "macro," another Latin term, means something big, large or huge. Hence, economics of large things, like decisions of the whole economy about how much to produce (GDP calculation), and behavior of all prices taken together (inflation) is studied under macroeconomics. Similarly unemployment of the labor force forms an important topic in macroeconomics.

Another useful definition that is frequently used in economics is the definition of "factors of production." Factors of production are those basic things needed for any productive activity to take place. In pure economic theory we recognize four factors of production: land, labor, capital and enterprise. Land needs no explanation, as it can be the basic piece of land either located in a field or on the top floor of a high-rise building. Labor involves the availability of manual labor or skilled labor input that is endowed in heavy human capital. Human capital is a concept that is used extensively in economic development theory that means the cultural, educational, or health conditions of a labor force. Clearly, there are differences in labor quality according to the human capital involved in it, but one can easily see that labor is a basic need for a productive activity.

Capital requires a special explanation because it can be of two types: financial capital and physical or real capital. Financial capital includes such things as liquidity (or cash), equity capital, bonds, stocks (or shares). Physical capital involves such things as machinery, tools, equipments, and natural resources, etc. Obviously, for a real productive activity, one needs physical rather than financial capital. The fourth factor of production is "enterprise." In short, enterprise can be a lot of things: it can be knowledge of technology, or it can be the willingness to be the first producer (innovator) of a good, or it can mean entrepreneurship. Clearly, without some enterprise, no production can be possible. At times this production can lead to initial financial losses when a producer is developing a new technology.

An important definition related to the factors of production is that of returns (or rewards) to the individual factors of production. For the use of land one must pay rent, hence rent is considered as a reward (or price) for land. Similarly for labor, the reward is wage rate; for capital, the reward is interest rate (one can borrow financial capital and use it to buy real capital) and for use of enterprise, one is rewarded with profits. Thus, there are specific rewards for each specific factor of production.

Opportunity cost is another concept that is used quite often in economic literature. What do we mean by an opportunity cost? In short it is the value of the second-best use of a resource. It is the alternate benefit one has to forego by using a resource for a specific purpose. For every decision there is an opportunity cost. Suppose, for example, time is a resource and taking an economics class at a certain time is your decision to use that time resource. Then what do you think is the opportunity cost of that decision? Of course, how you could have used this resource otherwise determines the answer to this question. Suppose you would have eaten at the cafeteria, or have watched TV, or have earned some money, or have done nothing at all with this time. The values of all these opportunities defines the second-best alternatives that are foregone by taking this economics class at this specific time. Economists always worry about opportunity cost calculation to make any decision because against opportunity costs there is an accounting cost of the direct cost of the decision being considered. Clearly the tuition you paid for the class, the cost of the textbook, or parking expenses are a part of accounting costs.

The concept of opportunity cost is quite useful for explaining the famous economic saying that, "There is no such thing as a free lunch." Even if a friend of yours asked you to go eat lunch with her and she is buying, many times you ignore that invitation because of the opportunity costs involved. One may ask, "What can be an opportunity cost of a free lunch?" Of course, the second best uses of that time will determine it, or perhaps the fact that you will have to listen to her boring stories throughout the meal. No wonder, then, that free lunch invitations are turned down all the time. (It is quite obvious that you will accept a free lunch invitation if the opportunity cost is less than the benefit you will receive from the free lunch.)

In a similar fashion, by using the concept of opportunity costs, one can also explain the frequently observed fact that at a boring ball game, a higher proportion (or percentage) of empty seats are seen in the more expensive sections. If we assume that the expensive tickets are bought by rich people (with high opportunity cost), and the cheaper tickets are bought by poorer people (with relatively low opportunity cost), then it is quite clear that people in the expensive seats will leave the boring ball game much earlier than those in the cheaper seats.

The economic system is another concept used quite often in economic literature. Economic system is technically defined as a "set of arrangements used by an economy to mobilize its resources [and] to answer three fundamental questions: What to produce? How to produce? and For whom to produce?." Answers to these basic questions determine production, technology, and income distribution in an economy. Clearly, the answer to the question of what to produce determines production combinations that will take place in an economy. Similarly, the answer to the question of how to produce determines the technology to be used to produce these production combinations. Third, when an economy answers the question of "for whom to produce," the income distribution in an economy is determined by deciding on the recipients of the produced goods and services. There are basically two types of arrangements any economy can make to answer these questions. One type of arrangement is to let the government sector control all resources in the economy and make the government policy makers responsible for answering these three basic questions. That type of arrangement is popularly called socialism or communism. Private property has little meaning in socialism. Another type of arrangement is to allow private individuals to determine the distribution of resources and make decisions about how to answer the three basic questions above. That arrangement is called pure capitalism. In this economic system, the governmental sector has little influence on the economy and private property is closely guarded.

Without government the most dominant sectors of pure capitalism, the consumer sector, and the producer sector have a constant flow of exchanges between them. This flow of exchanges is popularly called the circular flow. There are basically two types of circular flows to be recognized: real flow and money flow. In real flow, we do not consider the role played by money. In real terms, therefore, the consumer sector gives to the producer sector the factors of production, and in return gets from the producer sector goods and services. As shown in Figure 1.1 the real flow, therefore, recognizes this basic exchange between consumer and producer sectors.

However, if we consider the role played by money, then we can turn real flow into money flow. Consider that in monetary terms, for the giving up of factors of production, the consumer sector receives returns for the factor of production from the producer sector. Similarly in monetary terms the producer sector gets consumer expenditure for goods and services provided to the consumers.

Besides looking at economics in terms of micro and macro, economics can also be divided between normative economics and positive economics. Positive economics considers all those issues that have only information, data, historical events, etc., included in them without passing any value judgment on them. These can include such things as economic history of a country or information about institutions such as the Federal Reserve System or the government's behavior during wartime, etc. It also includes such things as surveys, data gathering, and other things that do not have any value judgments. In short, there is not much to disagree about in positive economics. However, in normative economics issues such as the policy options for the government, or forecasting of future economic growth or effects of certain policy action on other economic variables are included. Clearly in this area there is a lot of fuel for disagreement because each economist can come up with different answers depending upon his/her value judgments. Hence, when economists disagree with one another (as they often do), then they are basically discussing the normative economic issues.

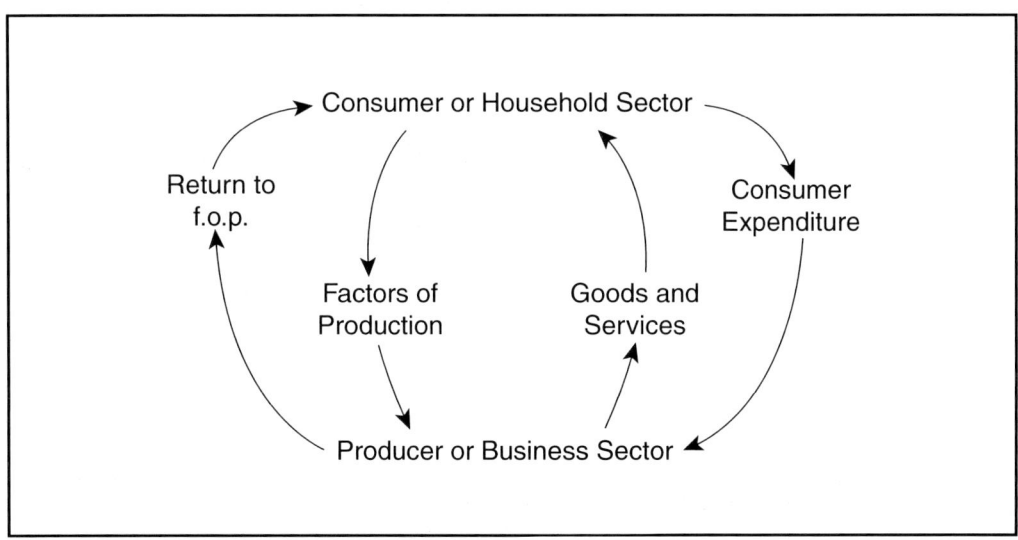

Circular Flow: Real and Money Flows ■ **FIGURE 1.1**

Another important concept is the production possibilities curve (PPC) or production possibilities frontier (PPF). PPC is defined as the locus of combinations of two goods an economy can produce by using all its resources.

In terms of Figure 1.2 suppose two goods, X and Y, are the only ones produced. By using all resources, suppose OK is the amount of good Y the economy can produce and OJ is the amount of good X produced, again using all resources. There can be a host of other combinations that can be produced, as represented by points along the PPC.

The shape of the PPC is "concave to the origin," which means if you calculate the slope of this curve, it increases as you move left to right along that curve. The main arguments are as follows: All points on PPC represent combinations of two goods that an economy can produce by using all of its resources. This also means that the combinations inside the PPC represent those productions that would leave some resources unused (or unemployed). If the economy is producing at a point inside the PPC, and if it attempts to move production toward points on the PPC, that process is called economic development. Hence, economic development

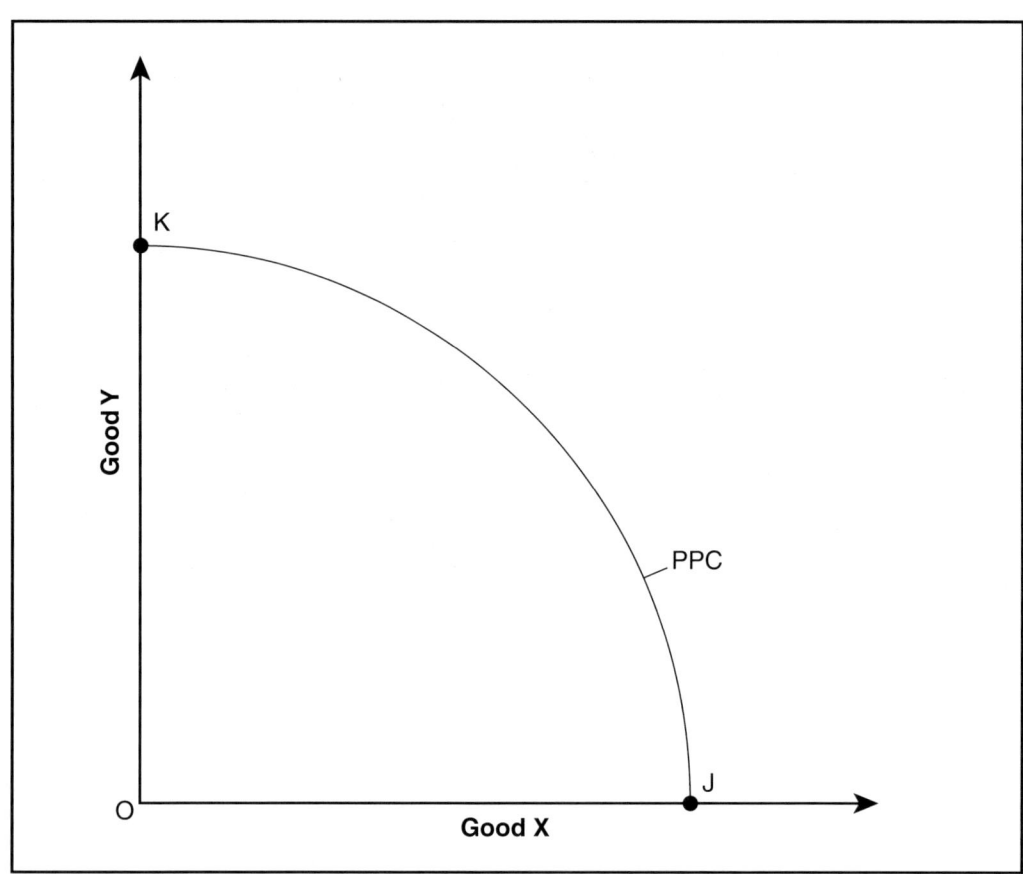

FIGURE 1.2 ■ Production Possibilities Curve (PPC)

essentially means the process of using the resources more efficiently and taking the economy toward full employment.

Similarly, points outside the PPC represent those combinations that are impossible to be produced by given resources. However, if more resources are available, or if the available resources are used more efficiently, then there is a shift of the PPC. This process is called "economic growth." Hence, the economic growth would make it possible for the economy to produce combinations represented by points outside the PPC. When you take advanced economics classes, using PPC to represent production decisions of the economy is a common practice, therefore the concept of PPC is important to introduce here.

In the next section, we introduce concepts related to drawing and reading graphs.

Technique of Drawing Graphs 1.2

If you think that your background in geometry is strong enough that you do not need information on the technique of drawing graphs, then you can skip this section without a loss of continuity. However, often students in economics principles classes come with little background in geometry, and hence find it useful to revise the concepts of geometry, which will help them to read and draw graphs that are used quite extensively in economic literature.

Technically the word "graph" only means a pictorial representation of a relationship between two variables. Then a question naturally arises: What do we mean by variables? A variable, as you may have heard in your first mathematics class, is any concept that can be measured in numbers. For example, the age of students in a class is a variable because it can be measured by changing numbers. Similarly, heights or weights of students in a class are other examples of variables. Thus, any concept that can be measured by changing values can be referred to as a variable. It is quite possible that if we conveniently pick several variables, their values will depend on each other's values. When this happens we say that two variables have a relationship. Consider, for instance, two variables: (1) income of a person and (2) the amount of saving he makes in a bank. As the values of income go up we shall expect that he will save more in a bank. Hence, values of saving depends upon values of income made by that person. Clearly then these two variables have a relationship.

There are basically two types of variables we recognize: (1) a dependent variable and (2) an independent variable. A dependent variable is the one whose values depend upon the values of other variables. In the above example then, the savings of a person is the dependent variable. On the other hand, an independent variable is the one whose values dictate the values of other variables. In our example, the income of the person is the independent variable.

Similarly there are two types of relationships variables can have with each another. The first type is called an inverse or negative relationship and the other type is called a direct or positive relationship. When the values of the independent variable increase and cause the values of the dependent variable to increase too, we say that the two variables have a direct relationship. For example, the above relationship (income and saving) is clearly a direct relationship, but we can think of several others as well. How about the relationship between interest rate (independent) and savings (dependent)? Or the one between height (independent) and weight (dependent) of a person?

When the values of the independent variable increase and cause the values of the dependent variable to decrease, we say that the two variables have an inverse or negative relationship. A classic example of an inverse relationship is the one between mortgage interest rate and the number of houses bought in a town. As the interest rate charged by bank for mortgages goes up, the number of houses bought in town will go down. Similarly, there is an inverse relationship between mortgage interest rate demanded by workers and the number of workers employed by businesses. In Table 1.1 we shall present the example of a positive relationship discussed above between a person's savings and income.

Our next job is to define the slope of the line. Generally speaking, the slope is a concept that tells us what will be the change in a dependent variable when there is a change in independent variable values. For example, how much will change in a person's savings when there is a change in income? In other words, by observing the above relationship, can we tell how much savings will increase if income increases by say, 100?

The slope usually gives us that answer. However, we can have a relationship whose slope is different at different points. That type of relationship is called a non-linear relationship and it is shown by a non-linear curve on the graph. The relationships that are shown by a straight line are called linear relationships and they have a constant slope at all points on that straight line.

TABLE 1.1 ■ Savings in Dollars

1000	200
2000	400
4000	800
6000	1200
8000	1600

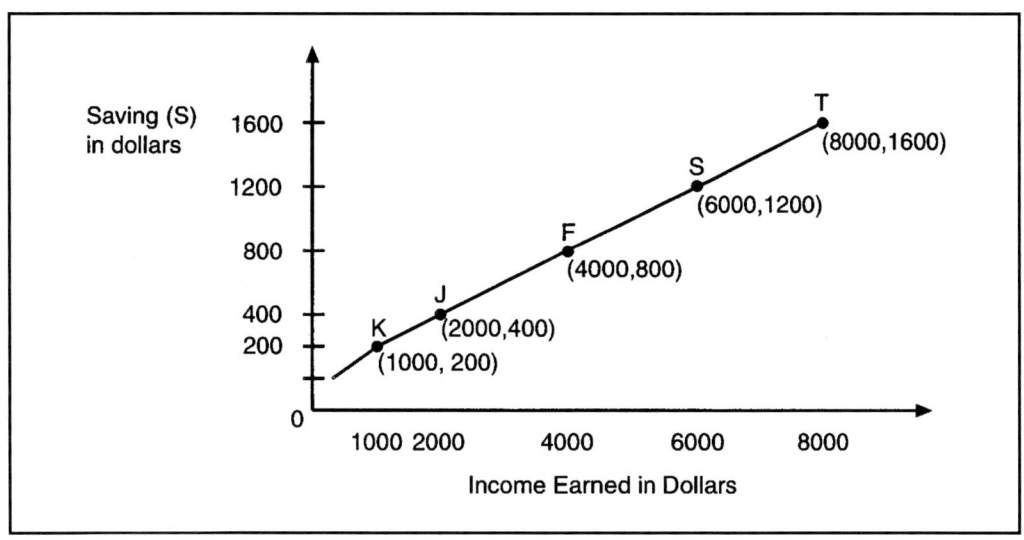

Graphing Variables from Table 1.1 ■ **FIGURE 1.3**

To define the slope of a linear relationship, consider once again the *savings line* plotted in Figure 1.3 that shows the positive relationship between a person's income and savings. The same relationship is reproduced in Figure 1.4. In general, the slope is defined by the ratio of rise and run, when we consider a movement on that line, from one point to another. Hence, consider two points on that line such as, say points F and S, and define their coordinates.

When a movement from point F to point S is considered, the rise is by the amount of change in saving that has occurred. It is measured by the distance ST and it is equal to 400. The run is measured by the distance FT and is equal to 2,000. Hence, the slope of this relationship is equal to 400/2,000 = .2.

Because the slope of a linear relationship is constant, it does not matter which two points we select to calculate the rise over run ratio. However, in the case of a

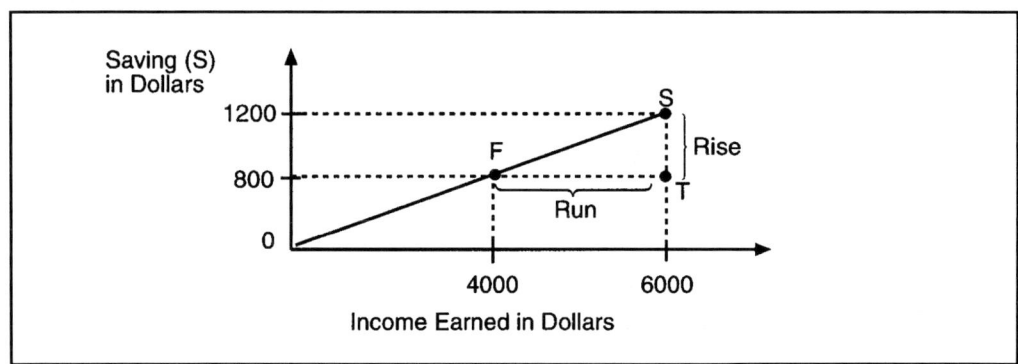

Slope of a Linear Relationship ■ **FIGURE 1.4**

non-linear relationship, we have to change the process of defining the slope. Consider a classic economic non-linear relationship between total product of a company and the number of employees it employs. As the number of employees goes up, the total product will increase but eventually the company will become over-crowded, and will cause the total product to decline. This is shown in Figure 1.5.

To calculate the slope of this relationship we must ask a question: Is the slope of this curve the same at all points? The answer is obviously no. Hence, we first need to determine at what point the slope of this curve is to be calculated. Suppose, therefore, that we want to define the slope at point L on this total product curve. The procedure to do that is to initially draw a tangent to this curve at point L. A tangent is a straight line that touches the curve at only one point. Once the tangent is drawn, the slope of the tangent is the slope of that curve at that point. Hence, at point L the slope of the non-linear total product curve is defined by the ratio LM/MN.

Economic hypothesis is a statement that hypothesizes human behavior. For example, an increase in the income of the consumer will lead to an increase in the consumer's consumption. A bunch of related economic hypotheses are used to construct the economic model. Hence, an economic model can be developed to show the behavior of humans or of an economy. We shall discuss such models in later chapters. Testing such models is a task economists do very efficiently.

This completes our review of the technique of drawing graphs. In economic analysis we use several relationships. To show these relationships economists make extensive use of graphs. One such relationship will be discussed in the next chapter.

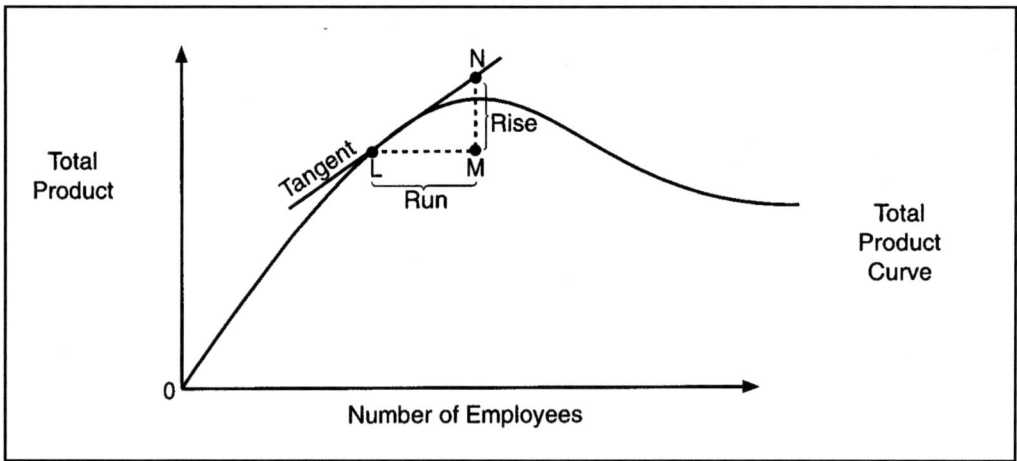

FIGURE 1.5 ■ Shifts of the Demand Curve

References

Arnold, R. 1996. *Macroeconomics,* 3rd ed., Chapter 1. West Publishing Company.

Baunol, W. and A. Blinder. 1995. *Economics,* 6th ed., Chapters 1 and 2. Prentice Hall.

Byrns, R. and J. Stone Jr. 1994. *Economics,* 6th ed., Chapters 1 and 2. Harper/Collins Publishers.

Case, K. E. and R. C. Fair. 1996. *Principles of Economics,* 4th ed, Chapters 1, 2, and 3. Prentice Hall.

Samuelson, P. and W. Mordhaus. 1994. *Economics,* l3th ed., Chapters 1, 2, and 3. McGraw-Hill.

Sharp, A. M., C. A. Register, and P. W. Grimes. 1996. *Economic of Social Issues,* 12th ed., Chapter 2. Irwin Publishers.

Stiglitz, J. 1996. *Economics,* 2nd ed., Chapter 2. W.W. Norton.

Tregarthen, T. 1996. *Microeconomics*, Chapter 2. Worth Publishers.

Chapter 2
Laws of Demand and Supply

SUMMARY

The laws of demand and supply and the relationship that exists between these two concepts are fundamental to the understanding of economics. This chapter explores the interaction between producers and consumers and the role of price and quantity as related to the laws of demand and supply and the functioning of the market mechanism within an economy.

The law of demand presents the inverse relationship between the price of a product and the quantity demanded for a product by an individual or market; thus, when price increases, quantity demanded declines. This section examines the income and substitution effects as justifications for the law of demand. Without the constancy of eight particular mechanisms, the law of demand will not be valid and a change in any of them will ultimately lead to a shift in the demand curve. Thus, this chapter presents the need for a clear distinction between demand (shift of the demand curve) and quantity demanded (shift along the demand curve). Finally, consumer satisfaction or surplus is briefly explained.

The law of supply presents the positive relationship between the price of a product and the quantity supplied by a producer. This section examines the profitability and substitution effects as a justification for the law of supply. As with demand, there are six principle mechanisms that must remain constant in order for the law of supply to be valid, and a change in any of them will lead to a shift in the supply curve. Once again, this leads into an explanation of the important difference between supply (a shift of the curve) and change in quantity supplied (a movement along the curve). Finally, satisfaction derived by producers from selling a good, or producer surplus, is also covered.

One can derive market demand for a good at a certain price by totaling individual quantities demanded by consumers. This section illustrates the graph of a market demand curve derived from individual demand curves or a horizontal summation of individual demand curves. Supply is derived in a similar fashion. The two together represent the equilibrium condition of a market for a good. Where they intersect is where quantity demanded equals quantity supplied, thus representing an appropriate equilibrium price for the good. When supply and demand are not in equilibrium, this will either represent a surplus or a shortage. This leads into a short discussion on the paradox of flexibility and the fact that supply and demand will not move back into equilibrium when unaffected by outside forces.

The final section explores outside forces on market mechanisms, including middlemen, arbitrators, and speculators as well as government policy of price control. In terms of price control, the implementation of price floors and ceilings are discussed, with the conclusion being that while these policies may be designed to help consumers, ultimately any type of government intervention in prices is not beneficial and the market mechanism should be left to its own devices.

2.1 Introduction

In Chapter 1, we defined economic hypothesis as the statement of human behavior. One of the most important and widely discussed economic hypotheses is the one that shows the relationship between the price of a product, the quantity demanded, and the quantity supplied. It was originally discussed in the writing of Adam Smith who is considered the "father of economics." In his famous book published in 1776, *Wealth of Nations,* he formulated the role of the price of a product. In a market system, the price of a product serves as a signal for producers to produce higher or lower quantity of that product. Mr. Smith was aware of the fact that when consumers need and are able to buy a certain commodity, then they cast their "price votes" for that commodity and as a consequence its market price goes up. Producers, whose self-interest is to maximize profits, take this price increase as a signal for producing higher quantity of that product. In order to reap new and increased profits in the production of that commodity they increase the production, and supply a higher quantity of the commodity. In this special way, a market system automatically satisfies the wishes of consumers. Smith refers to this mechanism as the "invisible hand of nature."

Other economists expounded on this original idea of Adam Smith to clarify what is popularly called "market mechanism." Strictly speaking, a "market" is a concept rather than a place or region as its name implies. It is, therefore, a conceptual space where producers (or suppliers) and consumers (demanders) meet to make their wishes known to each other. When the actual transactions take place there is a certain payment made by consumers for what they get, which we call a "price." Changes in price can dictate the changes in quantity the consumers are willing and able to buy. The willingness and ability of consumers signifies the demand for the products.

One has to recognize the difference between needs and demands. Only the needs that are backed up by purchasing power of a consumer can become demands. Clearly, consumers or individuals often need many things, but when they do not have the purchasing power to buy those things these individuals do not form a part of demand for those commodities. For example in order to come to my office I "need" a very expensive and roomy car, but do I make up a part of the demand for expensive cars? The answer is of course no, because my need is not backed by purchasing power for an expensive car.

Once we recognize the demands as separate from needs, then we can also see an inverse relationship between price of a product and the quantity demanded of that product by an individual or a market. Strictly the relationship can be seen in both directions. When the price is seen as the dependent variable, then an increase in quantity demanded can raise the price and a decline in quantity demanded can lower the price.

Hence, the relationship between quantity demanded and the price is positive, however, this is not what is depicted by the law of demand. In fact, in the statement of the law of demand the quantity demanded is treated as a dependent variable and price of a product is taken as an independent variable. In essence the law of demand is stated as follows: When the price of a product goes up, "by keeping all other things constant" the quantity demanded for that product will go down over time. Thus, the relationship between price and quantity demanded is inverse, if price goes up quantity demanded goes down, by keeping all other things constant.

The phrase "by keeping all other things constant" is expressed by the Latin words *ceteris paribus*. We shall see later what these other things are that must be kept constant for the law of demand to hold. Currently we need to notice a difference between demand schedule and demand curve.

"Demand schedule" is a table of values of price and quantity demanded that shows the inverse relationship between price and quantity demanded, as in Table 2.1. When this demand schedule is plotted on the graph it shows the demand curve as shown in Figure 2.1.

As can be seen in Figure 2.1, the inverse relationship between price of a product and quantity demanded is shown by the demand curve that has a downward-sloping from left to right shape. The main question is, "How can we justify the law of demand?" According to Alfred Marshall of Cambridge University, who is considered the father of the demand curve (and the law of demand), the two reasons that an increase in price will lower the quantity demanded are referred to as "substitution effect" and "income effect." When the price of a product goes up and the consumer has the same money income, his or her real income goes down and he or she feels poorer than before. This leads the individual to reduce the quantity demanded for all products, including that of the product whose price

TABLE 2.1 ▪ **Demand Schedule**

Price of a Product (T-Shirt)	Quantity Demanded of the Product (in one month from a store)
10	500
15	400
18	300
20	200

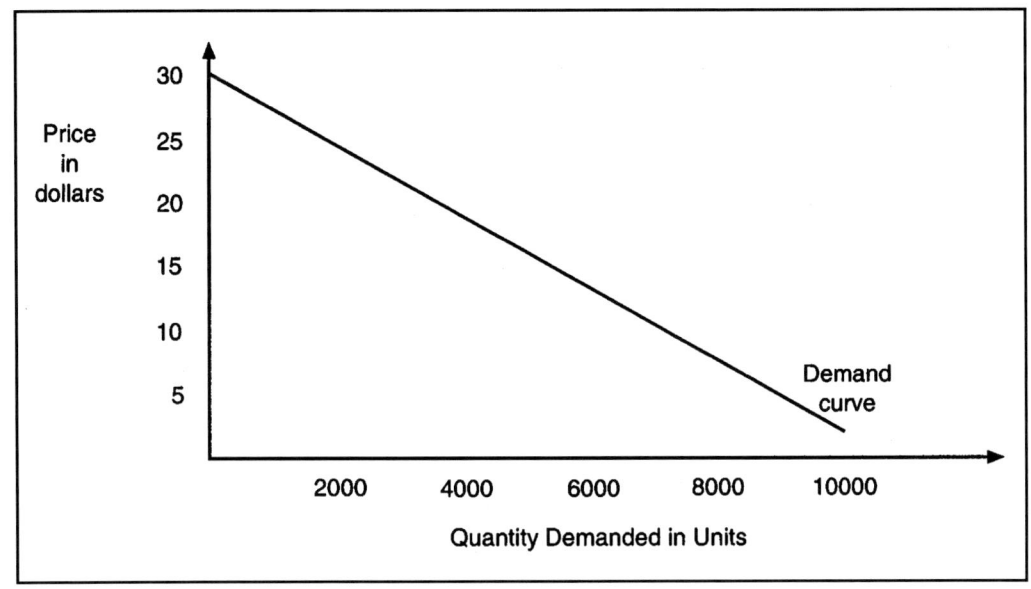

Demand Curve and Inverse Relationship ■ **FIGURE 2.1**

has increased. This effect of decline in real income on the quantity demanded is called the income effect.

The second effect, substitution effect, which is on the consumption side, is explained in a similar manner. When the price of a product goes up consumers will substitute its consumption by the consumption of other products. For example, if the price of coffee goes up then people will start drinking more cups of tea. This is called substitution effect on the consumption side. Thus, due to both income effect and substitution effects, the law of demand is justified.

Our next task is to explain the other things that must be held constant for the law of demand to be valid: (1) income of the consumer, (2) tastes of the consumer for the product, (3) prices of related products, (4) number of consumers in the market, (5) expectations of consumers, (6) income and population distribution of the consumers, (7) wealth of the consumers, and (8) government's policy of such things as income taxes. The important thing to remember is that if these things are allowed to change then the relationship between price and quantity demanded will change and the demand curve will shift from one location to another.

As the income of consumers changes there will be more or less quantity demanded at the same price. Hence, at the price of say $5, by looking at Figure 2.2 we can see that initially consumers demand 50 units of a product. With increase in income of consumers at the same price they will start demanding more than 50, perhaps 70 units of the product and point K of the original demand curve will move to the right to, say, point F. In a similar fashion all points of the original

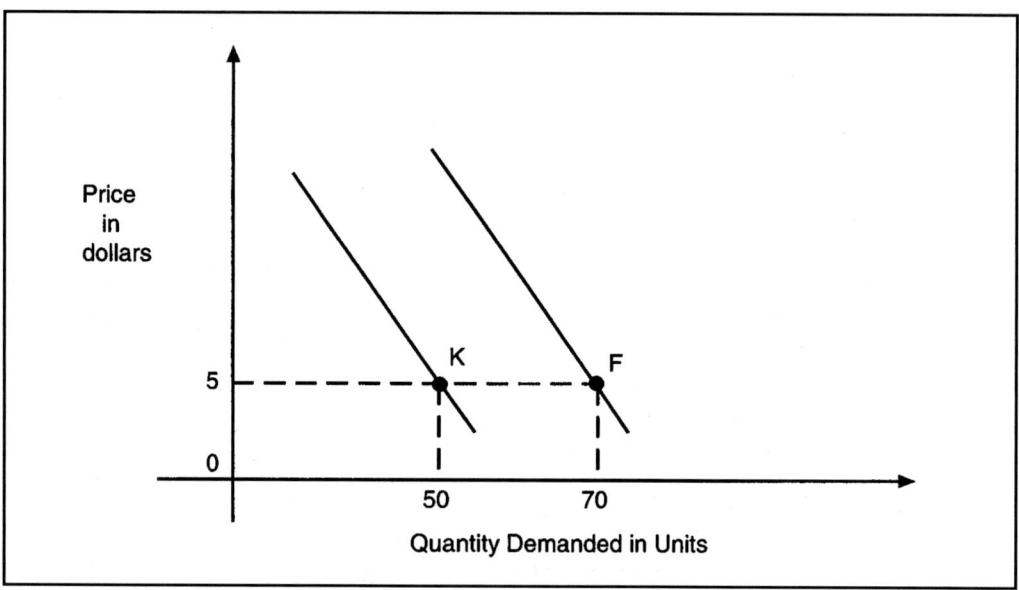

FIGURE 2.2 ■ Shifts of the Demand Curve

demand curve will move to the right and a new demand curve will be drawn to the right of the original one. Thus with increase in income there will be a rightward shift of the demand curve as shown in Figure 2.2.

However, not all products will be demanded with higher quantity when there is an increase in income of the consumer. Consider for example an economical product such as hamburgers. Suppose further that if an individual consumes five hamburgers in a week, then with an increase in her income she will start eating fewer than five hamburgers and switch to an occasional meal of steak instead.

Thus with increase in income of the consumer in this case the quantity demanded of hamburgers will go down. All these type of products whose quantity demanded declines with the increase in income of the consumers are popularly called "inferior goods." The goods that are consumed more after increase in income are called "normal goods" and, clearly, for normal goods with increase in income of the consumers the demand curve will shift to right. Note that with increase in income of the consumers for inferior goods there is a shift of the demand curve to the left. This is because with increased income, at the same price, consumers buy less of the inferior goods. For example, all the generic goods compared to brand names are inferior goods: people demand lower quantities of generic goods when their income goes up.

The second factor that has to be held constant for demand curve to be stable is the tastes of consumers for certain products. Clearly, tastes can change in favor of the product or they can change in a way that will make consumers stop consuming a product.

Consider for example a product like coffee. Suppose further that a new study finds that coffee consumption causes cancer. There should be a marked change in tastes of consumers to disfavor coffee consumption, and even if coffee stays at the same price consumers would start buying lower quantities of it. This would cause the demand curve of coffee to shift to the left.

The third factor that has to be held constant is the prices of "related" products. For any commodity there are two types of related products: substitutes and complementary. Two goods are said to be substitutes of each other if they can be consumed in place of each another. Examples of substitutes are such goods as coffee and tea, or Pepsi and Coke, automobiles and buses, or scooters and bicycles.

Now if we are looking at the demand curve of coffee and the price of tea goes up, then for the same price of coffee people will start drinking more cups of coffee and the points of coffee's demand curve will shift to the right. Thus, an increase in price of a substitute product makes a rightward shift in the demand curve of the product under consideration.

Complementary goods are those that have to be consumed together. Such combinations as cement and brick, tires and cars, toothpaste and toothbrush, or sanitizer and cleaning cloth complement each other. If two goods are complementary and the price of one of them increases then the demand curve of the other goods will shift inward to the left. This is because if the price of cement goes up then quantity demanded of cement will go down and even if the price of bricks is unchanged, people will demand a lower quantity of bricks. Hence, the demand curve of bricks will shift if the price of cement is changed.

The next thing to be held constant is the number of consumers. Clearly an increase in the number of consumers will shift the demand curve to the right and a reduction in the number of consumers will shift the demand curve to the left. The expectations of consumers for the future price of the product are also important. If the consumers expect price of the product to increase in the future, then even if the price currently remains unchanged, they will start demanding higher quantity of the product. Thus expectations of increase in price in the future can shift the demand curve to the right.

Income and demographic distribution of population can also have an effect on the position of demand curve of a certain product. This is because as income distribution changes in favor of a wealthy population, products such as perfumes, fancy cars, expensive motorboats, and luxurious housing will be demanded more. Hence, the demand curves of all these goods will shift to the right. Similarly as the poor become fewer in number the demand for such products as hamburgers, tacos, budget store items, and generic foods will go down. Hence, the demand curve of these products will shift to the left.

The demographic distribution of the population depends upon ages of the population. One can easily imagine that as baby boomers reach the age of retirement they will demand some specific product much more than some others. Clearly, with a greater number of older consumers in the population, products such as pain killers, pillows, and dentures will be demanded more and the demand curve of these products will shift to the right. The demand curve of such products as tours and vacations, motorcycles, and designer clothes, will shift to the left. Wealth of the consumers can also lead to some special consumption patterns. Increase in wealth makes the demand curve of all products that wealthy individuals use shift to the right.

The income tax structure can also change the location of the demand curves of inferior and normal goods in a predictable way. Increase in income taxes will make people demand lower quantity of all normal goods and higher quantity of inferior goods. Hence, for the normal goods the demand curves will shift to the left and for inferior goods the demand curves will shift to the right. All in all we have found several reasons why the demand curve can shift from one position to another. Of course, for the demand curve to be stable all these things must be held constant.

We can now make a clear distinction between the change in quantity demanded and the change in demand. When there is a change in price of the goods being examined there is a change in quantity demanded and the change in quantity demanded is explained by the movement along the demand curve (there is no need to shift the demand curve when this happens). On the other hand, when there is a change in one of the other things that have to be held constant, there is a "change in demand" for the product. Only the change in demand is explained by the shift of the demand curve.

Thus we should never talk about a change in demand when the price of the product under consideration is changing. Similarly, a change in quantity demanded never happens when there is a "change in one of the other things." It is important to master this terminology.

CONSUMER SURPLUS

The next important definition is of the term "consumer surplus." Consider in Figure 2.3 the demand curve for certain goods (e.g., goods X), and observe that the maximum price someone in the market is ready to pay for first unit of goods X is OJ. Suppose further that the market price of goods X is OK and the quantity demanded of goods X is OQ. Due to the fact that market price is OK, there are at least some consumers who are getting satisfaction that the price is less than what

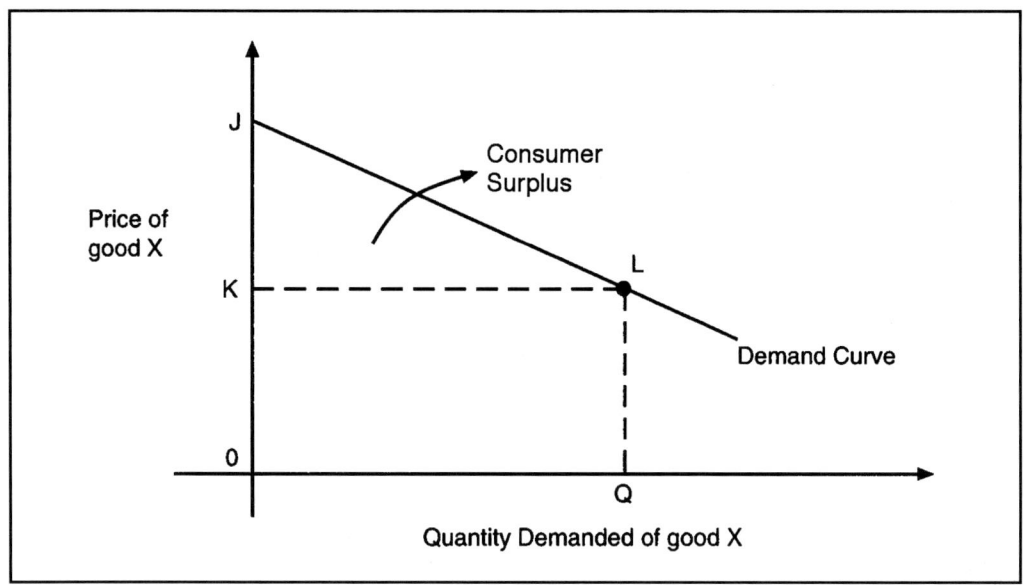

Consumer Surplus: Area under the Demand Curve ■ FIGURE 2.3

they would have paid for the first unit of it. A measure of this satisfaction is called consumer surplus. On the graph, consumer surplus is defined by the area of the triangle under the demand curve from market price to the maximum price that someone would have paid for that product. In terms of Figure 2.3, area of triangle KJL defines consumer surplus. Increase in consumer surplus represents a gain for the consumer class in the economy and a reduction in consumer surplus means loss to the consumer class.

Law of Supply 2.2

Just as there is a relationship between the price of a product and the quantity demanded, there is also a relationship between the price of a product and the quantity supplied by the producers. In short, the law of supply is expressed as, "When price of a product increases, quantity or supply (by producers, then suppliers) of that product increases by keeping all other things constant." Thus there is a positive, or direct, relationship between price and quantity supplied. Let us keep in mind however that in this relationship, the price is seen as the independent variable and quantity supplied is the dependent variable. (One could, of course, come up with an inverse relationship when quantity supplied is seen as the independent variable and price as the dependent variable, but that is not what law of supply is describing!)

The main question is, how can one justify the validity of the law of basic supply? There are two reasons, which are the profitability effect and the substitution effect on the production side. As price of a product goes up, suppliers (or producers) expect higher profits in the production of that product. Maximizing profits is a self-interest of producers so they increase the quantity supplied of that product to the market. This increase in quantity supplied is due to the profitability effect.

Second, one can argue that as price of a product increases, producers will substitute production of other products for the production of the commodity whose price has gone up. Hence there is a substitution effect on the production side. If a producer can manufacture two goods, (e.g., X and Y) and if the price of good X increases, then the producer will switch production from good Y to good X. And so, due to the substitution effect on the production side, the law of supply is justified. A direct relationship between price and quantity supplied is shown in Table 2.2. The table of values that shows positive relationship between price and quantity supplied is called "supply schedule." When the supply schedule is plotted on the graph it shows the supply curve.

Just as we should pay attention to the things that must be held constant in the case of the demand curve, the same is true for the supply curve. If any one of these things changes, there will be a shift of the supply curve. The factors that are important for determining the supply curve are: (1) number of suppliers of the product, (2) prices of related commodities on the production side, (3) technology of production, (4) resource cost or the cost of production, (5) expectations of the producers for future prices, and (6) business taxes.

The number of suppliers will obviously have an effect on the quantity supplied even if price stays the same. An increase in the number of suppliers will cause a higher quantity to be supplied at the same price and the points on the supply curve will shift to the right (or down). Hence, an increase in the number of suppliers will make the whole supply curve shift to the right.

TABLE 2.2 ▪ Supply Schedule

Price	Quantity Supplied
3	50
6	80
9	110
12	140
15	170
18	200

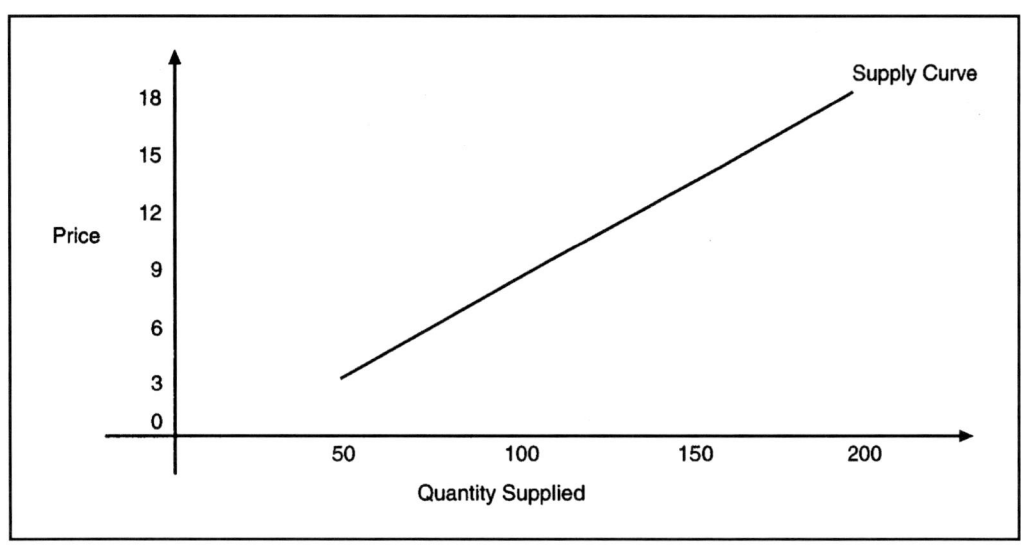

Supply Curve: Price and Quantity Supplied ■ FIGURE 2.4

On the production side products can be related to each other if they have to be produced jointly or they have to be produced one after the other. Examples of joint products are automobiles and tires, grapes and wine, oranges and orange juice, and so on. Clearly if products X and Y are jointly produced and price of good Y increases, then the quantity supplied of good X will increase even if there is no change in price of good X. Thus, all points on the supply curve of good X will shift to the right when the price of good Y increases. Technology of production can also change quantity supplied of any product. Consider the production of mining some resource, done by sending individuals to dig inside a mine. Suppose further that miners find a new machine that drills the mine faster and more effectively, so that there is an improvement in technology of mining production. Due to this improvement in technology, at the same price the quantity supplied of the product will increase and the supply curve will shift to the right.

Cost of production or resource cost can also influence the location of the supply curve. An increase in the cost of production will make it harder to supply the same quantity at the same price. Therefore, an increase in resource cost will force producers to lower the quantity supplied of the product, creating a leftward shift in the supply curve. Consider the supply curve of a product such as shirts, and suppose further that the price of cotton increases. Clearly at the constant price of shirts, the producers will produce a lower quantity of shirts, and the supply curve of shirts will shift to the left due to the increase in the price of cotton.

Last, but not least, business taxes can also dictate the position of the supply curve. An increase in business taxes will make it harder for producers to supply the same quantity at the same price of a product. So an increase in business taxes will shift the supply curve to the left. In the reverse case, a subsidy from the government can shift the supply curve to the right showing an increase in quantity supplied at the same price of the product.

There is an important difference between change in quantity supplied and change in supply. When the price of a product increases there is an increase in quantity supplied as shown by the law of supply. This is shown by a movement from one point to another on the supply curve and is called a change in quantity supplied. However, when there is a change in one of the other factors that have to be held constant, there is a change in supply and it is shown by a movement or shift of the supply curve or by a shift of the supply curve. Hence, one should not talk about shifting the supply curve when the price of the product changes. There is also no change in supply in this case, only a change in quantity supplied. When the technology changes, one should shift the supply curve and should talk about a change in supply. It is important to use this terminology correctly.

PRODUCER SURPLUS

Producer surplus is a concept that shows the satisfaction on the part of producers by having a market price greater than the minimum price that the first producer would have accepted for that product. Consider the minimum price of goods X in Figure 2.5 as OJ. At this price OJ some producer in the market would have produced the first quantity of good X. Suppose that the market price is OK and quantity produced at that price is OF.

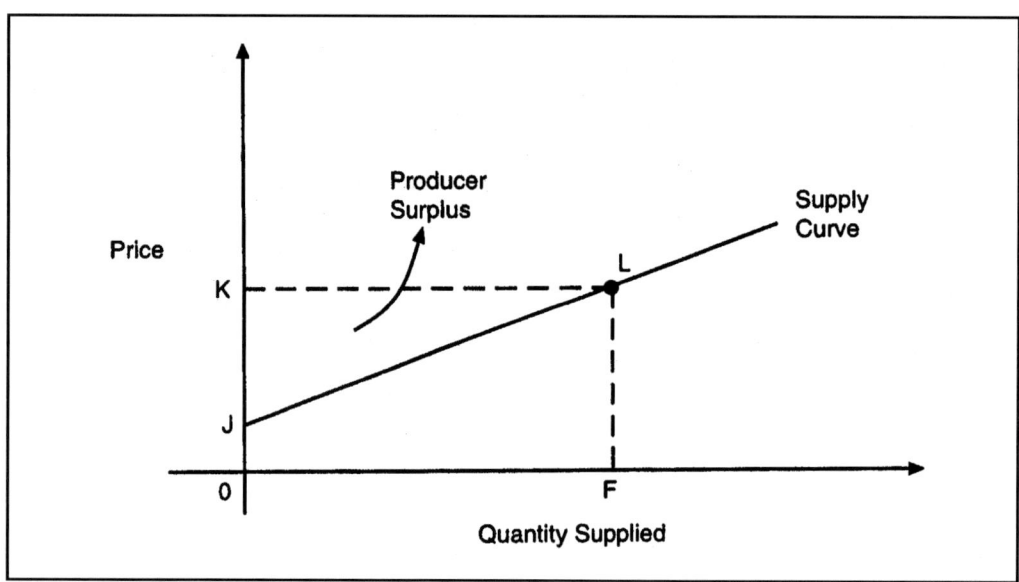

FIGURE 2.5 ■ Producer Surplus

Clearly all the producers who would have produced at least some quantity of goods X at prices below OK are satisfied that the market price is at OK. The measure of this satisfaction is called "producer surplus" and it is defined by the area above the supply curve up to the market price, as shown in Figure 2.5, triangle KJL. An increase in producer surplus leads to gains for the producer class and reduction in it causes losses for the producer class.

2.3 Market Supply Curve and Individual Supply Curve

Suppose there are three suppliers of a certain goods in a market: Mr. X, Mr. Y, and Mrs. Z. Suppose further their individual supply curves are as shown in Figure 2.6 and we need to derive the market supply curve from it. Consider the price of $5.00 when Mr. X supplies 50 units, Mr. Y supplies 100 units, and Mrs. Z supplies 30 units of this commodity. Then at the price of $5.00, the market as a whole shall supply 180 units of the commodity; in Figure 2.6 this is shown as point K. Similarly, we can get information for other prices and determine the quantity supplied by the whole market by adding the quantity supplied by the individual suppliers.

The process of adding individual supplier's quantities is called the "horizontal summation." Hence, the market supply curve is derived by horizontal summation of the individual supply curves.

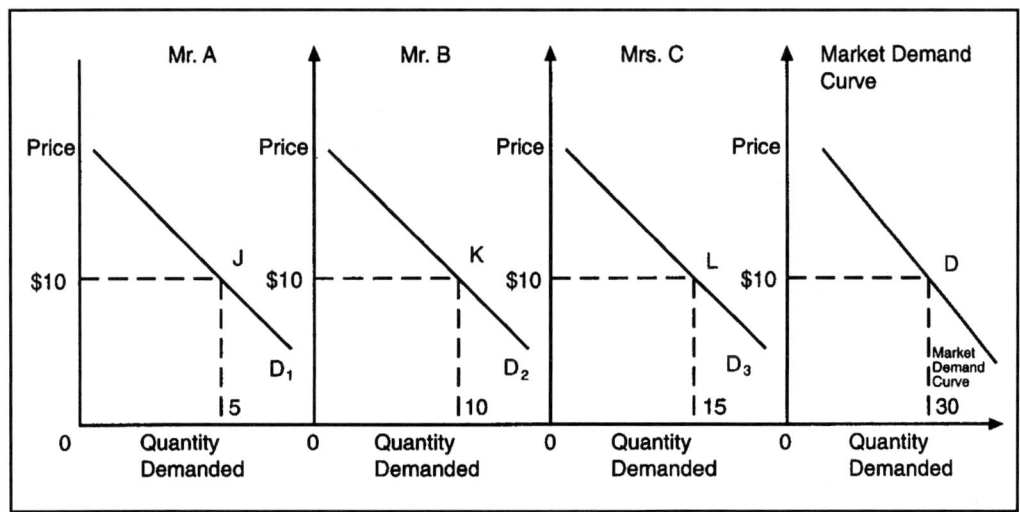

Market Demand Curve from Individual Demand Curves ■ **FIGURE 2.6**

A market demand curve is derived using the exact same procedure: horizontal summation of individual demand curves. A market demand curve is a horizontal summation of individual demand curves. By drawing both market demand curve and market supply curve on the same graph we can now determine the equilibrium stage of the market. Consider therefore Figure 2.7, which shows market demand and market supply curves for good X intersecting each other at point E where price is P_1 and quantity demanded and supplied are equal to each other at Q_1. In the absence of outside force on this market, the price of this commodity will have a tendency to move toward P_1. This is because at any price other than P_1 the market will exert a force on it to move toward equilibrium price. This phenomenon is newly termed the "paradox of flexibility," which in simple terms means that if a price is flexible, then it will remain at one level of equilibrium. To prove the paradox of flexibility, consider any price above equilibrium, say at P_2. At price P_2 the quantity demanded is OQ_2 and quantity supplied in the market is OQ_3.

Hence, with larger quantity supplied there is a surplus of good X in the market by the amount of Q_2Q_3. If there is a surplus of any commodity in a market, then the price will start going down, so the price of good X will decline from P_2 and start approaching P_1. In a similar fashion, at any market price below equilibrium (e.g., P_3) there is higher quantity demanded than quantity supplied by the producers. This creates a shortage of Q_4Q_5 of good X in the market. If there is shortage of a product, the price will start increasing and will move toward P_1. Thus, market equilibrium process makes it certain that the price of a product always moves toward equilibrium.

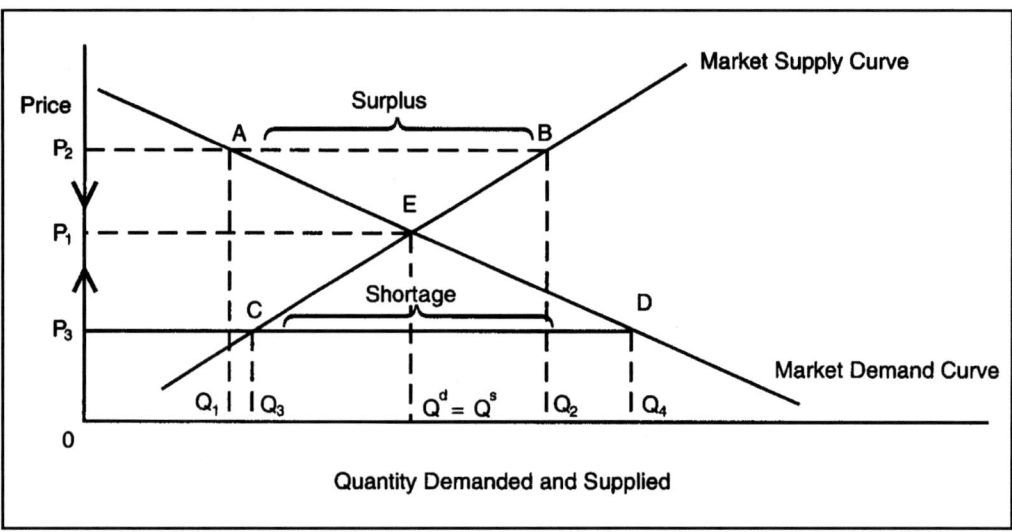

FIGURE 2.7 ■ Market Equilibrium

Obviously, no market is completely impenetrable by outside forces, which can be shown in terms of three groups of individuals who work in any market: intermediaries or middlemen, speculators, and arbitragers. Intermediaries are those individuals who buy from the producers and sell the products to consumers. Obviously, since producers and consumers do not meet with each other there is no one equilibrium price in this case. Nonetheless, a large number of middlemen is harmful for their profession. As one can imagine if there are a large number of intermediaries then the price charged by producers will be closer to price paid by consumers and that can reduce the profits of intermediaries. Of course, the main source of intermediaries' revenue comes from high information cost and high transaction cost that consumers have to pay for that exchange.

The second group of individuals is the group of speculators. They are risk-lovers and thrive on the uncertainty of changing future prices of the products. Speculators make profits by buying a commodity at a low price and selling it when the price is high. Hence, when speculators expect price to increase in the future they buy a commodity, and sell it when they expect the future price to be low. Similar to intermediaries, if there are a large number of speculators then price fluctuations can become smaller. These are called stabilizing speculations. In the case of a large number of speculators, when price increases there are some who think it will go down and start selling the commodity. As they sell the product the price actually does goes down and there are some other speculators who think the price will go up in the future and they start buying the product. The price fluctuations, therefore, become smaller due to an existence of a large number of speculators.

The third group of individuals are the arbitragers. Arbitrage activities involve buying of a product in one regional market and selling it in another regional market. Thus, if the price of a product is lower in one region than in another then arbitragers will buy in the first region and sell it in the second region. Of course, the activities of arbitragers help reduce the regional differences in the price of a product.

2.4 Using Demand and Supply Curves for Policy Decisions

One can use the simple model of demand and supply curves that was built in the earlier section to make policy decisions. One of the most relevant governmental policies is that of price controls. When governmental authority wants to control prices it has intention of helping the producers of that product or consumers of that product.

In either case however, our simple demand and supply model will show us that the opportunity cost of these policies is much higher than the benefits to be received. Therefore it is somewhat unnecessary and unfeasible to carry out price controls of any kind. Moreover if controlling prices on the governmental level can solve any (or all) economic problem, then life would be much easier! So, let us consider the economic consequences of a price ceiling policy such as rent control, or gasoline price control or insurance cost control, or some food price control. Price ceiling policy is adopted because the government thinks that the market-determined price is too high for (poor) consumers, so it wants to restrict the maximum price that producers can charge for the product.

Consider Figure 2.8. The market-determined price (P_1) is equating quantity demanded and quantity supplied, but the government finds this unacceptable so it pretends to help the consumers by controlling the maximum price. It is obvious that the government-controlled price has to be lower than the market price because it makes no sense to have the maximum price established at the equilibrium level (market would take the price to equilibrium by itself, no government control is necessary for that) and there is no help given to consumers if the maximum price

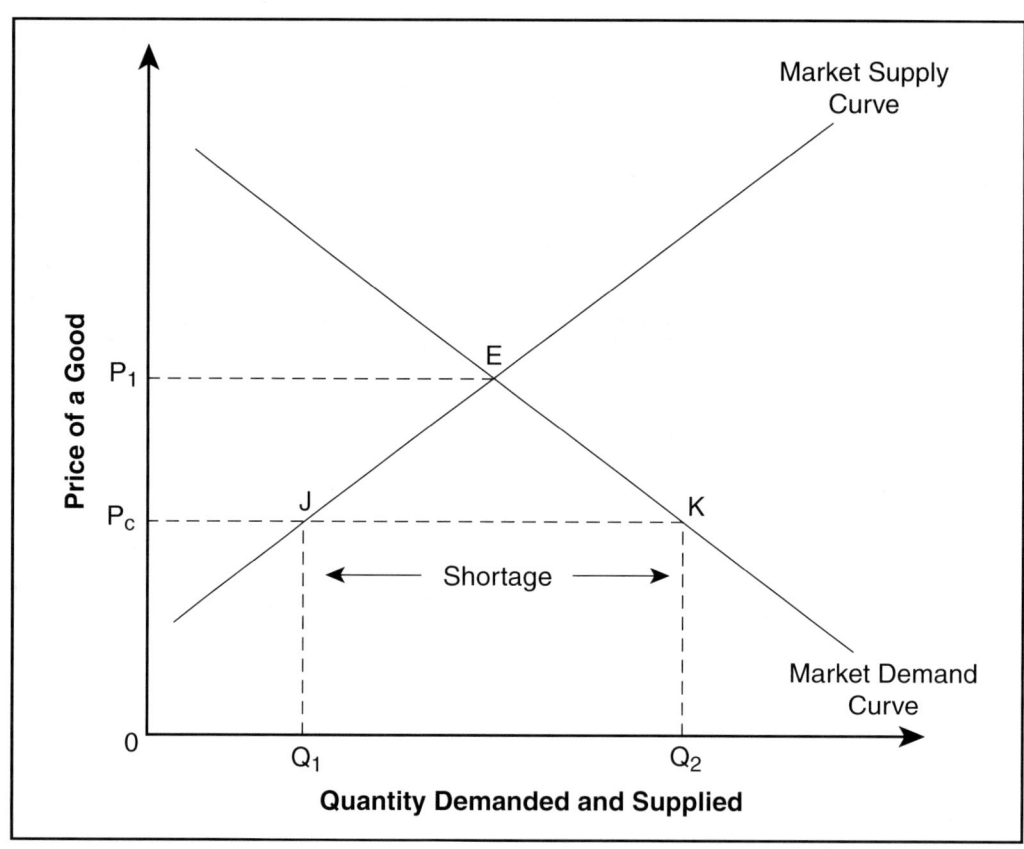

FIGURE 2.8 ■ Economic Consequences of Price Ceiling Policy

is established at a higher level than equilibrium (the market would do a better job of helping consumers in that case!). This essentially means that the price ceiling at any price below equilibrium would create higher quantity demanded than quantity supplied, leading to a shortage of the product.

Consider the case of airfares of recent years. In order to make it affordable for poor consumers to fly, suppose the government decided to help them by controlling the maximum airfare. The government's imposed maximum has to be less than the current fares if any help is to be given to the "poor" travelers. Then at the lower, government-controlled price, the quantity demanded would go up and quantity supplied would decline. While many consumers would decide to fly, it would be hard to find airlines ready to serve at these controlled maximum prices. This would lead to a shortage of the product, as shown in Figure 2.8. Besides this shortage one can also envision some other consequences of creating a price ceiling. To beat the shortage, some consumers who can afford to pay higher airfares would like to buy tickets at the higher fares, but this would be illegal. So there would be a tendency toward illegal transactions (sometimes called black market). To stop these illegal transactions, government has to install a police station near each airline office (or a travel agency), leading to a higher administrative cost. The quality of the product sooner or later would start deteriorating as airlines would find ways to cut the cost by taking more risky planes and cutting labor costs.

The economic consequences of so-called price floor policy can be seen in a similar way. A price floor is adopted to help the producers of the products, such as farmers (or rice or wheat) or milk suppliers. Consider Figure 2.9. The government policymakers think that the market-determined price is too low for poor farmers (or suppliers) to survive. So, government establishes the minimum price to be offered to the producers. This minimum price has to be above the equilibrium price, because at or below equilibrium price no help is offered to the suppliers. However, at any price above equilibrium, the quantity supplied is higher than the quantity demanded, leading to a surplus of the product. Hence, the price floor policy essentially creates the surplus of the product, as can be seen in Figure 2.9, at a price floor of P_f. Another consequence of this is that there will be some suppliers who are ready to offer the product at a lower price than P_f but the government would make it illegal to do so. Again, as there is a vast tendency for illegal transactions, the government would have to incur administrative costs in stopping this black market.

All in all we can conclude that price controls of any kind has no economic justification, as our simple demand and supply model shows. No wonder that a Nobel Prize-winning economist, Prof. Arthur Lewis, after researching the consequences of price controls (especially in the case of Ghana), concluded that "price control is a delicate instrument, easily misused."

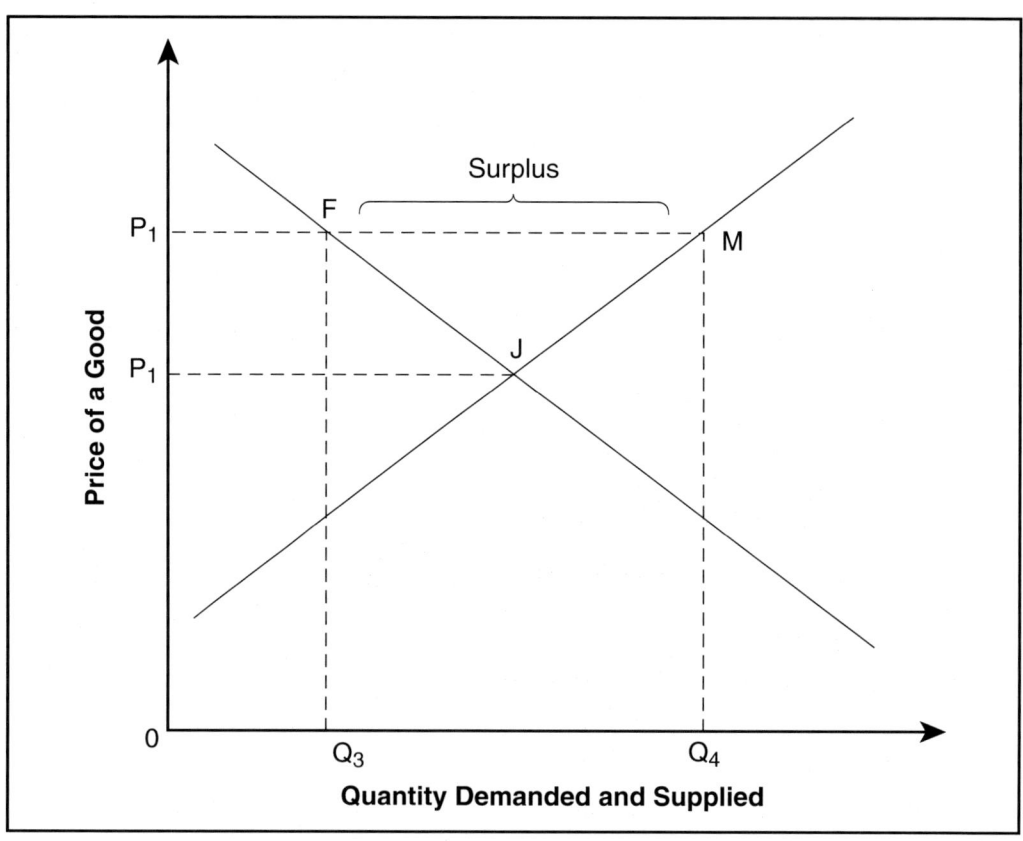

FIGURE 2.9 ■ Economic Consequences of Price Floor Policy

The law of demand and the law of supply are important statements of human behavior. This chapter has discussed the tendency of consumers and laws, shifts in demand and supply curves, and the effect of outside shocks to the market mechanism.

References

Arnold, R. 1996. *Macroeconomics*, 3rd ed., Chapters 2 and 3. West Publishing Company.

Banmole, W. and A. Blinder. 1996. *Economics*, 6th ed., Chapters 3 and 4. Prentice Hall Publications.

Byrns, R. and J. Stone, Jr. 1996. *Economics*, 6th ed., Chapters 3 and 4. Harper/Collins Publishers.

Kulkarni, K. and E. Dolan. 2007. *Understanding Microeconomics*, Chapter 3. Reddy, CA: Horizon Textbook Publishing.

Samuelson, P. and W. Nordhans. 1995. *Economics*, 14th ed., Chapter 4. Prentice Hall Publications.

Sharp, A. M., C. Register, and P. Grimes. 1996. *Economics of Social Issues*, 12th ed., Chapters 3 and 4. Irwin Publishers.

Stiglitz, J. 1996. *Economics*, 2nd ed., Chapter 4. W.W. Norton and Company.

Tregarthen, T. 1996. *Macroeconomics*, Chapters 3 and 4. Worth Publishers.

Chapter 3
National Income Accounting and GDP Calculation

SUMMARY

Just as individual firms keep a record of their performance to better inform their business strategy, economies also keep records of performance in order to better craft policy decisions. National income accounting and Gross Domestic Product (GDP) are the two most widely accepted means of doing so. As such, national income accounting and GDP are two pivotal concepts in the empirical assessment of aggregate economic performance within and among countries, over time.

The first section defines GDP as the market value of all final goods and services produced in an economy in a given time period. It is distinct from Gross National Product (GNP), which measures the value of all final goods and services produced by a country's national business entities, irrespective of their location in the world. In order to clarify this definition of GDP, the component concepts of *final goods* and *market value* are explained. Other useful concepts related to GDP are also presented, including *national income* and *net domestic product* (NDP). Moreover, the utility of a *price index* in offsetting the distorting effects of rising price levels on measurements of GDP is explored, and the basic mathematical construction of a price index is presented. There are three different price indices—consumer price index (CPI), producer price index (PPI), and GDP deflator. All perform similar functions, and these are considered in turn. Firstly, the price indices can be used to measure the *real GDP* by separating out the effect of price increases on the value of the GDP. Secondly, they measure the general price level of an economy. Thirdly, the price indices help one to ascertain the extent to which there is inflation in the economy.

It is unfeasible to calculate the actual market value produced by every firm in the economy; therefore, the second section presents two approaches used to approximate GDP: the total expenditure (aggregate demand) approach and the total income (aggregate supply) approach. Theoretically, the double-entry nature of national accounting ensures that both approaches equal the total value of all goods and services. Since each transaction involves both a sale and a purchase, one may consider either expenditures for output or the incomes that the production of output generates to calculate GDP. The total expenditure approach divides the economy into four sectors—consumer, producer, government, and foreign trade—and assumes that GDP is the sum of expenditures in these sectors. Thus, GDP is expressed according to the aggregate demand approach as: $Y = C + I + G + X - M$. Inversely, the total income approach assumes that the sum of the value of all activities representing income received should equal GDP, including wages of laborers, profits of firm owners, interest income from deposits, and taxes received by government at all levels. Despite their theoretical equivalence, the total expenditure approach is the more practical, and thus the most commonly used, method of calculating GDP.

Although GDP is the primary measure of economic activity in an economy, economic theorists still criticize its shortcomings as an economic tool. The final section details the limitations of GDP calculation and presents a few of the alternative measures that have been created to date. These include a measure of economic welfare that considers all negative externalities of production, net economic welfare (NEW), and a related measure of economic welfare (MEW) that adjusts all countries' GDPs. The conclusion is that such alternatives, despite their merit, have not become universally acceptable. Thus, one must remain cognizant of the fallibility of GDP data, but we need not reject the measure outright.

Introduction 3.1

Just as a firm keeps a record of the progress it makes over the years, an economy maintains its record of its performance using national income accounting. It is important for an economist to know how the economy is doing because several policy steps depend upon economic performance. For example, even the social security checks payable to elders are tied to the cost of living index (COLA). The economic growth rate can change the cost of living for all of us. So, the main question is, how do we keep track of economic performance? Are there practical problems with such recordkeeping? This chapter aims to answer these questions with the help of national income accounting, which involves calculating the Gross Domestic Product (GDP). GDP calculation serves two purposes. First, it is a measure of economic performance. Second, the GDPs of two or more economies can be used to compare developments in those economies.

In macroeconomics, the letter "Y" denotes GDP. However, before progressing, we need to point out the differences between GNP and GDP. While GDP measures the value of all final goods and services produced in a country's territory irrespective of the ownership of the entity producing the good or the service, GNP measures the value of all final goods and services produced by U.S.-owned entities irrespective of their location. Hence, the value of production of all final goods and services in the U.S. territories will be included in the U.S. GDP. Production by the Toyota plant in Mississippi will be included in the U.S. GDP but not in the U.S. GNP. This is because Toyota is a Japanese-owned firm, and GNP measure does not include value of production by non-U.S.-owned companies. In a similar way, the value of production of the IBM plant in Mexico City will be included in the U.S. GNP but not in its GDP, because Mexico City is not part of U.S. territory. However, if comparisons of the GDP and GNP are done, then it is clear that for United States, the numerical differences are insignificant. This is partly due to the fact that U.S. GDP is so large. We shall revisit this point in future discussion. Until 1991, the U.S. Department of Commerce, which keeps a record of U.S. economic performance, published Gross National Product (GNP) figures instead of GDP figures, as it does now.

The theoretical definition of GDP therefore can be summarized as the "total market value of all final goods and services produced in an economy in a given time period," usually that time period is one year. Two key concepts in the above statement are (1) final goods and (2) market value. Final goods are those goods that are used for final consumption or that directly satisfy wants. Examples of final goods include, apple juice, cars, gasoline, most grocery-store items, and houses. Consumption of these goods gives consumers satisfaction. Final goods therefore are sometimes called "consumer goods." As opposed to final goods, there are *intermediate goods* that are used in the production of some other goods. Examples of intermediate goods include rubber, plastic, machines, basic metals, and wood. Because the value of intermediate goods is already included in the value of final goods, intermediate goods are excluded from the GDP calculation to avoid double counting.

The market value of any good is the price of the good times the quantity produced. Thus the market value of ten cars would be $200,000 if each car is priced at $20,000. Hence

$$\text{Market value of a good} = \text{Price of the good} \times \text{Quantity produced}.$$

If we do this calculation for all final goods and add up all market values, then the total market value of all final goods should be the GDP of an economy. This GDP is labeled as *nominal GDP,* and, as you can see, the value of nominal GDP can be easily changed if there is only a change in the price(s) of commodities. For example, if prices go up (and the quantity produced stays the same), then market values will go up and then the nominal GDP will go up, making it a problem for us to conclude that the economy is developing when only prices in it are increasing. To avoid this problem, economists construct the price index.

The price index compares the prices of current year (the year for which the price index is constructed) with the prices of same goods in a base year (the common year used for comparison) and takes the following ratio:

$$\text{Price Index} = \frac{\text{Average Price Level in Current Year}}{\text{Average Price Level in Base Year}} \times 100$$

More technically, it can be written as,

$$\text{Price Index} = \frac{\Sigma p^c_i \times q_i}{\Sigma p^b_i \times q_i} \times 100$$

where p^c_i = Prices in current year
p^b_i = Prices in base year
q_i = Quantities of goods

Now the question is, which goods should we include in the price-index calculation? Depending upon the answer to this question, we can define three major price indexes:

1. *Consumer Price Index (CPI):* CPI uses only final goods for the price-index calculation. Hence, CPI gives us an idea of the change in the cost of living of *consumers from base year to the current year.*

2. *Producer Price Index (PPI):* PPI uses only intermediate goods in the price index calculation. In some older books PPI is referred to as the Wholesale Price Index. PPI therefore measures changes in cost of production of goods from base year to the current year.

3. *GDP Deflator:* This is the broadest type of price index because it includes all types of goods in price-index calculation. Hence, the GDP deflator is the most comprehensive price index; it measures changes in prices of all types of goods.

There are three major uses of price indexes calculated in this manner:

1. Real GDP = (Nominal GDP / Price index) × 100. The real GDP is conveniently defined as the ratio of nominal GDP and price index (multiplied by 100) to avoid the effect of prices on the value of GDP. Hence, if only prices go up, the price index will go up, nominal GDP will go up, and the real GDP may stay the same. Thus any increase in prices alone will not make a change in real GDP. In fact, in macroeconomic theory we traditionally separate the nominal and real variables by deflating them by their prices. For example, money wage/prices will be real wage. By defining real GDP we have now avoided the effect of prices on GDP.

2. Any one of the price indexes can be used to measure the "General Price Level" (P) of an economy. So, whenever a question of "how do you measure the price level of an economy?" arises, the answer usually is by one of its price indexes.

3. A percentage increase in general price level is popularly called inflation rate of the economy. Hence the 5 percent increase in general price level is the 5 percent inflation rate in the economy. Price indexes therefore have varied uses.

3.2

In reality, the Department of Commerce does not calculate GDP by taking surveys of the whole economy and calculating the actual market value produced by each and every firm. In fact, there is no way to contact each and every producer to inquire about the production he/she has made in a given month or a year. Hence, in practice, we have to make adjustment for the calculation of GDP. There are two approaches used for actual expression of GDP: (1) Total Expenditure or Aggregate Demand Approach and (2) Total Income or Aggregate Supply Approach.

In an aggregate (the word "aggregate" means "total") demand, or total expenditure approach, we approximate that the total expenditure generated by all sectors in an economy is the GDP of that economy. The argument here is that if someone has spent money to buy certain goods, they must have been produced, so the value of any expenditure should be included in the GDP of the economy. Therefore, in this approach:

GDP = Total expenditure generated by all sectors of the economy.

In any economy there are four major sectors that can generate expenditure: (1) consumer sector, (2) producer sector, (3) government sector, and (4) foreign trade sector.

1. The *consumer sector* is usually the largest sector of any economy; it generates roughly 65 percent of the total expenditure in the U.S. economy. There is a vast expenditure by consumers of final goods and services, and that expenditure is called "consumption" and it is represented by the letter "C." Therefore, consumption represents the expenditure of the consumer class on final goods and services on such activities as buying groceries, gas, shopping, houses, clothes, etc.

2. The *producer sector* has special expenditure on the purchase of machinery, tools, and equipment or on construction activities or the production of goods that are not yet sent to the market (popularly called *inventories*). In macroeconomic terms this expenditure is called *investment* and is represented by the letter "I." The term investment, therefore, has more than one meaning. When you tell your friend you are investing $100,000 in the purchase of IBM stock, that investment refers to the financial investment, and it is not a part of the real or macroeconomic meaning of investment. The real investment only includes the three activities we described above. Financial investment, such as the purchase of bonds, stocks, shares, and precious metals, etc., is important, but it is not a part of the macroeconomic meaning of investment. In the case of the U.S. economy, gross domestic investment constitutes roughly 20 percent of the total expenditure, and it is the most volatile part of total expenditure. It ranges from 17 percent to 22 percent, and its fluctuations are very important to changes in GDP, as we shall see in later chapters.

3. The *government sector* has expenditure on several activities such as welfare payments, defense expenses, paying off the interest on the national debt, education, transportation, national security, national parks and recreation, maintenance of the police force, prisons, housing and urban development,

and many other activities. All this expenditure by the government sector is called *government expenditure* and it is represented by the letter "G." In the United States, government expenditure has increased slowly in last fifty years. In 2008, for example, the U.S. government will spend as much as $2800 billion on all the different activities. Its main expenditure items however are (a) welfare payments, including Medicare and Medicaid, food coupons, the unemployment benefits program, and Social Security payments to the elderly; (b) defense expenditures; and (c) interest payment on government's debt, popularly called public debt or national debt. The U.S. government expenditure figure has been roughly 20 percent of the GDP for the last decade. We shall discuss these government expenditures further in chapter XX on fiscal policy. Fiscal policy is by definition government policy that makes changes in government expenditure (G) and taxes (Tx).

4. The *foreign trade sector* has two types of expenditures. The expenditure of domestic residents on foreign goods and services is called *imports* and is represented by "M." The United States is the largest importing country in the world. The expenditure of foreign residents on domestic goods and services is called *exports* and is represented by "X." The United States is the largest exporter in the world, with roughly $1700 billion worth of goods and services exported in 2007. (X − M) is popularly called, "net exports." From 1982 on, the U.S. economy's net exports have been negative, which creates the trade-balance deficit for the U.S. balance of payments. In recent years, this trade-balance deficit has been a major worry for policy makers because from 1998 to 2006, this trade-balance deficit has increased yearly at record-setting numbers. All-in-all, the total expenditure generated in the economy will be equal to GDP.

Therefore, via an expenditure approach,

$$Y = C + I + G + X - M$$

As previously mentioned, in a total expenditure approach this will be taken to be equal to the GDP (or Y) of the economy.

By using the second approach, the total income or aggregate supply approach, we can get the same numerical answer of the GDP because the rational argument can be made that any expenditure activity in an economy is an income activity to someone else. This is because if someone expends, someone else in the economy receives that expenditure. Therefore, if total expenditure is equal to the GDP then total income generated should also be equal to the GDP of an economy. Hence, in this approach we add up the value of all activities that represent income received. These activities include:

1. Rental income that is received by land owners.
2. Wages that are received by all the labor employed in the economy.
3. Profits received by all firm owners.
4. Interest income received by all depositors.
5. Taxes received at the governmental level.

The total of all monetary values of activities 1 through 5 should also be equal to the GDP (Y). Theoretically, this argument being very valid and logical, it does not really matter which approach one would use for calculating the GDP.

However, the total income approach (for practical purposes) is more complex than the total expenditure approach. This is primarily because taxes and profits do not appear in one lump-sum amount. We pay taxes at different levels to many different governments authorities. Taxes appear in the form of income taxes, sales taxes, property taxes, school taxes, inheritance taxes, import taxes, wealth taxes, capital gains taxes, and many more. Similarly, the profits of a firm can also take the form of proprietor's income, dividends to stock holders, or undivided corporate profits. Because of all these complicated forms of income items, one can conclude that total expenditure approach is more direct (only five items need to be considered). The following table shows the exact numbers of total expenditure items in billions of dollars (nominal terms) and the GDP figures of the U.S. economy from 1990 to 2007.

TABLE 3.1

	(All figures are in billions of dollars)					
Year	Consumption	Investment	Government Expenditures	Exports	Imports	GDP
1990	3,839.90	861	1,180.20	741.5	811.5	5,803.10
1991	3,986.10	802.9	1,234.40	765.7	752.3	5,995.90
1992	4,235.30	864.8	1,271.00	788	824.9	6,337.70
1993	4,477.90	953.4	1,291.20	812.1	882.5	6,657.40
1994	4,743.30	1,097.10	1,325.50	907.3	1,012.50	7,072.20
1995	4,975.80	1,144.00	1,369.20	1,046.10	1,137.10	7,397.70
1996	5,256.80	1,240.30	1,416.00	1,117.3	1,217.60	7,816.90
1997	5,547.40	1,389.80	1,468.70	1,242.00	1,352.20	8,304.30
1998	5,879.50	1,509.10	1,518.30	1,243.10	1,430.50	8,747.00
1999	6,282.50	1,625.70	1,620.80	1,312.10	1,585.90	9,268.40
2000	6,739.40	1,735.50	1,721.60	1,478.90	1,875.60	9,817.00
2001	7,055.00	1,614.30	1,825.60	1,355.20	1,725.60	10,128.00
2002	7,350.70	1,582.10	1,961.10	1,311.60	1,769.90	10,469.60
2003	7,703.60	1,664.10	2,092.50	1,377.60	1,889.80	10,960.80
2004	8,195.90	1,888.60	2,216.80	1,619.90	2,244.00	11,685.90
2005	8,707.80	2,077.20	2,363.40	1,853.50	2,588.50	12,433.90
2006	9,224.50	2,209.20	2,523.00	2,159.00	2,953.20	13,194.70
2007	9,540.50	2,117.30	2,608.30	2,302.00	3,058.10	13,551.90

SOURCE: Department of Commerce, U.S. Government. Various issues.

3.3

Besides GDP as the main measure of economic development, there are a few other useful concepts we can define. One such useful concept is the Net Domestic Product (NDP). The NDP equals GDP minus depreciation (or capital consumption allowance). Depreciation is the declining use value of equipment or a resource such as machinery. From NDP, we can also define national income (NI). NI equals NDP minus indirect business taxes (IBT).

After discussing the ways to calculate GDP and its components, we should now ask the question, is it worth spending all these resources in calculating GDP? Some economists, skeptical of the whole process of calculating and publishing GDP-related figures, answer this question with a big "no." In fact a group of economists, led by a former professor from Harvard University, Oskar Morgenstern, believes that the whole process of GDP calculation is a garbage-in-garbage-out (GIGO) process, because it leaves out so many important calculations and has quite a few limitations.

We can summarize the limitations of GDP calculation as follows: The first limitation of GDP as the measure of economic development is that the GDP calculation process does not consider the population of the economy; it only considers the production value. If we want to get the real measure of economic growth, we need to know not only production but also how many people are using that product. The real economic development occurs not just by higher production but also by few people having more production produced. Consider the GDP of the economy of India. India produces one of the ten largest GDPs in the world. So if you look at the GDP alone you may conclude that India is the tenth most developed country in the world. But that conclusion would be misleading. Because even if in 2008 India's GDP is roughly $1 trillion (without considering its purchasing power), when one considers India's population of 1.1 billion, its per capita income (PCI) is roughly $950. Ranked according to the PCI, India's rank is logically closer to 122, out of roughly 200 countries in the world. Hence, if GDP measure has to be an indicator of economic development, then it should consider the population of the economy, or to put it differently, PCI is a better measure of development than GDP itself (recall that PCI equals GDP/population).

Another limitation of GDP calculation is the fact that GDP does not consider "non-market" transactions, which are representatives of production activities that should be a part of GDP but are not. These are, therefore, productions that are produced but not sold in the market mechanism, and are therefore never valued. Consider, for example, a production like backyard gardening. When your friend has a vegetable garden and gives you some of the crop, if you do not pay for that gift, then the production has taken place, but there is no "marketed" exchange of that production, and therefore there is no value to that production that can be included in the GDP calculation. In reality, we can consider several other examples of non-market transactions. Some examples can include painting your own house (as opposed to having it painted by a company whom you will pay) or doing laundry at home (as opposed to having it done by a professional cleaner). Now, compared to developed economies, developing countries have many more non-market transactions. Consider the fact that per-farmer land holding in United States is roughly 550 acres while per farmer landholding in Bangladesh is only 2.5 acres. For the Bangladesh farmer, agriculture is essentially a backyard gardening production that his/her family uses for the whole year. Of course this type of production is neither valued nor marketed and therefore is not counted in Bangladesh's GDP. So our conclusion is that GDPs of less-developed countries (LDCs) are usually underestimates of their actual production due to the exclusion of non-market transactions in GDP.

The third problem with GDP calculation is its inability to include the bad side effects of higher production. The bad side effects are called the *negative externalities* or *diseconomies* of higher production. For example, when an economy produces a lot of cars, it obviously increases its GDP figure by a large number, but the large number of cars can add to pollution and make the air dirty. Dirty, polluted air is an excellent example of a bad side effect of higher production. Similarly, higher chemical production can cause the firm to dump the residues in the river. River pollution is another negative externality. Yet, another example of negative externality could be the danger of a radiation leak. In 1979, at the Three Mile Island Nuclear Generating Station in Pennsylvania, there was a great panic over a radiation leak from the nuclear plant. Of course, for the people living in the area, fear of radiation is a negative externality. (As one can argue in reverse, there are some positive externalities, or good side effects, of higher production, too. For example, when a big department store opens in your neighborhood, you will get to use newly paved and expanded roads. This may add some extra value to the GDP, too. But here we can make our point against GDP calculation by concentrating on the negative aspects of externalities). If GDP has to be a reliable measure of economic development, then the value of negative externalities should be subtracted from GDP value. Clearly, the GDP calculation in its present form does not discount externalities, hence it is limited in its usefulness as a reliable measure of economic growth.

Two attempts were made by some great economic researchers to overcome this problem. First, Professor Paul Samuelson, a retired professor at Massachusetts Institute of Technology (MIT), and Nobel prize winner in Economics, proposed a new measure of economic welfare called *net economic welfare* (NEW). NEW was set by considering all the negative values for externalities. Similarly, Professors William Nordhaus and James Tobin from Yale University, both Nobel prize winners, proposed the *measure of economic welfare* (MEW), which was supposed to do the same thing as NEW to adjust the GDPs of all countries. However, neither NEW nor MEW became very famous, partly because externalities are such subjective concepts that giving them monetary value was considered to be an abstract and arbitrary exercise.

Another problem with GDP calculation is its inability to recognize the difference between *what* is produced and *how much* is produced by an economy. While GDP does a good job of measuring how much an economy produces, it ignores what specifically that economy is producing. In reality, there can be an economy that uses many of its resources to produce products that are not very socially desirable. For example, if country A and country B have GDP figures of $500 and $700 billion respectively, then by looking just at GDP, we will conclude that country A is not as developed as country B. But if country A's production is mainly in necessities such as food, shelter, clothing and related goods, and very few luxury goods, such as big yachts, racy cars, or other luxury items, then country A's production is socially desirable. If country B is doing the reverse and has more production in luxury goods, producing only few necessities, then the social desirability of country B is questionable, despite the higher GDP. Would you consider country B more developed than country A in this case? The point is that higher GDP does not necessarily mean higher economic development if we do not know specifically what is being produced by the economy.

Another problem with GDP calculation is that it does not consider the distribution of production. For a complete idea of economic development, we need to know how the economy is doing in terms of taking higher production and prosperity to all classes of people. If one country, despite its higher production of goods and services, is letting its large poor population starve, and if the small minority of very rich people in it is taking a larger share of the GDP, then that country should not be considered very developed. Similarly, if another country is doing a great job of distributing its GDP to all levels of its population, then it should be considered better developed despite the lower value of its GDP.

Added to the above major limitations of GDP as a measure of economic development are other practical problems, such as discrepancies in collecting data, doing surveys, getting reliable information, and administering the yearly (if not quarterly) projects to do all these statistics. The question arises of how to solve the problem of illegal transactions, some of which may not be immoral, which will not be included in GDP. Transactions in many countries are often not recorded, even though they are legal and moral transactions, in order to evade taxes. This exclusion makes it even more difficult for GDP to serve as a good measure of economic growth. These practical problems would significantly add to the skepticism that some economists have for GDP calculation. No wonder then that some analysts want to abandon the whole exercise.

Nonetheless, as we know, almost all countries (even communist countries and dictatorships, which strictly control many of their economic variables) publish monthly, quarterly, and yearly data on GDP. All member countries of the International Monetary Fund (IMF) have their data printed in the famous publication *International Financial Statistics* and numerous other publications. So, why don't countries listen to Professor Morgenstern and his friends?

A simple answer to that question is that no one has yet found a more suitable, more reliable, and better substitute for GDP. Some attempts have been made by the World Bank to come up with alternative measures, such as the human development index (HDI). There is also a recalculation of GDPs according to the purchasing power of the money, which is an attempt to solve the problem of the dollar buying more in a developing country such as in India. These attempts, however, have not become very popular and universally acceptable. So our conclusion is what most of the economics profession (and statistics) agree upon. It is the feeling that we need to remember all the limitations of GDP calculation and take these figures with a grain of salt. The uses of GDP are so many and so far-reaching that we cannot just throw away its universal acceptability for minor problems in its expression.

In the next few chapters we shall discuss the measures of money supply in the U.S. economy and concentrate on the monetary sector. In Chapter 4, we shall start with the historical development of monetary systems, and begin by first reviewing the gold standard mechanism.

Chapter 4
Gold Standard Mechanism and Empirical Evidence

The monetary system underpinning the world economy has taken on various forms throughout history. As the first organized international monetary regime, lasting from 1871 to 1914 and intermittently thereafter until 1944, the gold standard is duly regarded as a defining period in world economic history. This chapter examines this regime from a historical perspective, explains its theoretical foundations, and empirically assesses its overall performance.

The gold standard required much discipline on the part of national governments, and each of its stringent rules is considered in detail. Firstly, governments had to establish a *mint price* in order to keep the value of gold constant in terms of the currency circulating as money. Secondly, governments were required to transact (buy and sell) any amount of gold supplied or demanded by the general public in order to ensure that the actual market price of gold equaled the established mint price. Finally, governments had to legalize the melting of gold coins so as to guarantee equality between the price of gold for monetary and non-monetary use. A simple supply–demand framework is presented to show how the money supply is completely dependent on the demand for gold for non-monetary purposes and the overall supply of gold in the country. The value of the money supply is then shown graphically to be the product of the mint price and the quantity of gold used as the money supply. This value of the money supply is likely to change because of shifts in the demand and supply curves, and events that could cause such shifts are cited.

The chapter then explores the benefits of the gold standard and the costs that ultimately led to its downfall. On the positive side, the system imposed a level of price discipline that provided a theoretical solution to the perennial problem of inflation. In short, money supply was insulated from any erroneous government policies. This insulation had the added benefit of eliminating those adverse business cycles caused by deeds of the national monetary authority. Likewise, the gold standard had an automatic cure for inflation via the incentives it provided to producers of gold. Finally, the system is beneficial for international price equalization. This chapter demonstrates this by presenting the *law of one price*. To its detriment, however, the gold standard fostered the contempt of national governments who had to follow its strict rules without garnering any modicum of control over money supply. More ominously, the system gave countries implicit incentives to break the rules of the game. A country supplying more money than warranted by its gold reserves could still import goods and services from abroad, as its price level would necessarily rise above that of other countries. This severely reduced the level of trust countries had in one another to convert their currencies into gold when necessary. Empirical evidence shows that price stability was indeed not achieved either in the short run or in the long run, even though stable exchange rates were maintained between the major currencies.

The final section reflects upon recent developments in international monetary relations. A basic outline of the Bretton Woods agreement is sketched, and the contributions of the gold standard to its successor are highlighted. A survey of the European Monetary System cites it as a possible harbinger of future turbulence in the world monetary system. The conclusion is that although the international monetary regime is constantly in flux, the gold standard and Bretton Woods will have enduring influence.

4.1 What Is the Gold Standard?

The gold standard is a monetary system that existed in various forms throughout history. The classical gold standard existed in the United States and in several other countries in the years between 1880 and 1917, although aspects of it persisted in various forms until the 1971 breakdown of the Bretton Woods system. In the classical gold standard monetary system, each country was committed to keep the value of their monetary unit constant in terms of gold. Before 1821, most countries were on a bimetallic standard based on silver and gold. After the Napoleonic War inflation episode, and Great Britain returned to a gold standard. Throughout the period between 1821 and 1880, the gold standard steadily expanded as more and more countries turned to it and by 1880, the majority of the countries in the world were on a gold standard. According to Bordo, "the period from 1880 to 1914 known as the 'heyday' of the gold standard, was a remarkable period in world economic history, characterized by rapid economic growth, the free flow of labor and capital, virtually free trade, and in general, world peace. These external conditions coupled with the elaborate financial network centered in London are believed by many observers to be the *sinequanon* of the effective operation of the gold standard."

After 1914, the gold standard temporarily broke down because of World War I, but was re-established from 1925 to 1931. However, due to large outflows of gold stock from the U.K. and the U.S. economies, the gold exchange standard broke down again in 1934. Another reason for this breakdown was the unwillingness of most of the countries to let the gold outflow happen. The Bretton Woods system (which existed from 1944 to 1971) was the most recent attempt to adopt some kind of gold standard mechanism. Bordo summarized the reasons for the breakdown of this system by saying, "In the post-World War II period, persistent U.S. balance of payments deficits helped finance the recovery of world trade from the aftermath of depression and war. However, the steady growth in the use of the U.S. dollars as international reserves, and persistent U.S. deficits steadily reduced the U.S. gold reserves and the gold reserve ratio—which in turn reduced confidence in the ultimate ability of the U.S. to redeem its currency in gold. This so-called confidence problem, coupled with the aversion of many countries to paying seigniorage to the United States as well as paying an 'inflation tax' to the United States in the post-1965 period, ultimately led to the breakdown of the Bretton Woods System in 1971." Thus, even though the gold standard does not exist now, it has been the most influential monetary system of the past. It, therefore, deserves a careful examination in this chapter.

4.2 The Working of the Pure Gold Standard: Rules of the Game

In the gold standard, governments of each member country had to adhere to at least three strict rules. First, each government had to keep the price of gold constant in terms of the currency circulating as money. This fixed price was established as US$35 per ounce of gold. Second, at the mint price, the government must be ready to buy or sell any amount of gold offered to it by the general public. The readiness of the government to do these activities guaranteed the equality of the actual market price and the announced mint price of gold. This is because, if the actual price of gold happened to be lower than the mint price of gold, then the public would tend to sell gold to the government. Consequently, the supply of gold in the market would go down and the actual price of gold would move upward.[1] In the reverse case, if the actual price of gold was greater than the mint price, then the public would buy gold from the government. In turn, the supply of gold in the market would go up, lowering its market price. Due to this second rule, therefore, the mint price was no different than the market price. Third, the governments under the gold standard also had to legalize the melting of gold. Because of this rule, the price of gold for monetary and non-monetary use was made equal, and this rule supported the equality of the mint and the actual price of gold.

With the help of the these three rules and Figure 4.1, let us now determine the exact value of the money supply under the gold standard. Notice that in Figure 4.1 the horizontal axis denotes the quantity of the total gold supplied in the economy and the quantity demanded of gold for non-monetary purposes such as for jewelry or simply for hoarding. On the vertical axis, we plot the price of gold per ounce. The inverse relationship between the price and the quantity demanded of gold for non-monetary purposes is shown by the downward sloping demand curve from left to right. As the price of gold increases, people would tend to demand a lower quantity of it because of the famous income and substitution effects.[2]

The supply curve of gold for the economy would be upward sloping from left to right. This is so because a higher price of gold makes the producers of gold, who supply the quantity, work harder and produce more.

As the principles of economics may have taught you, due to an increase in the price of a good, the real income of the consumer goes down, making the consumer demand less of all goods. Second, an increase in the price also makes the consumer substitute the consumption of gold by the consumption of related commodities such as silver. In ordinary terms, an increase in the price of gold would make people wear more silver and less gold.

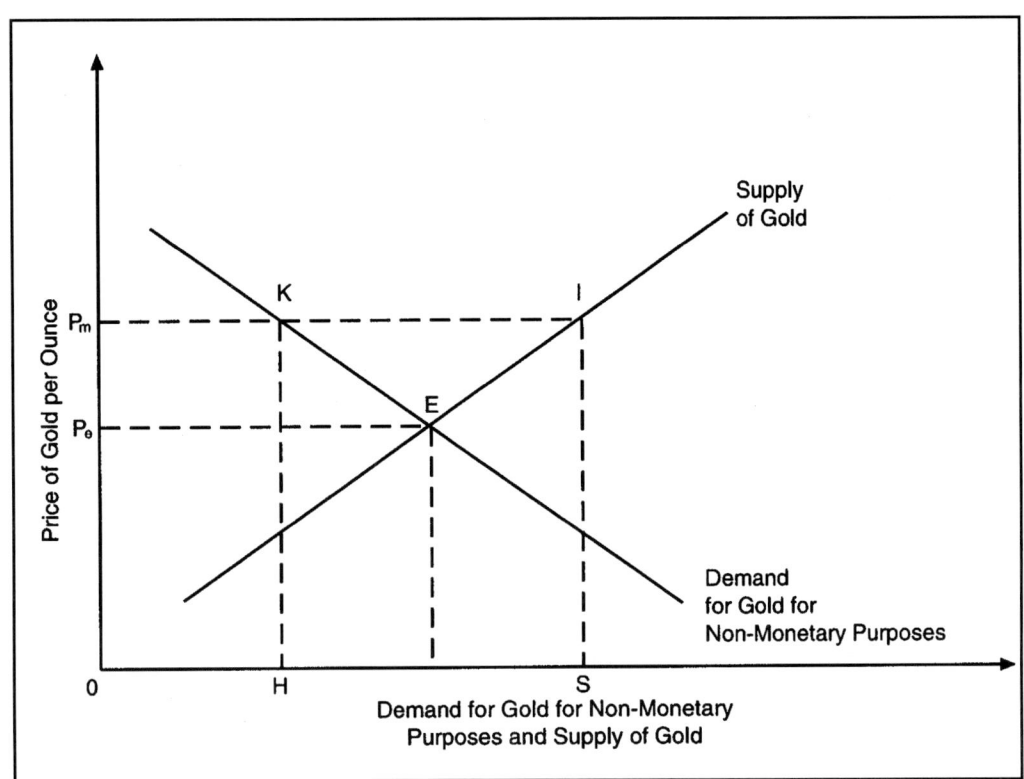

FIGURE 4.1 Quantity Supplied of Gold and Quantity Demanded of Gold for Non-Monetary Purposes

At the point where these two curves intersect, the equilibrium price P_e, is determined. Interpreted carefully, this means that at price P_e, all of the supply of gold in the economy is being demanded for non-monetary purposes such as making jewelry. Obviously that means there is no excess supply of gold left to make coins. Hence, a rational government would fix the mint price about P_e (certainly not equal to or below P_e because in those cases, there would be no gold left to support the money supply of the economy). Let us assume that the government in question fixes the mint price at the level P_m. At P_m, the quantity of gold supplied in the economy is OS (P_m), given by the supply curve, and the quantity demanded of gold for non-monetary purposes is P_mK (or OH), given by the demand curve. This results in an excess of gold supply of HS (or KI) to be used as the money supply. In a pure gold standard, the quantity HS is available for coin making. Now, if we define the value of the money supply as the product of the price of gold and the quantity of gold used as money, then the value of the money supply, in terms of Figure 4.1 is OP_m (price) × HS. The product of OP_m and HS defines the area of the rectangle KISH. Thus, the value of money supply under the gold standard can be expressed as the area of KISH.

Does this mean that it is only the locations of the demand and supply curves in Figure 4.1 that determine the amount of the money supply under the gold standard? Or to ask the question differently, does this mean that the money supply (under the gold standard) is likely to change if there are shifts in these curves? The answers to both questions are, importantly, yes. Hence, the sources of changes in the money supply under the gold standard are derived from the factors that shift the demand for gold and supply of gold curves. Our preliminary understanding of the principles of economics tells us that the demand curves for gold shifts if there is an increase in the income of the consumers. Because the demand for gold we are considering here is the demand by the whole economy, it is the income of the nation or economy (national income) that would be influential in this case. A higher income tends to make consumers demand more gold at a given price. Hence, an increase in income would indicate a shift of the demand curve to the right. It would reduce the area of KISH, which means the value of the money supply would go down.

Second, the price of related commodities, silver in this case, can also influence the location of the demand curve. If the price of silver goes up, people would demand more gold (less of silver) and the demand curve of gold would shift to the right. This reduces the value of the money supply under the gold standard. Similarly, the tastes of the consumers, prices of complementary goods, and expectations of the consumers also have an effect on the location of the demand curve. Refer to Figure 4.2 for shifts in the demand curve due to changes in demand.

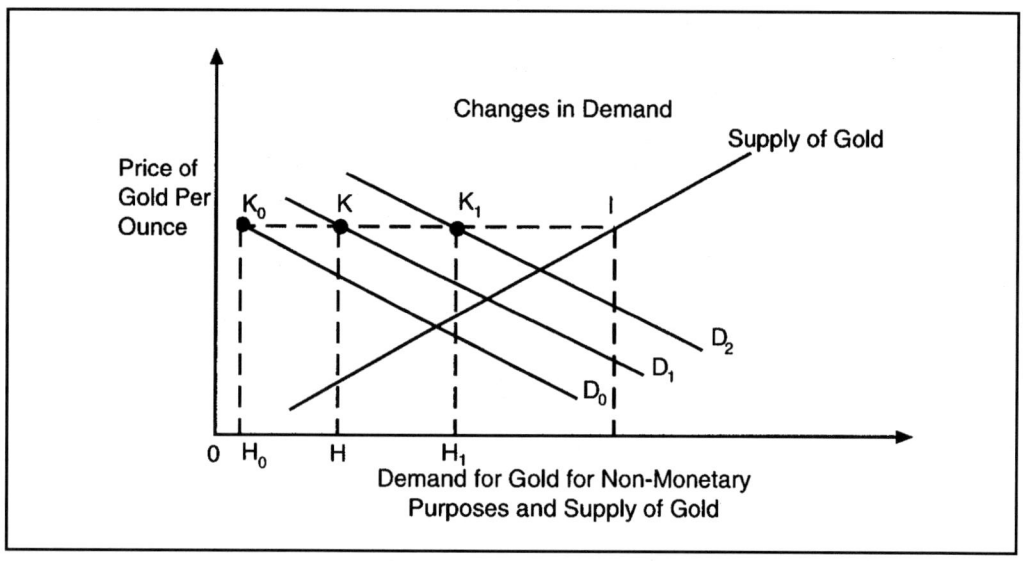

FIGURE 4.2 ■ Demand for Gold for Non-Monetary Purposes and Supply of Gold

In general, when the demand curve shifts to D_2 from D_1, the value of the money supply goes down from KISH to K_1ISH_1 and when the demand curve shifts downwards from D_1 to D_0, the money supply increases from KISH to K_0ISH_0.

The supply curve of gold may shift because of the changes in any of the factors that affect the quantity supplied (dependent variable) except the price of gold. These factors include changes in the cost of production, discoveries of new gold mines, expectations of producers, and changes in the technology of production. For example, an increased cost of production would reduce the gold supply, causing the supply curve to shift to the left. This reduces the area of rectangle KISH, making the value of the money supply under the gold standard lower. Similarly, the discovery of a new gold mine, optimistic expectations of producers, and improved technology of gold production may shift the supply curve to the right, increasing the area of rectangle KISH, and increasing the value of the money supply. In theory, one may argue that by announcing a different mint price of gold, the government can exercise some control on the money supply. However, in practice, each member country had agreed to keep the mint price unchanged for an indefinite period.

In Figure 4.3, the rightward shift of the supply curve from S_1 to S_2 increases the value of the money supply from KISH to KI_0S_0H. A leftward shift of the supply curve from S_1 to S_0 is responsible for a decrease in the money supply from KISH to KI_1SH_1. Notice carefully the consequences of the above shifts in terms of making changes in the money supply.[3] Because the money supply determination was left for a free-play of demand and supply curve location, it was obvious that the government had no control on it. However, it is interesting to note that the system in

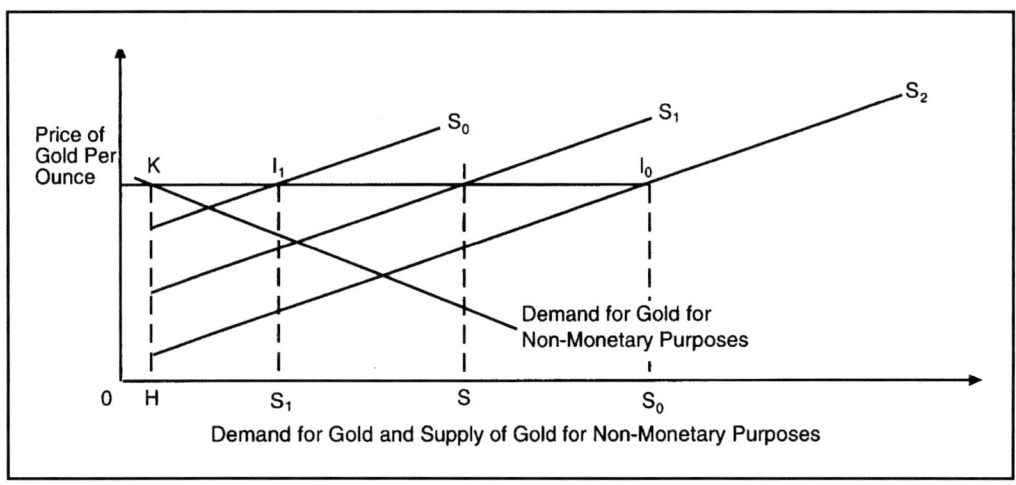

Supply for Gold and Demand for Gold for Non-Monetary Purposes ■ **FIGURE 4.3**

which governments could not change the money supply at will functioned efficiently for a long time. There were some apparent benefits to the gold standard.

First, because governments could not increase money supply excessively, the gold standard was an era of price stability. It provides evidence for the belief that excessive increases in the money supply are the only reason for inflation, always and everywhere. It can also be deduced that if governments cannot control the money supply, then any business fluctuations whose basic cause is the governmental actions, were absent under the gold standard. That gives us one less reason for having business cycles in the economy. Evidently, governmental actions were not the only cause of business cycles, for even in the era of the gold standard there were some business cycles.

Second, even if there happens to be inflation (defined as an increase in the general price level of goods and services), there is an automatic cure for it under the gold standard system. For example, in the case of inflation, producers would tend to divert their resources from the production of gold to the production of goods and services. In the long run, this would lead to an increase in the supply of goods and services, and also to decreases in the gold supply. Both of these consequences lead to a decrease in the general price level of goods and services because a higher supply of goods would bring their prices down and a lower gold supply would lead to a lower money supply in the economy, which also makes the inflation stable. Thus, some economists believe that in the gold standard system, inflation should be no problem in the first instance, and even if it happens to become a problem, it would be cured automatically.

Third, the gold standard system is also beneficial for price equalization on an international basis. (This is sometimes referred to as 'the law of one price.') The price equalization happens in the following manner. Suppose there are two economies, A and B, and the price level in the country A, say P_A, initially happens to be greater than the price level in the country B, say P_B. In this situation, assuming free trade, country A will import more from country B. As country A does so, it will have to pay money for the goods and services she is importing. Hence, the money supply in country A will go down and the supply of goods and services will go up. Both forces would reduce prices in country A. As far as country B is concerned, it would lose goods and services and obtain additional money supply. Hence, the tendency of the general price level would be to go up in country B. Theoretically, the process would continue until the price levels in both economies are equal. Hence, on an international level, the countries could achieve the same price level for their goods and services. It appears that this was probably the most significant benefit of the gold standard, for even in modern times (as late as 1980) several economists have argued for returning back to the gold standard to solve the problem of world-wide inflation. Now the questions are, if there are so many benefits of the gold standard, in theory, then why did it break down in the first place? Are there any economic causes for this breakdown or were they all purely political? Questions like these can be answered by looking at the costs that were incurred in the adoption of the gold standard.

First, under the gold standard, the government authorities were trapped in a strange situation. They had to follow the stringent rules we mentioned before, and in return, had no control over the money supply. This gave rise to contempt on the part of the government and an unwillingness to obey the rules. In the long run, they realized even more fiercely that an active government has to influence the money supply to carry out an increase in activities. Thus, more and more governments became reluctant to obey the rules of the gold standard and that endangered its existence.

Second, the government that was able to defect from the system benefited from its actions. To make this point clear, let us continue with the same example of country A and country B as before. Let us assume that country A, which is importing goods and services from country B, decides to move away from the gold standard and not abide by its rules. Then it is possible for country A to continue importing from B and make the payment for the increased imports by printing more currency. Country A would keep on obtaining more goods and services from country B by giving up a lower cost commodity, its money. It is, thus, possible for a defector (country A) to be at an advantage by failing to observe the rules of the gold standard. Several economists feel that this was the basic reason why many countries were suspicious of other members under the gold standard, and it was the major reason why the gold standard broke down.

The third reason for the breakdown of the gold standard was a greater awareness on the part of governments about the necessity of providing a greater supply of the medium of exchange in order to achieve economic growth. The reasoning behind this is as follows. A higher number of transactions in the economy are needed for a greater level of Gross National Product because only more exchanges can best do the job of producing higher output by encouraging specialization. Exchanges are facilitated only by more money—not by a constant or declining money supply. Hence, it appears that by not having more money, there is a guarantee of economic stagnation. It is, therefore, a strict mandate on governments not to be able to increase the money supply according to their own liking, which constituted a serious drawback in the gold standard system. No wonder it failed in the past, and no wonder in modern times, when governments are so active in the process of economic advancement, very few economists support re-adopting the gold standard. Having reviewed this, let us now consider some of the major developments in the present monetary system in the world economy.

4.3 Empirical Evidence on the Gold Standard Mechanism: A Critical Appraisal

Having discussed the theoretical foundation underlying the gold standard mechanism, now we will critically review the performance of the gold standard era and put it in historical perspective.

THE CLASSICAL GOLD STANDARD (1879–1914)

The use of precious metals as a medium of exchange can be dated back several centuries. However, gold was particularly popular due to its scarcity, durability, and the relative ease with which it could be minted into coins of uniform value. As economies grew over the years and the volume of transactions expanded rapidly, slowly currency (paper money) replaced gold as a medium of exchange. This is because paper money was safer and lighter to transport, while each unit could still be converted into gold on demand. Thus, the so-called gold standard in which currency, fully backed by gold, served as the medium of exchange emerged simultaneously in many countries as a viable monetary arrangement.

The international gold standard was not consciously established through international treatises. Instead it evolved over time, partly due to the series of unforeseen events leading to gold discoveries, and partly due to the economic problems inherent in maintaining a bimetallic standard. Under a bimetallic standard, a nation's currency would consist of a specified amount of one metal (gold) or another (usually silver). For example, the United States Coinage Act of 1792 stipulated that a dollar should consist of 24.75 grains of gold or 371.25 grains of silver. This, in turn, fixed the mint ratio of silver to gold at 15:1 (371.25/24.75 is approximately 15), i.e., 15 ounces of silver for 1 ounce of gold. Thus, whenever the market price of gold (in terms of silver) differed from the mint price of gold, profitable arbitrage opportunities existed. The market price, in turn, depended on the relative supplies of gold and silver, which were tied to the unforeseen circumstances concerning the timing of gold and silver discoveries. For example, in the United States, the market price of a unit of gold fluctuated between 15.6 and 15.8 units of silver after the 1820s. This prompted traders to buy gold cheaply at the U.S. mint for 15 ounces of silver and sell it high in the market. As the U.S. mint lost gold and acquired silver, the new coins had to be struck in silver, despite the government's official commitment to a bimetallic standard. The situation reversed itself when the Coinage Act of 1834 changed the mint price of gold to 16 ounces of silver, in response to a shortage of gold coins in circulation. Because gold was not overvalued (relative to the market price) at the mint, it drove the silver coins out of circulation.[4]

Great Britain was one of the first countries to tie the pound sterling more closely to gold than to silver as early as the seventeenth century. Toward the latter half of the eighteenth century, Germany, Japan, and other major countries followed suit, attracted by Britain's economic dominance and hoping to achieve similar economic success by imitating British institutions. The United States officially joined the gold standard in 1879 when it restored full convertibility of the paper dollar into gold, which was temporarily suspended to finance the Civil War. With Britain, the United States, and major European nations on a domestic gold standard, the international monetary system evolved toward the gold standard in 1879 and lasted until the outbreak of World War I.

The monetary authority in each country defined the value of its domestic currency in terms of gold, commonly referred to as the 'par value.' For example, the U.S. dollar value of an ounce of gold was defined as $20.67 compared to £4.24 per ounce in Britain. The monetary authorities stood ready to buy or sell gold at the stipulated price to keep the par value of domestic currency fixed. Such practices, in essence, fixed the mint exchange rate between any pair of currencies through their ties to the gold. For instance, the mint exchange rate between dollars and pounds was $4.87 per pound sterling.[5] The arbitrage activities ensured that market exchange rates between currencies did not deviate from the official mint exchange rates more than the amount of transportation costs incurred in shipping gold across national boundaries. Thus, the gold standard came to represent a special type of fixed exchange rate system among nations' currencies.

The viability of the gold standard also required that the monetary authority issue no more currency than it could back by gold. Besides, the way the classical gold standard system was designed, as discussed in the theory section, money supply was allowed to change passively in the face of balance of payment difficulties. This, in turn, meant that nations could not actively use monetary policy to achieve domestic full employment with price stability. However, this did not undermine the confidence of the classical economists in the gold standard, who held that in the long run, there is an automatic tendency for a market-oriented system to achieve full employment without inflation.

In retrospect, how well did the classical gold standard work? The economists, by and large, agree that the gold standard was successful in maintaining a stable exchange rate between major currencies. During 1879–1913, there were no changes in the mint exchange rates between the U.S. dollar, British pound, French franc, and the German mark.

The United States also experienced rapid economic growth accompanied by a low inflation rate, whereas nations unable to maintain gold convertibility (e.g., Latin America) suffered from frequent devaluations of their currency. Such empirical evidence has prompted some economists to conclude that the gold standard also contributed to price stability.

However, a closer examination of behavior of prices during the eighteenth and nineteenth centuries reveals that price stability was not attained, either in the short run or in the long run. According to Richard Cooper, "Price stability in the sense of a return to earlier levels of prices was obtained over longer periods only by judicious choice of the years for comparison. If one chooses 1822, 1856, late 1915 and 1931, for instance, the U.S. wholesale price level indeed appears unchanged. But between these dates there were great swells and troughs" (1982, p. 7). In retrospect, this is not surprising, because the growth of the gold stock itself has been historically erratic due to unforeseen circumstances relating to gold discoveries or new extraction technologies. So even if the monetary authorities had followed the rules of the gold standard closely in creating no more money than they could back by gold, the growth in the money stock and the associated price movement would be expected to be quite volatile. To make matters worse, the monetary authorities frequently circumvented the rules by changing the laws to require less gold backing for each unit of currency when it was in their national interest to do so.

To summarize, it appears that during the tranquil period of pre-World War I, the nations under the gold standard indeed enjoyed economic prosperity and low inflation rates, but the question remains as to whether the gold standard was responsible for such economic prosperity or was it the prosperity of these nations that allowed them to remain faithful to the gold standard? It is worth noting that the gold standard era coincided with a period of rapid technological evolution that improving the overall living standard of the masses. Besides, the world economy was still not subjected to severe shocks such as World War I and II, the Great Depression of the 1930s, or the OPEC oil price shock of the 1970s, which would have profound influence in shaping the international monetary system of later years.

THE INTER-WAR YEARS

The classical gold standard era came to an abrupt end with the outbreak of World War I. Financing the war became the prime focus of the belligerent nations. Most of the nations accomplished it by issuing paper currency. In the absence of new gold to back the paper currency, the nations were forced to suspend the convertibility of their currency into gold. However, the United States returned to gold immediately after World War I in 1919. Attracted by the comparative financial stability of the gold standard era, other European nations followed suit. Austria and Sweden restored convertibility in 1923, followed by Germany in 1924. Fearing isolation and a loss of its dominance as the world's leading financial center, Great Britain restored the convertibility of the pound to gold in 1925 at the pre-War price of gold. With return of all the major nations to gold, the international monetary system was back on the gold standard once again.

In retrospect, Great Britain's return to gold at the pre-War parity level proved fatal. Although prices had been generally falling since the War, in 1925 it was still much higher than it was in the pre-War days of the gold standard. As had been correctly predicted by John Maynard Keynes, at the pre-War parity level, the British pound was seriously overvalued. This adversely affected Britain's international competitiveness and in turn, caused slow economic growth and high unemployment rates. An overvalued pound also led to higher imports and lower exports resulting in current account deficits and consequent gold outflow. Given that Britain's gold reserves were limited, the persistent outflow of gold undermined the confidence of other nations in Britain's ability to honor its commitment to exchange pound for gold at the pre-War parity level. Thus, the panic-stricken foreign holders of pounds began converting their pounds to gold, and Britain was eventually forced off gold in 1931.

At around the same time, the world economy was plagued by the international monetary system. International monetary cooperation took a backseat as country after country suspended the convertibility of its currency to gold. To 'protect' domestic jobs from foreign competition, countries erected trade barriers, instituted quotas, and more importantly, resorted to predatory devaluations to increase their own international competitiveness at the expense of foreign countries. Such currency devaluation often provoked foreign retaliation and left all countries worse off in the end. For example, it is often argued that the U.S. devaluation of 1933, when the dollar price of gold was raised from $20.67 per ounce to $35 per ounce (nearly 60 percent devaluation of the dollar in terms of gold), was undertaken in response to the pound's devaluation of 1931. The turbulence in the world markets continued until the outbreak of World War II in 1939, the period of which was characterized by great instability stemming from flexible exchange rates.

According to many economists, such inter-war experience prompted the Allies at the close of World War II to establish an international monetary system with some degree of exchange rate flexibility, but with primary emphasis on some sort of exchange rate stability that was prevalent during the classical gold standard era.

THE BRETTON WOODS SYSTEM (1944–1971)

Unlike the gold standard, the Bretton Woods system was a deliberate creation. In 1944, representatives of 44 nations including the United States and Great Britain (led by Harry White of the U.S. Treasury and John Keynes, respectively) met in Bretton Woods, New Hampshire in the United States, in an effort to lay out the rules of a stable and open international trade and monetary system that would preserve the fixed exchange rate aspects of the gold standard within a framework allowing for moderate exchange rate changes. The International Monetary Fund (IMF) was created to serve as a forum through which countries could meet to solve their exchange rate and balance of payment problems.

Under the rules of the agreement, the U.S. dollar had to be pegged to gold within 1 percent of its par value of $35 per ounce of gold. This required that the Federal Reserve of the United States stand ready to buy or sell gold in unlimited amounts to maintain the fixed price of gold. In contrast, other nations participating in the IMF had the choice of tying their currencies either to the dollar or to gold. In practice, other nations chose to peg their rate of exchange to the dollar and thus were indirectly tied to gold. It was the responsibility of these nations to keep the dollar values of their respective currencies unchanged at the agreed upon pegged rates through buying and selling of dollars. In essence, the Bretton Woods system was a gold exchange standard rather than a pure gold standard in which the dollar played a central role as the reserve currency.

The Bretton Woods agreement, in theory, incorporated the desirable features of a flexible exchange system into a gold exchange standard. Following World War II, some nations were growing rapidly, while other nations were struggling to recover from the devastations of the War. The agreement recognized the need for some sort of flexibility in the international monetary system to periodically realign currencies of nations in widely divergent circumstances. Nations could change the exchange rate between the dollar and their own currency by less than 10 percent of par value through intervention in the foreign exchange market. A larger change in the exchange rate stemming from a fundamental disequilibrium[6] in balance of payments required IMF consent. Thus, the Bretton Woods agreement was referred to as an 'adjustable peg'; exchange rates were to be pegged but adjustable.

In retrospect, how did the Bretton Woods system work? Despite the flexibility, most of the nations suffering from current amount deficits were reluctant to devalue their currencies because of national pride. Instead, the deficit nations would wait until a devaluation was long overdue. By then, the individuals fearing an imminent devaluation would sell the nation's currency and exacerbate the deficit. On the other hand, those nations enjoying current account surpluses were equally reluctant to revaluate their currencies fearing that such a move would adversely affect their international competitiveness. This, in effect, robbed the Bretton Woods system of the flexible adjustment mechanism that was designed to correct the balance of payment disequilibria. The adjustable peg regime of Bretton Woods turned into a de facto fixed rate regime.

The Bretton Woods system also meant contradictory responsibilities for United States. On the one hand, the central banks of other nations needed large stocks of dollars to carry out large-scale intervention in the foreign exchange market in order to keep the dollar price of their currencies fixed. But the accumulation of large sums of dollars in the hands of foreign central banks, if not backed by adequate gold reserves, would undermine confidence in the convertibility of the U.S. dollar to gold. During the 1960s, the United States began experiencing huge balance of payment deficits, partly resulting from overly expansionary monetary policies pursued to ease the impact of the Vietnam War. Fearing that the United States would be unable to maintain the dollar price of gold, the foreign central banks were reluctant to accumulate dollars at the rate at which they were being created. Because the United States did not have the option under the Bretton Woods agreement to devalue the dollar, it tried to persuade the surplus nations (particularly Germany and Japan) to revalue their currencies, but without success. Eventually, on August 15, 1971, President Nixon was forced to suspend the convertibility of dollars into gold. Recognizing the end of the Bretton Woods system, many nations let their currencies float against the dollar and the era of flexible exchange rates began.

The Future of the International Monetary Regime 4.4

The sharp exchange rate fluctuations since the 1980s have rekindled interest in the pegged rate systems of earlier years. Despite its limitations, the Bretton Woods system, in retrospect, appears to have coincided with a period of exchange rate stability and rapid economic growth. Inflation was moderate and the national income in the G7 countries rose more rapidly than in any comparable period before or since. According to Bordo and Eichengreen, "it is tempting to assume, as many have done, that the key to this admirable performance lay in the international monetary agreement concluded in 1944" (1993: preface). The European Monetary System (EMS) was the first serious attempt at another adjustable peg system since the demise of Bretton Woods in 1971. The EMS was established in March of 1979 under the auspices of the European Economic Community (EEC)[7] to create a 'zone of monetary stability' among its members. Many of the member nations have established fixed par values among their currencies and agreed to maintain market exchange rates within a band around these par values. Their currencies float jointly against the dollar and together they comprise a composite currency (the so-called European Currency Unit, or ECU) representing a very large economic area. (In 1999, it was renamed Euro.)

After numerous initial doubts, the EMS is now widely viewed as a resounding success. It is likely to evolve into a full economic and monetary union (EMU) by the end of this century with a single currency. If successful, the EMU is likely to induce a substantial portfolio adjustment away from the dollar into the ECU or the common currency. The resulting appreciation of European currencies against the dollar will distort the pattern of trade, invoke protectionist sentiments, and destabilize global arrangements. According to many economists (for example Bergsten, 1993), the United States and Japan should engage Europe in negotiations on the global monetary system while the latter is still working out its regional arrangements.

In that spirit, Bergsten and Williamson have advanced a 'target zone' proposal. They suggest that a limited number of major countries (e.g., the United States, Germany, and Japan, to begin with) negotiate a set of mutually consistent targets for their real exchange rates. The participating countries would be expected to conduct their macroeconomic policies with a view to limiting exchange rate fluctuations within 10 percent (approximately) of the target rates. As Williamson puts it, "there is no point in pretending that the world economy can perform satisfactorily . . . to achieve sensibly aligned and reasonably stable exchange rates without the official sector explicitly asking itself what those rates are and being willing to adjust monetary policy to achieve them" (Williamson, 1987, p. 204).

McKinnon (1988) has advocated for a new monetary regime centered on fixed exchange rates between major currencies 'a gold standard without gold,' as he calls it. He believes that the great variation in exchange rates among the industrial nations in recent years can be attributed to the fact that the investors continually shift their preferences between yen, mark, dollar, and sterling assets according to their expectations as to how each exchange rate will move in the future. According to McKinnon, the appropriate solution to this portfolio instability would be for the U.S. Federal Reserve System, the Bank of Japan, and the Bundesbank to adhere to a common monetary standard by announcing fixed nominal targets between yen/dollar and mark/dollar exchange rates (within narrow bands). The three central banks would adjust their domestic money supplies from time to time to maintain the nominal exchange parities and, concomitantly, maintain roughly the same rates of domestic inflation as under the classical gold standard.[8]

To conclude, the international monetary regime is evolving over time. The newly liberalized economies of Eastern Europe and the Commonwealth of Independent States are presenting challenges never experienced before. Whatever the shape of the future monetary regime, the lessons learned from the fixed exchange rate system of the classical gold standard or the Bretton Woods system are certainly going to play a crucial role in its formation.

Notes

1. See Bordo in the Suggested Reading List.
2. As the principles of economics may have taught you, due to an increase in the price of a goods, the real income of the consumer goes down, making the consumer demand less of all goods. Also, an increase in the price also causes the consumer to substitute for the consumption of gold by the consumption of related commodities such as silver. In ordinary terms, an increase in the price of gold would make people wear more silver and less gold.
3. Following the effects of income changes, an interested reader may want to analyze the effects of these changes on the money supply under the gold standard.
4. In theory, one may argue that by announcing a different mint price of gold, the government can exercise some control on the money supply. However, in practice, each member country had agreed to keep the mint price unchanged for an indefinite period.
5. Such a situation illustrates Gresham's law—that bad money (i.e., the money that is overvalued at the mint) drives out the good money (i.e., the money that is undervalued at the mint.) $20.67 = 1 ounce gold = £4.24 or $4.87 = £1.
6. The term "fundamental equilibrium" was nowhere clearly defined in the agreement; however, it was broadly defined as large and persistent balance of payment deficits and surpluses.
7. Includes the United States, Germany, Japan, France, the United Kingdom, Canada, and Italy.
8. The aim would be to set targets such that the nations' current accounts will be in balance and, at the same time, fastest domestic economic growth will be achieved without igniting new inflation.

References

Aghevli, B. 1975. The balance of payments and money supply under the gold standard regime: U.S. 1879–1914. *American Economic Review:* 40–58.

Barro, R. J. 1979. Money and the price level under the gold standard. *Economic Journal:* 13–33.

Bergsten, C. F. 1993. The Collapse of Bretton Woods: Implications for International Monetary Reform. In *A Retrospective on the Bretton Woods System: Lessons for International Monetary Reform,* eds. M. D. Bordo and B. Eichengreen, 587–593. Chicago: University of Chicago Press.

Bordo, M. D. 1982. The classical gold standard: lessons from the past. In *The International Monetary System: Choices for the Future,* ed. Michael Connolly, 229–65. Praeger Special Studies, Praeger Publishers.

Bordo, M. D. 1993. *A Retrospective on the Bretton Woods System: Lessons for International Monetary Reform.* Chicago: University of Chicago Press.

Cooper, R. N. 1982. The gold standard: historical facts and future prospects. *Brookings Papers on Economic Activity:* 1–56.

Enders, W. and H. E. Lapan. 1987. *International Economics: Theory and Policy.* Prentice-Hall Inc.

Ford, A. G. 1960. *The Gold Standard 1880 to 1914.* Oxford: Claredon Press.

Kemmerer, E. W. 1994. *Gold and the Gold Standard.* New York: McGraw-Hill.

Krugman, P. R. and M. Obstfeld. 1994. *International Economics: Theory and Policy,* 3rd ed. New York: Harper Collins College Publishers.

Lindert, P. H. 1991. *International Economics,* 9th ed. Richard D. Irwin, Inc.

McCloskey, D. N. and J. K. Kecher. 1978. How the gold standard worked. In *The Monetary Approach to the Balance of Payments,* eds. J. Frenkel and H. G. Johnson. Toronto: University of Toronto Press.

McKinnon, R. I. 1998. Monetary and exchange rate policies for international financial stability: a proposal. *Journal of Economic Perspectives* 1:83–103.

Salvatore, D. 1993. *International Economics,* 4th ed. Macmillan Publishing Company.

Tew, B. 1997. *The Evolution of the International Monetary System: 1947-1977.* Hutchinson Press: London

Thomas, L. 1979. *Money, Banking and Economic Activity,* Chapter 2. Prentice-Hall.

Williamson, J. 1987. Exchange rate management: the role of target zones. *American Economic Review Papers and Proceedings* 2:200–04.

Chapter 5

Essence of Classical Economics: Pre-1930s Era

In this chapter we set the stage for the theories of the earliest economists, the Classical Economists. While there was a common thread of argument until the 1930s, economic theory evolved most progressively in the late nineteenth century and into the early twentieth, in countries such as the United Kingdom, France, and to a somewhat larger extent, the United States. This early thought held that economic strength is greatest when markets are allowed to function by themselves. In fact, so strong was their confidence in the market mechanism that economists argued for the cliché that the "best government is the one that governs least." In French terminology this meant, "Let the economy function by itself" or *laissez faire*. This concept was a direct product of French economist J. B. Say's Law of Market, which implies that on the macro level, "Supply creates its own demand." Once this law is taken as an article of faith, it is easy to see that prices ought to have an inherent tendency to stay stable and all disequilibria can thus be considered as "purely temporary."

Classical economists were also aided by their firm belief in the full flexibility of all prices in all markets. As we learned in Chapter 2, if the price level is flexible, it always stays at the equilibrium level. As you will learn from this chapter, classical economists were champions of showing that all three major markets of an economy—namely the labor market, the capital or money market, and the commodity of product market—will automatically be in equilibrium if their respective prices are fully flexible. This again leads to the same conclusion that market disequilibrium is a temporary phenomenon. Therefore, in the long run all markets will move toward a permanent state of equilibrium. The main bump in classical economists' thinking was experienced during the era of the Great Depression. In Europe, the depressionary forces operated throughout the late 1920s and, because of protectionist policies pursued by many countries, the situation spread all over the world, including, of course, to the United States. As the Great Depression was a time of prolonged and significant disequilibrium in all markets, the prevalent classical macroeconomic theory had no answer to explain it. There was no theoretical reasoning as to why depression in an economy can occur, and there were definitely no economic theories to explain why it could last so long. Hence, this disarray set the stage for a brilliant explanation by John Maynard Keynes and, by doing so, he furnished a revolution against classical economics. This chapter, consequently, reviews this background thoroughly. Likewise, it provides an explanation for the process of market equilibrium for all three major markets of the economy and explains Say's Law of Market in detail.

Introduction 5.1

Before the 1930s, macroeconomic theory was based on universally held economic thought that the role of government should be limited as much as possible, and the best government was thought to be the one that governed least. Freedom of expression and freedom of making choices on an individual level were considered the work of the Mother Nature, and individuals were thought to be sole decision makers for their well-being. The classical economists tradition began in 1776, when Adam Smith proposed that individual's self interest drives decision making and when everyone worked according to self interest the whole economy can work smoothly, too. Adam Smith thought this was the best way of achieving economic efficiency. Influenced by the Smithian way of thinking, other economists such as David Ricardo (1817), and John Stuart Mill (1848) proposed theories to support this fundamental argument that the government's role essentially was undesirable for smooth functioning of market mechanisms.

Much of classical economics also came out of French economists' monumental works such as that of J. B. Say. In French, the two words that best express the feelings of classical economists for policy making are *laissez faire,* which call for letting the economy function by itself, and preventing governmental interference. In other words, the best thing for the government to do is to stay out of the market mechanism. In this chapter we shall discuss the main reason why classical economists felt this way about economic behavior.

We also need to answer another question: What level of GDP does an economy produce by itself? Classical economists traditionally answered this question as: A capitalistic economy, when left to itself, produces full employment level of GDP. A full employment level of GDP is that level of GDP which when produced buy the economy, enough jobs are created for everyone who wants one. It is in other words the "potential" level of GDP, produced by using all resources of the economy. Usually, resources mean the stocks of all factors of production—namely, land, labor, capital, and enterprise. However, the most important resource we should consider is the labor, because it is the employment (or unemployment) of labor that is most worrisome for us. Resources such as capital or land do not complain if they are left unused, but leave labor unemployed and it starts making significant noise. So for a long time economists have worried about labor employment (or unemployment) more than other factors of production.

In reality, there are some wealthy individuals who will "voluntarily" stay unemployed. This so-called voluntary unemployment does not create problems for anyone, neither for the labor supplier nor for the labor demander. There is some frictional unemployment in the economy too. For example, if there are sufficient jobs available in some distant place or state to which few individuals are interested in relocating, its unwilling labor suppliers are frictionally unemployed. Both types of unemployed labor comprise 3–4 percent of the total labor force, so in case of a big economy such as the United States, the full employment is defined as 4 percent unemployment to give concession to about 4 percent of the frictionally and voluntarily unemployed labor force. So on a theoretical level we can argue that the classical economists believed that a capitalistic economy produces full employment level of GDP.

5.2

There were two reasons why classical economists held this belief. The first one was due to Say's Law of Market, a theory that originated from the work of French economist John Baptiste Say. John Maynard Keynes had summarized Say's Law of Market in five words: "supply creates its own demand." When we say "supply creates its own demand" these days, we do not mean that if the supply of one good increases the demand for it will go up too. In fact, it is wrong to even try to argue such a law. As we saw in Chapter 2, the factors that determine supply of a good are entirely different from the factors that guide the demand for a good. No one can prove that if supply of Denver Broncos hats is increased, then their demand would go up. The demand for Denver Broncos hats would depend upon how they generate enthusiasm (change of tastes, expectations, income, and the number of the consumers) in their fans by winning games. The same thing is true for other goods. Hence, on a microeconomic level Say's Law of Market cannot be proved. But Say did not imply this, either. Rather, he meant that if the supply of one good is increased then the demand for the *inputs* of that good would automatically increase. For example, if the supply of Broncos hats is increased, then the demand for the inputs of Broncos hats—the cloth material, sewing machines, paints, labor, packaging, trucking etc.—is automatically raised. But recognize that the inputs of one industry are the outputs of another industry. An increase in supply of one good automatically increases the demand for another. In a hypothetical case, if the supply of "all" goods is raised simultaneously, then the demand for "all" goods would also be increased automatically. Therefore, Say's Law of Market would not work for one good but has some logical explanation for "all" goods. It is essentially a macroeconomic law: it works for "all" goods taken together and implies that in a capitalistic economy,

Aggregate demand = Aggregate supply.

According to Say's law, any increase in the aggregate supply would automatically create an increase in aggregate demand. Prices in general would have a tendency to stay stable. Moreover, if prices do change in the short run, there will be forces that act to bring them back to equilibrium and will guarantee stability in the long run. In general, there is no reason to believe that the economy would experience instability by itself and all disequilibria are purely temporary.

5.2

The same conclusion that all disequilibria are temporary can also be reached by considering the individual market mechanism. According to classical economic theory, if we consider three major markets—namely labor, money or capital, and commodity (or product or goods)—all can exist simultaneously in equilibrium due to the assumed flexibility of their respective prices. The price flexibility that guarantees the market equilibrium is already discussed in Chapter 2, but we shall use the same idea to prove that all three major markets of the economy can be in equilibrium without governmental influence.

The Walras Law concludes that even if there were a fourth market, that market would be in equilibrium so long as the other three markets are in equilibrium. Walras was another French economic thinker who proposed that if there are "n" number of markets in an economy, and if at any given point "n – 1" markets are in equilibrium, then the nth market at that point is also in equilibrium. This law is not hard to prove. It only says that if on a grand level, aggregate demand equals aggregate supply, and if in all markets except one demand equals supply, then the remaining market should also have demand equaling supply.

We shall now prove how each of the three markets are ensured equilibrium if their respective prices are assumed to be flexible. Consider the labor market with its "price" of wage rate (W).

As shown in Figure 5.1, the wage rate will be the determinant of quantity of labor demanded. An increase in wage rate would mean those who demand labor (namely corporations, firms, and other employers) would demand a lower quantity of labor, so the demand for labor curve is downward sloping from left to right. Similarly, the workers are the labor suppliers and an increase in wage rate means the quantity of labor supplied would go up; more labor being ready to work, and those already working being ready to work longer hours. Therefore the labor supply curve slopes upward from left to right. At point "E," where the labor demand curve and labor supply curves intersect, we have the labor market equilibrium.

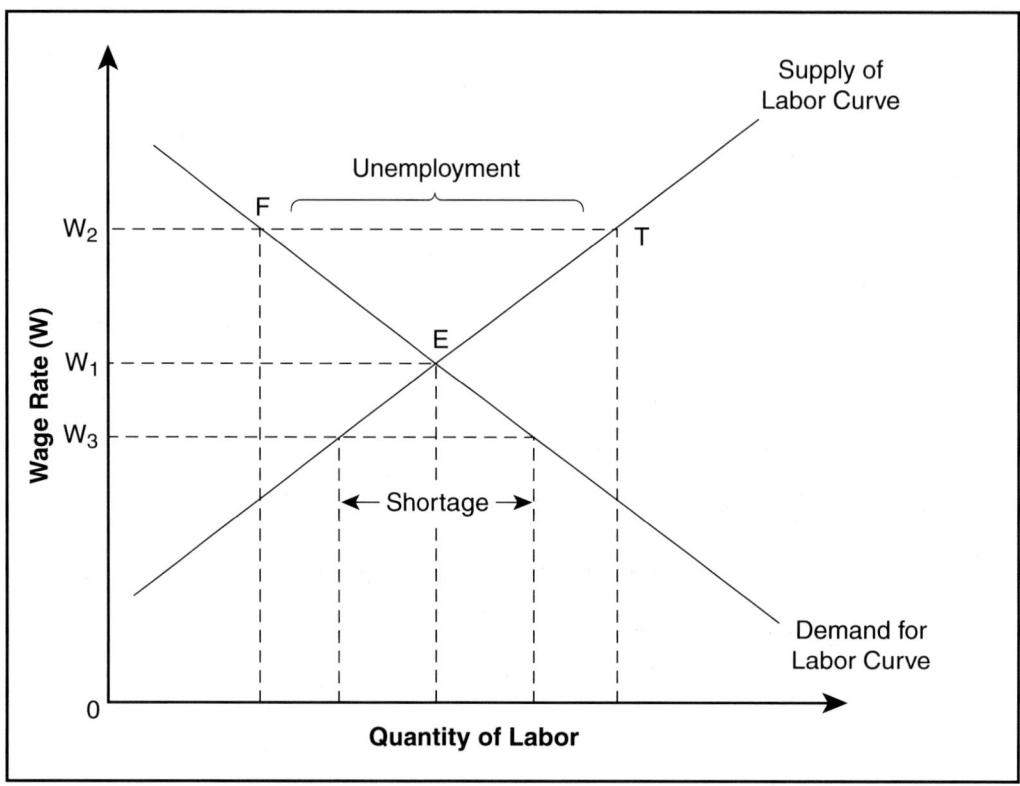

FIGURE 5.1 ■ Wage Rate vs. Quantity of Labor

According to classical economists, if the labor market is left to itself, it would automatically reach equilibrium stage if the wage rate is fully flexible, at least in the long run. This market clearing process is mentioned in Chapter 2 as the "Paradox of Flexibility," and classical economists have complete faith in its validity.

Consider any wage rate away from the equilibrium wage rate (W_1 on the graph), say W_2 wage rate, which is above equilibrium. The W_2 wage rate will not exist for a long time because at W_2 there is higher quantity supplied of labor (by workers) than the quantity demanded of labor by employers. This creates a surplus of labor (or unemployment), and when a surplus of labor meets a flexible wage rate, that rate will start going down from W_2 to W_1. Therefore the unemployment stage in an economy will be purely temporary; it is cured by the automatic decline in wage rate and in the long run unemployment is impossible to occur.

Similarly, if the wage rate happens to be lower than the equilibrium level such as W_3 wage rate, then there is a higher quantity of labor demanded than quantity of labor supplied. This creates a shortage of labor as shown in Figure 5.1. Therefore, classical economists were in firm belief that labor market equilibrium is guaranteed by flexible wages.

In a similar fashion we can also prove the market equilibrating mechanism in money or capital markets. That job was done in a sophisticated explanation of the Loanable Funds Theory by Irving Fisher of Yale University during the 1910s. We reproduce that explanation here.

5.4 The Loanable Funds Theory

The classical theory of the interest rate pointed to the interaction of saving and investment schedules as the basic determinants of the interest rate, which created a problem. However, in classical theory it may be that no solution is possible, because the position of the saving schedule will vary with the level of national income. As income rises, the saving curve will shift to the right. Hence, no one will be able to determine saving unless one knows income and one cannot know income unless one knows the interest rate (and investment). Thus, classical theory could not explain how the interest rate could be finitely determined.

The *loanable funds theory,* on the other hand, hypothesizes that the interest rate is decided by the intersection of demand for and supply of loanable funds. The loanable funds approach emphasized the availability of total credit in the economy. A producer who sells bonds to borrow money creates the demand for loanable funds and the supply of bonds. One who invests money in buying bonds creates the demand for bonds and the supply of loanable funds. Thus, the demand and supply forces in the loanable funds market operate in opposite directions to the demand and supply forces in the bond market. Next, we should note that the supply of loanable funds can come from a surplus in the budget of any entity in the economy. If we consider the economy to be composed of two major sectors, the private sector and the public sector, then the supply of loanable funds can be augmented if the private sector saves more than it invests. In the public sector, the supply of loanable funds can be augmented in two ways. First, because of the surplus in the budget of the government (when government tax revenue is more than the amount of government expenditure), and second, because of the excess supply of money created by the monetary policy. Thus, saving surplus in the government budget and an excess supply of money are the primary sources of the supply of loanable funds.

On the opposite side of the market, the demand for loanable funds is created by the private sector if it invests more than it saves, and by the public sector if the government runs a deficit in its budget and/or if there is excess demand for money. With an increase in the interest rate at a given time, there will be a reduction in the quantity of loanable funds demanded and an increase in the quantity of loanable funds supplied. Hence, as shown in Figure 5.2, the supply of the loanable funds schedule will slope upwards from left to right, and the demand for loanable funds will slope downward from left to right.[1] The intersection point of these two schedules determines the equilibrium interest rate. According to Dennis Robertson and other loanable fund theorists, at the end of a transitory (or adjustment) period, r_E is the only rate that would persist. This is because at any interest rate above r_E (like at r), the supply of loanable funds given by $r_E I$ (or OS_0), and the demand for loanable funds given by $r_0 K$ (or OD_0) to create an excess supply of loanable funds, would lead to the reduction in the interest rate. On the other hand, if the interest rate happens to be below r_E, such as $r_1 J_1$ (or OD_1), there will be pressure on the interest rate to move up. In the long run, r_E is the only interest rate that would exist. Thus, according to the loanable funds theory, the interest rate can be determined by looking at the supply and demand forces in the loanable funds market. However, as Hansen points out, the loanable funds theory does not escape the criticism leveled against the *classical theory*. If there is a change in national income, Hansen points out that the saving part of the total supply of loanable funds does not remain constant and the supply schedule shifts. One cannot determine saving (or supply of loanable funds), unless the interest rate is predetermined and one knows income, to determine the level of investment and income.

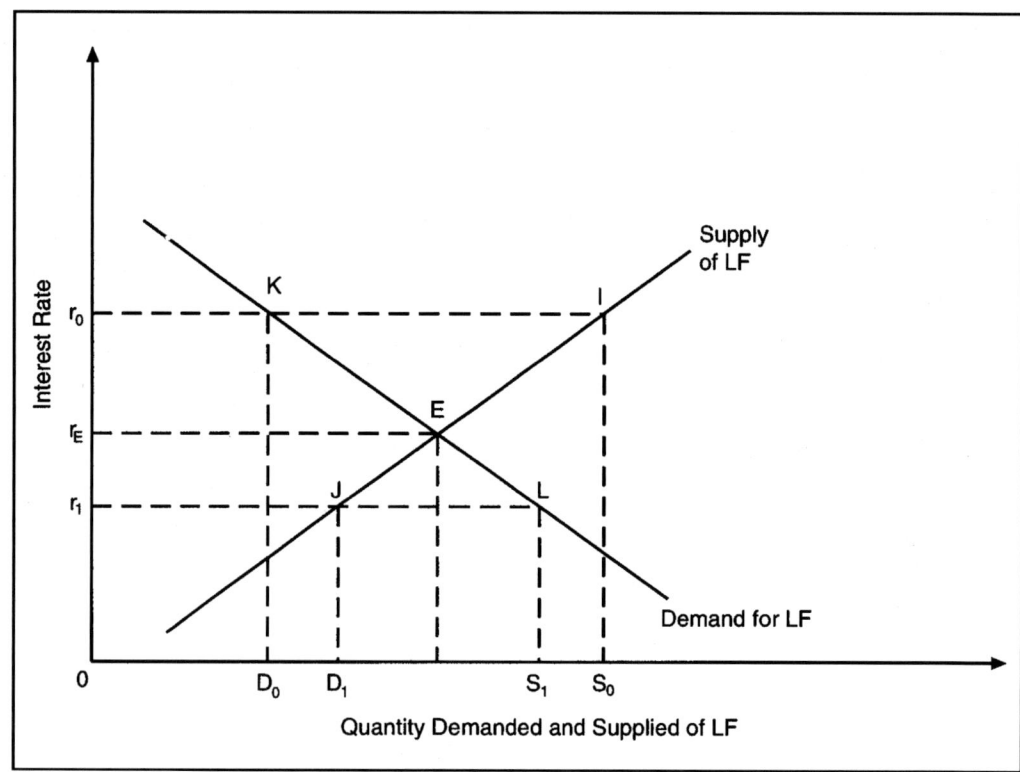

FIGURE 5.2 ■ Supply and Demand for Loanable Funds

According to Irving Fisher (1930), the expectation of inflation can make it necessary to modify the conclusion of the loanable funds theory. If people expect that the inflation rate is going to be higher in the future, then both the demand for and the supply of loanable funds can be affected. The quantity demanded of loanable funds in general will increase and the quantity supplied will go down. Hence, the demand curve for loanable funds will shift rightward and the supply curve of loanable funds will move leftward. As shown in Figure 5.3, this would create a higher interest rate than (r). According to Fisher, we should differentiate between the nominal interest rate (which we do observe) and the real interest rate (which we should observe, but do not because of the expected inflation rate). The following relationship is established:

Real interest rate = Nominal interest rate − Expected inflation rate.

Today it is believed that it is the real interest rate that is crucial in making decisions about the real investment and bond market.

There is a third market that needs to be analyzed to show the automatic market equilibrium in classical economic theory. That market is the *goods market* (or *product market* or *commodity market*). In the goods market two forces operate: the demand for overall goods, called "aggregate demand," and the supply of all goods

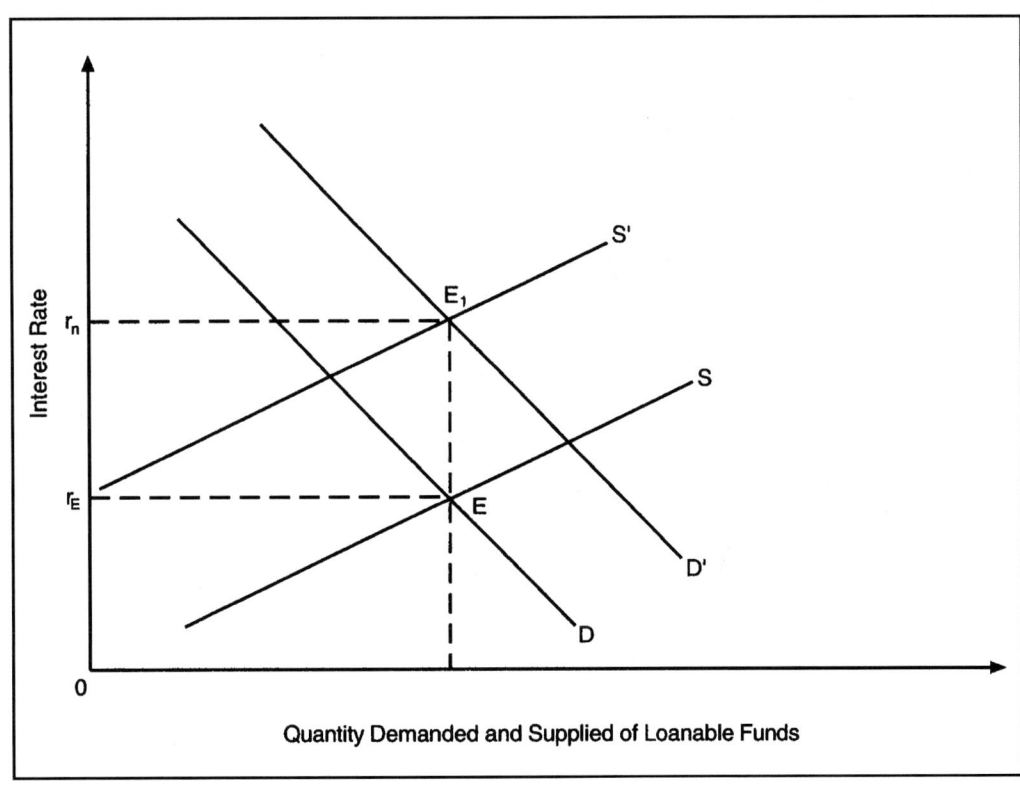

Demand for and Supply of Loanable Funds ■ **FIGURE 5.3**

taken together, known as "aggregate supply." These forces determine the general price level (P) or the average price level of all goods and services, as measured by one of the Price Indexes in the case of the United States. As shown in Figure 5.4, as the general price level increases, the quantity of goods and services demanded by consumers would go down as the aggregate demand curve slopes downward from left to right.

Similarly, as the general price level increases, the quantity of goods and services supplied by producers increases and the aggregate supply curve slopes upward from left to right. At point J there will be goods market equilibrium with equilibrium price level of P_1. The quantity demanded of all goods and services is equal to the quantity supplied of all goods and services at price level P_1. The logic of proving that in the long run the only price level that can exist is P_1 uses the same logic of any other market to prove the Paradox of Flexibility. So if no other price level is possible, and if general price level is higher than P_1, there is a excess supply (or surplus) of goods and services that would bring the general price level back to P_1. At any price level below P_1 there is excess demand (or shortage) of goods and services making the price level go back. Thus, the forces of shortage and surplus ensure

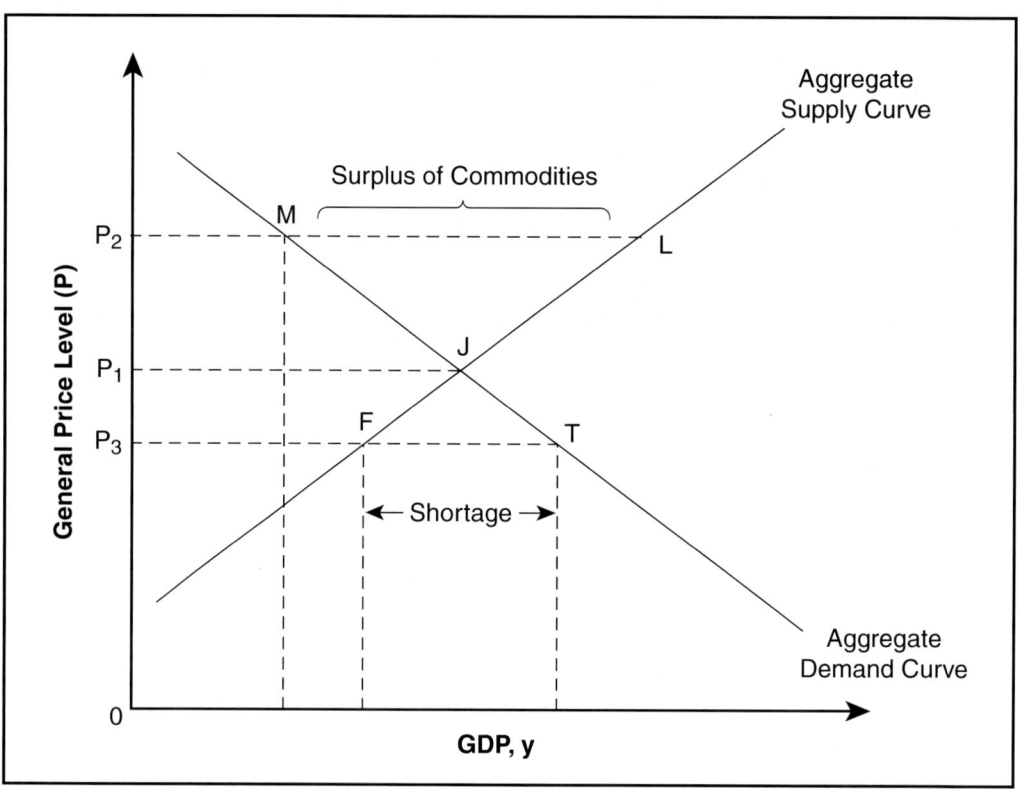

FIGURE 5.4 ■ Product Market Equilibrium

that in the long run there is no possibility of disequilibrium in this market. In general, therefore, classical economists believed that:

1. All disequilibria are purely temporary.
2. A capitalistic economy functions smoothly by itself.
3. There is no need for government to interfere in market forces.
4. The best government is the one that governs least, and therefore *laissez faire* is the best policy for the government.

As we have mentioned throughout this chapter, these theories of classical economists have had tremendous effects on pre-1930s economics policy, especially before and during the Great Depression.

5.5

The economic situation of the Great Depression era created both practical and theoretical challenges for classical economists. Table 5.1 gives some crucial data. In the four years of the real depression in the United States, the real GDP declined by 33 percent, the general price level declined by 35 percent, and unemployment increased from roughly 4 percent in 1929 to roughly 24 percent in 1933.

The interest rate charged by the Federal Reserve Banks for loans to the commercial banks (popularly called "discount rate") was 1 percent in 1931, and remained that way until 1941. Thus, all three markets that should have automatically returned to equilibrium showed pathetic signs. The money market was in a shambles due to the very low interest rate, the labor market was in permanent disequilibrium due to a very high unemployment rate, and the significant decline in value of the general price level made a mess of the commodity market. Almost all arguments by classical economists were seriously challenged or (much worse) were shown to be futile by these economic events. Classical economists were baffled. They had no answer to the question of if the disequilibria were expected to be of a persistent, long-term nature, then, what could the government do to solve the problem. Policy makers and politicians were in a similar situation. In a September 1931 radio address, President Herbert Hoover declared to the American public that "the worst is over" and that they were going to see a much better tomorrow. In reality, at that time in 1931 the worst had not even started; the situation continued to decline until 1933. The state of the macro-economy was so greatly confused that we were in need of a revolutionary new theory. That theory was offered by John Maynard Keynes in his monumental book, *General Theory of Employment, Interest and Money*. In the next chapter we shall discuss the main

TABLE 5.1 ■ U.S. Economy in the Great Depression Era (1929–1942)

Year	Unemployment Rate (%)	Output Growth Rate (%)	Price Level	Nominal Money Stock
1929	3.2	−9.8	100.0	26.6
1930	8.7	−7.6	97.4	25.7
1931	15.9	−14.7	88.8	24.1
1932	23.6	−1.8	79.7	21.1
1933	24.9	9.1	75.6	19.9
1934	21.7	9.9	78.1	21.9
1935	20.1	13.9	80.1	25.9
1936	16.9	5.3	80.9	29.5
1937	14.3	−5.0	83.8	30.9
1938	19.0	8.6	82.2	30.5
1939	17.2	8.5	81.0	34.1
1940	14.6	16.1	81.8	39.6
1941	9.9	12.9	85.9	46.5
1942	4.7	13.2	95.1	55.3

NOTE: The price index is normalized to 100 in 1929. The money stock is measured in billions of dollars.
SOURCE: Historical Statistics of the United States, U.S. Department of Commerce.

Keynesian criticism of classical economics and study a way out of the depressionary situation.

Note

1. Strictly, any direct relationship between two variables is shown by an upward sloping curve, and any inverse relationship is shown by a downward sloping curve from left to right.

Chapter 6

The Keynesian Macroeconomics: Commodity or Product Market

SUMMARY

In this broad chapter we intend to summarize the Keynesian arguments about the commodity market functioning in a capitalistic economy. While the Keynesian main message is about the involvement of the government sector, a conclusion to that effect needs background information from the commodity market. According to Keynes, in a commodity market the force of total expenditure (aggregate demand) is the most important one. It consists of consumption (C) by consumers, investment (I) from producers, and government expenditure (G) undertaken by the government's fiscal policy.

In consumption determination, the crucial factor is the equation called the *consumption function*. From the consumption function we also show the derivation of the savings function. Then, the chapter moves on to the investment determination in a special Keynesian way. Some other important concepts defined are:

1. Autonomous investment (or expenditure) multiplier, and

2. The equilibrium level of GDP, which is the level capitalistic economies tend to produce naturally. If they do not produce equilibrium GDP, they have to pay the price of either an inflationary gap or recessionary gap. Once equilibrium level of GDP is determined in algebraic and geometric terms, we introduce the concept of autonomous investment multiplier, which is the multiple of change in investment that is responsible for a change in equilibrium GDP. To show that the value

of this investment multiplier is always 1/MPS (in our simple Keynesian model), we considered the multiplier process. This process explains the different expenditure streams that an increase in investment goes through.

Our next job in this chapter is to introduce the role of the government sector and find out what changes we would have to make to analyze the commodity market. The important concept here is the one of GDP gap. It is the difference between potential GDP and the actual (or equilibrium) GDP produced by an economy. To close the GDP gap Keynes showed effectively that "a somewhat comprehensive socialization of investment is the only means. . . ." We consider this to be the main message of Keynes in this chapter.

Keynes was not only a strong academician (for a few years, he even taught economics in King's College, Cambridge University, in the United Kingdom), but also a very strong policy maker for the United Kingdom, an activist, and a great debater. His policy advice was instantly popular in most of the world's economies. But as we see in the last part of this chapter, there were some blips in his analysis of the commodity market.

6.1 Introduction

The main aim of this chapter is to analyze the Keynesian system in the most crucial market of an economy: the product market. Monetary theory gained significantly from the Keynesian ideas of the autonomous investment multiplier, the marginal efficiency of capital (MEC), the marginal propensity to consume, and several others. Keynesian thoughts were quite different from his predecessors, whom we referred to as the classical economists in the last chapter. The classical economists had no answers to the crucial questions posed by events of the Great Depression of the 1930s. In the context of events in 1936, Keynes wrote the most groundbreaking macroeconomic book of modern times, the *General Theory of Employment, Interest and Money*. It was a very difficult job to explain the paradox of poverty in the midst of potential plenty. On the one hand, Keynes challenged the critical, but crucial assumptions of classical theory, and on the other, he developed his own ideas about the consumption, investment, and saving behavior of people in a capitalistic economy. From Keynes' perspective, the most important factor in determining the level of GDP an economy will produce was the aggregate demand (or total expenditure) an economy was able to generate.

If we assume that a typical economy is composed of four major sectors, namely, a consumer sector, a producer sector, a government sector, and a foreign trade sector, then each of these sectors has its own expenditure, and the total expenditure in an economy consists of the following elements.

The consumer sector expends on final goods and services. Its expenditure is known as consumption (represented by letter "C"). The producer sector has its own expenditure on purchase of machinery, tools and equipment, on construction activities, and on increase in inventories. Its expenditure is known as investment (represented by letter "I"). The government sector's expenditure is known as government expenditure (represented by letter "G"). This includes expenditure of government sector on welfare programs, education, health, development projects, defense, etc. Usually all economies have an increasing role played by government expenditure in the total expenditure stream. In the foreign trade sector, expenditure takes place in two parts. When the residents of our economy expend on foreign goods, it becomes imports (represented by letter "M"), and when foreigners expend on our goods, their expenditures are seen as our exports. Exports are usually represented by the letter "X." If all of the above categories of total expenditure are taken into consideration, then the aggregate demand in an economy is represented as Consumption (C) + Investment (I) + Government Expenditure (G) + Exports (X) − Imports (M). It is important to notice that imports are subtracted from the total expenditure stream because they represent expenditure on foreign products. Hence, foreign countries should include that production in their GNP. Having pointed out what constitutes aggregate demand, we can concentrate on each of its components.

6.2 Consumption Behavior

As mentioned before, consumption constitutes the expenditure done by the consumer class on such final goods as groceries, homes, cars, medicines, clothing, etc. In the whole expenditure stream, consumption is by far the largest category and thus the most important. The general behavior of consumption is stable and households tend to consume even when very little income is earned. Nonetheless, the most crucial explanatory variable for consumption is the total income. If income increases, then a typical household is likely to consume more in absolute terms. In other words, the relationship between income and consumption is seen as a direct one. In the consumption theory of Keynes, what seems logical for household behavior is also assumed true for national behavior. Hence, in general, consumption of an economy depends upon the national income. The relationship is direct because as (Y) goes up, (C) is expected to increase and is also assumed to be linear. Denoting consumption by (C) and national income (or GDP) by (Y) we can write this relationship as:

$$C = a + bY \qquad (1)$$

The linear, direct relationship shown by Equation (1) is known as the consumption function. This relationship, when plotted on the graph, is depicted by an upward sloping curve from left to right. In Equation (1), letters "a" and "b" deserve more explanation. Letter "a" is the constant term in the equation. Geometrically, it is the intercept of the Y-axis (or vertical axis) and it becomes equal to consumption (C = a) when income (Y) is zero. In other words, "a" is the bare minimum consumption an economy makes even when GDP is zero. In economic literature, "a" is called autonomous consumption. Hence, autonomous consumption is the value of "a" constant in the consumption function.

The second letter, "b," algebraically is the coefficient of (Y) in the consumption function. In geometric terms, it is the slope of the consumption function. Just like any other slope, it is measured by considering a movement on that line from one point to another (like from point G to G in Figure 6.1). In such a movement we consider the value of the rise (i.e., KG) and the run (GK), and define the slope as rise/run. In the case of Figure 6.1, the slope of the consumption function is KG'/GK. In another notational form (KG') is denoted as (C) because it is

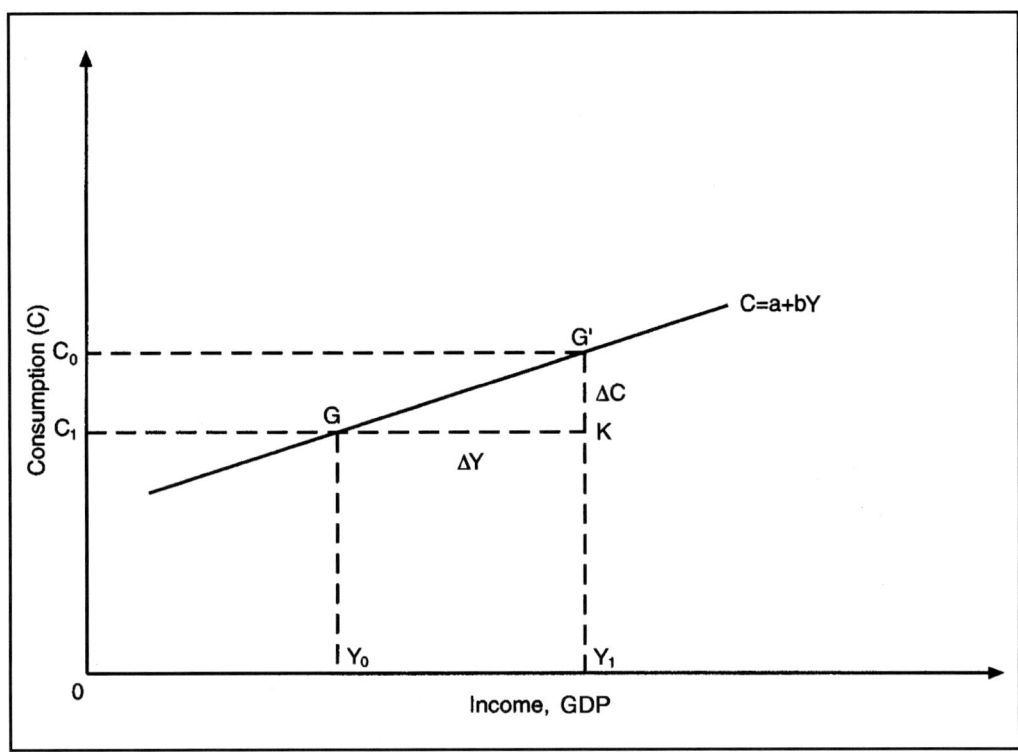

Consumption Function ■ **FIGURE 6.1**

the "change in consumption." Also, (GK) is denoted as (Y) as it is the "change in income." Hence, the slope of the consumption function (b), is equal to C/Y. In economic terms, it is known as the marginal propensity to consume (MPC).

Thus, MPC is the slope of the consumption function and is the coefficient of the Y term in the equation. What is the "propensity" to consume? As Heilbroner and Thurow (1984) put it, "it means that the relationship between consumption behavior and income is sufficiently dependable so that we can actually predict how much consumption (or how much saving) will be associated with a given level of income." When the numerically value is found, the marginal propensity to consume gives us an idea of the exact increase or decrease in consumption when income increases or decreases. However, one should not get the impression from the above discussion that income is the only determinant affecting the consumption of an economy. There are many others, even if GDP is the primary determinant of consumption.

Before we examine these other variables closely, we have to acquaint ourselves with another important concept called the average propensity to consume (APC). While the "marginal" propensity to consume considers a movement from one point to another on the consumption schedule, the "average" propensity to consume concentrates on only one point of that schedule. Hence, at any given income level, the level of consumption gives us APC. In notational form, APC is the ratio of the level of consumption (C) at a given Y level. Hence, APC = C/Y. The relationship between APC and MPC can be shown by the following simple derivation:

$$\text{Consider that APC} = C/Y$$

From the consumption function, putting the value of C = a + bY we get:

$$APC = a + bY/Y = a/Y + b = a/Y + MPC$$

Hence,

$$APC = a/Y + MPC \qquad (2)$$

From Equation (2) it is obvious that APC and MPC are different concepts. Nonetheless, they will be equal to each other in a special case when a = 0. Thus, when the vertical axis intercept is zero—that is, if the consumption function passes through the origin—then APC = MPC. Another good way of differentiating APC from MPC is to remember that MPC relates to the ratio of "changes" in consumption and income levels, while APC concerns itself with the ratio of those variables at a given point with no changes involved. To further clarify, let us analyze a numerical example.

Suppose a consumption function of an economy is represented by an equation C = 150 + .6Y and the following queries are made:

1. What is the value of autonomous consumption?
2. What is the value of APC at income level 2000?
3. What is the value of MPC?

By mere examination, one can say that autonomous consumption, the constant value in the consumption function, is 150. To calculate APC we have to find the consumption at 2000 income. This can be done by the following:

$$
\begin{aligned}
C &= 150 + .6Y \\
&= 150 + .6\,(2000) \\
&= 150 + 1200 \\
&= 1350
\end{aligned}
$$

Hence, APC = 1350/2000 = 135/200 = .67. The value of MPC can be found easily because it is the coefficient of Y in the consumption function. Hence, MPC = .6.

OTHER DETERMINANTS OF CONSUMPTION

Just as price is the major determinant of the quantity demanded, income is the crucial determinant of consumption. However, there are certain determinants other than income that might cause people to consume more or less at each level of national income. Any change in these other determinants would cause the consumption function to shift from one position to another:

Stock of Assets In general, a stock of liquid or illiquid assets can change the consumer consumption rate. The higher the stock of assets—bank deposits, stock, bonds, etc.—owned by consumers, the greater the proportion will be spent out of their income. Hence, the consumption function is likely to shift to the left/upward with a higher stock of assets held by consumers.

Inflation Rate or Expected Price Level In case of an inflationary situation, the real consumption of the household is expected to go down. Hence, the expected or actual price level can affect consumption. An increase in the price level would be responsible for shifting the consumption function upward. Changes in the price level also have an effect on the value of assets, which again affect the level of consumption as mentioned above. Thus, the inflation rate is another determinant of the consumption rate of an economy.

Stock of Durable Goods An economy that has consumed a lot before and has a high stock of durable goods is expected to consume with a lower rate currently than an economy that has a small stock of durable goods. Many households would not take a major part in consumption activities if they have had a stock of durable goods. A shift of the consumption curve to the right (downward) with lower stock of durable goods and to the left (upward) with higher stock of consumer goods is obvious.

Consumer Credit or Indebtedness A higher amount of consumer credit means that consumers may be obliged to retrench on current consumption. Hence, the indebtedness of the consumer may negatively affect consumption at the present time.

Taxes The government can influence the consumption level of an economy by making changes in taxes. A higher tax burden would necessarily reduce people's disposable income, thus reducing their consumption. Income taxes, for example, directly affect the income, which in turn influences consumption. On the other hand, a lower tax rate is expected to boost the consumption and total expenditure of the economy.

In general, the above-mentioned "non-income" determinants of consumption are also important to determine the consumption behavior of an economy. Any change in the above determinants, would cause the shift of the consumption function, as seen in Figure 6.1. On the other hand, with a change in income, we may observe a movement from one point to another on the consumption function of Figure 6.1.

DERIVATION OF SAVING FUNCTION

With the help of our discussion on the consumption function, we can also clarify the saving behavior. Saving is, in essence, the income that is not consumed. Hence, any saving behavior can be easily found by observing the consumption behavior. Initially, in algebraic terms, it can be derived as follows:

$$\text{Saving (S)} = \text{Income (Y)} - \text{Consumption (C)}$$

$$S = Y - C$$

Substituting the value of consumption from the consumption function:

$$S = Y - (a + bY)$$

$$S = Y - a - bY$$

$$S = -a + (1 - b)Y \tag{3}$$

Equation (3) is known as the saving function. Hence, if the consumption function is given as $C = a + bY$, the saving function is derived as $S = -a + (1 - b)Y$. In numerical terms, if the consumption function is $C = 150 + .7Y$, then the saving function is $S = -150 + .3Y$. This obviously illustrates the idea that the saving function is the relationship between saving and income, just as the consumption function is the relationship between consumption and income.

In geometric terms, from the consumption function, the saving function can easily be derived. Consider Figure 6.2, which has two parts. On both parts of the X-axis we measure income, on the upper part of the Y-axis we plot consumption (C), and on the lower part we measure saving (S). The upper quadrant is no different than Figure 6.1 except that in the former, we see an extra curve labeled as a 45° line. There is a special reason why we have drawn it there. As one of the characteristics of a 45° line, we know that all the points on that line are equidistant from both axes. In other words, at all points on the 45° line of the graph, the consumption level is equal to the income level. Obviously, the relationship shown by the 45° line (i.e., C = Y) is purely imaginary (or hypothetical). But by using this hypothetical relationship, it is easy to derive the saving-income relationship in the lower part of the Figure 6.2.

Notice from the consumption function that at zero income, consumption is "a," which means that saving is "–a." Hence, we get one point, "K," on the lower quadrant, which is the saving function. Also notice that at income level "Y_0," consumption is equal to income (because at "Y_0" income, the actual consumption, given by point E, is equal to income because point E is also on our hypothetical 45° line). This means that at income "Y_0," saving is zero, giving us point "I" on the lower graph. Now consider another GDP level, say Y_1, consumption at Y_1 is given by point "B." Because point "A" is on the 45° line, we can also say that

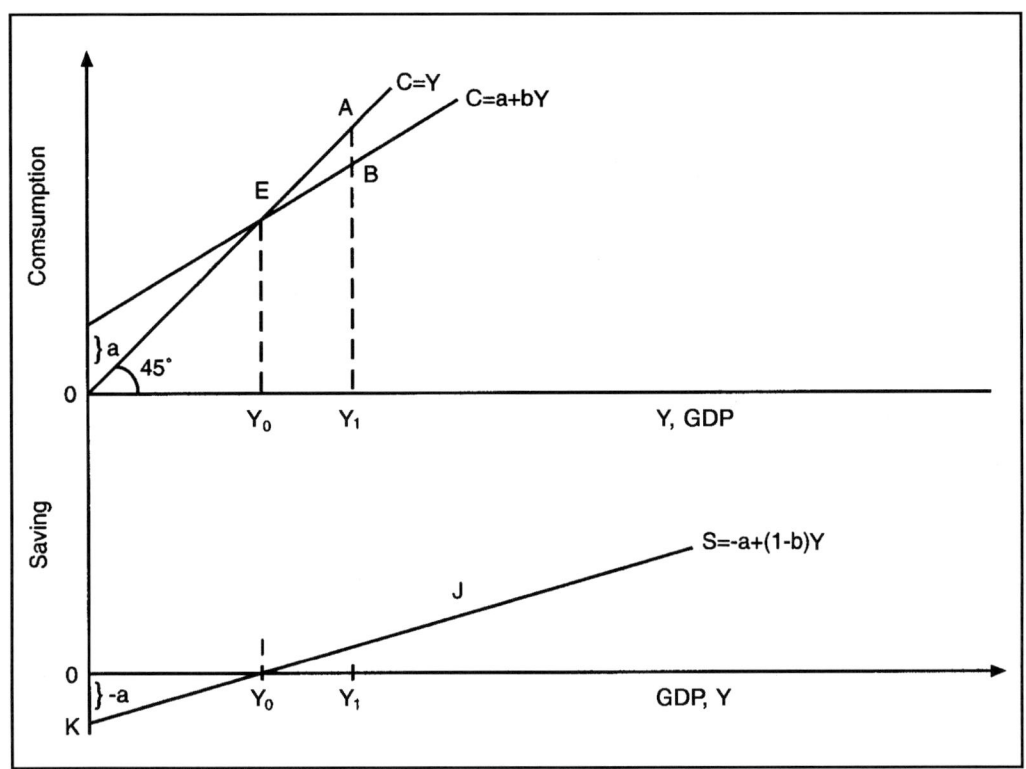

Saving Function Derived from Consumption Function ■ FIGURE 6.2

$AY_1 = OY_1$, meaning that AY_1 is also the income. Hence, with AY_1 as income and BY_1 as consumption, we can say that saving is "AB." In the lower part of the graph, we can take point "J" in such a manner that $JY_1 = AB$. By joining the points K, I, and J, we can draw the saving function.

From the saving function, we can now define some other important concepts, such as the marginal propensity to save (MPS) and average propensity to save (APS). Like MPC, MPS is the slope of the saving function and is defined as the ratio of change in saving to the change in income and it is the coefficient of the income term in the saving function. But looking at the saving function we can say, MPS = 1 − b, and b = MPC. Therefore, by definition, MPC + MPS = 1.

Average propensity to save (APS), like APC, is defined as the ratio of saving to income (S/Y = APS). By simple derivation it is possible to show that APC and APS also add up to unity. Let us define initial income as consumption plus saving:

$$Y = C + S$$

Dividing both sides by Y, we get:

$$Y/Y = C/Y + S/Y$$

therefore:

$$1 = APC + APS$$

Among the non-income determinants of savings, the interest rate seems to be the most important one. The higher the interest rate offered on the deposits, the higher its saving will be. The saving curve drawn in Figure 6.2 would shift from one place to another due to changes in the interest rate. One would also note that all the determinants of consumption are also the determinants of saving because saving is just the income that is not consumed. Hence, these non-income determinants of consumption listed above also indirectly affect the saving behavior of the economy.

6.3 Investment Determination, Equilibrium Level of GDP, and Multiplier Analysis

While consumption constitutes the most important and the largest part of total expenditure of the economy, the second most important part is investment (I). Investment, in real terms, is made up of one of the following three factors: (a) expenditure on buying of machinery, tools, and equipment, (b) construction activities, and (c) changes in the stock of inventories. Inventories are the stocks of goods that are produced by a company, but not sent to the market. The above definition of investment is special and important to remember. This "real" investment also has to be differentiated from the purchase of bonds, stocks, or precious metals, which constitute "financial" investment. According to Keynes, an investment activity undertaken by the producers would depend upon two "rates." One is the "rate" of expected returns from the use of the machine the producer is thinking about buying (or not buying). This is popularly called the marginal efficiency of capital (MEC). The second relevant rate is the interest rate charged by banks for their loans (represented by "r").

If the interest rate happens to be lower than the expected profit rate, producers would realize that the rate that they would repay their loans from the bank would be less than the profit rate expected from their investment. The producer would go ahead and borrow from the bank and actively carry out the investment. Under these circumstances, investment would go up. Investment in the economy would tend to go down if the expected profit rate happened to be less than the interest rate charged by the banks. The optimum level of investment is determined by that point at which MEC = r.

This expected profit rate in economic literature is referred to as the marginal efficiency of capital (MEC) or marginal efficiency of investment (MEI). In practice, it is hard to measure this rate in numerical terms. In order to tackle this problem, Keynes defines this rate as "that rate of discount which would make the present value of the series of annuities given by the returns expected from the capital asset during its life just equal to its supply price." The relationship between marginal efficiency of capital and investment is seen as inversed. With higher investment the rate of profit is expected to decline.

Hence, in Figure 6.3 the MEC curve is sloping downward from left to right. Assuming the constant interest rate charged by banks ($r = r_0$) irrespective of the borrowing amount or investment, we can determine optimum amount of investment (I_0) at point "K." I_0 is considered the optimum investment amount, because at another amount of investment there is an inequality between MEC and the interest rate, meaning a tendency for investment to either increase or go down. For example, at investment I_1, MEC > r, and so the tendency of investment will go up. At investment I_2, MEC < r, and so investment would go down from I_2.

There are several factors in the real world that would have an effect on the value of MEC. Notable among these are (1) the expected revenues from an investment, (2) taxes, (3) the cost of production, and (4) expected inflation rate. All of these factors would be responsible for a shift in the MEC curve in Figure 6.3.

For instance, a higher tax rate would force producers to increase the supply price of capital equipment, and the discount rate (MEC) that makes the supply price equal to the present value would have to be lowered. Hence, the MEC curve

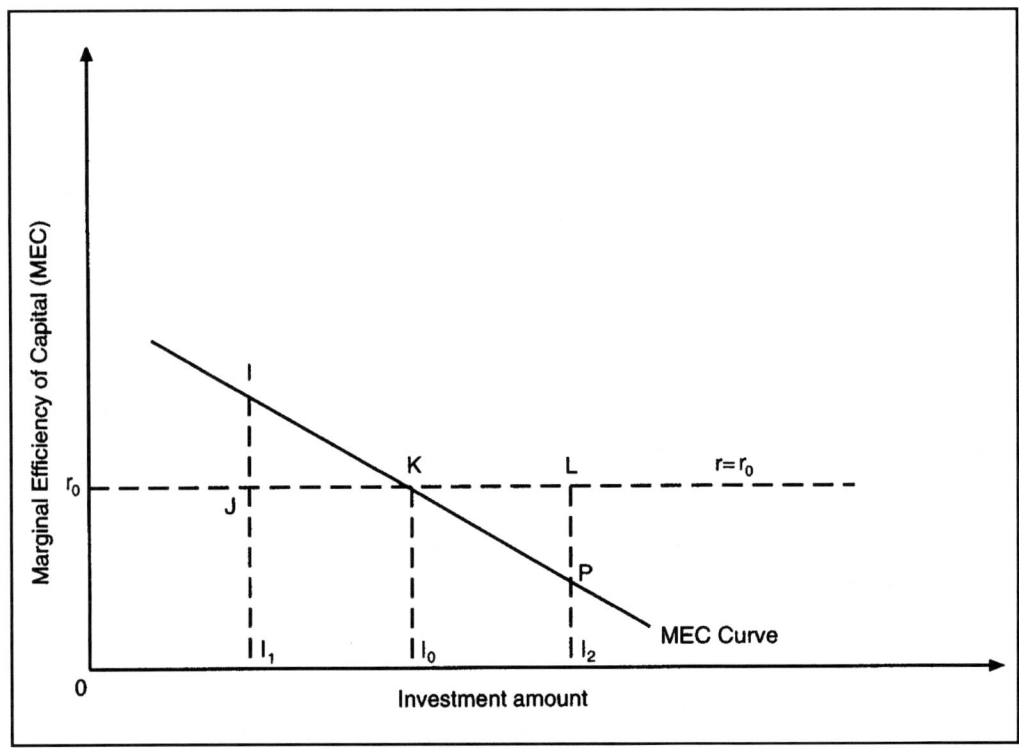

Optimum Investment Determination ■ **FIGURE 6.3**

would shift downward, determining lower investment than 10 as the optimum amount. The expectation of inflation (or reduction in the value of money, as Keynes sees it) has a similar effect on investment. In Keynes' words,

> ... the expectation of changes in the value of money influences the volume of current output. The expectation of a fall in the value of money stimulates investment, and hence employment generally, because it raises the schedule of the marginal efficiency of capital, e.g., the investment demand schedule; and the expectation of a rise in the value of money is depressing, because it lowers the schedule of the marginal efficiency of capital.

It is crucial to realize that to a Keynesian mind, since investment is dependent upon the relationship between the interest rate and the marginal efficiency of capital, investment is independent of income. Hence, changes in GDP have no effect on investment. In other words, investment is completely autonomous of GDP. If we assume a closed economy (no international trade) where the government plays no role, then its aggregate demand (or total expenditure) is just consumption (C) plus investment (I). To draw such an aggregate demand curve in Figure 6.4 is easy because when autonomous investment is added to consumption, the consumption function will not change its slope. The (C + I) curve lies to

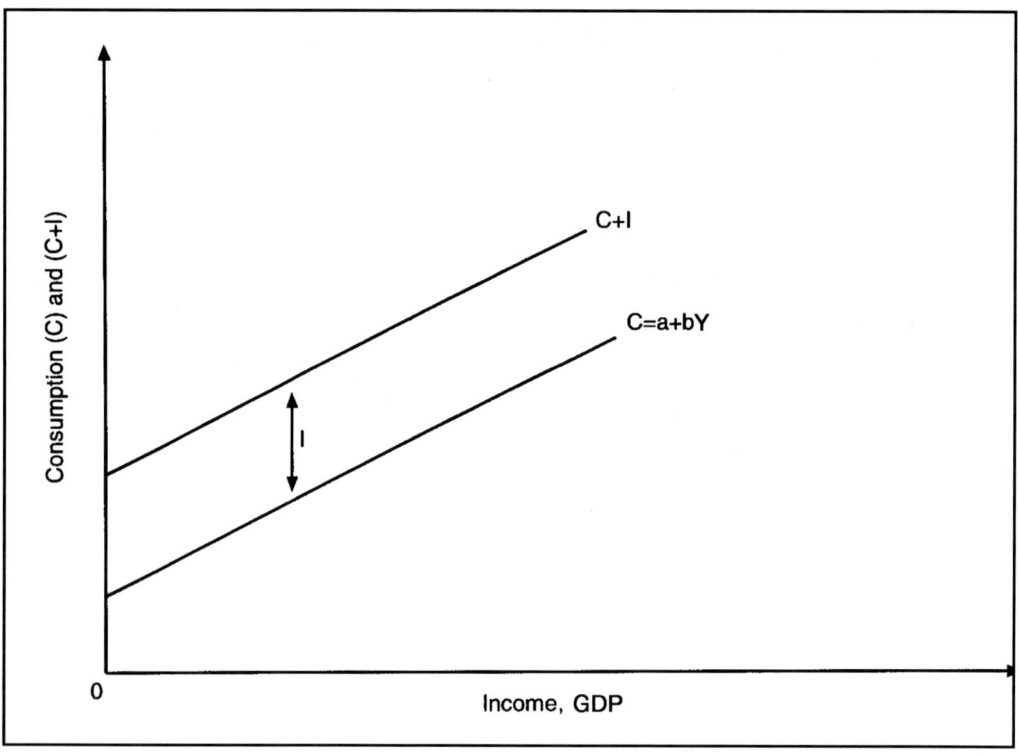

FIGURE 6.4 ■ Total Expenditure Curve

the upper side of the consumption curve by the amount of investment. A mathematical derivation is carried out through the following simple calculation:

Define

$$Y = C + I$$

substituting consumption's value as (a + bY):

$$Y = a + bY + I$$

The (C + I) curve is also called the aggregate demand curve or total expenditure line. It is used to define another important concept of the equilibrium level of income. In order to determine the equilibrium level of income, we must first understand its meaning. In general, the equilibrium level of income is defined as that level of income where the aggregate demand/total expenditure in the economy is equal to its aggregate supply. Notice, however, that aggregate supply is same as the level of GDP produced.

Hence, in notational form, the equilibrium level of income needs (C + I) = (C + S). Specifically in a closed economy, it is the level where investment is equal to saving. There is yet another way of defining the equilibrium level of GDP. Consider that investment is seen as an "injection" in the expenditure stream because any increase in it increases the total expenditure of an economy. On the other hand, saving is called a "leakage" from the total expenditure of an economy. From this approach, the equilibrium level of income is that level where an economy's leakages are equal to its injections.

In the Keynesian system, in order to determine the equilibrium level of income, we use Figure 6.5, known as the *Keynesian Cross*. In the above graph, the (C + I) line is the same as what we derived in Figure 6.4. Together with this (C + I) line, which we call the actual aggregate demand line, we would also plot a 45° line. As a hypothetical case, in this graph the 45° line represents all those points at which aggregate demand is always equal to aggregate supply. However, at point "E" where both lines intersect, we have an equality of actual aggregate demand and aggregate supply. Hence, point "E" decides the equilibrium level of income as Y. In numerical form, the equilibrium level of income can be determined as follows: Suppose the consumption function of an economy is given as:

$$C = 400 + .75Y$$

and the investment determined by MEC and the interest rate relationship is given as 500 currency units. A question of equilibrium level of income can be answered by noticing that equilibrium income level needs:

$$C + I = C + S$$

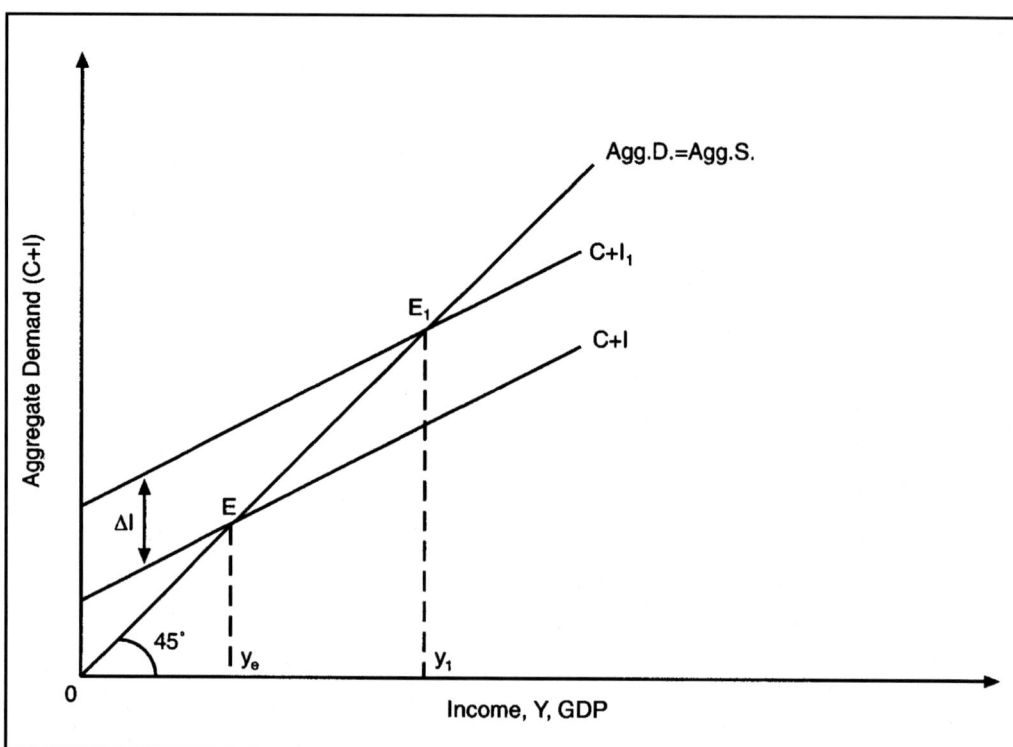

FIGURE 6.5 ■ Equilibrium Income Determination

i.e., C + I = Y

Equilibrium income (GDP) needs:

$$C + I = Y$$

i.e., a + bY + I = Y
i.e., 400 + .75Y + 500 = Y
i.e., 900 = .25Y
i.e., 3600 = Y

Therefore, the level of income of $3600 is the equilibrium level. The next issue we want to discuss is how changes in equilibrium income can be caused by changes in investment levels. Let us suppose that investment increases from the level shown in Figure 6.5 to a higher level. (Let us call the original level of investment I_0 and the new level of investment, I_1.) In other words, investment increases by ΔI amount. With higher investment, in Figure 6.5 we may have to draw another aggregate demand line. Obviously, the new level of equilibrium income would be higher than (Y_0), say (Y_1). Let us denote this increase in income by ΔY. Thus, we can see from Figure 6.5 that with an increase in investment equilibrium income increases.

In mathematical terms derivation of this change in GDP is easy to see. Consider that for Equilibrium GDP, we need

$$Y = C + I$$

or

$$Y = a + bY + I$$

Rearranging

$$Y - bY = a + I$$

or

$$(1 - b)Y = a + I$$

and

$$\Delta Y = (a/1 - b) + (1/1 - b) \times \Delta I$$

Totally differentiating the above, keeping in mind that "a" and "b" are constants, we get:

$$\Delta Y = 1/(1 - MPC) \times \Delta I = (1/MPS) \times \Delta I$$

Therefore, any change in investment will be multiplied by this factor of 1/MPS to give us the amount of change in the equilibrium GDP.

The value of the factor $[1/(1 - MPC)]$ (or 1/MPS) is called the autonomous investment multiplier (or the investment multiplier) and is denoted by the letter "K." By definition, the investment multiplier is the multiple of change in investment, which gives rise to the change in the equilibrium level of income. In algebraic terms, it is equal to the inverse of the marginal propensity to save (MPS), or one divided by one minus the marginal propensity to consume. In numerical terms, the value of the multiplier would always be greater than unity because marginal propensity to consume (and also to save) is always less than one. This is because it is improbable that ($\Delta C/\Delta Y$) can be greater than one. This means that any change in investment would create a larger change in the equilibrium level of income.

A NUMERICAL ILLUSTRATION

Suppose the consumption function of an economy is given as C = 150 + .75Y and the initial investment is 500. If the investment increases from 500 to 600, what is the change in the equilibrium income? A question like this can be answered by initially calculating income as:

$$Y = C + I$$
$$= 150 + .75Y + 500$$

or .25Y = 650

or Y = 2600

and with new investment:

$$Y = 150 + .75Y + 600$$
$$= 750 + .75Y$$
$$.25Y = 750$$
$$\text{or } Y = 3000$$

Due to an increase in investment by 100, the equilibrium level of income increases by 400. This necessarily means that the value of the investment multiplier is 4, which can be verified by $1/MPS = 1/.25 = 4$.

Now we must understand why there is a multiple increase in the equilibrium GDP of an economy when investment increases by a certain amount. For example, when there is an investment activity of 100 units (of buying either machinery, tools, equipment, or construction activity) there is an increase in income of 100 units created in the first period. Those people who receive this income are obviously going to spend a part of it and save the remaining part. Their action of consuming more from the increased income will be dictated by the value of marginal propensity to consume (MPC).

Hence, they would consume $MPC \times 100$ in the next period and would become the income of someone else. In the economy as a whole up to this point, there is an increase in income of $100 + MPC \times 100$. However, those who receive income of $MPC \times 100$ would consume in the next round by $MPC \times MPC \times 100$ and the process would continue for the fourth, fifth, sixth time periods. All in all, at the end of the process (i.e., equilibrium), the increase in income would be:

$$\Delta Y \text{ or change in } Y = 100 + MPC \times 100 + MPC_2 \times 100 + MPC_3 \times 100 + \ldots$$
$$= (1 + MPC + MPC_2 + MPC_3 + \ldots) \times 100$$
$$= 1/(1 - MPC) \times 100$$
$$\Delta Y = [1/(1 - MPC)] \times \Delta I$$

Any increase in investment is responsible for a multifold increase in the equilibrium income level. However, the multiplier principle works in both directions. Any decrease in investment also causes a multifold decrease in the equilibrium level of income. Also, the multiplier process can be ignited by a change in any part of the total expenditure. Hence, similar to the investment multiplier, there is a government expenditure multiplier (and actually change in any part of aggregate demand creates a multiplier effect on the equilibrium level of income). In fact, as the multiplier process is started by a change in any autonomous factor, the multiplier is sometimes called the "autonomous spending multiplier."

Full Employment, Active Government Sector, and Keynesian Analysis

6.4

So far we have discussed GDP determination with simplified assumptions, including an inactive government sector. In realistic terms however, the role of government is not only important, but also more prominent in the modern era. It is necessary to find out the changes needed to accommodate an active government sector in our Keynesian model. When the active government sector is considered, two things happen: First, government injects a lot of its own expenditure in the total expenditure stream. This means the definition of total expenditure has to be modified as equal to consumption (C) + investment (I) + government expenditure (G).

Secondly, the government is also responsible for imposing taxes (Tx), which appear in several forms. There are direct taxes such as income taxes at different levels, gift and property taxes, as well as numerous indirect taxes such as sales taxes, excise taxes, transportation taxes, etc. Even if we consider the simplest taxes, namely, lump-sum income taxes, we can envision that taxes act as leakages from the expenditure stream and to increase them would reduce total expenditure by their effect on consumption. The government policy that decides the levels of government expenditure and taxes is fiscal policy. Each country has a separate arrangement on how these changes are activated. It is safe to assume, however, that decisions of fiscal policy are done according to the wishes of its makers. They increase (and rarely, decrease) government expenditure whenever they feel an increase is warranted.

Hence, we can easily argue that decisions of fiscal policy are independent of GDP levels (or G is autonomous to GDP). Theoretically, the addition of government expenditure to (C + I) only makes it another autonomous factor added to (C + I) and the resultant total expenditure line in Figure 6.6 is parallel to the (C + I) line that we drew before. Hence with an active government, our geometrical way of defining equilibrium GDP remains the same. The equilibrium level of the GDP is defined by the point where the (C + I + G) line, or newly defined total expenditure line, intersects the 45° line in Figure 6.6.

In algebraic terms also, the active government sector changes little. Here is a numerical example: Suppose initially consumption function is given as C = 500 + 2/3Y. The investment (I) level is 300 and the government expenditure (G) level is 200. What is the equilibrium level of GDP that the economy would produce? To get the answer, consider that for equilibrium GDP we need (Y = C + I + G). Hence, we need (Y = 500 + 2/3Y + 300 + 200). Solve this for Y and you will get (Y = 3000) as the equilibrium level of GDP. As mentioned before, an economy

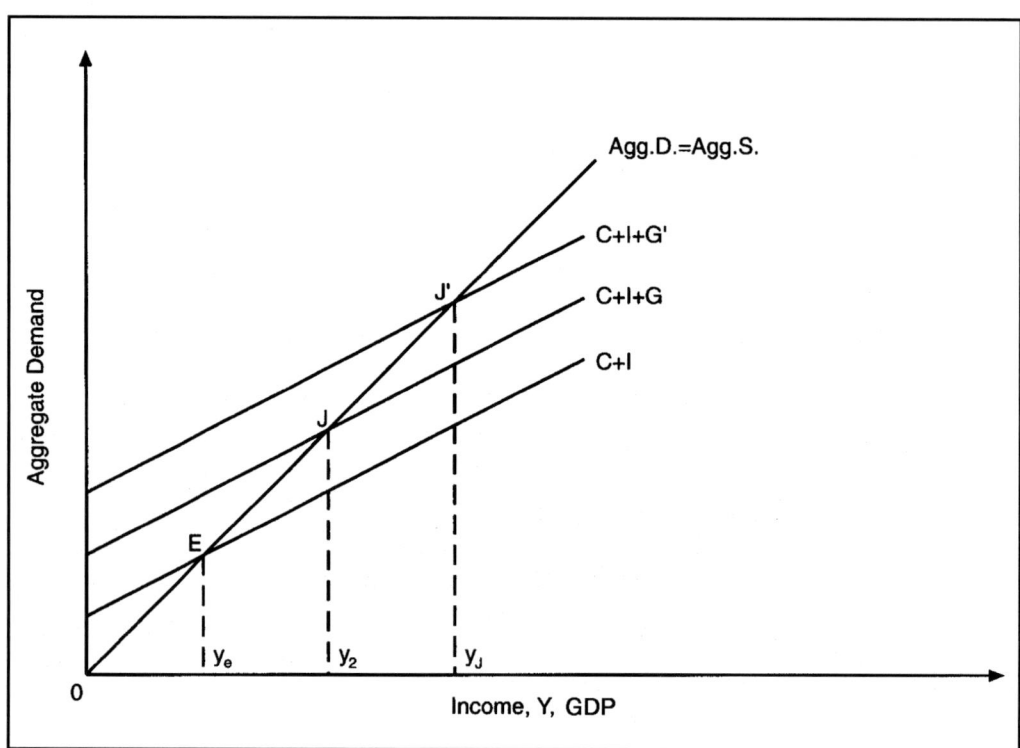

FIGURE 6.6 ■ Aggregate Demand with Active Government

will always produce the equilibrium level of GDP because otherwise there would be either recessionary or inflationary gaps.

The basic thrust of the Keynesian analysis is not to get to the equilibrium GDP that the economy produces if there is no outside force on it, but to determine how to achieve full employment in the economy. Keynes was probably the first economist to emphasize that the equilibrium level of income may not be equal to the full employment income. This may be so, if only for the simple reason that the equilibrium level of GDP is defined as the GDP level with equal aggregate demand and aggregate supply, and the full employment level of income is defined as the level where all persons in the economy willing to work can find a job. There is not *a priori* reason why both income levels may be the same. According to Keynes, classical economists erred in not realizing this point. Now the basic reason why the economy may not achieve full employment could be the lack of aggregate demand. While the economy may attain the Y level of income in Figure 6.6 on its own, it is likely that full employment income could be greater than Y_e.

Therefore, the economy, left to itself, does not have any mechanism to lead to full employment. The government that is anxious to achieve this has a definite role to play under these circumstances. Its main task has to be to influence the aggregate demand structure and raise it to the appropriate level. We should not analyze the role of an active government. As mentioned before, the moment the government becomes active, aggregate demand is defined as C + I + G. Government expenditure, like investment, is autonomous, independent, and exogenous of changes in the income of the economy.

Hence, in Figure 6.6 the shape of the C + I line would remain unchanged. Only its location would change according to the amount of government expenditure. The new aggregate demand will then be represented by the C + I + G curve and a new equilibrium level of income would be given by point "J" (and its level is Y on the horizontal axis).

Let us assume that full employment level of income, as shown in the graph, is Y_j. In order to achieve that level, according to Keynes, the government must take the initiative in starting new social programs and raising the aggregate demand level to C + I + G' that is appropriate for full employment. In Keynes' words:

> The state will have to exercise a guiding influence on the propensity to consume partly through its scheme of taxation, partly by fixing the rate of interest, and partly, perhaps, in other ways. Furthermore, it seems unlikely that the influence of banking policy on the rate of interest will be sufficient by itself to determine an optimum rate of investment. I conceive, therefore, that a somewhat comprehensive socialization of investment will prove the only means of securing an approximation to full employment; though this need not exclude all manner of compromises and of devices by which public authority will cooperate with private initiative.

Nothing can be clearer than this quote. This distinctly shows Keynes' aim: giving the government a larger share of responsibility for the attainment of full employment. The government policy that makes the changes in taxes and government expenditure is its fiscal policy. From the above quotation, it is clear that Keynes regarded fiscal policy to be very efficient. This was partly due to his belief in the multiplier process. When government expenditure is increased, Keynes believed that the same multiplier process is put into action as one after an increase in investment. This is because when the government expends, it begins new construction projects, like building highways or dams. All of these activities start the same multiplier process as investment activity does. Moreover, the same multiplier (1/MPS) explains the increase in the equilibrium GDP by increasing government expenditure. Hence, $\Delta Y = (1/MPS)\Delta G$.

Due to universal application of the multiplier process, fiscal policy is always effective in increasing real output of the economy. In case of changes in taxes, however, the effect on the GDP is a little more complex. When lump-sum income taxes are raised, there is a decline in the consumption expenditure of the economy. However, this decline is less than an increase in taxes, because people would pay increased taxes by reducing consumption as well as by reducing saving. If taxes are increased by 100, for example, then people's disposable incomes would decline by 100, consumption would decline by MPC × 100, and saving would decline by MPS × 100. Furthermore, the multiplier (1/MPS) is applied to this consumption in a reverse direction to find the total decline in the equilibrium GDP due to taxes. In equation form this means:

$$\text{Change in equilibrium GDP} = -\left(\frac{MPC}{MPS}\right) \text{Change in taxes}$$

or

$$\Delta Y = -\left(\frac{MPC}{MPS}\right) \Delta Tx$$

In fact, (MPC/MPS) is called the tax multiplier. [As you can see, the strength of the tax multiplier is smaller than the autonomous investment multiplier (1/MPS) that is applied for an increase in G]. Therefore, an equal increase in G and increase in taxes would have a positive effect on the equilibrium GDP.

Further modifications in this simple Keynesian model also show that if a government is committed to balancing the budget, so that $\Delta G = \Delta Tx$, then the balanced budget multiplier is always 1, irrespective of the values of MPC or MPS.

Followers of Keynes (popularly called Keynesians) in the 1940s and 1950s were busy solving numerical problems of how much increase in G (or reduction in Tx) is needed to raise the GDP from where it is to where one needs to take it. After the publication of *General Theory* in 1936, the main message of Keynes, namely, "to reach to the approximation of full employment, the only means is to have a somewhat comprehensive socialization of investment," was accepted the world over. Many countries adopted Keynesian policies without hesitation. Moreover, what government wouldn't like to increase its expenditure especially if it is the only means of achieving full employment? Additionally, Keynes was a very active political economist. He not only single-handedly designed the economic policy of the United Kingdom, but also visited European countries and the United States to sway policy makers on his new ideas. There are numerous examples of Keynesian policies in action in many countries, especially the United States and the United Kingdom. In conclusion, the main message received from the commodity market analysis by Keynes is the one which emphasizes the active role of government toward reaching full employment.

6.5 Influence of Keynes on Policy Making in the U.S.

In this section we discuss the application of Keynesian policy to the United States economy. At the time that Keynes had begun forming his theories, the United

States economy was in its darkest years ever—the Great Depression of 1929-1933. Also, as we discussed, classical economics could not explain, let alone solve, the problems of the U.S. economy, when Keynes' ideas achieved both. His ideas, however, were not ushered in with a great deal of enthusiasm. President Franklin Roosevelt and his administration had been looking for quick solutions to the smaller individual problems at hand rather than a complete theoretical change of economic ideals. Even with this skepticism, however, Keynes' ideas filtered into the policies of the New Deal.

The New Deal was a watered down version of the type of policies suggested by Keynes. Keynes would have liked the president to run a much higher federal deficit. Roosevelt, however, was wary of such an unbalanced budget, and did not enact expansionary fiscal policies to the extent that Keynes would have liked. It wasn't until 1941, when American entered the Second World War, that President Roosevelt, out of necessity, ran the type of deficit implied by Keynes. During the war years, the United States quickly pulled out of its economic depression. This leads many to believe that had the United States accepted Keynes' theories earlier, the depression might not have been as great.

The Great Depression era can be scrutinized for trends using many different analytical techniques, but the most convincing is Keynesian analysis. Keynesian economics gave us a completely new way of looking at macroeconomics. *General Theory* did more to change the landscape of macroeconomics than any other economic work in history.

KEYNES' LIFE

John Maynard Keynes was one of the most interesting and influential people in the history of economics. His theories on macroeconomics have influenced countless government economic policies, including the United States. His most recognized work, *The General Theory of Employment, Interest and Money,* almost immediately changed the way the world looked at the role of government in society and the economy.

John Keynes was raised in a very academic family. His father, John Nevile Keynes, lectured on logic and political economy at Cambridge. His mother, Florence, was a great advocate of social reform as well as a successful author. Through attendance in the best schools, along with lessons given at home, little John was able to propel himself to the top of his class by 1894. His academic prowess allowed him to attend Eton academy, a very exclusive school, where he excelled, winning numerous prizes in mathematics and placing first in virtually everything he attempted. Because of Keynes tremendous academic success, in

1902 he was given a scholarship to study mathematics and classics at King's College, Cambridge.

In 1905, Keynes acquired an interest in economics and began attending lectures given by the famous economist Alfred Marshall. In August 1906, he was employed by the India Office but dissatisfied with the job he spent most of his time there working on his own theories. He returned to Cambridge in June 1908, and was elected to a fellowship in March 1909.

Keynes then began to teach economics at Cambridge. He published numerous papers on statistics and on the Indian economy. In 1913, he was appointed to a commission that examined Indian finance and currency. Keynes continued working there until the start of the First World War. In 1915, Keynes started working at the Treasury to help manage the wartime economy. However, he resigned from the position in 1919 because he did not agree with the proposals for German reparations.

After his resignation from the Treasury, Keynes wrote *The Economic Consequences of the Peace*, which criticized the Versailles Peace Conference and attacked leading political figures. During the 1920s Keynes worked on his *Treatise on Probability*, and by the 1930s was drawn back toward economics, due in part to the unemployment and depression that was sweeping many economies in the world. Classical economics did not have an answer or reason for this new type of depression. It was a phenomenon that needed to be explained by a new theory, a theory that Keynes supplied in his most famous and influential work, *The General Theory of Employment, Interest and Money*, in 1935-1936.

By 1937, Keynes' health had begun to fail, but he remained an influential voice in the Treasury throughout the Second World War. His most important project during this time was the creation of the International Monetary Fund in the famous Bretton Woods Conference in 1944.

Keynes died of a heart attack in 1946 at the age of sixty-three at his home in Sussex. Although he died at a relatively young age, his influence was far reaching and he is arguably the most influential macroeconomists in the history of economics.

U.S. POLICIES DURING THE DEPRESSION AND WORLD WAR II

When Keynes was working on *The General Theory of Employment, Interest and Money* in the 1930s, the United States was in the middle of an unprecedented economic crisis: the Great Depression. Over the course of just four years, unemployment had skyrocketed from 3.2 percent in 1929 to 25.2 in 1933. At the same time, the nominal GDP dropped by 46 percent and the general price level by 24 percent. Needless to say, the U.S. economy was in shambles, and there was nothing in classical economic theory that could explain, let alone solve, these problems. America was in desperate need of a revolutionary macroeconomic policy change. The answer came from the mind of John Maynard Keynes.

Although many of the policies ushered in by President Roosevelt during the Great Depression were Keynesian in nature, most historians do not believe that the he was a true Keynesian. According to Lord Robert Skidelsky, author of the definitive biography on Keynes, Keynes had visited Roosevelt in 1934 to look over the New Deal and advise him on ways to revive the American economy. After that meeting, Keynes wrote, "Washington . . . is the laboratory of the New World. It's the laboratory of economics." Though Keynes was sympathetic to the New Deal, his relationship with President Roosevelt was not close. Roosevelt felt that Keynes was trying to tell him how to run his administration while Keynes felt that Roosevelt was being stubborn. Lord Skidelsky believes that Keynes "didn't affect President Roosevelt directly, but did so indirectly." Even if Keynes didn't directly influence the president, he influenced an entire generation of economic thinkers. Lauchlin Currie was one such economic mind, and he become Roosevelt's special advisor. So there remained undeniably Keynesian voices in the White House during this time.

Keynes' proposals also left Roosevelt in a political conundrum. In the election of 1932 Franklin Roosevelt campaigned that he would work to balance the budget, but under Keynes' ideas the government must run a large deficit. Because of this situation and some possible stubbornness on the part of the president, the New Deal and other policies before the Second World War were watered down versions of the policies proposed by Keynes. Keynes would have liked to see a much higher deficit, but Roosevelt was unwilling to operate with a highly unbalanced budget.

The U.S. Fiscal Policies 6.6

THE NEW DEAL

The New Deal was the name for the sweeping governmental changes issued by President Roosevelt. It consisted of three separate parts: relief, recovery, and reform. According to Lord Robert Skidelsky, many of these policy changes were not a Keynesian response to the economic crisis, but rather a response to many different individual problems in the United States.

Despite this, some policies were purely Keynesian in nature, and had the expected outcome. The government expenditures on large-scale public works such as dams, roads, and major sanitation projects proved to be highly effective Keynesian policies. For every additional dollar per capita spent on these types of projects, the per capita income increased by roughly $2. In Keynesian analysis this phenomenon can be explained by the multiplier process.

The Tennessee Valley Authority and most of the second New Deal (started in 1935) didn't have anything to do with Keynes or his ideas. These policies were the type of "quick fix" policies mentioned earlier. Policies like the National Health Program and Civilian Conservation Corps (CCC) were met with greater rewards.

THE CIVILIAN CONSERVATION CORPS

The Civilian Conservation Corps (CCC) had two major purposes: to reduce unemployment and preserve the country's natural resources. To accomplish these goals, the CCC offered jobs to poor young men between the ages of eighteen and twenty-five to work on useful, large scale, public works projects such as soil conservation, road construction, and forest preservation. The men were employed for six months at a time and paid $30 a month.

The CCC provided over 500,000 poor American men with at least a temporary job to get their feet back on the ground. The CCC worked with different outfits in each state performing tasks, such as clearing brush, planting trees, building roads and small dams, creating and protecting state and federal parks, stringing telephone wire, digging ditches, fighting fires, educating the people on soil conservation, and many more important jobs.

This was an ingenious way to increase the government expenditure and offer unemployment relief. Through a statistical analysis, it can be shown that for every dollar the government put into these large-scale projects the local total income would increase by $2. Needless to say, this was a very effective economic policy.

THE NATIONAL HEALTH PROGRAM

Public health and unemployment were probably the two social issues that President Roosevelt and his staff most concerned themselves with in the 1930s. The president's advisors had differing views on whether unemployment insurance or public health insurance should be given more consideration. On top of that, there were differing views of what should happen to health insurance. Many felt that all health insurance should be federalized and government funded, but medical professionals lobbied against federalization claiming it would decrease the quality of medical care. After much debating, the two sides were finally able to agree on some type of health insurance at the National Health Conference in 1938.

At this conference, official representatives of major interest groups, including editors, civic and industrial leaders, and representatives of medicine, labor, agriculture, welfare, education, and foundations were brought together to discuss the health needs of the nation and the National Health Program. The National Health Program gave recommendations to legislators. These recommendations called for an extra $850 million a year and were the beginnings of the public health system the United States has today. Even though most of the participants in the conference of 1938 probably weren't aware of Keynes' economic ideas, they unwittingly enacted a Keynesian policy that caused a large increase in government spending.

6.7 A Critique of Keynesian Conventional Wisdom in Commodity Market

While Keynes arguably is the most applied macroeconomist of the twentieth century, his analysis was not without some glaring shortcomings. In fact, Keynesian philosophy was severely criticized by economists in the 1960s. In this section we shall summarize some critical issues of Keynesian argument in the commodity market. In future chapters we shall provide a few more criticisms in other markets and policy issues.

MARGINAL PROPENSITY TO CONSUME

One of the disturbing points about Keynesian framework of commodity market as previously summarized is that it depends heavily on the value of marginal propensity to consume (MPC). MPC is not only a slope of the consumption function but also the unique link between the consumption analysis and the multiplier analysis of Keynes.

There are empirical doubts about the behavior of the value of MPC as the national income changes. If MPC is unstable in magnitude, so is the investment multiplier. Hence, the actual effect of expansionary fiscal policy on the national income is not as easily and specifically achieved as Keynes would have liked. There are several attempts to estimate the value of MPC. Notable among them are Kuznets (1946), Modigliani (1966), Friedman (1956), and Duesenberry (1952). Depending upon the individual views taken by these authors, the consumption in general is seen as a function of national income, but there is no evidence that this relationship has a constant slope (i.e., constant MPC).

INVESTMENT FUNCTION

Last but not least, the investment function derived by Keynes can also be criticized. The marginal efficiency of capital depends solely upon the "expected" gains from a capital asset, and any expectations are difficult to measure, so we have little indication how the investors would rationalize their decisions about investment. Investment demand has been a subject of several studies including those of Jorgenson (1971), Clark (1979), and Jaffee and Rosen (1979).

None of these have fully supported the Keynesian analysis that unless we know MIEC, the optimum investment level cannot be determined. Furthermore, MEC and its relationship with the interest rate are not the only determinants of investment. As accelerator theory proposes, the gross investment is also dependent upon the desired capital stock and/or GDP. Hence, the main assumption of Keynesian economics that investment is determined completely autonomously to GDP levels is questionable.

Further work in this area by other economists (especially Paul Samuelson) assumes that investment is in fact determined by GDP and that effect is called accelerator. In fact, combination of accelerator and multiplier give us the compounding effects of GDP on investment and of investment on GDP leading to the reason for business cycles in the economy.

FOREIGN TRADE IMPLICATIONS OF EXPANSIONARY FISCAL POLICY

The analysis in this section is carried out with the help of an important article by Walter Eltis (1976). According to Eltis, expansionary fiscal policy will have serious ramifications. Let us see how that happens. Including the international trade, the basic aggregate demand and aggregate supply identity can be written as:

$$C + I + G + X = C + S + Tx + M \qquad (4)$$

where C = domestic consumption in real terms
   I = domestic investment in real terms
   G = government expenditure in real terms
   X = real exports
   S = domestic savings
  Tx = taxes in real terms
   M = real imports

Adjusting the equation or identity, we get

$$(G - Tx) + (I - S) = (M - X) \qquad (5)$$

Given the fact that there is an expansionary fiscal policy (increase in G, which is not financed completely by raising taxes) in terms of Equation (5), there are either adjustments in (I − S) or (M − X). In other words, any increase in government expenditure in real terms has to be compensated by an equal decrease in (I − S) or an increase in deficit on the current account of the economy's balance of payments. Assuming that the investment and saving amounts of an economy do not change substantially by changing government expenditure, we have to conclude that an expansionary fiscal policy almost always leads to deficit on the current account. This is a crucial point that was ignored in *The General Theory* (Keynes, 1936).

The economic reasoning behind why the deficit will occur as a result of an expansionary fiscal policy is overwhelming. An increase in government expenditure increases the equilibrium national income of the economy by several times, depending upon the value of the multiplier. Assuming a positive marginal propensity to import, an increase in national income boosts the economy's imports, which leads to the deficit in the balance of payments. Hence, the most bothersome point of the Keynesian argument is that it ignores international trade. In the words of Walter Eltis: "The ultimate effect of the Keynesian deficit-financed expansion is to destroy the balance of payments."

On theoretical grounds, there are at least two solutions to the above syndrome. One way is to create an additional instrument to achieve the additional objective of maintaining the balance of payments. That instrument is offered by the exchange rate adjustment policy. As international economic principles would tell us, given the satisfaction of the Marshall-Lerner condition, a devaluation of a currency leads to a decrease in the balance of payments deficit (or increase in surplus). Thus, if the government is ready to allow the domestic currency to devalue in the international market, Keynesian conventional wisdom would achieve the same popularity as it did in the earlier years. But when the big question is, "Do the governments accept the unfortunate results of devaluation?" The answer almost always is "maybe not."

The second solution is more theoretical than practical. It comes from the idea that if all countries of the world pursue expansionary fiscal policies, then in the global sense there is no need to experience balance of payments deterioration.

To quote Eltis again, "For the world as a whole there is no (imports-exports) term in the equations that were set out earlier, so if all countries together raise government expenditure and cut taxation, they will achieve expansion without collective balance of payments deterioration." It is possible that in the midst of diverse world opinions and ideologies, the governments of the whole world cannot and would not act together. Hence, the above solution has little practical implication. However, it does show the need for collective decision making at the international level.

All in all, the criticism of Keynesian conventional wisdom on the international level is the most serious. Many countries that have adopted the Keynesian policies (e.g., the United Kingdom, the United States, and India) have experienced the unwanted result of devaluations of their currencies or in the absence of depreciation of the currency they have suffered from huge balance of payments deficit. Part of this deficit can be attributed to the expansionary Keynesian policies as shown by the above equation.

Another serious problem for Keynesian philosophy was created by events of late 1960s when many of the world economies faced the unprecedented problem of stagflation. This simultaneous occurrence of inflation and unemployment was mainly due to the excessive increase in money supply created in the 1940s and 1950s. A strong believer in Keynesian arguments could not explain why stagflation can occur. In fact monetarists succeeded in providing the reasons for stagflation as well as in giving us the solutions to this problem. We shall visit monetarists in a separate chapter.

References and Suggested Readings

Boyes, W. 1994. *Intermediate Macroeconomic Theory,* 3rd ed., Chapter 3 and 4. Southwestern Publications.

Gordon, R. 1994. *Macroeconomics,* 4th ed., Chapter 6. Boston: Little Brown and Company.

Heilbroner and Thurow. 1984. *The Economic Problem,* 7th ed., Prentice-Hall.

Hicks, J. Mr. Keynes and the classics: A suggested interpretation. *Econometrica,* 5 April 1937: 147–59.

Johnson, I. C. and W. W. Roberts. 1982. *Money and Banking: A Market Oriented Approach,* Chapter 20. New York: The Hyden Press.

Keynes, J. M. 1936. *The General Theory of Employment, Interest and Money,* Chapters 1, 6, 8, and 10. New York: Harcourt, Brace and World.

Mayer, J., J. Duesenberry, and R. Aliber. 1984. *Money and Banking and the Economy,* 2nd ed., Chapter 13. W.W. Norton.

Scott, R. H. and N. Nigro. 1982. *Principles of Economics,* Chapter 21. Boston: Macmillan Publishing.

Smith, W. L. 1974. "A graphical exposition of the complete Keynesian system," In *Readings in Money, National Income and Stabilization Policy,* W. L. Smith and R. L. Tergen (eds.). Homewood, Illinois: Irwin Publishers, pp. 61–67.

Thomas, L. 1982. *Money Banking and Economic Activity,* Chapter 18. Prentice-Hall.

Walter, E. 1976. The failure of the Keynesian conventional wisdom. *Lloyds Bank Review,* No. 122, October: 1–8.

Chapter 7

Money, Money Supply, and Banking Business in the United States, and the Money Creation Process of Banks

SUMMARY

Money supply is an important macroeconomic variable that affects the economy in general and induces interest among economists in its evolution, functions, and creation. This chapter concentrates on the information about money in the U.S. economy and looks at the function of banks before and after the 1980s. It starts with an explanation of what money is, and then describes the evolution of money. While the Federal Reserve System some time ago announced four different measures of U.S. money supply, today they use only two, M1 and M2. In this chapter we investigate the components of M1 and M2. We recognize that these measures are extremely dynamic and many financial assets that can indirectly serve as money are not included in any of these measures. These financial assets are called near monies.

In the survey of the historical evolution of money, we explain such important concepts as the Gresham's law, commodity money, seigniorage, credit money, and legal tender. In describing the functions of money, we realize that four are important: money serves as a medium of exchange, a store of value, a standard of value, and a means of postponing our payment. We compare the money economy with the barter economy and see that because of the existence of money, the efficiency and productivity of contemporary economies are much higher.

In considering the banking industry in the United States, we recognize that the crucial years of banking regulations were 1980 and 1982. Before 1980, there were five distinctly different types of banking institutions, but since 1982 those differentiating characteristics have disappeared. Hence, modern banks are called financial institutions (FIs). They serve the same functions, are regulated by Federal Reserve System in the exact same fashion, and they obey common rules. However, due to their function of giving loans to the public, FIs are able to change the money supply level in the United States. This is popularly called "money creation by banks." In the last part of the chapter we construct a model of a simplified process of banks' money creation. The simplifying assumptions allow us to see the exact process in which new money supply is created. We derive the potential money multiplier by explaining the money creation process. This chapter is therefore another important contribution to our understanding of the monetary sector of the economy.

7.1 Introduction

"Money" or "money supply" has been a mystery to mankind for a few centuries. On the one hand, it is just a piece of paper and on the other hand, it is something we all would love to have because it can buy almost everything we wish. However, to describe fully what money is, is a cumbersome process. Problems arise as soon as we try to understand the meaning of the word, partly because there is no single acceptable definition of money. Money is often defined conceptually as something generally accepted as a medium of exchange. This can be labeled a "behavioral" or "functional" definition of money because it emphasizes the unique function of money, namely, to serve as the medium of exchange.

This brings us to the question: How do we define medium of exchange itself? We may get some help from P. Wickstead (1936) who writes "the special characteristic of a medium of exchange is that it is acceptable by a man who does not want it, or does not want it as much as what he gives for it, in order that he may exchange it for something he wants more."[1] However, this functional definition does not pinpoint the exact amount of money supply that we see in day-to-day transactions.

Hence, we must search for another definition of money in order to learn what constitutes the modern money supply. Another (probably better or more acceptable) definition defines money as the total debt of government and commercial banks. Debt on the part of the government sector in all countries is in terms of coins and notes, or bills, or, in general, currency. Also, debt on the part of commercial banks is primarily in terms of deposits held by the public. Note that all the deposits we hold with banks are our assets and the bank's liability. Hence, money defined in this way should include the coins, currency, and deposits of the banks. Therefore,

Money or money supply = Coins + Currency + Deposits

This definition of money can be termed a *physical* definition. In contrast to the *behavioral* definition, it pinpoints exactly what money supply is in modern economies.

However, our problems are not over until we decide whether or not all deposits of all banks are included in the money supply. So, the next question is: Should we include all checking deposits or should we include only saving deposits? Obviously, banks everywhere in the world have:

a. Demand deposits (called checking accounts or money market funds in the United States)
b. Time deposits (called saving accounts in the United States)
c. Certificates of deposits or fixed deposits, etc.

In most countries, this problem is resolved by defining money in several ways, such as M1, M2, and M3, depending upon what types of deposits are included in the money supply measure. Therefore, governments have to mandate that at least some part of money supply should be accepted as a means of liability payment. The part of the money supply that is legally made acceptable as a medium of exchange is called *legal tender*. We shall visit the concept of legal tender later in this chapter.

Obviously, bank deposits are not a legal tender because anyone can refuse to accept other person's check, and that is perfectly legal. (In this case, the payee cannot do anything but offer cash as payment.) However, cash payments are typically a part of legal tender, as your currency bill may state clearly. So, we resolve the issue by attempting to include some deposits in M1, some others in M2, and some other forms of monetary assets in M3.

Table 7.1 shows the real numbers for M1 and M2 money supply in the United States. M1 money supply typically includes all coins, currency bills, traveler's checks, and checkable deposits at all financial institutions. There are basically three types of checking deposits:

   a. ***Ordinary checking deposits.*** Those that all of us hold with the bank and that pay interest.

   b. ***Negotiable order of withdrawal (NOW) accounts.*** These are interest-earning checking deposits. As the name suggests, funds are withdrawn from FIs only after a (negotiable) notice. They carry market-determined interest payments and have minimum balance requirements.

   c. ***Automatic transfer to saving (ATS) accounts.*** These checking accounts have an ability to move funds automatically from saving to checking. They also carry market determined interest payment and have minimum balance requirements. There are a few other things included in the M1 definition of U.S. money supply, but we can ignore them for being too small in size.

The money supply measure called M2 includes all of the things that go into M1 plus mainly the saving deposits of small denomination. By "small denomination," the Federal Reserve System means less than $100,000. Other things that go into M2 are money market deposit accounts, and shares in retail money market mutual funds net of retirement accounts. Before 2006, the Federal Reserve used two other definitions of money supply M3, which included (mainly) saving deposits of large denominations and a few other small components. The broadest money supply measure ever used was called (not M4, but) "L," which included such items as:

TABLE 7.1 ■ U.S. Money Supply Data: Money Stock Measures

| | Billions of dollars | | | |
| | Seasonally Adjusted | | Not Seasonally Adjusted | |
Date	M1(1)	M2(2)	M1(1)	M2(2)
2006				
June	1375.4	6831.9	1378.4	6834.0
July	1370.7	6857.4	1367.8	6851.8
Aug.	1370.1	6878.1	1369.8	6867.4
Sep.	1361.0	6901.5	1346.5	6892.2
Oct.	1367.9	6954.0	1359.4	6934.0
Nov.	1371.0	6989.9	1367.5	6993.6
Dec.	1366.5	7031.9	1387.3	7067.6
2007				
Jan.	1372.2	7081.8	1368.4	7064.9
Feb.	1367.1	7109.0	1346.9	7075.5
Mar.	1369.3	7159.4	1378.2	7181.8
Apr.	1377.2	7206.8	1391.6	7266.5
May	1374.8	7227.0	1383.6	7206.3
June	1365.4	7243.6	1367.9	7248.6
July	1368.0	7267.5	1365.2	7251.5
Aug.	1369.5	7319.2	1368.6	7309.9
Sep.	1366.1	7346.5	1350.8	7335.1
Oct.	1369.2	7369.7	1361.3	7345.6
Nov.	1365.7	7398.0	1361.8	7399.5
Dec.	1366.3	7428.0	1386.0	7466.1
2008				
Jan.	1367.0	7477.4	1364.1	7463.3
Feb.	1370.3	7581.9	1349.1	7549.7
Mar.	1372.0	7661.6	1381.4	7692.6
Apr.	1367.7	7676.7	1383.7	7738.0
May	1363.6	7684.0	1372.5	7666.5

Percent change at seasonally adjusted annual rates	M1	M2
3 Months from Feb. 2008 to May 2008	−2.0	5.4
6 Months from Nov. 2007 to May 2008	−0.3	7.7
12 Months from May 2007 to May 2008	−0.8	6.3

1. M1 consists of (a) currency outside the U.S. Treasury, Federal Reserve Banks, and the vaults of depository institutions; (b) traveler's checks of nonbank issuers; (b) demand deposits at commercial banks (excluding those amounts held by depository institutions, the U.S. government, and foreign banks and official institutions) less cash items in the process of collection and Federal Reserve float; and (d) other checkable deposits (OCDs), consisting of negotiable order of withdrawal (NOW) and automatic transfer service (ATS) accounts at depository institutions, credit union share draft accounts, and demand deposits at thrift institutions. Seasonally adjusted M1 is constructed by summing currency, traveler's checks, demand deposits, and OCDs, each seasonally adjusted separately.
2. M2 consists of M1 plus (a) savings deposits (including money market deposit accounts); (b) small-denomination time deposits (time deposits in amounts of less than $100,000), less individual retirement account (IRA) and Keogh balances at depository institutions; and (c) balances in retail money market mutual funds, less IRA and Keogh balances at money market mutual funds. Seasonally adjusted M2 is constructed by summing savings deposits, small-denomination time deposits, and retail money funds, each seasonally adjusted separately, and adding this result to seasonally adjusted M1.

NOTE: Components may not add to totals given due to rounding.

- Special Drawing Rights (SDRs), issued by International Monetary Fund and used extensively as an international medium of exchange

- Eurodollars, which are dollar deposits anywhere outside the United States

- Commercial Paper, which are "I owe you" papers issued by large corporations and traded in a special commercial paper market

- Bankers' Acceptances, which are letters of credit originated at the financial institution level and are very useful for international transactions such as importing and exporting activities

There were a few other minor items included in the measure of L.

Starting in 2006 the Federal Reserve System stopped publishing figures for M3 and L. Most recent money supply levels are listed in Table 7.2.

Financial assets that are not included in any measure of money supply, but which can readily be converted into a medium of exchange, are called "near monies." These assets are things like bonds, stocks, commercial papers, shares and equities, etc. The big question is: Should we or should we not include these assets when considering money supply? Hence, the money supply measures are not completely inclusive of all financial assets, and no matter how you describe the measure, some assets are excluded.

TABLE 7.2 ■ Recent U.S. Money Supply Figures

	M1	M2	M3
1995	1,142.99	3,566.34	4,518.28
1996	1,106.80	3,738.02	4,824.60
1997	1,070.20	3,924.33	5,224.77
1998	1,080.65	4,207.45	5,765.94
1999	1,101.44	4,517.97	6,270.34
2000	1,103.57	4,785.44	6,860.51
2001	1,140.21	5,203.35	7,648.49
2002	1,196.23	5,592.88	8,259.04
2003	1,273.48	5,983.78	8,787.33
2004	1,344.43	6,266.34	9,234.73
2005	1,371.78	6,553.41	9,786.47
2006	1,374.38	6,858.67	
2007	1,369.23	7,263.04	

Measured in billions of dollars.
Average of monthly values.
SOURCE: federalreserve.gov
M1 and M2: www.federalreserve.gov/releases/h6/hist/h6hist1.txt
M3: 2006 and 2007 values not available

It is useful to point out the consequences of the existence of near monies. First, due to their existence, the definition of money supply still remains very arbitrary because it is still not possible for us to decide what exactly is the money supply and any attempt to do so is likely to fail over a period of time. Moreover, no matter how the money is defined, it is going to be very dynamic in nature. This is because on a daily basis (sometimes even hourly), there is a change in quantity of money as people shift their assets from cash to bonds to stocks to saving deposits, etc.

Second, the existence of near monies can change the consumption habits of people. If there are substantial amounts of near monies (such as bonds and stocks) in existence, then people are likely to consume a higher proportion of their current income. The effect of this stock of financial assets on people's consumption is known as the real balance effect.[2]

One can imagine real balance effect being positive, because with a higher stock of near monies, consumers would tend to spend higher proportions of their incomes. Third, the existence of near monies is likely to widen the fluctuation of business cycles. For example, in an inflationary stage of a business cycle, if people have stocks as near monies, then they are likely to convert them into the medium of exchange (or cash) to consume more. This obviously increases the demand for goods and services and makes inflation even worse. In the case of a recession (or deflation), people tend to convert their money into near monies and consume less, which reduces the demand for goods and services and brings down the price level even further. Thus, due to near monies, business cycle fluctuations are made wider. Fourth, the existence of near monies makes the job of monetary policy—the policy that makes changes in the money supply—much harder. This is because it is much more difficult to pinpoint the target level for the money supply that, due to near monies, fluctuates over a period of time.

Today, we are left with several definitions of money supply depending upon which near money component we include or exclude. The availability of several definitions of money (and measures of money supply) is one of the reasons for the confusion between words like "money," "wealth," "income," and "property." Once and for all, let us erase these confusions one by one.

There is a basic conceptual difference between money and income. Money is a stock concept, and income is a flow concept. A stock concept is something we have to measure "at a point in time." Hence, it is meaningful to say that the money supply is "such and such," in "such and such" currency unit on "such and such" date. We do not have to measure it per week or per month. Income, on the other hand, is a flow concept and has to be measured over a period of time, such as per week, per month, or per year. Hence, if someone mentions to you that he or she is making a lot of money, what someone really means is that he or she is earning a high income. Money, as a stock, can be changed (or made) only by banking authorities on a central or commercial level. The difference between money and wealth should also be understood. Both money and wealth are stock concepts, however, wealth consists of several physical things and has a meaning only in real terms. Money, on the other hand, has no meaning in physical terms (it is just a piece of paper), but has meaning only in monetary terms or in terms of exchange. Wealth, like property, consists of things like buildings, machinery, resources, etc.

Despite the above distinctions, money as a commodity is desired by every adult on earth. There is glamour associated with its control and severe economic consequences are attached to its increase or decrease. Why is it, then, that money is so important? What are the origins of its modern form? These questions are answered in the following sections.

7.2 Evolution of Money

In traditional society, metal or any other commodity that served as a monetary unit had an unchanged value for both monetary and non-monetary uses. Because it was possible to use the metal for both purposes, the stability of its value was almost guaranteed. This also increased its general acceptability as a means of payment. In other times, cattle, tobacco, tea, and liquor have served as a medium of exchange, but, in a short time, metal became more popular than any other media because of its properties. First, metals were scarce in availability and were stable in supply. Both these characteristics guaranteed a constancy of their value (assuming no drastic changes in its demand); hence, rapid and shocking inflations were not possible. Second, metals are more durable than any other form of monetary unit mentioned above. According to Lloyd Thomas, Jr., "This property enabled metallic coins to serve the store-of-value function effectively and thereby to permit the separation of purchases and sales over time."[3] This was obviously not possible for tobacco or cattle. Third, using metals as a monetary unit was much easier because metal coins could be conveniently minted and transferred from one place to another. All these properties gave metals a distinct advantage over any other form of money. Among metals, iron, silver, copper, and gold have served as money in one time period or another. Iron and copper eventually encountered the problem of abundance of supply. Hence, in order to keep the value of these metals the same for monetary as well as non-monetary purposes, the coins had to be bulky and heavy. Gold was too scarce to be used as money. Hence, silver became popular for a long time. The monetary system in which the metal serving as money has the same value for monetary and non-monetary purposes is called *full-bodied commodity money.*

Over time, governments realized that it was also sufficient to introduce a monetary unit whose value was backed up by a stock of precious metal. This gave rise to representative commodity money. In this system, the value of the monetary unit was higher for a monetary purpose than for a non-stock purpose of the precious metal. When representative commodity money was introduced, it ultimately replaced all the metal coins over a period of time. This case is an application of the Gresham's law, which can be stated as: "When good and bad money circulated at the like value, people would prefer to hoard the good and pass away the bad; so that the former would disappear from, and the latter remain in circulation."[4] Gresham's law, originally written in 1552, still holds its meaning.

Depending upon how many metals are used in making coins for circulation, there were three distinct monetary standards in the past: mono-metalism, bimetalism, and symmetalism. As the name suggests, mono-metalism used only one metal to redeem the coins; bimetallism used two metals to make two separate coins; and symmetalism used two metals to make the same coin. The gold standard was the classic case of a monometallic system and its operation will be discussed in detail in the next chapter.

In modern times, governments realized that as long as people accept a currency as a medium of exchange, there is absolutely no reason why it has to be backed up by any amount of a precious metal. The very fact that currency that is not backed by any precious metal can work for all of the purposes that it is supposed to serve, has led to the new monetary system known as fiduciary money system. Money whose value in physical terms is less than its value in monetary terms and is not backed up by any precious metal, which can be exchanged with it, is known as fiat or credit, or fiduciary money.[5]

In Lloyd Thomas' words, "In a real sense, the backing of our money today consists of an implicit faith and confidence that our government will keep the supply of money in reasonable control so that the buying power of a dollar (monetary unit) does not deteriorate appreciably in a given week of a month. Given the existence of this faith, money can serve its functions effectively without any commodity backing. All it needs is the confidence of the public for its efficient functioning and the responsibility of the monetary policy to keep the money supply under check. In case of the United States, the confidence of the public in monetary system is protected by calling a part of money supply a "legal tender." Legal tender is that part of money supply that is a legally made medium of exchange. In other words, one can repay all kinds of debt by paying the legal tender.

Consider again the M1 money supply in the United States, which is made up mainly of coins, currency bills, checkable deposits at all financial institutions, and traveler's checks. Out of these, coins and currency bills are clearly a part of legal tender, because your payment of debt in coins and currency bills cannot be legally denied by the receiver. Checkable deposits on the other hand are not a part of legal tender because anyone can refuse your check and there is nothing legally you can do but offer the cash for payment.

An interesting phenomenon has occurred since 1973, when the modern money supply system became functional all over the world. In this system, because the government does not have to have backing of any precious metal for the money supply, governments (or monetary policies in particular) are essentially free to just go ahead and "print" as much money supply as they want. This practice can also give the governments tremendous profit, which is aptly called "seigniorage." Therefore in modern times governments can earn seigniorage by printing more money supply (which was not possible under the gold standard, where the money supply had to be backed by gold stock with the government). In the post-1973 era, governmental polices became irresponsible, allowing the money supply to increase to some outrageously irresponsible rates, too. Several examples of such irresponsible monetary policies include Brazil and Argentina, which in the early 1990s had money supply annual growth rates above 800 percent. Similarly, the Southeast Asian crisis of the late 1990s occurred when the money supply in Indonesia increased by 700 percent per year. Let us consider the consequences of such policy action.

First, with such an increase in money supply, there ought to be a very high rate of inflation leading to what is appropriately called, "run-away inflation." No wonder, then, that these countries have witnessed inflation rates as high as 1,400 percent for some time. The consequences of inflation are discussed in Chapter 12, but suffice it to say that hard problems need hard solutions, so the solutions of run-away inflation are not easy. Second, the tremendous increase in money supply not only lowers the international credibility of the governments, but also leads to depreciation of the domestic currency. Hence, the currency value in the international financial market declines as fast as the inflation arrives in these countries. It is easy to recall several examples of these situations happening all over the world. Fortunately, the U.S. monetary policy has never gotten into such an irresponsible money supply growth and has not been too greedy about the seigniorage.

In the modern monetary system, a few new developments have taken place in recent years. For example we have started moving toward a "check-less" society where many of our bills are automatically paid by bank accounts. The automatic withdrawal facility has become somewhat popular where no check needs to be written to make a payment. Similarly electronic transactions are removing the need for sending drafts or checks to repay our debts. Hence, the future monetary system may be computer operated with most of our transactions done by computer manipulations.

After this short survey of monetary systems, it is now time to look at the different functions that money performs.

7.3 Functions of Money

There are four major functions of money that are basic and useful for us to know more about:

1. Medium of exchange
2. Standard or measure of value
3. Store of value
4. Means of transfer payments

The first important function that money performs is to serve as a medium of exchange. The importance of this function is best understood by imagining an economy without money, namely, a barter economy. In a barter economy, "all exchanges are to be made in physical terms," which means that good X has to be exchanged directly for good Y. Moreover, in order for an exchange to take place, a barter economy requires what is known as "double coincidence of wants." A possessor of good X must have information about the existence of a seller who would offer the good desired and be ready to accept good X in exchange. In other words, both individuals should have enough information to answer the following questions:

- Who should offer the goods desired to be purchased?
- In what quantity is the offer made?
- Is the ratio of exchanges acceptable to both parties?

To collect the needed information is a costly, time-consuming, and inefficient process. Therefore, the requirement of a double coincidence of wants in a barter economy makes exchange particularly difficult.

It is obvious that in a money economy, a person can transfer goods and services for money and then exchange money for any other desired commodity. There is not as great a need for information in a money economy as there is in a barter economy. Because acquiring information is a costly endeavor, exchanges in a money economy are less costly and therefore much easier. Moreover, this reduction is transaction costs for exchange leads to more exchanges, and a higher number of exchanges is better for the economy. A higher number of exchanges facilitates the "specialization" process in the economy, and specialization is beneficial because, given enough competition everywhere, by specializing one can use one's resources in the most efficient way. Without money, exchanges are so costly and rare that growth and prosperity are out of the question. Service of the monetary unit as a medium of exchange is, therefore, the most important and desirable function that money performs and is tied into to the efficiency and growth of an economy.

The second important function of money is that it also serves as a measure of value. All goods and services can be expressed in terms of money. When the values of goods and services are expressed in terms of money, they become "prices." Money serves as a standard or as a "numeraire" in measuring the value of goods and services in exchange. Due to this function of money, economic life is much more efficient in a money economy than in a barter economy. In a barter economy, all goods would have to be measured and their value expressed in terms of all the other remaining goods. Hence, if there are "n" goods, each good would have to be expressed in terms of those remaining (n – 1). The number of exchange rates needed in such an economy would be given by the formula:

$$J = n(n-1)/2$$

where J = total number of exchange rates needed in the barter economy;
n = number of different goods in the economy.

To use a simple example, a barter economy with only 100 goods would need

$$[100(100-1)]/2 = 50 \times 99 = 4{,}950$$

exchange rates (or price) expressions!

In the case of a money economy, this can be done with only 100 prices. In reality, we have tens of thousands of goods. Hence, one might imagine how cumbersome it would be to deal with a very large number of prices. Thus, the money economy is much more convenient than a barter economy because the former has a standard of value.

The third function money performs is to serve as a store of value. Because people are aware of the fact that money can always function as a medium of exchange, they can store their wealth in terms of money. Thus, this function is related to the first function performed by money. However, in a modern society, because income is received periodically, there is a need to save purchasing power for a time. However, there are other assets that can also serve as a store of value, such as bonds, stocks (shares), equities, real estate, etc. Given a wide spectrum of other financial assets, in which purchasing power can be stored, there is a special reason why people prefer money to several other assets. This is called the "liquidity" property of money. By liquidity, we refer to the "ease with which we can convert a financial asset into a medium of exchange." Liquidity is the greatest for money as an asset because money itself is a medium of exchange. Compare this with any other financial asset like bonds or stocks. It takes some time period to convert these assets into something that can be exchanged for goods. Obviously, there are some people who do not have a very high "liquidity preference" and who store their wealth in terms of other non-liquid assets. The decision about the choice of financial assets according to liquidity risk and returns is called a *portfolio decision.* However, we can be confident that when using money as a medium of exchange is necessary, money also performs the useful function of a store of value.

Lastly, money serves the function of a measure of deferred payment. Often people engage in exchanges that involve payments over some period of time. There will be some inconvenience inherent in the receipt of payments at a later date because people prefer liquidity in a shorter time over liquidity in a longer time. To measure this inconvenience and to pay for this waiting time, money is useful. We refer to this "additional reward for waiting" as the interest rate. The contracts which involve such waiting time and interest rates are known as *debt contracts.*

It is important to get acquainted with some other concepts related to money. One such concept is the value of money measured by the amount of goods and services one unit of money can buy. In other words, the value of money is nothing but its purchasing power. It is inversely dependent upon the supply of money. If the supply of money becomes scarce, then the value of money increases. But more about this will be considered in other chapters.

Another important concept is called "postponement of payments." This is done by the use of credit cards. Strictly speaking, the use of credit cards solves only the problem of carrying cash on one's person. Although credit cards sometimes are used indirectly as a medium of exchange, they are not considered a part of the money supply.

7.4 The Commercial Banking Business in the United States

Banking business in the United States has gone through several regulatory and structural changes over the point of time. Historically the banking business has its origin in private goldsmiths in the United Kingdom who started collecting gold deposits from people in exchange for the loans they issued. As time progressed, the U.S. Department of the Treasury was created with an ability to deposit gold (that is why the name includes the word "treasury") from the public. As mentioned before, gold certificates were issued by the Treasury, which became an efficient medium of exchange. In the pre-Federal Reserve Era, individual commercial banks issued their own bank certificates and, even though travel was not very prevalent, it quickly became confusing for different media of exchanges to survive.

In modern times, the most crucial years for banking regulation were from 1980 to 1982. Before 1980 there were basically five distinctly different banking institutions governed by different levels of regulatory authorities. At the helm of the banking structure were banks called commercial banks.

1. *Commercial banks* were the largest institutions within the banking structure, controlling roughly 80 percent of banking deposits in 1980. They numbered around 14,000 scattered all over the United States.

    Commercial banks chartered by individual states (called state banks) had the option to choose whether or not to become a member of Federal Reserve System. Those that opted to be non-member banks were governed by individual state banking authorities that typically had much more liberal rules of regulation than the Federal Reserve System for "member banks." For example, the State of Michigan started the "free banking system" in 1939, which meant that any group of individuals could start a banking firm if it had enough initial financial capital. Other states then had to adopt the same type of liberal rules to be competitive with the state of Michigan. Naturally, among commercial banks, there was a tendency to shift from membership to non-membership, one of the reasons why the U.S. Congress changed the bank regulations in 1980.

    Commercial banks were the only type of financial institutions that were allowed to offer checking deposits. Other types were supposed to do business only in saving deposits.

2. The second most important banking institutions were the *mutual saving banks,* numbering 800 in the country. They did business mainly of a shorter term nature and specialized in accepting deposits and giving loans of less than 5 years term.

3. *Saving and loan associations* (S&Ls) specialized in long-term business so their main function was to give mortgages and accept long-term saving deposits.

4. *Credit unions* (CUs) specialized in business for their members. The members had some common attribute, such as being employees of the same firm etc. Before 1980, credit unions did business only by accepting saving deposits and by giving loans to its members and were therefore at a much smaller scale than they are today.

5. *Insurance companies* were scattered all over the United Sates, some of them so vulnerable that their life span was less than five years. However, they took saving deposits and insured people's life, health, property, real estate, etc.

These were the financial institutions—banks and non-banks—with different definitions of function but still competing with each other for attracting deposits. Sometimes the competition was unfair; it was not a case of a level playing field and the competition drove some institutions bankrupt. As the U.S. economy experienced severe stagflation problems in the late 1970s, more and more banking institutions experienced hardships and Congress realized the need for action, which led to a drastic change. The change was brought by the passing of the Depository Institutions De-regulation and Monetary Control Act (DIDMCA) of 1980, which was further supported by the St. Germain Act of 1982.

Both these acts made it clear that there will be no difference between banks and non-banks after 1982: all institutions will have the authority to offer checking deposits, they all will be controlled by the same rules, and they will be regulated by the same regulatory requirements. Therefore, all banks after 1982 are more appropriately called financial institutions (FIs) because they perform common functions and their differences are only in name. The U.S. banking system allows banks to have each other's accounts, and it also allows them to borrow from each other. This banking system is called a "correspondence banking" system. In the correspondence banking system, competing U.S. financial institutions are heavily controlled and regulated by the Federal Reserve System, but they can correspond with each other. They are all members of the Federal Reserve System in the post-1982 era.

The functions of a typical financial institution can be summarized as follows:

- Accept deposits, keep them safe, and offer some interest on these deposits
- Give loans to all sections of the society—to individuals, to businesses, to commerce, to importers and exporters, and to governmental agencies
- Pay bills automatically (electronically) from the accounts
- Help wealthy individuals manage their portfolios by suggesting different financial investment channels
- Carry out foreign exchange transactions, which involve changing one currency into any other currency.

There are a few additional functions of a modern bank, but the most important function that enables them to "create" additional money supply in the economy is the second function—giving loans to the public. So, banks or financial institutions are able to increase money supply of an economy by giving loans. This ability in the hands of banks may sound a bit frightening; therefore, it is worth our while to investigate the exact process of money creation by financial institutions.

7.5 Money Creation Process by Banks

When we say that banks have an ability to increase money supply we essentially mean that they can increase the amount of deposits held with the banking system. However, notice that bank deposits are a part of all measures of money supply (even M1) in the United States. If you consider that M1 consists of coins plus currency bills plus checkable deposits with the financial institutions, it is clear then that banks are not able to change the coins amount because coins are minted by the Department of Treasury in the United States, and no one is allowed to change that amount. Nor can banks change the amount of currency bills floating in the economy because currency bills are printed by the Department of Federal Reserve System and no one else is allowed to print the bills. Hence, banks' money creation is essentially the process of deposit creation.

To understand this process further in simplistic terms, let us construct a simplified money creation model with some rational but simplifying assumptions as follows:

ASSUMPTION 1

Suppose all money supply in the economy is made up of only checkable deposits, which means that there are no coins, no currency bills, and no saving accounts in the system. At the outset this assumption may seem far fetched but in reality, out of M1 money supply in the United States, about 3 percent is in coins and about 21 percent is in currency bills. So roughly 75 percent of the money is in checkable deposits, which means Americans do roughly 75 percent of total transactions by checks and about 25 percent in cash. These percentages can be different in other countries but overall, developed countries carry out the majority of their transactions in checks. Therefore, this assumption of having all money supply in checkable deposits is a pretty rational assumption.

ASSUMPTION 2

Suppose all financial institutions have to obey the same legal requirement ratio (LRR) and say that ratio is 10 percent. This assumption needs an explanation: The legal requirement ratio (LRR) is the percentage of total deposits that banks have to keep with the Federal Reserve Bank account. As a rule of Federal Reserve

Banking, all financial institutions have to keep a certain proportion of their total deposits (sometimes called total reserves) with their account with the Federal Reserve Bank that oversees their region. In reality LRR differs according to size of the financial institution and type of the deposit. Large-sized banks have to keep a larger percentage with the Federal Reserve and have to therefore obey a larger LRR. This arrangement is designed to give some competitive advantage to the smaller-sized financial institutions that must compete with large-sized financial institutions to attract deposits and run a similar business. In fact, very small-sized financial institutions are even guaranteed to have an LRR, such as 3 percent, on checking deposits.

In reality, the LRR is also higher for saving deposits than for checking deposits. This is partly because the Federal Reserve realizes that saving deposits are more stable than checking deposits. All in all, to understand the process better, for this simplified model of money creation we shall assume that LRR is the same for all financial institutions.

ASSUMPTION 3

Suppose all banks or financial institutions are fully loaned up. A fully loaned up bank is the one that has no excess reserves left to give out as loans. One can define excess reserves as follows:

$$\text{Excess reserves} = \text{Total reserves} - \text{Required reserves to be kept with Federal Reserve Banks}$$

Thus, each financial institution has total reserves out of which some have to go to the Federal Reserve Bank and the remaining can be used for giving out loans to the public. These loanable reserves are called *excess reserves*. A fully loaned up bank by definition is one that gives all excess reserves as loans to the public and has no excess reserves left.

Given these assumptions, suppose a person, Mr. X, walks to his bank, bank A, and deposits a check of $100.00. Then bank A's managers realize that their total reserves have gone up by $100, out of which $10 should be deposited in the Federal Reserve Bank to satisfy the 10 percent LRR. This makes an increase in excess reserves of $90. Due to Assumption 3, these $90 will be used by bank A to give loans to someone else in the economy, say another individual, Mr. Y.

Mr. Y will borrow $90 to pay off his bills to an individual, Mr. Z, who will deposit $90 in his bank, bank B. Now bank B managers realize the increase in total reserves of $90 out of which $9 should go to the Federal Reserve Bank. This gives $81 as the excess reserves to bank B, which will be used to give loans to another individual, Mrs. Z. Mrs. Z will borrow $81 to pay her bills and, as you can imagine, the process will continue until these amounts become close to zero.

In this process, however, the banking system as a whole has created additional deposits. To realize these additional deposits, recognize that the initial deposit (ID) of $100 by Mr. X was his own money, which he is free to claim from bank A. But the same $100 acted as a $90 deposit of Mr. Z in bank B and the process was going to have a few more additional deposits to it as well.

All in all, in the banking system as a whole, the same $100 can do the job of many more deposits and every time there is a new deposit, banks are able to create new money supply! (Recall that deposits are a major part of money supply.) Therefore, the whole banking system is able to create additional money supply in the economy. This may sound serious to non-economists, but then consider the money you deposited in your bank recently. Do you think the bank keeps it as cash? The answer is, of course not. The bank has already used a part of total deposits as a loan to others. Or consider this possibility: If all the depositors go to the bank at the same time, and demand their deposits collectively, there is no money with the bank to satisfy these withdrawals. This is technically called a "run on the bank." In the Great Depression era (1929–1933), 4,400 banks had to close their doors because this type of run on the banks occurred so frequently.

In the above process, therefore, the total money supply (MS) that can be (potentially) created by all banks is given as follows:

$$\text{MS created in simplified model} = 100 + 90 + 81 + \ldots$$

If we denote Initial Deport (ID) as the first 100, then 90 can be expressed as:

$$= ID(1 - LRR) \text{ and } 81 = (1 - LRR) \times (1 - LRR)ID.$$

In notational form therefore, we can write:

MS created in the simplified model

$$= ID + ID(1 - LRR) + ID(1 - LRR)^2 + ID(1 - LRR)^3 + \ldots$$

$$= ID\,[1 + (1 - LRR) + (1 - LRR)^2 + (1 - LRR)^3 + \ldots]$$

$$= ID\,[1/(1 - (1 - LRR))] = ID[1/LRR].$$

This last term in the above equation [1/LRR] is popularly called "simplified money multiplier" or "potential money multiplier"; "potential" because it is the maximum potential of the banking system to create additional money supply in the economy. By using the above formula, we can also deduce that the simplified money multiplier in our model is [1/LRR] = 1/.1 = 10, and the initial deposit by Mr. X in bank A was 100. Therefore the total money supply the banking system would have created is equal to 10 × 100 = 1,000.

Our conclusion here is that financial institutions do possess the ability to change the money supply, so they have to be heavily regulated. This regulation and control over the U.S. money supply (and to some extent interest rate) is the main job of the Federal Reserve System. We will discuss how this system works in the next chapter.

Notes

1. Wickstead P. 1993. *The Commonsense of Political Economy,* Vol. 1, p. 136. London: Routledge and Kegan Paul.
2. Several studies of the real balance effect have been done. See Kulkarni (1979). Studies conclude that the real balance effect does not occur as much as it was initially thought.
3. Lloyd Thomas, Jr., p. 13; see Suggested Further Reading.
4. Alexander Del March 1968, p. 68. Gresham's Law is named after Sir Thomas Gresham. He was an English textile merchant who served King Edward VI, Queen Mary I, and Queen Elizabeth I as a financial representative in Antwerp. Though he was certainly not the first to explain it, the law is always credited to him.
5. Following Lloyd Thomas (1979, p. 19), even if we use the three words synonymously, technically credit and fiduciary monies are broader than fiat money.

Suggested Further Reading

Armen, A. 1977. Why money? *Journal of Money, Credit and Banking,* February.
Brunner, K. and A. Meltzer. 1971. The uses of money: Money in the theory of an exchange economy. *American Economic Review,* Vol. 61, No. 5.
Chetty, V. K. 1969. On measuring the nearness of the near monies. *American Economic Review,* June.
Fisher, D. 1978. *Monetary Theory and the Demand for Money,* Chapter 1. New York: John Wiley and Sons.
Goldfeld, L. V. and S. M. Chandler. 1979. *The Economics of Money and Banking,* 7th ed., Chapter 1. New York: Harper and Row.
Johnson, I. C. and W. W. Roberts. 1982. *Money and Banking: A Market Oriented Approach,* Chapters 1 and 2. New York: The Dryden Press.
Kulkarni, K. G. 1979. Comparison of the existence of real balance effect in six countries. *Economic Affairs,* Vol. 24, No. 8-9, August–September: 193–203.
Thomas, L. 1979. *Money, Banking and Economic Activity,* Chapters 1 and 2. Prentice-Hall.
Thorn, R. S. 1976. *Introduction to Money and Banking,* Chapters 1 and 2. New York: Harper and Row.
Tullock, G. 1975. Competing monies. *Journal of Money, Credit, and Banking,* November.

7.6 Chapter 7 Appendix

CONVENTIONS

Because (in principle) money is anything that can be used in settlement of a debt, there are varying measures of money supply. Since most modern economic systems are regulated by governments through *monetary policy,* the supply of money is broken down into types of money based on how much of an effect monetary policy can have on that type of money. *Narrow money* is the type of money that is more easily affected by monetary policy, whereas *broad money* is more difficult to affect through monetary policy. Narrow money exists in smaller quantities, while broad money exists in much larger quantities. Each type of money can be classified by placing it along a spectrum between *narrow* (easily affected) and *broad* (difficult to affect) money. The different types of money are typically classified as *Ms*. The number of Ms usually range from M0 (most narrow) to M3 (broadest) but which Ms are actually used depends on the system. The typical layout for each of the Ms is as follows:

- **M0:** Physical currency. A measure of the money supply that combines any liquid or cash assets held within a central bank and the amount of physical currency circulating in the economy. M0 is the most liquid measure of the money supply. It only includes cash or assets that could quickly be converted into currency. This measure is known as *narrow money* because it is the smallest measure of the money supply.

- **M1:** This is M0 plus demand deposits, which are checking accounts. This is used as a measurement for economists trying to quantify the amount of money in circulation. The M1 is a very liquid measure of the money supply, as it contains cash and assets that can quickly be converted to currency.

- **M2:** M1 plus small time deposits (less than $100,000), savings deposits, and non-institutional money-market funds. M2 is a broader classification of money than M1. Economists use M2 when looking to quantify the amount of money in circulation and trying to explain different economic monetary conditions. M2 is a key economic indicator used to forecast inflation.

- **M3:** M2 plus all large time deposits, institutional money-market funds, short-term repurchase agreements, along with other larger liquid assets. The *broadest measure of money;* it is used by economists to estimate the entire supply of money within an economy.

SOURCE: "Why Reporting of M3 Does Not Matter" from *Droke Reports* by Clif Droke. Reprinted by permission of the author.

FRACTIONAL-RESERVE BANKING

The different forms of money presented in government money supply statistics come from the practice of fractional-reserve banking. Whenever a bank gives out a loan in a fractional-reserve banking system, a new type of money is created. This new type of money is what makes up the non-*M0* components in the *M1–M3* statistics. In short, there are two types of money in a fractional-reserve banking system:

1. *Central bank money* (physical currency)
2. *Commercial bank money* (money created through loans), sometimes referred to as *checkbook money*

In the money supply statistics, *central bank money* is *M0* while the *commercial bank money* is divided up into the *M1–M3* components. Generally, the types of commercial bank money that tend to be valued at lower amounts are classified in the narrow category of *M1* while the types of commercial bank money that tend to exist in larger amounts are categorized in *M2* and *M3*, with *M3* being the largest.

MONEY SUPPLIES AROUND THE WORLD

United States

The Federal Reserve previously published data on three monetary aggregates, but now it only publishes data on two of them. The first, M1, is made up of types of money commonly used for payment, basically currency (M0) and checking

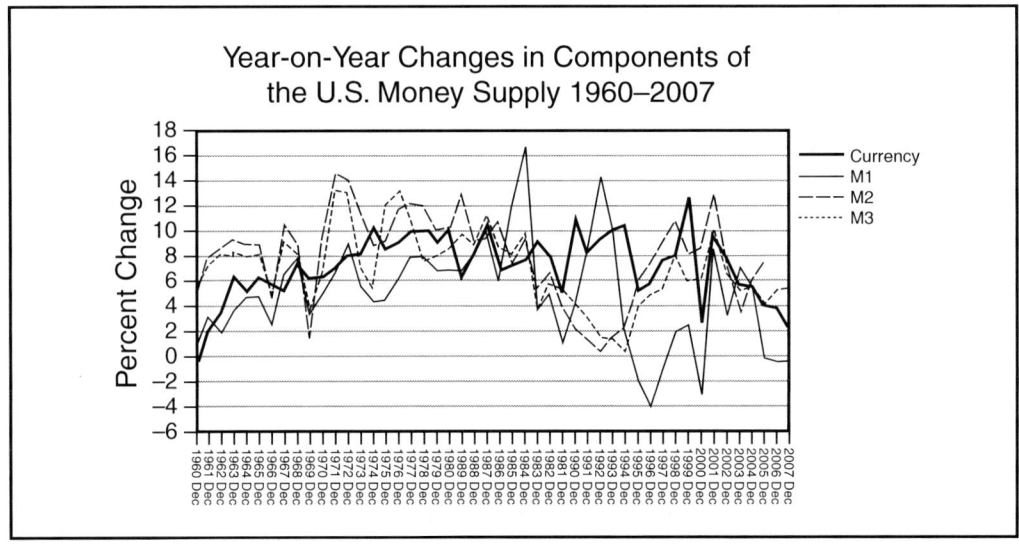

Components of U.S. Money Supply ■ FIGURE 7.1

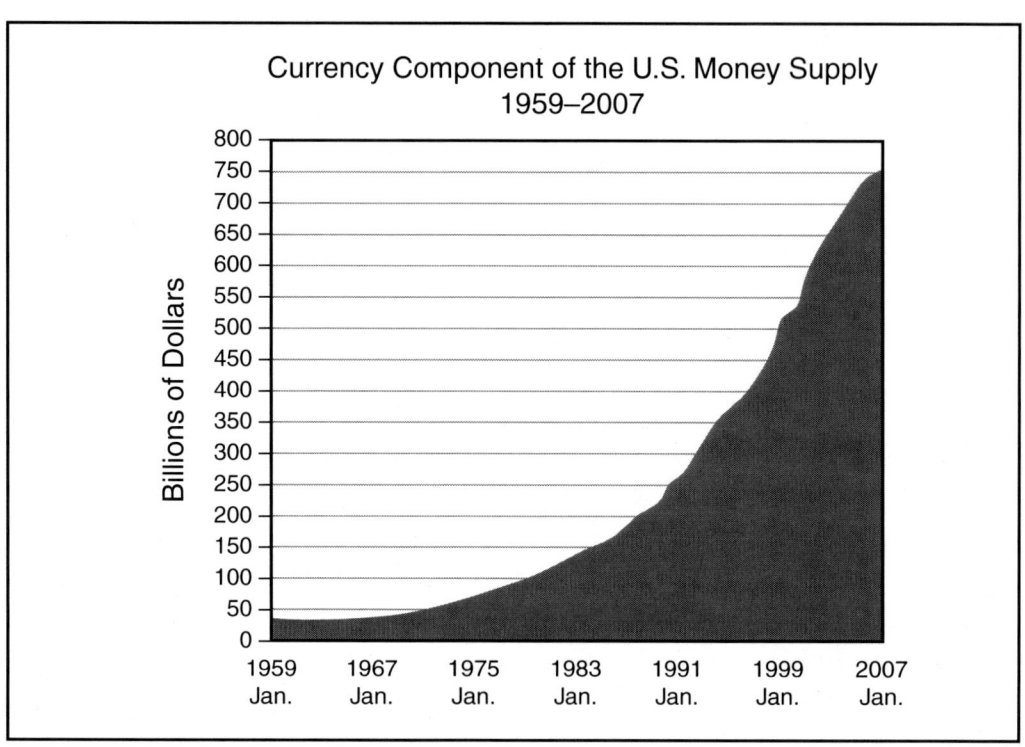

FIGURE 7.2 ■ Currency Component of the U.S. Money Supply, 1959–2007

deposits. The second aggregate, M2, includes M1 plus balances that generally are similar to transaction accounts and that, for the most part, can be converted fairly readily to M1 with little or no loss of principal. The M2 measure is thought to be held primarily by households. The third aggregate, M3, is no longer published; it included M2 plus certain accounts that are held by entities other than individuals and issued by banks and thrift institutions to augment M2-type balances in meeting credit demands. It also included balances in money market mutual funds held by institutional investors. The aggregates have had different roles in monetary policy as their reliability as guides has changed. The following details their principal components

- **M0:** The total of all physical currency, plus accounts at the central bank that can be exchanged for physical currency.

- **M1:** Those portions of M0 held as reserves or vault cash + the amount in demand accounts ("checking" or "current" accounts).

- **M2:** M1 + most savings accounts, money market accounts, and small denomination time deposits (certificates of deposit of under $100,000).

- **M3:** M2 + all other CDs (large time deposits, institutional money market mutual fund balances), deposits of eurodollars and repurchase agreements.

The Federal Reserve ceased publishing M3 statistics in March 2006, claiming that M3 did not appear to convey additional information about economic activity compared to M2, had not been used in determining economic policy, and that the costs to collect M3 data outweighed the benefits. Some politicians have spoken out against the Federal Reserve's decision to cease publishing M3 statistics and have urged the U.S. Congress to take steps requiring the Federal Reserve to do so. Congressman Ron Paul claimed that "M3 is the best description of how quickly the Fed is creating new money and credit. Common sense tells us that a government central bank creating new money out of thin air depreciates the value of each dollar in circulation." Some of the data used to calculate M3 are still collected and published on a regular basis. Current alternate sources of M3 data are available from the private sector

M4 Money Supply of the United Kingdom

There are just two official UK measures. M0 is referred to as the "wide monetary base" or "narrow money" and M4 is referred to as "broad money" or simply "the money supply."

- **M0:** Cash outside the Bank of England + banks' operational deposits with the Bank of England.

- **M4:** Cash outside banks (i.e., in circulation with the public and non-bank firms) + private-sector retail bank and building society deposits + private-sector wholesale bank and building society deposits and Certificate of Deposit.

European Union

The European Central Bank's definition of euro area monetary aggregates:

- **M1:** Currency in circulation + overnight deposits

- **M2:** M1 + deposits with an agreed maturity up to 2 years + deposits redeemable at a period of notice up to 3 months

- **M3:** M2 + repurchase agreements + money market fund (MMF) shares/units + debt securities up to 2 years

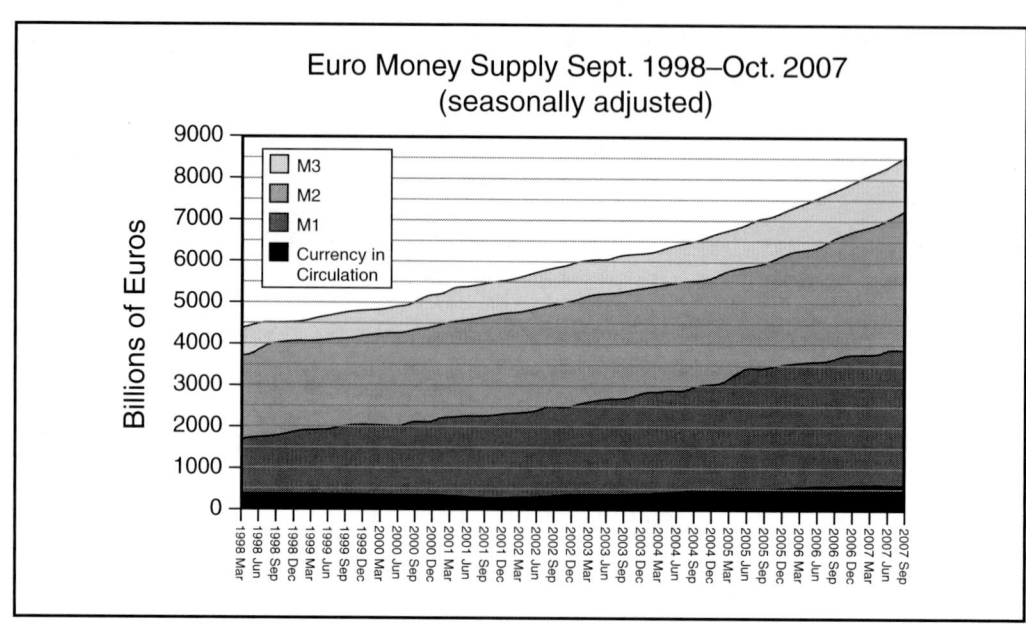

FIGURE 7.3 ■ Euro Money Supply

Chapter 8

Federal Reserve Banking and Monetary Policy Making in the U.S.

SUMMARY

The policy of government that leads to changes in the money supply is called *monetary policy*. In the United States, monetary policy is carried out by the Federal Reserve. This chapter explains the structure of the Federal Reserve and the ways in which the money supply can be changed. There are three layers of authority in the Federal Reserve System: (1) the Federal Reserve Board, or Board of Governors; (2) the Federal Open Market Committee (FOMC); and (3) Federal Reserve Banks.

In the discussion of the Federal Reserve Board, we not only evaluate the criteria for appointments of the Board members (i.e., Governors), but also summarize the performance of some Federal Reserve Board Chairmen. In terms of public scrutiny and being in the media glare, the FOMC is the most active layer of the Federal Reserve System. It meets roughly eight times per year and each meeting's actions are closely watched by financial market participants. The FOMC determines the discount rate, and is in charge of determining the level of open market operations to be carried out. These decisions are considered to be valuable because they have a direct effect on the level of money supply in the economy.

Twelve Federal Reserve Banks form the next level of authority in the Federal Reserve System. Each bank controls a "District" and is responsible for being a bank for the financial institutions (FIs) in that district. They also help FIs in their district to clear checks, and in general the Federal Reserve Banks are responsible for implementing all applicable regulations in their district. Bank examiners visit each branch of a FI to make sure that all rules are followed.

The major and minor weapons of money supply change in the U.S. economy are also discussed in this chapter. We evaluate the importance of each weapon and conclude that when money supply is to be changed, it is changed by using one of these weapons, and never by just printing more currency. To understand the workings of the Federal Reserve System, it is important to recognize the way U.S. monetary policy works, and it is this chapter's main goal to provide that understanding.

Introduction 8.1

In the last chapter we analyzed the process by which financial institutions (FIs) are able to change the money supply level in the economy. Because banks have the power to affect the economy in this way, they must be regulated efficiently. In the United States, that job is performed by the Federal Reserve System as a whole. In this chapter we will examine the structure of the Federal Reserve System and the method it uses to control the money supply, interest rates, and other monetary aggregates.

The following information is derived from http://www.u-s-history.com/pages/h1052.html and clearly states the reasons and events that led to the origin of the Federal Reserve System.

> Public sentiment had been supportive of national monetary reform since the Panic of 1907. The National Monetary Commission, created under the Aldrich-Vreeland Act, issued a report in 1912, which called for creation of what many regarded as a third string of Banks of the United States. All major European powers had developed centralized controls over their banking systems, but the U.S. remained alone in failing to do so. Full centralization of banking had not proved popular earlier in the country's history, but the recurring bank panics and instability of the currency clearly pointed to the need for major reform.
>
> Following President Wilson's victory in 1912, Arsène P. Pujo of Louisiana, chairman of the House Banking Committee, led the so-called Pujo Commission in a wide-ranging examination of the nation's financial ills. Among other actions, Pujo brought in J. P. Morgan to testify and eventually came to the conclusion that a 'money trust' existed in the country and the central banking solution offered by the Monetary Commission would not work.
>
> In 1913, the Democrats controlled both houses of Congress and crafted a regional, rather than fully centralized, approach to banking reform. Carter Glass of Virginia headed matters in the House and Robert L. Owen of Oklahoma did so in the Senate. The final legislation created 12 Federal Reserve Banks that would act as central banks for all national banks and other member state institutions. The Banks would not be federal bodies, but private ones owned by the member banks. A Federal Reserve Board was formed to oversee the system and establish policy. Members of the Board would be appointed by the President, providing a considerable measure of federal direction over the system.
>
> A new form of currency was created—the Federal Reserve Note—as a means to solve the problem of inelasticity. The notes were to be backed by commercial credit and reserves of gold of at least 40 percent of the amount of the notes issued. Government funds were to be deposited in the Banks, which ended the old sub-treasury system.

The greatest power bestowed on the new Federal Reserve System was establishment of the *discount rate*—the rate of interest charged by the Banks when lending to member institutions. The ability to raise the discount rate was to have the tendency to slow down the economy, while dropping rates would tend to stimulate economic activity.

The Federal Reserve Act was an important reform measure, but it failed to produce overnight miracles. Banks, or the "money trust," would remain supremely powerful and draw the attention of later federal regulation.

8.2 Structure of Federal Reserve System

MEMBERSHIP TO FEDERAL RESERVE BOARD (FRB) AND ITS FUNCTIONS

As the quotation above mentions, there are basically three layers of authority in the Federal Reserve System. At the top of the system is the Federal Reserve Board (FRB), sometimes called the Board of Governors (BOG). There are seven members for the BOG, all appointed by the U.S. President for a non-renewable fourteen-year term. In fact, their contracts are staggered such that one governor finishes his or her contract every two years. Therefore, during a four-year term, a U.S. President can appoint only two governors to the BOG. Hence, it is believed that the majority of the BOG is outside the control of a particular White House administration. This is one reason behind the argument that the Federal Reserve System is independent of a President's Administration.

In reality, however, this independence is not as clear-cut as it may sound. This is partly because BOG members can always resign. Job offers from the private sector are more lucrative than staying for fourteen years on the BOG's government salary. When a governor resigns, the President has another opportunity to appoint someone for the remainder of that term. In practice, therefore, the last President to appoint only two governors was John F. Kennedy. Additional considerations arise when a President is re-elected, as was the case with Presidents Reagan, Clinton, and George W. Bush. Therefore, the independence of the Federal Reserve System is questionable.

The Chairman of the Federal Reserve System is also appointed by the U.S. President for a regular (but renewable) term of four years. Since 2006, Ben Bernanke has been the Chairman of the Federal Reserve Board, succeeding Alan Greenspan. Mr. Greenspan was the longest-serving Chairman, from 1987 to 2006. While his career was marred by the events of September 11, 2001, he also served during the unprecedented growth of the U.S. economy in the 1990s. While it is too early to judge the success or failure of work by Mr. Bernanke, Mr. Greenspan's functions have been severely criticized by some (a Google search on the words "Greenspan follies" will give a better understanding). Many critics blame Mr. Greenspan for the financial crisis of 2007. Another influential Chairman of the Federal Reserve Board was Paul Volcker, who served from 1979 to 1987. Recall that 1979 was a very inflationary year, with a roughly 14 percent inflation rate; Volcker is given much credit for taking this rate down to roughly 7 percent by 1987.

Mr. William McChesney Martin, Jr., is another Chairman of the Federal Reserve Board who single-handedly helped design the monetary policy of the U.S. from 1951 to 1970. He was a very efficient economist who made many useful and correct decisions. He was appointed as the Chairman at the early age of 40, and his performance was such that he was re-appointed four successive times by five different U.S. Presidents.

The main decisions made by Federal Reserve Board members are:

1. Determining the level of Legal Requirement Ration (LRR);
2. Suggesting to the Congress changes in bank regulations; and
3. Most importantly, serving on the second most important committee in the Federal Reserve System, namely, the Federal Open Market Committee (FOMC).

The following information taken from http://www.federalreserve.gov/pubs/frseries/frseri2.htm outlines the membership, structure, and functions of the FOMC, which makes up the second layer of authority in the Federal Reserve System.

- **Membership**—The FOMC is composed of the seven members of the Board of Governors and five Reserve Bank Presidents. The president of the Federal Reserve Bank of New York serves on a continuous basis; the presidents of the other Reserve Banks serve one-year terms on a rotating basis beginning January 1 of each year. Rotation is such that each year one member is elected to the Committee by the boards of directors of Reserve Banks in each of the following groups: (1) Boston, Philadelphia, and Richmond; (2) Cleveland and Chicago; (3) Atlanta, St. Louis, and Dallas; and (4) Minneapolis, Kansas City, and San Francisco.

- **Organization**—By statute, the FOMC determines its own organization. Each year at its first meeting, the Committee elects its Chairman and Vice Chairman and selects staff officers to serve the Committee for the coming year. Traditionally, the Chairman of the Board of Governors is elected Chairman and the president of the Federal Reserve Bank of New York is elected Vice Chairman. Staff officers are selected from among the officers and employees of the Board of Governors and the Federal Reserve Banks.

- **Meetings**—By law, the FOMC must meet at least four times each year in Washington, D.C. Since 1981, eight regularly scheduled meetings have been held each year at intervals of five to eight weeks. If circumstances require consultation or consideration of an action between these regular meetings, members may be called on to participate in a special meeting or a telephone conference, or to vote on a proposed action by telegram or telephone. At each regularly scheduled meeting, the Committee votes on the policy to be carried out during the interval between meetings.

    Attendance at meetings is restricted because of the confidential nature of the information discussed and is limited to Committee members, nonmember Reserve Bank presidents, staff officers, the Manager of the System Open Market Account, and a small number of Board and Reserve Bank staff.

- **The Decision-Making Process**—Before each regularly scheduled meeting of the FOMC, System staff prepare written reports on past and prospective economic and financial developments that are sent to Committee members and to nonmember Reserve Bank presidents. Reports prepared by the Manager of the System Open Market Account on operations in the domestic open market and in foreign currencies since the last regular meeting are also distributed. At the meeting itself, staff officers present oral reports on the current and prospective business situation, on conditions in financial markets, and on international financial developments. In its discussions, the Committee considers factors such as trends in prices and wages, employment and production, consumer income and spending, residential and commercial construction, business investment and inventories, foreign exchange markets, interest rates, money and credit aggregates, and fiscal policy. The Manager of the System Open Market Account also reports on account transactions since the previous meeting.

After these reports, the Committee members and other Reserve Bank presidents turn to policy. Typically, each participant expresses his or her own views on the state of the economy and prospects for the future and on the appropriate direction for monetary policy. Then each makes a more explicit recommendation on policy for the coming inter-meeting period (and for the longer run, if under consideration). Finally, the Committee must reach a consensus regarding the appropriate course for policy, which is incorporated in a directive to the Federal Reserve Bank of New York—the Bank that executes transactions for the System Open Market Account. The directive is cast in terms designed to provide guidance to the

Manager in the conduct of day-to-day open market operations. The directive sets forth the Committee's objectives for long-run growth of certain key monetary and credit aggregates. It also sets forth operating guidelines for the degree of ease or restraint to be sought in reserve conditions and expectations with regard to short-term rates of growth in the monetary aggregates. In general, the future growth of money supply is dependent upon the decisions made by FOMC in its meetings.

FOMC meetings are also responsible for determining the "discount rate"—the interest rate charged by Federal Reserve Banks for their loans to the FIs. In fact, the loans to FIs from the Federal Reserve Banks are called "discounts and advances" and the interest rate on them is called the discount rate. "Federal funds rate" is another important term, referring to the interest rate charged by one financial institution for its loans to another financial institution. The U.S. banking system allows FIs to correspond with each other regarding each other's accounts, to help each other on various services such as foreign exchange transactions, and borrowing to balance their books every night. FIs that are short of funds can many times borrow from other FIs on an overnight basis; these loans are known as "federal funds."

The third interest rate of importance is the "prime rate." This rate is determined by each FI and is applied to loans made to a large customer such as a big corporation. All of these interest rates generally move in the same direction. Hence, when the FOMC increases the discount rate, all interest rates go up, and vice versa.

The Federal Reserve Banks are the third layer of authority in the Federal Reserve System. The United States is divided into twelve "Districts" and each Federal Reserve Bank controls one District. The twelve Federal Reserve Banks are scattered across the country and are located in Boston, New York, Richmond, Philadelphia, Atlanta, Dallas, St. Louis, Kansas City, Chicago, Minneapolis/St. Paul, San Francisco, and Cleveland. The main Federal Reserve System office is located in Washington, D.C., and each bank has corresponding regional offices in all major cities of the U.S.

The following information is derived from the Federal Reserve Board website.

ORGANIZATION OF THE FEDERAL RESERVE BANKS

Federal Reserve Banks operate under the general supervision of the Board of Governors in Washington. Each Bank has a nine-member Board of Directors that oversees its operations. There is one President and two Vice-Presidents. Nine members are derived from all sections of society, such as the banking community and the business community, to assure representation from all sections. Federal Reserve Banks generate their own income, primarily from interest earned on government securities that are acquired in the course of Federal Reserve monetary policy actions. A secondary source of income is derived from the provision of priced services to depository institutions, as required by the Monetary Control Act of 1980. Federal Reserve Banks are not, however, operated for a profit, and each year they return to the U.S. Treasury all earnings in excess of Federal Reserve operating and other expenses.

MONETARY POLICY ROLE

The primary responsibility of the central bank is to influence the flow of money and credit in the nation's economy. The Federal Reserve Banks are involved in this function in several ways. First, five of the twelve presidents of the Federal Reserve Banks serve, along with the seven members of the Board of Governors, as members of the Federal Open Market Committee (FOMC). The president of the Federal Reserve Bank of New York serves on a continuous basis; the other presidents serve one-year terms on a rotating basis. The FOMC meets periodically in Washington, D.C., and determines policy with respect to purchases and sales of government securities in the open market, actions that in turn affect the availability of money and credit in the economy.

Second, the boards of directors of the Federal Reserve Banks initiate changes in the discount rate, the rate of interest on loans made by Reserve Banks to depository institutions at the "discount window." Discount rate changes must be approved by the Board of Governors. All depository institutions that are subject to reserve requirements set by the Federal Reserve—including commercial banks, mutual savings banks, savings and loan associations, and credit unions—have access to the discount window.

Each Federal Reserve Bank has a research staff to gather and analyze a wide range of economic data and to interpret conditions and developments in the economy. This research assists the FOMC in the formulation and implementation of monetary policy. It also contributes to informed decision-making by the Federal Reserve Banks on bank supervisory matters and other areas. Most Reserve Banks publish a monthly or quarterly journal devoted to basic research and analysis of current economic issues in their District.

SUPERVISION AND REGULATION

In addition to its money and credit responsibilities, the Federal Reserve Bank has broad supervisory and regulatory authority over the activities of state-chartered member banks and bank holding companies, including their foreign activities, Edge corporations, and foreign banks operating in the United States. It is also charged with writing regulations for the major federal consumer credit laws.

Some of these supervisory responsibilities are delegated to the Reserve Banks by the Board of Governors. These responsibilities include conducting field examinations and inspections of state-chartered member banks, bank holding companies, and U.S. foreign bank offices and the authority to approve certain types of bank and bank holding company applications.

GOVERNMENT SERVICES

The Federal Reserve System, through the Reserve Banks, performs various services for the U.S. Treasury and other government, quasi-government, and international agencies. Each year, billions of dollars are deposited and withdrawn by various government agencies from the operating accounts of the U.S. Treasury held by the Federal Reserve Banks.

The Federal Reserve Banks hold, in their vaults, collateral for government agencies to secure public funds that are on deposit with private depository institutions. In addition, Reserve Banks receive for deposit to the Treasury's accounts such items as federal unemployment taxes, individual income taxes withheld by payroll deduction, corporate income taxes, and certain federal excise taxes.

The Federal Reserve Banks also issue and redeem instruments of public debt, such as savings bonds and Treasury securities. They have certain responsibilities for allotment and delivery of government securities and for wire transfer of securities. In addition, the Reserve Banks make periodic payments of interest on outstanding obligations of the U.S. Treasury, federal agencies, and government-sponsored corporations.

DEPOSITORY INSTITUTION SERVICES

Currency and Coin

The Federal Reserve Banks distribute currency (paper money) and coin to depository institutions to meet the public's need for cash. During periods of heavy cash demand, such as the Christmas season, institutions obtain larger amounts of cash from the Federal Reserve Banks. When public demand for cash is light, institutions deposit excess cash with the Reserve Banks, for credit to their reserve accounts. Currency and coin received at the Federal Reserve Banks are sorted and counted. Unfit currency and coin are destroyed and replaced with new currency and coin obtained from the Treasury Department's Bureau of Engraving and Printing and Bureau of the Mint.

Check Processing

The Federal Reserve serves as a central check-clearing system, handling approximately 18 billion checks a year. Using high-speed sorting machines, the Federal

Reserve Banks process these checks, route them to the depository institutions on which they are written, and transfer payment for the checks through accounts that depository institutions maintain with the Federal Reserve Banks.

Wire Transfers

The Federal Reserve Banks and about 7,800 depository institutions are linked electronically through the Federal Reserve Communications System, a network through which depository institutions can transfer funds and securities nationwide in a matter of minutes.

Automated Clearinghouses

Federal Reserve Banks and their branches operate automated clearinghouses, computerized facilities that allow for the electronic exchange of payments among participating depository institutions. Automated clearinghouses are used primarily to effect recurring transactions, such as direct deposit of payrolls and payment of mortgages, and serve as a replacement for checks. The Treasury Department uses automated clearinghouses extensively to make Social Security, payroll, and vendor payments.

The above information provides a summary of the work and functioning of the Federal Reserve Banks, and how these three layers of authority make up the Federal Reserve System as a whole. The specific ways in which the money supply in the U.S. economy is changed by the Federal Reserve System is analyzed below.

8.3 Tools of Money Supply Change

For someone with no economics background, an increase in the money supply can be perceived to be brought about by just printing more units of currency. For example, one may guess that an increase in the money supply can be brought about simply by running the printing presses a little longer. However, this perception is totally wrong. In practice, to increase the U.S. money supply, the Federal Reserve uses one of three major or three minor tools discussed herein.

OPEN MARKET OPERATIONS (OMO)

The first major tool, Open Market Operations (OMO), involves buying (and sometimes selling) Treasury bonds (technically called "Treasury securities") by the New York Federal Reserve Bank from the dealers on Wall Street who essentially work for FIs and the general public. Hence, OMO is the purchase and sale of Treasury bonds by the Fed from the public and banks. In the 1930s and 1940s there was a desk at the N.Y. Federal Reserve Bank that did the job of calling the dealers, so traditionally it is said that the N.Y. Federal Reserve Bank "Desk" carries out the OMO. When money supply is to be increased, the FOMC would suggest that the N.Y. Fed Desk should buy Treasury securities in the open market for a desired amount. As the N.Y. Federal Reserve Bank Desk gets the quotations of bond prices from the dealers, it buys at the lowest price. The dealers have to be paid for the sale of these bonds, which is done by issuing checks from the N.Y. Federal Reserve Bank. As the dealers deposit these checks into their respective banks, the deposits act as the Initial Deposits (ID) in our simplified money creation model discussed in Chapter 7. By using these initial deposits and by giving more loans, the banking system as a whole would create additional money supply for the U.S. economy.

Using OMO is the most active way of changing the U.S. money supply because in almost every FOMC meeting there is a new amount of securities that the FOMC decides to buy (or sell) until the next meeting. As mentioned before, the FOMC normally meets eight times per year, meaning that a change in OMO can occur as quickly as six weeks. While the accurate change in money supply is almost impossible to predict, the changes in OMO can give a firm direction to the future money supply level, and in that sense it is a powerful weapon and is often used.

DISCOUNT RATE CHANGES

The second major weapon of money supply change involves making changes in the discount rate. As previously defined, the discount rate is the interest rate charged by Federal Reserve Banks for their loans to financial institutions. When the money supply is to be increased, the discount rate is lowered. A reduction in the discount rate gives the signal to the FIs that the loans to them will be available at a lower rate than before. Even if the loans from the Federal Reserve Banks are not freely given to the banks, and even though they are not given in unlimited amounts, the reduction in the discount rate acts as a signal to the banking system. Hence, banks will lower the interest rate charged to customer loans, and more lending will occur. As we have seen, an increase in loans would mean more money is created by the banking system, and the money supply would go up. Until 1991, changes in the discount rate were not seen to be a very active weapon of money supply change. There were on average only two to three changes in the discount rate in a year. But after 1991, the Federal Reserve System seemed to realize the greater value of this weapon and now discount rate changes occur much more frequently. In fact, in 2007 there were a record number of seven changes in the discount rate. This illustrates that a change in the discount rate can be an effective weapon of money supply change.

CHANGES IN LEGAL REQUIREMENT RATIO (LRR)

The most powerful weapon of money supply change is the change in LRR. When a LRR change is activated it is mandatory on the part of FIs to obey it; therefore, its effectiveness is almost always guaranteed. When money supply is to be increased, the Federal Reserve System would lower the LRR so that FIs have to keep a smaller percentage of their total reserves with the Federal Reserve banks. Thus, they would be able to give more loans to the public. As the amount of loans increases, the money supply in the economy goes up. However, changing the LRR is such a powerful weapon that it is rarely used or used only in emergencies. As it is, the LRR does not change for small banks, guaranteeing that they do not have to predict any changes in the LRR. Large banks have been assured of a range within which the LRR can change. Of course, too many changes in the LRR would directly affect the banks' functions, and the bank managers would have to guess the next move by the Federal Reserve, so these LRR changes are kept to a minimum.

Besides these three major weapons of money supply change, there are three minor weapons that can also be used. Because they change the money supply in interesting ways, we should consider them here as follows:

1. **Moral Suasion.** By using this weapon, Federal Reserve Banks sometimes activate a desirable change in money supply. Suasion (or persuasion) means a deliberate action to have some pre-determined objective fulfilled. For example, if the Federal Reserve wants to have an upward change in money supply, then it would send a memo to FIs in a certain region to do a specific function. For example, suppose there are drought conditions in Iowa and farmers are getting hurt. By sending memos, banks in that region can be persuaded to give extra loans to the farming community. If banks follow the Federal Reserve's advice, the money supply will go up. Of course, the change in the money supply will be small, and that is why suasion is considered a minor weapon of money supply change.

2. **Changes in Margin Requirements.** A margin requirement refers to the cash down payment one is required to make to buy a bond or a company stock. So, a 10 percent margin requirement means that to buy a stock of $100, one needs to put down cash of $10 and the remaining $90 can be borrowed from a bank. When money supply is to be increased, the Federal Reserve would lower the margin requirement so that people could borrow more to buy bonds and stocks. As they borrow more, the money supply would go up. When there is inflationary pressure and if money supply is intended to be reduced, the margin requirement is increased.

3. **Jawboning.** The third minor weapon of money supply change is "jawboning," which essentially means giving signals to the banking and financial community about intentions of monetary policy in the future. These signals are provided by a high level administrator, such as the U.S. President or Chairman of the Federal Reserve Board. Sometimes these signals are not even meant to be very serious, but the press and media read too much into them and they become a case of jawboning. Every month the Chairman of the Federal Reserve Board has to answer questions before the Senate Banking Committee, and this session is closely monitored. In fact, most of the speeches by all members of the Board are closely monitored for any signals of future change in the money supply. A classic case of jawboning is the famous speech by Alan Greenspan in 1996, where he criticized too much stock market activity by calling it "Irrational Exuberance." His intention was to dissuade stock buyers from taking too much risk, so he argued that borrowing money to play in the market was a risky business that would have ups and downs. The next day there was a significant decline in market activity, which also resulted in a small decline in money supply. In recent years, the stock market has responded to information provided by many major policy makers. Hence, minor changes in money supply can occur based on such information.

In summary, we can argue that when money supply is to be changed, monetary policy (the policy that makes changes in money supply, carried out by the Federal Reserve System in the United States) can use one of the above weapons to change money supply in the economy. The next obvious question becomes: If these are the ways in which money supply is changed, what are the consequences of such money supply change on the economy as a whole? In other words, how would GDP, interest rates, prices, exchange rates, investments, and other economic variables change when there is a change in money supply? The theory that claims to know the answer to these questions is called "monetary theory." Economists have thought about these consequences for a long time, right from the early days of David Hume (1752). However, the most celebrated monetary theory was proposed by Irving Fisher (Yale University, circa 1905). In the next chapter, we consider the development of Fisher's quantity theory.

Chapter 9

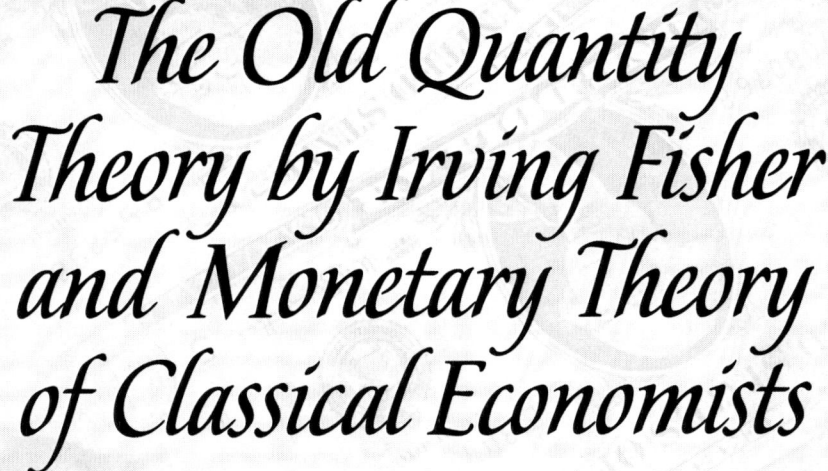

The Old Quantity Theory by Irving Fisher and Monetary Theory of Classical Economists

SUMMARY

This chapter extends the discussion first presented in Chapter 5 of the general economic thought of classical economists and offers a more detailed analysis of classical monetary theory. As mentioned previously, classical economists wholeheartedly believed that all markets possessed an automatic mechanism of establishing general equilibrium; therefore, excess supply or demand can only be a temporary phenomenon. Among the first persons to formally express these beliefs was Jeremy Bentham, when he sourced the persistent inflation of the early 1800s in Great Britain to increases in money supply. By describing how money supply affects other economic variables, Bentham laid the foundation for the classical economists' monetary theory.

Among the most famous of the classical economists is Irving Fisher, whose life and contributions to the field of economics and society are explored in depth. Although his first love was mathematics, Fisher's understanding of economics was so profound that we eventually codified Bentham's early thoughts into the modern quantity theory of money. The chapter explains his equation of exchange, expressed as MV = PY, where M is the money supply, V is the velocity of money, P is the general price level, and Y is real output. By finding that real output and velocity of money—or the rate at which a unit of currency is spent on final goods and services—are independent of money supply, Fisher concluded that an increase in the quantity of money results in an exactly proportional increase in the general level of prices. Thus, according to Fisher, expansionary monetary policy is responsible for inflation in an economy and is ineffective in influencing the level of real output. True to classical economic sentiments, this implies that national monetary authorities ought to remain as inactive as possible regarding money supply, as an active policy stance can actually be counterproductive to the economy.

Despite his contributions to classical economic thought, the chapter highlights the criticisms lodged against Fisher's analysis by a number of his contemporaries. Many cite the equation of exchange as a mere truism, in which a cause-and-effect relationship between money supply and the price level cannot be ascertained; thus, the quantity theory of money cannot be used to derive policy consequences. In addition, Keynes disproved Fisher's assumption that real output is independent of money supply by pointing to the impact of involuntary unemployment, the existence of which guarantees that real output (Y) cannot stay constant when there is an increase in money supply. Finally, a group of economists crafted the Cambridge equation, $M = KPY$, where K represents the proportion of national income kept in money terms, which questions Fisher's assertions that the velocity of money is independent of the money supply and that money functions only as a medium of exchange. However, despite the shortcomings in Fisher's quantity theory of money, the chapter concludes with an affirmation of his theory's continued applicability in the realm of monetary analysis.

9.1 Historical Background of Classical Economics

As mentioned in Chapter 5, economists before the 1930s are called "classical" economists because they held special feelings about how any macro economy, but especially a capitalistic economy, determines the level of its GDP. Strictly speaking, classical economists were neither organized in their writing nor did they communicate with each other to come up with any identical philosophy. Nonetheless, some common ideas persist in the writings of John Stuart Mill (1806–1873), David Ricardo (1772–1823), Alfred Marshall (1842–1924), Irving Fisher (1867–1947), and J. B. Say (1767–1832). Because it was the classical school of thought from which Keynes so strongly disassociated himself, and since criticisms of classical writing led to special Keynesian feelings, it is imperative that we initially review the main contentions of the classical economists in this chapter.

Just as the classical economists were experts in showing an automatic mechanism of establishing general equilibrium in the economy, they were also staunch advocates of the laissez-faire policy. In other words, the most common thread that runs among all classical economists is their faith that the capitalistic economy possesses a built-in force that leads to automatic general equilibrium. Hence, no action on the part of the government is needed to cure business fluctuations, since in the long run, they will probably not persist. Hence, all disequilibria are purely temporary. In all markets, excess supply or excess demand do not last for a very long time. However, as mentioned in Chapter 5, the major jolt to the classical economists' beliefs was given by empirical changes that occurred all over the world.

Starting in the 1920s, the major industrial economies of the world experienced one by one what is rightly called the Great Depression. As discussed in Chapter 5, that was the start of the Keynesian revolution. Thus, we are in a position to observe carefully, in classical economists' terms, the process by which the money supply affects other economic variables. The theory that explains this process is known as "monetary theory." The oldest monetary theory that is popular with economists of modern times is the one developed by classical economists such as Henry Thornton, Jeremy Bentham, David Hume, and Irving Fisher. Other notable names are John Gray in England in the 1830s and 1840s and Paul Douglas of the University of Chicago in the United States in the 1930s.

Jeremy Bentham's work can be traced back as early as the 1800s. It was a time when England had undergone price inflation and Bentham attempted to explain it. In his writings, one can see some seedlings of the quantity theory of money. His statements such as "the sum of all prices given for all the saleable articles sold within a year cannot be anything but the total of money given of them" or "the rapidity of circulation must also enter into account" gives us the impression that Bentham had described the modern quantity theory which Irving Fisher eventually elaborated. Thus, quantity theory clearly proposes that an increase in the price level of the economy is caused only by an excessive increase in money supply. Hence, for reasons which we will discuss later, quantity theorists believe that the effect of a change in the money supply is seen in terms of change it causes in the general price level. Bentham's earlier work was the first to recognize the equality of aggregate demand (the money side of his equation) and aggregate supply (the real side of his equation). Given this equality, Bentham argued, "we can look for the cause of the permanent increase in prices only in the increase of the effective force, i.e. the quantity and the rapidity of circulation, of the mass of money." This was his attempt to explain England's inflation of the early 1800s. Economists also see the origins of monetary theory in Henry Thornton's book: *Paper Credit* (1802). In it, one can find statements like, "the effect produced by paper credit on the price of articles depends not merely on the price of paper in existence, but also on the rapidity of circulation." It is clear from this statement that Thornton was aware of the changes in the velocity of money. As argued by Harris (1981), there were several other economists of earlier years, like Wicksell and J. S. Mill who also attempted to describe the effect of the money supply on the price level.

9.2 Life of Irving Fisher

Irving Fisher, born in Saugerties, New York, was truly one of the most pioneering economists of the twentieth century. Ragnar Frisch, a Norwegian economist, wrote of Fisher:

> The most salient feature of his work is, I think, that in everything he was doing, he has been anywhere from a decade to two generations ahead of his time. He had indeed been a pioneer. (Frisch, 1952)

After a studious childhood, Irving soon realized his interest in the field of mathematics, and finished his doctorate degree in mathematics at Yale University. Nonetheless, his dissertation entitled "Mathematical Investigations in Theory of Value and Prices" had a grafting of economic theory in it. He used vector analysis to solve the problem of price and value differential and his use of mathematics was so advanced that even the professionally trained mathematicians of the day found his techniques quite challenging. Fisher was known in mathematical circles immediately after his dissertation.

Fisher's first job was to be a tutor in the mathematics department, but he contacted Prof. William Graham Summer who persuaded him that economics was a more suitable profession. Even if economics was his second love, as history notes quite well, Fisher prospered in it tremendously. His active research program and his hard work earned him a full professorship at Yale at the relatively tender age of 31. However, just after his promotion, he caught tuberculosis and had to be on academic leave for five years. It was only in 1903 that he resumed his duties at Yale. Within a few years he published *The Theory of Interest Rates* and an international reputation followed him everywhere thereafter.

Irving Fisher was not only an outstanding mathematician and economist, but also a very renowned investor. In 1910, Fisher received a patent from the United States Patent Office for inventing a device that improved the performance of pianos. In 1910, Fisher also published a new system called "The Making of Index Numbers" in his book *Elementary Principles of Economics*. His index number formula was a comprehensive study of index number formulae wherein he tested other formulae and arrived at his "Ideal Formula." Later in 1923, Fisher established the Index Number Institute, a business to prepare and sell index numbers and other economic data for publication. The business of preparing and selling index numbers to the public became so popular that he profited up to $10 million, which he used very efficiently in donating to promotional activities for monetary stabilization and public health, including research for tuberculosis. Because Fisher contracted tuberculosis and his father died of the same disease, he spent considerable time (from 1904–1911) as the Secretary of the Anti-Tuberculosis Association in New Haven, Connecticut. In 1913, Fisher founded the Life Extension Institute to improve public health through publicity and by promoting periodic health examinations. He tried to convince insurance companies that it would be to their advantage to provide low-cost medical checkups. In 1916, Fisher was among the first to recognize the importance of insurance against large medical expenditures. However, the crash of 1929 was devastating for Fisher. He lost much of his wealth in the Great Depression but still remained optimistic about the future. In fact, he wrote a book titled *How to Live,* where he discussed the importance of keeping up with health-related activities. This book was just one indication of how widespread his thought process was and how involved he was in issues other than pure economic theories.

Fisher's life also illustrates what a determined and able man can accomplish in the long run. Fisher left a long-lasting imprint on economic nomenclature. Words and phrases such as "equation of exchange," "dance of dollar," "ratio chart," "distributed lags," "ideal formula," "index wage," "commodity dollars," "utils," "Fisher Effect," and "check-book money" are all attributed to Irving Fisher. Certainly, he is one of the most cited economists after Keynes, and his books were translated into several foreign languages. In 1910, Fisher was instrumental in suggesting the use of double-entry bookkeeping techniques for national income and product estimates. Because of his contributions in this field, he was known as the organizer and father of national income accounting systems. He wrote another book outlining the details of his ideas on national income accounting, *The Nature of Capital and Income*. Besides being a prolific writer, Fisher was also an eloquent speaker. He went on a lecture series to the University of London, the University of California, and the Geneva School of International Studies, and studied in Berlin and Paris in 1893 and 1894. His tremendous contributions earned him honorary degrees from the University of Athens and the University of Luzanne.

Very few economists have served in as many associations as Fisher had served by the early 1900s. He was the President of the American Economic Association, the Econometric Society, the American Association of Labor Legislation, the National Institute of Social Sciences, and the Chairman of many other important national commissions. He was the founder of the American Eugenics Society, the Life Extension Institute, the Vitality Records Office, and the Stable Money League.

In the five years after 1925, Fisher went from being a university professor to a business publicist to a financial tycoon to a small businessman, to a board member of important corporations, to a stock market prophet. Besides staying busy in his life through all these activities, Fisher remained a scientist, scholar, and educator. He continued his propaganda for prohibition, economic monetary stabilization, good health and eugenics, and monetary reform. Money was a special passion for Fisher. He wrote many books and articles on money-related topics. After teaching a course on money at Yale, he wrote a related textbook. His books on capital and income were famous, but his book entitled *The Purchasing Power of Money* was groundbreaking. Therein he details the famous quantity theory of money and the medium of exchange function of money. With one of the most exciting lives lived by an economist, Fisher fell seriously ill in January of 1947 and doctors diagnosed his illness as cancer. Nonetheless, he participated in the American Economic Association meeting in January of 1947 and wrote to President Harry Truman, urging him to adopt monetary reform.

9.3 The Quantity Theory of Money by Irving Fisher

The most elegant and elaborated analysis of the effect of the money supply on other variables was done by Irving Fisher of Yale University in 1903. He formulated a theory known as the "quantity theory of money," in terms of an equation called the "equation of exchange." Since Fisher used this equation so extensively, it is also called the "Fisherian equation." And because this equation is used to analyze the quantity theory of money, it is also referred to as the "quantity theory equation." This equation is expressed in the following form:

$$MV = PY$$

where M = the amount of money expended in the economy during a given period of time;

V = the velocity of money, defined as the turnover rate of money. More technically, "velocity of money completes the circular flow in the given time period";

P = General Price Index measured by one of the price indexes discussed earlier;

Y = real output or total transactions in the economy in a given time period.

Hence, if P_i is the price of the ith commodity and q_i is the quantity transacted (bought or sold) of that commodity, then $\Sigma P_i q_i$ is called the market value of all commodities, which is on the right-hand side of the Fisherian equation:

$$P_1 q_1 + P_2 q_2 + P_3 q_3 + \ldots + P_n q_n = \Sigma P_i q_i = PY$$

By analyzing this relationship, Fisher concluded that, "a normal effect of an increase in the quantity of money is an exactly proportional increase in the general level of prices." The first observation he thought we should make is that "velocity of circulation, as an institutionally determined factor influenced primarily by such things as the public's payment habits, the extent of the use of credit, the speed of transportation and communication as it influences the time required to make a payment, and other technical factors that bear no discoverable relation to the quantity of money in circulation." In simpler terms, this means that the velocity of money is independent of the stock of the money supply. Similarly, Fisher viewed real income (Y) of the whole economy to be determined by such exogenous factors as the stock of natural resources in the economy or the labor productivity. In short, the real output (Y) can also be considered to be independent of changes in the money supply. Hence, under these conditions, with any change in money supply (M), the price level (P) would have to change in an equal and direct proportion to warrant the equality specified by the Fisherian equation. A doubling of money supply will be responsible for the doubling of the price level. This obviously means that the expansionary monetary policy of any government is responsible for the price increases an economy experiences. The effect of any consistent expansionary monetary policy will be to create inflation in the economy. A conclusion of this sort gives a message to the monetary authorities to be as inactive as possible because any action of increasing the money supply, on its part, would be ineffective in influencing the level of real output of the economy.

Nonetheless, anxious economists attempted to search for inconsistencies in Fisher's arguments. To summarize the criticisms of the quantity theory of money, we note the following points. First, in the equation of exchange, some may observe that the left-hand side (money supply times the velocity of money) represents the value of total income generated (price level times total real output). In "ex-post," since this indicates an identity (tautology, truism, or an equation which is true by definition), that total expenditure for the economy, as a whole, is always equal to total income generated in it. Hence, the quantity theory equation cannot be used to derive policy consequences. For instance, one should not (and cannot) argue that an increase in the money supply causes the price level to go up. As an identity, any increase on the left-hand side of the equation must be compensated by an equivalent increase in the right-hand side. In other words, an identity cannot be used to assert a cause and effect relationship. The matter of the quantity theory equation being an identity did not escape Fisher's mind, and he had an answer for it in the following manner:

> One of the objectors to the quantity theory attempts to dispose of the equation of exchange . . . by calling it a mere truism. While the equation equivalence, in all purchases, of the money or check expended, on the one hand, and what they buy on the other, . . . this equation is a means of demonstrating the fact that normally, the Ps (price levels) vary directly as M, this is, demonstrating the quantity theory. "Truisms" should never be neglected. The greatest generalizations of physical science, such as that forces are proportional to mass and acceleration, are truisms, but when duly supplemented by specific data, these truisms are the most fruitful sources of useful mechanical knowledge.

The second criticism of the quantity theory's conclusion comes from a group of economists from Cambridge University in Cambridge, England. Notable economists in this group were A. C. Pigou, Alfred Marshall, and R. G. D. Allen, who on their behalf, created a modified version of the quantity theory equation known as the "Cambridge equation." The main thrust of this equation was its emphasis on the store of value function of money. The equation can be stated as follows:

$$M = K \times P \times Y$$

where K is defined as the proportion of national income kept in money terms. The above equation is also a definitional identity. According to Pigou and others, people have several reasons to keep money in terms of cash. In his words, ". . . everybody is anxious to hold enough of his resources in the form of titles to legal tender (money) both to enable him to affect the ordinary transactions of life without trouble, and to secure him against unexpected demands due to a sudden need, a rise in the price of something he cannot easily dispense with." If the money supply goes up, the value of K is expected to increase, because with more liquidity available, people will tend to use more money as a store of value.

By comparing the Cambridge equation (M = KPY) and the Fisherian equation (MV = PY) we can deduce easily the value of K as being equal to the inverse of the velocity of money. Hence, K = 1/V; as the money supply (M) increases, the value of K will go up (as discussed before), which obviously would mean that the velocity of money would fall. Hence, the Fisherian contention that the velocity of money is independent of changes in the money supply is questionable. The observations that money also serves as a store of value, and that a money supply increase would make people use money more and more as a store of value, are indeed a challenge for the quantity theory's conclusion. According to Havrilesky and Boorman, "This orientation led the Cambridge economists to formulate a first line of monetary inquiry from which emanate many of the modern developments in monetary economics. By emphasizing the individual's demand for money and the utility which money balances may yield, Cambridge economists were led to examine choices facing the individual."

However, being a clever economist as he was, Fisher did not miss the point that any increase in the money supply may "temporarily" affect the value of velocity of circulation. But he ignored any significant consequences of this because they occur only in the transitory periods. (In modern times, economists have picked up the idea of money serving as a depository asset and not merely as a medium of exchange. The velocity of money is believed to be dependent upon the extent to which money performs the store of value function).

The third criticism of the conclusion of the quantity theory was put forward by John Maynard Keynes in his revolutionary book, *General Theory of Employment, Interest and Money* (1936). The main thrust of his argument is that a capitalistic economy is characterized by underemployment of aggregate demand so as to warrant employment of all resources including, of course, that of labor. The type of unemployment caused by insufficient demand for business output is labeled as involuntary unemployment. An existence of involuntary unemployment guarantees us that the real output (Y) cannot stay constant when the money supply is increased. Moreover, Keynes proved in a rather systematic process how an increased money supply can be effective in raising the level of economic activity. He believed that the Fisherian conclusion does not hold because of the likelihood of an increase in real output (Y) on the right-hand side of the equation.

In spite of these strong criticisms against its conclusion, the quantity theory is credited tremendously for its observation of the dependence of price level on the money supply. As Friedman pointed out later in 1956, whether we believe in the absolute proportionality of Fisher's conclusion or not, the fact still remains that the major cause of consistent increases in the general price level is an excessive growth in the money supply. As we will examine in later chapters, the revised version of the quantity theory of money holds a crucial position in modern monetary theory. One has to admire the efficiency and depth shown by Fisher in noticing the fact that the money supply may cause an increase in price levels, at least in the long run. The long-run observation of several capitalistic economies have shown that increases in price levels were, in fact, associated with a wide increase in money supplies. This book will later explore the other factors that can cause inflation in the economy, but thanks to Fisher's work in the early 1900s, we have realized already that one of the important factors in that list is an excessive money supply.

In summary, classical economists believed laissez faire was the best policy. They also thought that all disequilibria in all markets were purely temporary. However, the main shock to their belief was provided by the Great Depression and thereafter we needed a new way of thinking of the process that determined the GDP production in any economy. That job was done by the pioneering work of Lord J. M. Keynes. In the next chapter, we start discussing Keynesian macroeconomics.

Suggested Further Reading

Bentham, J. 1801. *The True Alarm,* London.

Blaug, M. 1995. Why is the quantity theory of money the oldest surviving theory in economics? In *The Quantity Theory of Money from Locke to Keynes and Friedman,* ed. Blaug. Aldershot, England: Edward Elger.

Fisher, I. 1935. *100% Money.* New York: Adelphi Publishers.

Fisher, I. 1922. *The Purchasing Power of Money: Its Determination and Relation to Credit, Interest and Crises.* New York: Macmillan Publishers, New York. Reprinted 1963, New York: Augustus M. Kelley.

Fisher, I. 1920. *Stabilizing the Dollar.* New York: Macmillan Publishers.

Friedman, M. 1989. The quantity theory of money. In *Money, The New Palgrave,* eds. J. Eatwell, M. Milgate, and P. Newman. New York: W.W. Norton.

Friedman, M. 1956. *Studies in Quantity Theory of Money.* Chicago: The University of Chicago Press.

Friedman, M. 1969. *The Optimum Quantity Theory of Money and Other Essays.* Chicago: Aldine Publishing Company.

Frisch, R. 1952. Frisch on Fisher. In *The Development of Economic Thought: Great Economists in Perspective,* ed. H. W. Spiegel. New York: John Wiley.

Harris, L. 1981. *Monetary Theory,* Chapters 4, 5, and 6. New York: McGraw-Hill.

Havrilsky, T. M. and J. T. Boorman. 1982. *Money Supply, Money Demand and Macroeconomic Models,* 2nd ed. Harlan Davidson Publishers, Inc.

Humphrey, T. 1974. The quantity theory of money: Its historical evolution and role in policy debates. *Economic Review,* Federal Reserve Bank of Richmond, May/June: 1–19.

Humphrey, T. 1997. Fisher and Wicksell on the quantity theory. *Economic Quarterly,* Federal Reserve Bank of Richmond, Vol. 83, No. 4: 71–90.

Keynes, J. M. 1936. *General Theory of Employment, Interest and Money.* London: Harcourt, Brace and World.

Kulkarni, K. *First Principles of Macro-Monetary Theory,* 3rd ed. Chapter 7. Dubuque, Iowa: Kendall/Hunt Publishing Company.

Laidler, D. 1991. *The Golden Age of the Quantity Theory: The Development of Neo-classical Monetary Economics, 1870-1914.* The Princeton University Press.

Mill, J. S. 1848. *Principles of Political Economy.* London: J.W. Parker Publishers.

Patinkin, D. 1993. Irving Fisher and his compensated dollar plan. *Economic Quarterly,* Federal Reserve Bank of Richmond, Vol. 79, Summer: 1–33.

Pigou, A. C. 1917. The value of money. *The Quarterly Journal of Economics,* Vol. 32, November: 41.

Tavlas, G. 1977. Some initial formulations of the monetary growth rate rule. *History of Political Economy,* Vol. 9, Winter: 535–47.

Wicksell, J. G. K. *Interest and Prices.* Translated by R. F. Kahn. New York: Macmillan Publishers.

Chapter 10

The Keynesian Macro-Monetary Theory and the Keynesian Chain

SUMMARY

The weaknesses of classical monetary theory discussed in the last chapter prompted Keynes to craft a new macro-monetary theory, which could take account of the money market and comprehensively explain the effects of money supply on the economy. This chapter explores this theory, including Keynes' analysis of both interest rate determination and the effectiveness of monetary policy, while also explaining important Keynesian concepts, such as the demand for money.

Unlike the classical economists, Keynes asserted that money serves as a store of value in addition to its role as a medium of exchange. Hence, Keynes laid forth three important motives for keeping money in cash or in non-interest bearing bank accounts. Also classified as the three types of money demand, these include transactionary demand, precautionary demand, and speculative demand for money. This chapter defines these terms and explains their main determinants as well. The transaction demand for money is money needed to make transactions, and it is primarily determined by income level and the time interval between two income receipts. Precautionary demand for money, as the name suggests, is the amount of money kept in cash as a precaution against unforeseen contingencies requiring sudden expenditure, including unforeseen opportunities of advantageous purchases. It is primarily determined by the risk of illiquidity and the cost of money, or the interest rate. That is, the higher the risk of being illiquid, and the higher the cost of getting additional cash, the higher is the precautionary demand for money. Finally, the speculative demand for money is the amount of money people hold for making speculations in the bond market. The interest rate is the only determinant for speculative demand of money; hence, as the interest rate increases, the buying of bonds also increases and less money is held in cash for speculation of the bond price—which is always the inverse of the interest rate in the economy.

The discussion of money demand leads to a formal analysis of money market equilibrium, which is represented graphically by the point where the overall demand for money curve and the money supply curve intersect. The importance of this point is derived from the fact that it determines the equilibrium interest rate in the money market. According to the paradox of flexibility, if the interest rate is flexible, then it will stay at this equilibrium level.

The chapter then examines the effectiveness of monetary policy within the Keynesian framework. Accordingly, changes in monetary policy, which are principally changes in money supply, must be interpreted in terms of their effect on aggregate demand and real GNP. In short, a higher money supply creates a lower interest rate, assuming that the demand curve for money is held constant. This in turn creates higher investment, as the Marginal Efficiency of Capital (MEC) now exceeds the new, lower interest rate. This increased investment sparks the multiplier process that generates higher levels of real income, and it is only through the multiplier process that any policy action can affect real GNP. This conceptualization of a Keynesian chain, whereby changes in money supply create several knock-on effects that ultimately impact real GNP, puts Keynesian analysis at odds with that of the classical economists, who saw increases in money supply as only creating inflation.

Finally, the chapter concludes with a discussion of the special circumstances that lead to a breakdown of the Keynesian chain. A so-called liquidity trap occurs when interest rates in the economy are so low that the speculative demand for money is very, very high, almost to infinity. In such a case, any expansionary monetary policy ceases to be effective, as the increase in money supply is unable to reduce the interest rate and increase real investment and real income. That is, the increase in money supply will no longer exert an impact on aggregate demand and GNP. Keynes was cognizant of this potentiality, leading him to famously state that, "Money does not matter." Due to the existence of liquidity traps, the best monetary policy is one that keeps money supply consistently at the level at which the interest rate is as minimal as possible.

10.1 Introduction

In the last chapter, we focused our attention only to the classical economists' monetary theory. However, that theory (i.e., quantity theory) was heavily criticized by Keynes and his other friends from Cambridge University. In the writings of *General Theory,* Keynes did not forget to explain his feelings about the effects of money supply on the economy, nor did he omit the discussion about what he considered to be the critical market for money supply change, namely, the money market. We will devote this chapter to discussing money market mechanisms as explained by Keynes. Accordingly, the main aims of this chapter include:

1. The introduction of some important Keynesian concepts such as the demand for money,
2. Analysis of the interest rate determination according to Keynes, and
3. Keynesian analysis of the effectiveness (or the lack thereof) of monetary policy.

It is often argued that in the Keynesian system, nominal or monetary factors have had less importance than real variables such as real GDP, real consumption, real investment, etc. This is because with few exceptions, monetary factors are believed to have little influence on real factors like real consumption, real investment, real GDP, etc. In the pure Keynesian view, the most important factor was obviously aggregate demand, and monetary forces were to be examined in accordance with their effect on aggregate demand or total expenditure.

In Keynesian analysis, the real interest rate was thought to be the link between the monetary and real factors. Hence the changes in money supply have initial reflections in the money market, and in the money market, the "price" of money, namely, the "interest rate," was supposed to be determined by the intersection of demand for and supply of money curves. As you know from Chapter 8, we have gained a lot of information about the process by which money supply is determined in the United States. (HINT: It is measured by M_1 or M_2.) In this chapter we will discuss the process of how demand for money is determined.

10.2 Demand for Money

Here it is important to understand how we define the demand for money. The definition of "demand for money" was crucial because demand for money, unlike demand for any other goods, was not given by the willingness or ability of a person to buy it, but by the actual holding of it. Hence, demand for money is the amount of money people would like to keep in terms of cash (or in non-interest earning checking accounts) at a given time period, or the hoarding of money.

Now, if money serves as the medium of exchange, why would someone hoard it? According to Keynes, there are three important motives (reasons) why people would keep money in cash or in non-interest bearing bank accounts. Also classified as the three types of money demand, these include *transactionary demand, precautionary demand,* and *speculative demand* for money. We shall analyze these motives of demand for money in detail.

THE TRANSACTION DEMAND FOR MONEY

Because money functions as a medium of exchange, one of the important reasons for holding money is having it available for making transactions. In Keynesian words, "one reason for holding cash is to bridge the interval between the receipt of income and its disbursement." Depending upon how much money is received by a person and the time available to disperse that income, one can always determine the transaction demand for money. If we assume that uniform income is received every month and total payments are equal to total receipts, then by using Figure 10.1 we can determine the average transaction demand for

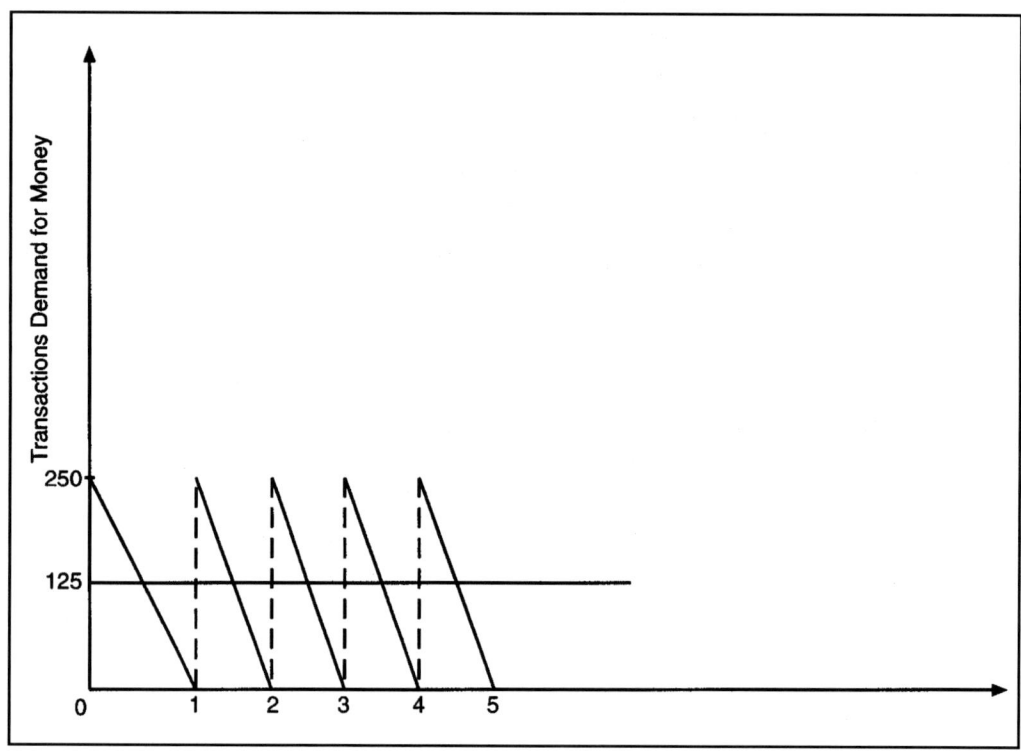

FIGURE 10.1 ■ Transactions Demand for Money

money. The time interval for receipt of income and the income one receives per month can decide the amount of money demanded by the person. As the interval between the time income is received and the time it is spent is shortened, average cash balances held will decline. In general, the transaction demand for money by a person who receives 250 money units of income would be 125 on the average over a month. The longer the time period, the larger the demand for money. A higher income would create a higher transaction demand for money. Thus, the transaction demand for money is primarily determined by the income level and the time interval between two income receipts.

The most significant contribution to the determination of transaction demand for money in the post-Keynesian era was done by Baumol (1952) and Tobin (1956). In the simplest version, Baumol's model can be summarized as follows. Consider an individual (or an institution) who receives income over a certain period of time, say a month. Suppose the person also spends that income at a constant rate and saves nothing at the end of the period. Then, at any given time, the individual will hold assets (say bonds) worth the unspent income. The main question Baumol and Tobin attempt to answer concerns how the person holds different assets, given that interest-yielding bonds can be owned as well as cashed, and that there is a fixed cost involved in exchanging bonds for cash. Of course, the individual would like to arrange assets so as to minimize costs over the period.

The problem can be hypothesized and solved in the following way: Suppose T is the value of the total income of a person. Then T is also equal to the real value of the volume of transactions carried out, r is the interest rate, b is the real cost of turning bonds into cash (or brokerage fee), and K is the real value of bonds turned into cash every time such a transfer takes place. There are two types of costs incurred by the agent. First, every time bonds are sold in equal lots of size K, the outlay in brokerage fees is equal to b (T/K). At the same time, if money is held instead of bonds, interest is foregone, and this too, must be treated as a cost. Because expenditure is a constant flow, the agent's average money holding over the period is K/2, that is, half the amount of his/her receipts from the sale of bonds. The average money holding over the period multiplied by the rate of interest per period gives the opportunity cost of holding money.

The total cost of making a transaction, where X is the cost, can be written as:

$$X = bT/K + rK/2 \qquad (1)$$

To find the value of K that minimizes the cost explained in Equation (1), one needs to take the derivative of X with respect to K and set it equal to zero to solve it for K. Hence, we get

$$dX/dK = -bT/K^2 + r/2 = 0 \qquad (2)$$

so that

$$K = d2bT/r \quad (3)$$

Because, at any given time, money holdings have an average value of K/2, the demand for money for transaction purposes is obtained by dividing the right-hand side of Equation (3) by 2; to get

$$Md/P = K/2 = \tfrac{1}{2} 2bT/r \quad (4)$$

Thus, in Baumol and Tobin's analysis, the transaction demand for money is determined by Equation (4). Besides the transaction demand for money, Keynes also specified other "motives" for money demand, such as precautionary and speculative motives.

THE PRECAUTIONARY DEMAND FOR MONEY

The precautionary demand for money, as the name suggests, "is the amount of money kept in cash as a precaution." This money is needed "to provide for contingencies requiring sudden expenditure and for unforeseen opportunities of advantageous purchases, and also to hold an asset of which the value is fixed in terms of money." The volume of this type of demand for money would depend upon the reward for holding money in any other substitute form (e.g., interest rate on bonds) and the risk of being illiquid. The higher the risk of being illiquid, and the higher the cost of getting additional cash, the higher is the precautionary demand for money. To elaborate with an example, let us suppose you are traveling far away from your home (and back) and the cost of getting cash is high (and the risk of being illiquid is high as well). In this situation, you would tend to keep more money in your pocket. That money is obviously the demand for money for precautionary purposes. Also, a higher interest rate on the substitutes of money would mean people would keep more of these substitutes and less of money holdings. Hence, the demand for money is inversely related to the yields on the substitutes of money.

THE SPECULATIVE DEMAND FOR MONEY

The most important type of demand for money, according to Keynes, is the speculative demand for money. It is the amount of money people hold for making speculations in the bond market. If people have a choice of holding wealth in the form of either money or bonds, then the interest rate on bonds is the only determinant of the speculative demand for money. In general, people would prefer to hold money to buying bonds, since money has higher liquidity than bonds. This is known as "liquidity preference." It is only when the interest rate in the economy increases that people would be ready to buy bonds at a higher price and reduce their speculative demand for money. Hence, more bond buying occurs at higher interest rates, with less money held in cash for speculation of bond prices. Keep in mind that the price of bonds is always inverse to the interest rate in the economy. It is very easy to prove that relationship. Consider, for example, if you have a bond that has the price of 100 dollars paying a 6 percent interest rate. Suppose that after one year, interest rates in the economy increase. Then if you want to sell your bond, which pays only 6 percent, you need to bring its price down (and sell it for lower price that 100 dollars). Hence, as the interest rate goes up, the bond price comes down. The reverse is true too. If the interest rates go down, your bond's price will go up.

This inverse relationship between the interest rate and the speculative demand for money is depicted by the downward sloping curve from left to right, shown in Figure 10.2. Keynes called this curve the "liquidity preference curve":

> This component of money demand is highly volatile since it depends heavily upon the changing nature of the public's expectations. If the outlook for stock and bond

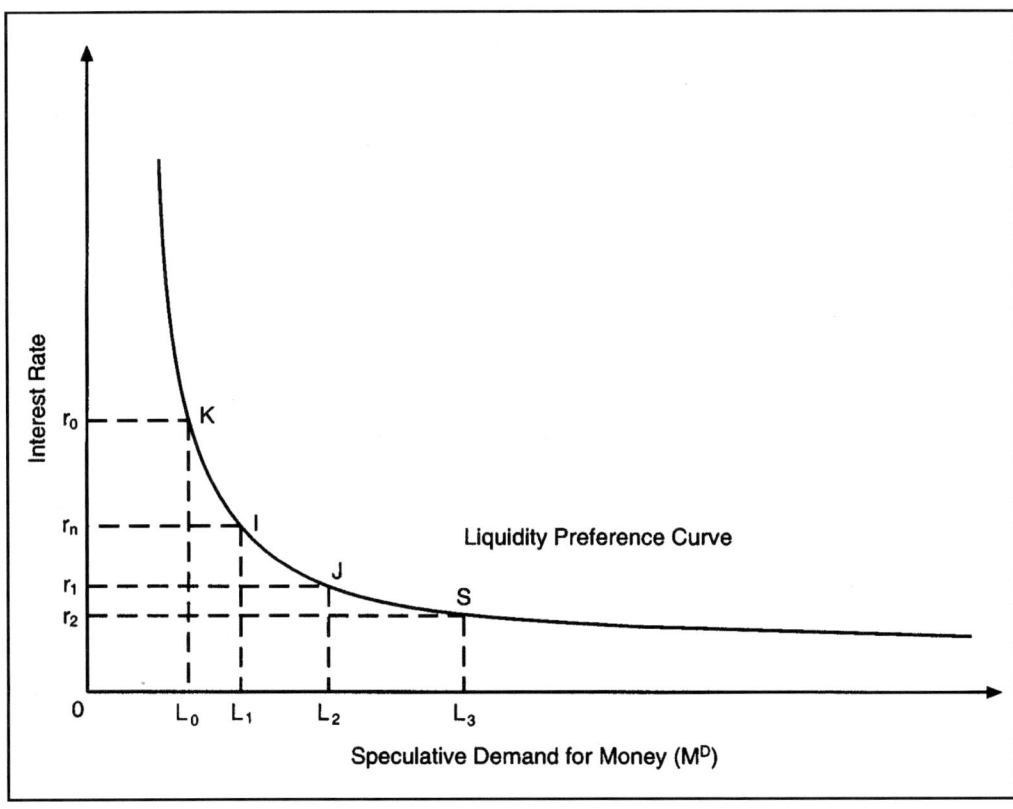

Liquidity Preference Curve ■ **FIGURE 10.2**

markets becomes increasingly gray or cloudy, speculative demand for money increases as people seek to unload securities. As the outlook clears up and becomes more favorable, the speculative demand for money declines and people take the plunge and utilize money balances to purchase stocks and bonds.

Furthermore, one should notice from Figure 10.2 that the shape of the liquidity preference curve becomes flatter at lower interest rates. This is because Keynes believed that the interest elasticity of speculative demand for money increases as the interest rate declines. With lower interest rates, there is greater responsiveness of demand for money for interest rate changes. This needs more explanation. According to Keynes, people always hold in their minds a certain rate of interest which they think should normally prevail. Hence, the "normal" interest rate is the level toward which people expect the interest rate to gravitate.

The normal interest rate in people's minds is generated from past experience. If the current interest rate is much below the normal interest rate, people will expect the current rate to move back to normal. This is because movements in the current interest rate do not make people substantially revise expectations to the level of the normal interest rate. Now, if this theory applies to an individual, it also applies to a large extent to the economy as a whole. Thus, Lloyd Thomas clarifies it by stating:

> When one goes from the analysis of an individual to aggregate analysis, it is necessary to allow for the fact that different individuals have different conceptions regarding the normal level of interest rates. Keynes argued that the lower the current level of interest rate, the greater the number of people that will be convinced that the current rate is below the normal rate and, therefore, the greater number of people that believe the interest rate will rise and bond prices will decline. Therefore, according to Keynes, the lower the current interest rate, the lower will be the demand for bonds and the greater will be the demand for money.

In terms of Figure 10.2 at interest rate r_0, the normal interest rate "r_n" is lower than current; hence, the demand for money for speculation is quite low. At interest rate r_1, the normal interest rate (r_0) is above the current rate; hence, people expect the interest rate to move up in the future.

MONEY MARKET EQUILIBRIUM

In the money market, the demand for money and supply of money interact to determine the price of money, namely, the interest rate. Equilibrium in the money market is defined by an equality of demand and supply of money quantities. Demand for money, as we have just seen, is determined, in general, by national income (Y) and the interest rate. It holds a direct relationship with income and an inverse relationship with the interest rate. The supply of money is determined by the policies of a country's Central Bank. It is possible that their policies are dependent upon interest rates, but there is no reason for us to know it *a priori*. Hence, money supply is determined independently of the interest rate (or money supply is decided autonomously or exogenously). In Figure 10.3, we draw the downward sloping demand curve for money to show the inverse relationship between the interest rate and the demand for money. The money supply is shown by a vertical straight line to indicate the absence of a relationship between the supply of money and the interest rate. At the point of intersection of these straight lines, at point E, equilibrium in the money market is established. If interest rates are sufficiently flexible, then in the long run, r_0 is the only interest rate that would persist. As we have seen in the classical economists' case (Chapter 5), this is because at any interest rate above or below r_0, there would be pressure generated on the interest rate (by excess demand or excess supply) to move back to the r_0 level. The paradox of flexibility has application here. If the interest rate is flexible, then it will stay at equilibrium level.

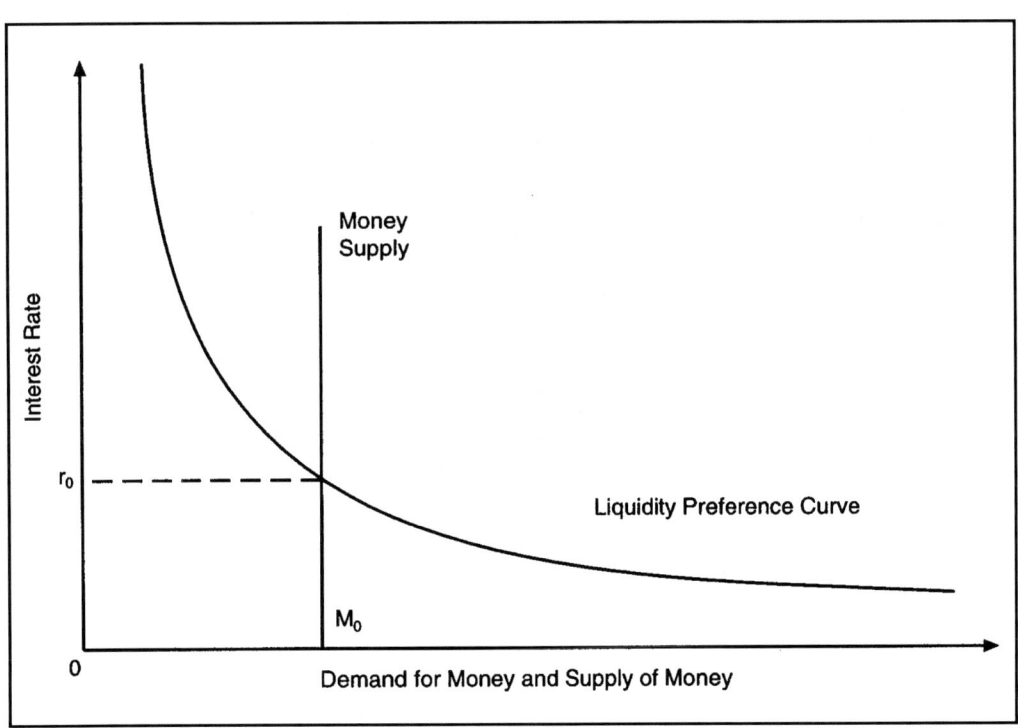

Equilibrium of Money Market ■ **FIGURE 10.3**

10.3 Effectiveness of Monetary Policy According to Keynes

In the Keynesian mind, monetary policy is effective only if it is able to affect the aggregate demand. Effectiveness of any policy is measured in terms of the change in real GDP that the policy can cause. In the Keynesian way of thinking, real GDP increases only if there is an increase in real aggregate demand. It is only through the multiplier process that any policy action can affect real GDP, after that policy change is able to increase the real aggregate demand of an economy. Monetary policy, which makes changes in the money supply, is responsible for the shifts in the vertical straight line in Figure 10.4.

A higher money supply would create a rightward shift in the money supply curve (and a lower money supply would create a leftward shift.). Assuming the same demand curve for money, we may conclude that higher liquidity in the economy creates a lower interest rate as equilibrium moves from point E to E'. In more practical terms, it is easy to prove that a higher money supply would create a lower interest rate. There are primarily two reasons for this effect. First, as money supply is raised, total bank deposits would go up, since the majority of the money supply is in the form of bank deposits. As bank deposits increase, the competition

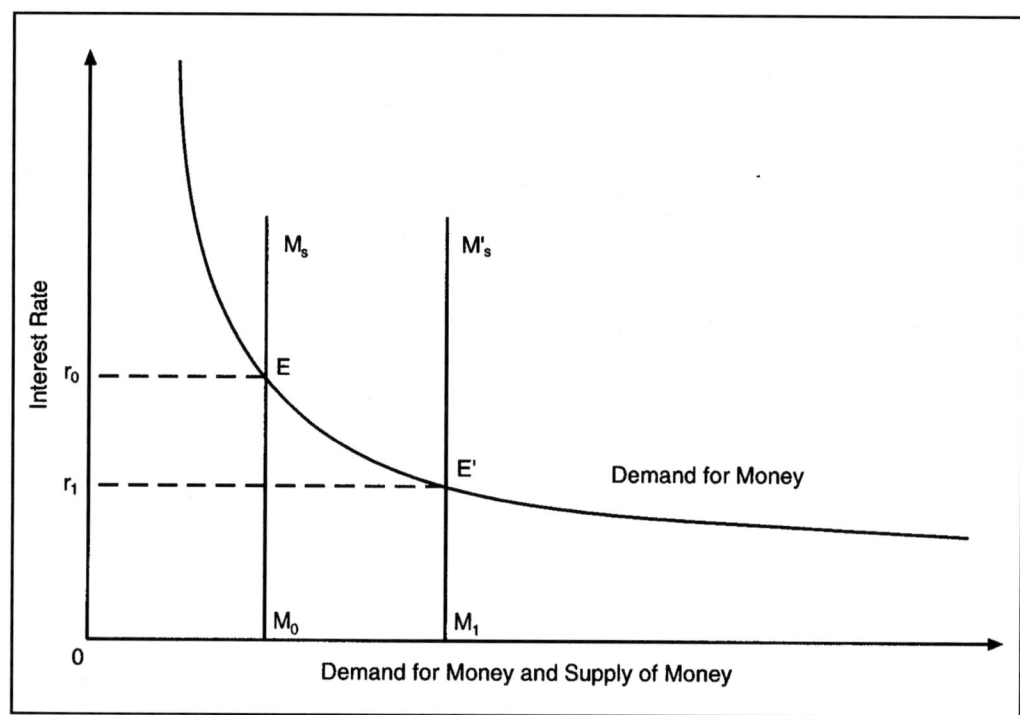

FIGURE 10.4 ■ Effectiveness of Monetary Policy: Keynesian View

of giving loans to the public would force the financial institutions to lower their interest rates. Hence, an increase in money supply would create lower interest rates. Second, the most active way to increase the money supply is by buying Treasury securities (or bonds) from the dealers on Wall Street via open market operations. However, as more Treasury bonds are bought by the Federal Reserve, the demand for bonds increases and the price of bonds increases. As we have learned before, the price of bonds is always inverse to interest rates, so as the bond price goes up, interest rates need to decline.

In the Keynesian system designed in Chapter 6, a lower interest rate would create a situation where Marginal Efficiency of Capital (MEC) would be greater than r_1. In this situation, producers would realize that it would be profitable to carry out investment activity; hence, the investment level would increase. In terms of Figure 10.5, with interest rate r_0, the optimal investment was I_0 and with the lower interest rate of r_1 the new investment would be I_1 which is higher than I_0.

Thus, in the Keynesian system, a higher money supply creates a lower interest rate, which creates higher investment. This increased investment sparks the multiplier process, which generates higher levels of real income. Therefore, in notational form, a chain of events of a change in M, causing a change in r, causing a change in I, causing a change in Y, can be designed and is elaborated upon by Keynes. This chain of events sometimes is referred to as the *Keynesian chain*.

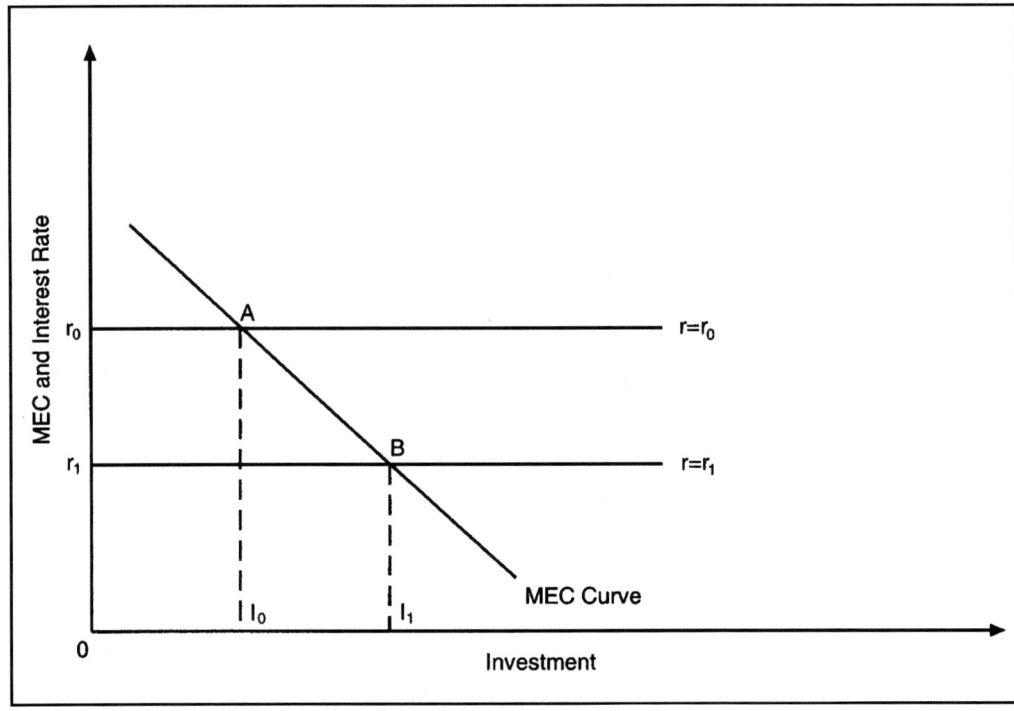

Investment Determination ■ **FIGURE 10.5**

According to Keynes, monetary policy is effective *via* the Keynesian chain alone. This explanation is in sharp contrast to the conclusions of quantity theory of the classical economists. In the classical economists' world, there was no need for the money supply to be changed because all it does is create inflation. In the Keynesian world, however, an increase in money supply has an ability to raise the GDP of the economy via the Keynesian chain.

Having said so much about the effectiveness of monetary policy, now is the time to ask ourselves the question: Why is Keynes popular for saying "Money does not matter"? To answer this question, we must consider a special case under which the Keynesian chain breaks down. This case is given by the existence of the liquidity trap.

Consider an extreme case when the interest rate becomes very, very low such as at the r_2 level. All persons in the economy would then expect that the normal interest rate level being r_0, cannot go down further in the future. It is, therefore, quite likely that in this special case no one in the economy would be interested in buying bonds. The demand for money for speculative purposes would be very, very high, almost to infinity. Obviously, the shape of the demand curve for money would become horizontal in this special case. This horizontal part of the demand curve for money is given a special name by Keynes. It is called the *liquidity trap*.

When interest rates are very low (as they were in the Great Depression), Keynes could easily visualize the existence of the liquidity trap. But here, the explanation of the liquidity trap's existence is not the main contribution of Keynes. Noticing the policy consequences of the existence of the liquidity trap is even more important. However, in order to understand that, we must first explain money market equilibrium.

In terms of Figure 10.6, let us assume that at a very low interest rate, like at r_3, a liquidity trap exists. When there is an increase in money supply before the liquidity trap (say from M_0 to M_1 to M_2), the Keynesian chain explains the effectiveness of monetary policy. However, after the money supply has reached the M_2 level (or the interest rate has become r_3), any expansionary policy ceases to be effective.

In other words, at point E_2, where the interest rate is r_3 and the money supply is M_2, any increase in the money supply is unable to reduce the interest rate; therefore, it is unable to increase investment and real income. In Keynes' view, in the case of liquidity trap, since the interest rate fails to decline, the increase in money supply will exert no impact on aggregate demand and GDP. The economy is stuck in what Keynes called the liquidity trap. It is in this case that Keynes would wholeheartedly say that money does not matter.

A situation like this was probably the reason why no monetary policy could become effective during the Great Depression of 1929–1933. To analyze problems

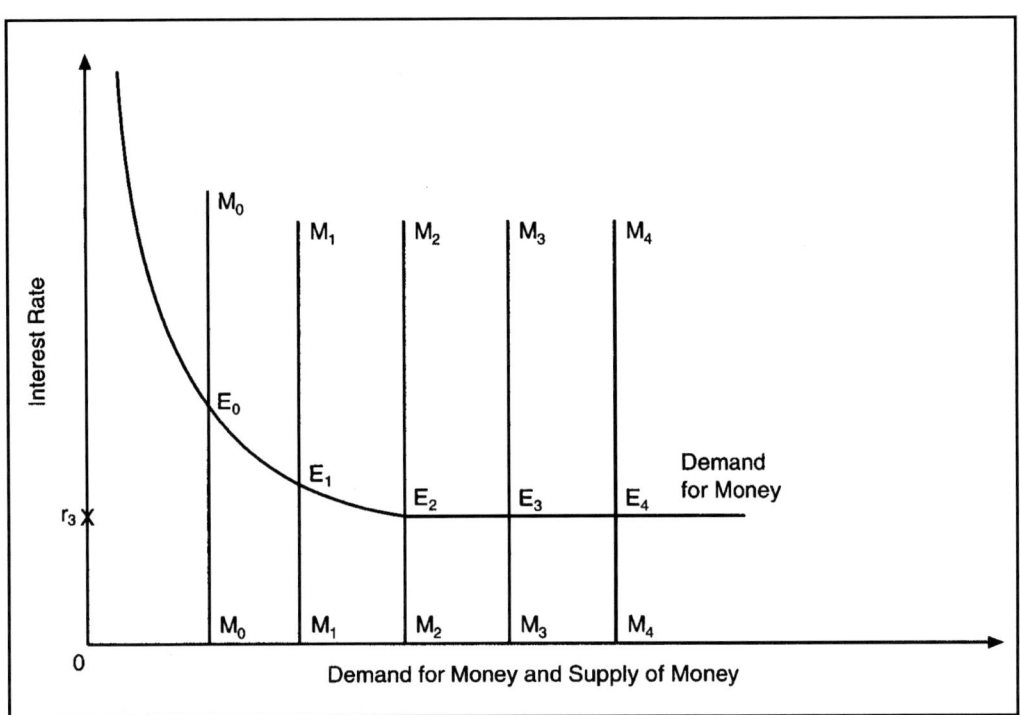

Liquidity Trap and Monetary Policy ■ FIGURE 10.6

faced by the world in the Great Depression, let us examine a sample case of the U.S. economy one more time here, by noting a few facts. From October 1929 to March 1933, the real GDP fell by about 30 percent, the unemployment rate increased from less than 4 percent to 25 percent, and the consumer price index fell about 25 percent. Money supply, defined as M_1 or M_2, showed a considerable decline, probably because of a large number of bank failures. Nonetheless, the monetary base, which is defined as bank reserves plus currency with the public and which is believed to be controllable by the Central Bank, showed an overall increase of 20 percent. If we extend the period through the end of 1935, the growth of the monetary base exceeded 75 percent.

Observing the above facts, Keynes would argue that a policy of "easy money" (increase in monetary base) was in fact instituted by the Federal Reserve but was unsuccessful. What was required in this case, according to Keynes, was massive fiscal actions such as an increase in government expenditure or tax reductions. Given these conditions, there was nothing the Federal Reserve could have done to extract the economy from depression.

Money market analysis described in this chapter was the basic interpretation of Keynes regarding the demand and supply of money. We have also seen that due to the existence of a liquidity trap, monetary policy becomes completely ineffective.

Hence, the best monetary policy can do is to keep money supply consistently at the level at which the interest rate is as minimal as possible. If the interest rate happens to be greater than r_3 in Figure 10.5, monetary policy should pump more money into the economy to bring it down. In short, monetary policy should keep interest rates at a certain minimum level. This type of policy recommendation is known as "pegging the interest rate."

According to Keynes, optimum monetary policy will always follow the "pegging the interest rate" recommendation, since the economy will eventually be stuck in the liquidity trap. In the liquidity trap, money does not matter, and the existence of the liquidity trap sets a limit to the effectiveness of monetary policy. This analysis clearly places fiscal policy above monetary policy. The former does not have any limit to its effectiveness, as changes in government expenditure directly affect the aggregate demand and real GDP of the economy by getting the multiplier process underway. Thus, fiscal policy should be the primary policy of the government, which is anxious to take its economy to full employment. The monetary policy is subordinate, secondary, and inferior to fiscal policy, and should be used as a supplement to the fiscal policy.

Having seen these special Keynesian feelings about government activism, our task is to move one step further and find out what could be the criticisms of such a recommendation. But we take up that task in future chapters when we consider the monetarist analysis. Monetarists are a group of people who believe in a very passive government compared to Keynes, and who rely on market mechanisms to solve economic problems. They obviously disregard the Keynesian analysis of government activism on theoretical, as well as practical, bases.

Suggested Further Reading

Baumol, W. J. 1952. The transactions demand for cash: an inventory theoretic approach. *Quarterly Journal of Economics,* Vol. 66, November: 545–56.

Brunner, K. and A. Meltzer. 1968. Liquidity traps for money, bank credit and interest rates. *Journal of Political Economy,* Vol. 76, February: 1–37.

Goldfeld, S. 1973. The demand for money revisited. *Brookings Papers on Economic Activity,* Issue 3: 577–638.

Havrilesky, T. and J. Boorman. *Monetary Macroeconomics,* Chapters 7 and 8. Chicago, Illinois: Harlan Davidson Inc.

Jones, D. 1965. *The Demand for Money: A Review of the Empirical Literature,* Staff Economic Studies of the Federal Reserve System.

Kaufman, G. 1969. More on an empirical definition of money. *American Economic Review,* Vol. 59, March: 78–87.

Keynes, J. M. 1936. *General Theory of Employment, Interest and Money,* Chapters 13 and 15. New York: Harcourt, Brace and World, Inc.

Konstas, P. and M. W. Khouja. 1969. The Keynesian demand for money function. Another look and some additional evidence. *Journal of Money, Credit and Banking,* Vol. 1, November: 765–77.

Laidler, D. 1977. *The Demand for Money—Theories and Evidence,* 2nd ed. New York: Dun-Donnelly Publishing Corp.

Thomas, L. 1982. *Money, Banking and Economic Activity,* Chapter 14. Prentice-Hall Inc.

Tobin, J. 1956. The interest elasticity of transactions demand for cash. *Review for Economics and Statistics:* 241–47.

Chapter 11

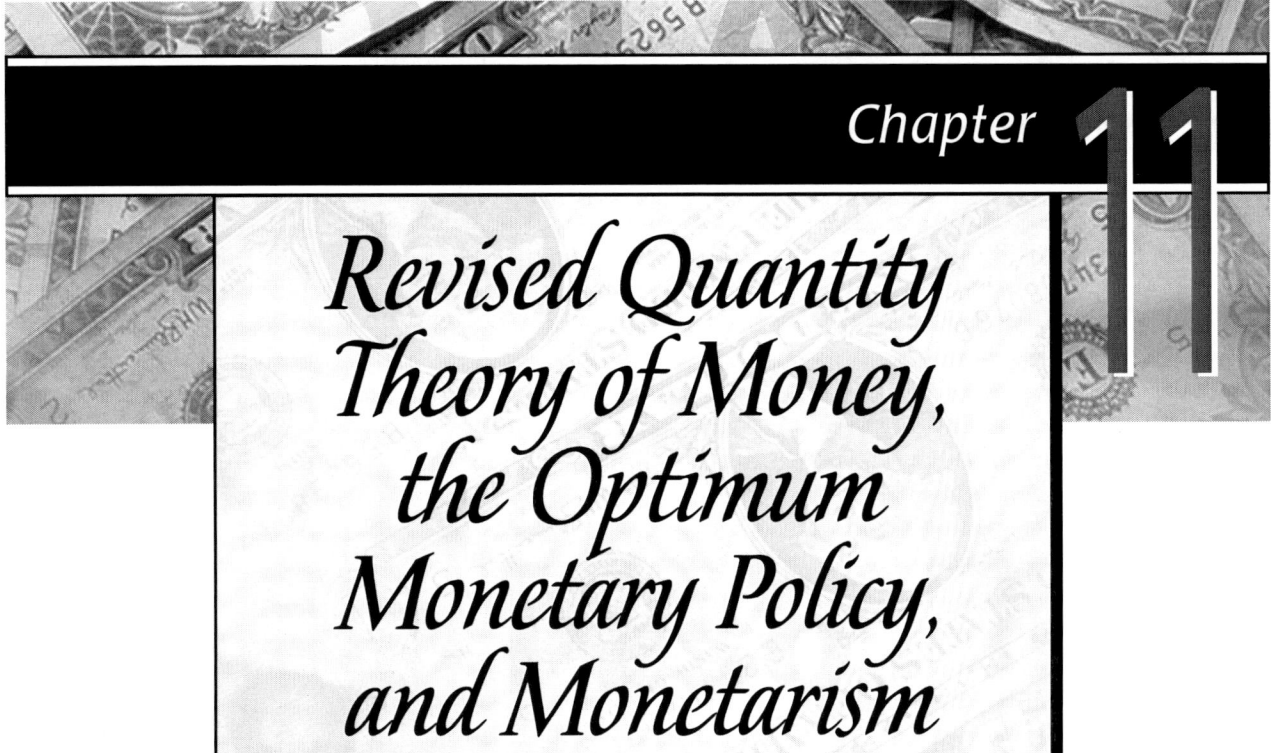

Revised Quantity Theory of Money, the Optimum Monetary Policy, and Monetarism

SUMMARY

The widespread application of Keynes' recommendations of government activism in the economy helped spread growth and prosperity in the immediate decades subsequent to World War II. By the late 1960s, however, this prosperity came to a standstill as stagflation began to rear its ugly head. Because Keynesians could not proffer a solution to the simultaneous existence of inflation and unemployment, an updated quantity theory of money was sorely needed.

The monetarists, led by Milton Friedman, provided such a theory. Monetarism did not arise out of a single text, but rather has its roots in a variety of studies that extended the earlier work of Irving Fisher. Monetarists assert that the extensive growth of money supply, a consequence of government economic activism, stimulates inflation in the long run. To prove these assertions, monetarists revised the equation of exchange introduced in Fisher's quantity theory of money, MV = PY, to show the stability of the velocity of money. According to the monetarists, the velocity of money is determined by the demand for money, such that the velocity of money declines as people demand more money in terms of cash. Because the main components of money demand, permanent income and the general price level, are stable, the demand for money is also stable—and by extension the velocity of money must also be stable. Hence, they successfully demonstrated that because the velocity of money (V) is stable over the long run, then any increase in money supply (M) can either increase the general price level (P), or raise national income

(Y), or both. Logically, any excessive increase in the general price level is due to an excessive increase in the money supply.

One can distinguish a few significant differences between the Keynesian and monetarist frameworks. For example, Keynes believed that the interest rate was the primary determinant of money demand. As mentioned above, monetarists perceive permanent income and the general price level as the main determinants of money demand. This conceptual difference is due to the broader monetarist definition of wealth, which includes all assets rather than just money and bonds. Consequently, money demand in the monetarist framework is less sensitive to the interest rate. Moreover, monetarists believe that the transmission mechanism for monetary policy is more direct than what Keynes presumes. The demand for money curve will shift as a result of an increase in money supply, rather than remain fixed like Keynes argues. This curve shifts because of three important effects: liquidity effect, income effect, and price effect. While the liquidity effect reduces the interest rate much like Keynes asserts, this is only temporary. The income and price effects exert upward pressures on the interest rate, and if these latter effects are greater in magnitude than the first, this will lead to higher, not lower, interest rates. Hence, the monetarist approach is much broader than that of Keynes, who only considered the liquidity effect. Finally, unlike Keynes, monetarists contend that expansionary fiscal policy crowds out private investment and stifles economic activity, leading to economic stagnation. This is known as the crowding out hypothesis.

Unsurprisingly, the new quantity theory of money implies that fiscal and monetary policy should be very conservative and non-interventionist. Monetarists recommend that national monetary authorities implement a strict monetary rule—an annual increase in the money supply of only 4 percent. Several potential benefits of adhering to this strict monetary rule have been put forward, including a cessation of severe business cycle fluctuations and an ability to achieve stability in aggregate demand with greater ease. These professed benefits of the monetary rule notwithstanding, monetary authorities are reluctant to adopt it because there are a number of practical problems with its implementation. It is quite difficult to estimate the velocity of money, and the money supply is also difficult to define and measure. Lastly, adoption of the monetary rule does not spell the end of inflation. This is because monetary rule can cure only one type of inflation, namely the demand-pull inflation.

11.1 Introduction

As we mentioned before, Sir John M. Keynes was not only the most prolific contributor of macro-monetary theory of the 1930s, he was also an influential practitioner of his advocacies. He traveled extensively to introduce the theories he developed to policymakers. He actively influenced the governmental authorities to practice his solution directly or indirectly in their policy actions, and was involved in a great share of policy making in the United Kingdom.

In several ways, Keynes (and his followers after his death, aptly termed "Keynesians") became successful in his persuasion. On the political side, the Keynesian recommendations looked too attractive to avoid their practical implementation. In essence, Keynes advocated that an active government that undertakes social projects of reconstruction is beneficial for economic growth and is a step forward in achieving the objective of full employment. What government would deprive itself of an opportunity of spending more and being politically popular? Classic examples of governments that wholeheartedly approved of Keynesian philosophies are the governments of several industrialized economies, including those of the United States, United Kingdom, Italy, France, the Netherlands, and Canada. Keynesianism was also adopted by some developing countries such as India, Pakistan, Kenya, and Ghana.

For several years, the policy recommendations by Keynes were profitable in terms of achieving economic growth and prosperity. In general, for about 20 to 25 years, the capitalistic economies overwhelmed themselves with the gains of government activism and by the adoption of a new line of economic thought proposed by the Keynesian revolution. Together with this increased governmental role in the economy, and due to the destruction created by World War II in the 1940s, the continued industrial development in those days, the relatively lower population compared to modern times, and the availability of several unused natural resources, the 1950s and 1960s were the most glamorous years of economic prosperity for the Western world.

However, by the late 1960s, the era of prosperity started to see some sparks. As over-anxious government activism created an excessive growth in the money supply and government expenditures, economies started approaching a saturation point, world population started increasing faster, and inflation and unemployment existed simultaneously. The Keynesian advocacy of an active government sector started yielding greater harm than good to economies, and the time started approaching when Keynesian economists could not find an answer to the mysterious phenomenon of simultaneous inflation and unemployment, popularly called "stagflation." At about this time, the University of Chicago gave birth to a new economic philosophy, which claimed that the answer to the question of stagflation lay in the disregard held by Keynesians to the quantity theory equation and overactive governments all over the world.

A group of economists, then partly at the University of Chicago and partly elsewhere, who regarded excessive money supply growth as a basic reason for inflation, were known as "monetarists," and Professor Milton Friedman of the Hoover Institution at Stanford University (who completed substantial work at the University of Chicago and died in 2006 at the age of 94) was considered to be the leader of this group. The economic theories espoused by monetarists are termed "monetarism" (initially coined by Professor Karl Brunner of Rochester University).

Among several theories put forward by Professor Friedman before and after receiving the Nobel Prize in Economics in 1976, the most relevant idea for the present chapter is the "Revised Quantity Theory of Money."

11.2 Further Developments in the Quantity Theory of Money

Even if Friedman's work was that of a pioneer in the quantity theory of money, contributions are also attributed to several other economists. Notable among these are Don Patinkin of Hebrew University, who had his own statement of quantity theory, Anderson and Jordon who showed the impact of money supply on income and prices, and Brunner and Meltzer who presented empirical evidence that the demand for money is stable in a way that supports the quantity theory.

Thus, monetarism has evolved not out of any single book, but from a variety of studies and theories supporting the basic fact that in the long run, extensive growth of the money supply is the fundamental reason for economic problems. In general, the monetarists concentrate on the long-term effects of the policies, while Keynesians believe that "in the long run, we are all dead."

The main reason why Friedman feels that "all inflations always and everywhere are a monetary phenomenon" is his argument that the quantity theory equation, if correctly interpreted, is not a bad equation after all.

From the quantity theory equation developed in earlier chapters and expressed as $MV = PY$, if the velocity of money is shown to be stable in the long run, then any increase in money supply (M) can either increase the general price level (P) or raise national income (Y), or raise both P and Y.

When the economy is close to full employment, changes in Y are much more difficult and an increase in M leads to a higher increase in P than in Y. On the other hand, if the economy is far from full employment, then an increase in Y is quite possible; hence, expansionary monetary policy leads to a higher increase in Y than in P. Therefore, it is wrong to presume that "Money does not matter" as Keynes implied in his writings, especially in the case of the liquidity trap.

In fact, according to Friedman and monetarists, monetary policy is quite a powerful policy, and "money does matter." Hence, monetarists argue that if the velocity of money is proven to be stable, then changes in the money supply are quite effective in making changes in P and/or Y. Moreover, anytime one observes an excessive increase in P (say inflation), the main cause is an excessive increase in the money supply.

In the above analysis, the important part is to show the stability of velocity of money. It can be easily recognized that the unique determinant of velocity of money is the demand for money. If people wish to hold more money in terms of cash, the turnover rate of money declines; hence, velocity also declines. The demand for money is therefore negatively related to its velocity. Thus, to show the velocity of money to be stable, we need to show that the demand for money is also stable.

Hence, the stability of demand for money becomes an important condition to show the effect of the money supply on general price levels. In the words of Peterson, "We may characterize income-expenditure theory as a theory of the demand for output as a whole cast in the framework of the aggregate demand function (C + I + G, in a closed economy)."

By analogy, the modern monetarist theory can be characterized as a similar theory cast in the framework of a demand for money function that explains how the money supply affects the performance of the economic system. The demand for money is the fundamental behavioral relationship in monetarist theory. According to Friedman, "The demand for money is a stable function of a set of variables that affects the demand for any other good."

Moreover, monetarists believe that the demand for money function is more stable than the multiplier (K) that Keynes has heavily emphasized, and therefore an effect of money supply is more direct and consistent (than the effect of investment) on the output and employment of an economy. But defining money as a "temporary abode for generalized purchasing power," Friedman claims that people demand money for the same reasons as they demand any other good. The most significant determinants of demand for any other goods are: (1) total wealth of the household or firm, (2) the opportunity cost of holding the goods, and (3) the tastes and preferences of the wealth holding unit.

The wealth of the household or business firm consists of the permanent level of income (Y) the household earns in a given time period and the ratio of non-human to human wealth (H). The permanent level of income, according to

Friedman, is the level of income that is adjusted for transitory changes like windfall losses or gains. Hence, it is defined after omitting the sudden increase in income due to factors like a Christmas bonus or lottery gain and sudden losses like those due to natural calamities.

The second part of wealth, viz. human capital, consists of an individual's inherited and acquired skills and training. This may also include the psychological factors such as habits of the public for making transactions, work culture, health of workers, etc. So, inclusion of this explanatory variable was to be consistent with the Fisherian way of explaining the determinants of velocity of money. In principle, the value of human capital would be equal to "the discounted value of the future income stream that an individual could expect to obtain from all of his education and training." Friedman believes that holding money balances, like the demand for education and recreation, is a luxury. Therefore, as wealth increases, the demand for money is expected to increase more than in proportion to the increase in wealth.

In more technical terms, this means that the elasticity of demand for money with respect to wealth is greater in proportion than the increase in wealth. This also means that the expected elasticity of demand for money with respect to wealth is greater than one. Besides wealth, Friedman essentially regards "permanent" level of income (GDP) as another determinant of money demand. There is a difference between "current" or actual level of GDP and the permanent level of GDP. The latter excludes all the transitory (short-term) changes in current GDP. For example, when there is only a two week disturbance in current GDP (say if there is an earthquake or floods), would the whole economy change the demand for money? The answer, according to monetarists, is no. Hence, the expected determinant of money demand is the permanent level of GDP calculated as the current GDP-transitory changes in current GDP.

The next expected determinant of money demand is the general price level (P). The effect of the price level on nominal demand for money is positive and is straightforward to explain. An increase in the price level will result in a proportionate increase in the demand for money. This must occur if people wish to keep money balances constant in real terms. The general price level's effect is more important when price changes are larger than when they are by a few percentage points. The direct cost of holding money is, of course, the rate of interest. To accept on a theoretical level that the interest rate is a determinant of demand for money is to align oneself with Keynesianism.

As we saw while discussing the Keynesian theory of liquidity preference, the demand for money for asset purposes changes inversely with the interest rate. According to Friedman, the cost of holding money can also be seen in terms of an increase in the "expected" price level. An increase in it has an effect of making the demand for money more costly, since the market value of other assets would rise if the demand for real balances is reduced.

Lastly, the third major determinant of demand for money as seen by Friedman is tastes and preferences. However, Friedman contends, "the tastes and preferences of wealth owning units . . . must in general simply be taken for granted in determining the form of the demand function. . . . it will generally have to be supposed that tastes are consistent over significant stretches of space and time." Hence, the short-run changes in the demand for money are not expected to occur due to habitual or taste changes of the money-holding persons.

All in all, Friedman sees the demand for money to be a function of:

a. permanent income,
b. the general price level,
c. the rate of interest on equities,
d. the interest rate on bonds,
e. wealth, and
f. human capital.

Among the six determinants above, when tested for empirical evidence, the most significant are general price level and permanent income. The effect of the interest rate on the demand for money is negligible, if at all. One reason for this low interest rate elasticity of demand for money is the definition of wealth, which includes all assets, rather than Keynes' assumption that the choice is between money and bonds.

Monetarists' definition of assets includes both producer and consumer durable goods. A low interest rate elasticity of demand for money results because given several (assets) options, people do not have the willingness to hold money as an asset. Hence, the demand for money is less responsive to the rate of return being obtained on other financial assets, especially bonds. As we saw before, in Keynesian analysis, people only have two options for holding several assets; bonds and money. And when people have limited choices, the demand for money becomes very sensitive to changes in interest rates. In terms of Figure 11.1, the Keynesian demand curve for money is shown to be flatter than the monetarists' demand curve for money. This shows that money demand is more sensitive to changes in the interest rate in Keynesian analysis than in monetarists' analysis. In fact, in an extreme case of a liquidity trap, demand for money is very sensitive to changes in interest rates, making the elasticity of money demand with respect to interest rate changes to be equal to infinity.

Friedman and monetarists believe that since people have several financial assets to choose from, any excess money balances "will spill over directly into the spending stream for goods and services, primarily because the substitution effect

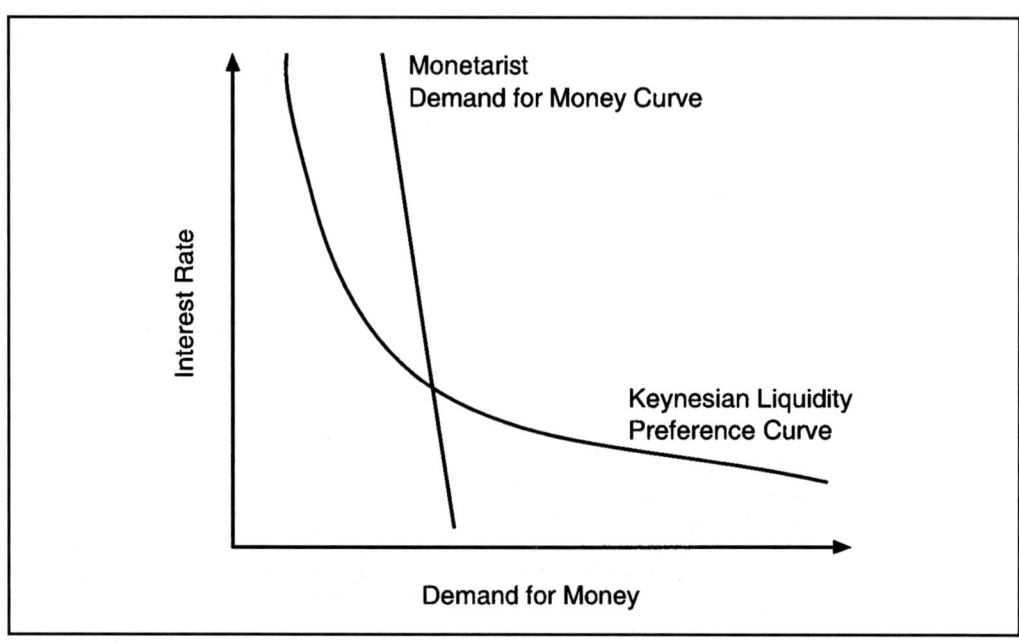

FIGURE 11.1 ■ Demand for Money: Two Interpretations

between money and the range of financial assets available to the firm or the household is small" (see Peterson, listed in the Further Reading list, p. 381). Thus, monetarists believe that money demand is not very sensitive to interest rate changes.

When tested empirically, Friedman finds that there are two significant determinants of money demands; permanent level of income and the price level. Since permanent level of income by definition is stable, and since price level can be stable if money supply is stable, the demand for money is inherently a stable function. And since demand for money is shown to be stable, the velocity of money is also stable. Thus, the main reason for revising the quantity theory was to show the stability of demand for money and therefore, in essence, the stability of velocity of money.

11.3 Transmission Mechanism for Monetary Policy: Monetarists' View

The next important question to ask the monetarists is: How does an increase in the money supply make changes in other economic variables? In other words, what is the transmission mechanism for the monetary policy change? That question can be answered in terms of Figure 11.2, where money market equilibrium is at point J and where the quantity of money demanded is equal to the quantity of

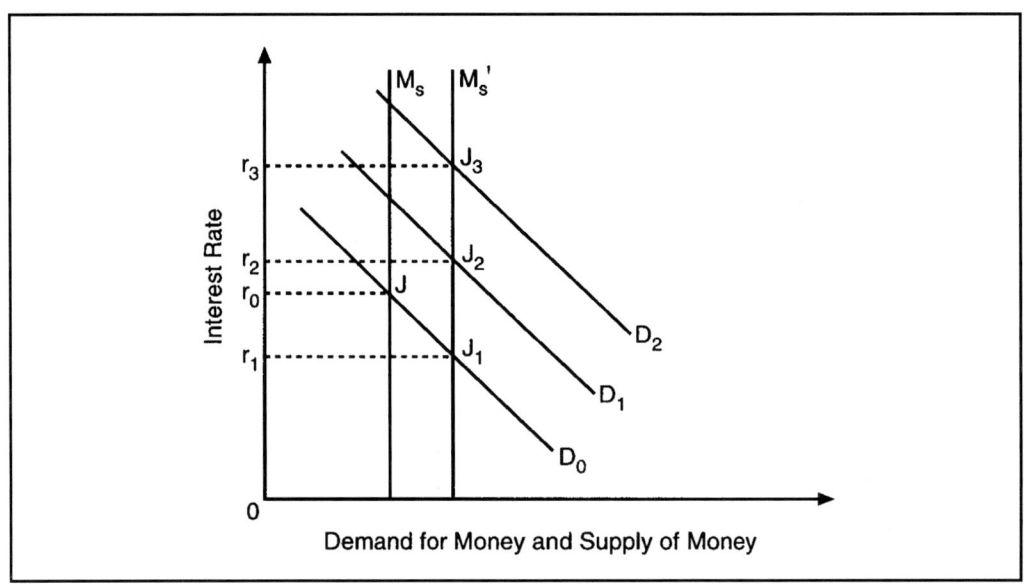

Money Market-Equilibrium ■ **FIGURE 11.2**

money supplied. According to monetarists, the Keynesian view that with the increase in money supply there is a reduction in the interest rate is oversimplified. In Friedman's view, when there is an increase in money supply, the demand for money curve does not remain fixed but is likely to shift. There are three separate effects of a change in money supply upon the interest rate, viz. liquidity effect, income effect, and the price effect.

LIQUIDITY EFFECT

Due to an increase in the money supply, the vertical line in Figure 11.2, representing money supply, moves to the right. This establishes a new temporary equilibrium at point J_1 with a lower equilibrium interest rate of r_1. The result of a lower interest rate due to the liquidity effect can easily be explained through common sense. The increase in overall liquidity of the public would require banks to charge lower interest rates. This is the same effect that was initially explained by Keynes (and which we saw in Chapter 6). So in this instance, monetarists are in agreement with Keynesians that there is a liquidity effect after an increase in money supply.

INCOME EFFECT

With higher liquidity available, however, and with lower interests rate temporarily resulting from higher money supply, people tend to increase their spending on goods, services, securities, etc. There is also higher investment that results in higher national income. Moreover, as one can observe from the quantity theory equation, an increase in the money supply is directly responsible for an increase in real GDP. This higher national income becomes responsible for shifting the demand for money curve to the right. In terms of Figure 11.2, the rightward shift of the demand for money curve establishes the new equilibrium, which also happens to be temporary, at point J_2 with a higher interest rate of r_2.

PRICE EFFECT

The increased money supply also has a positive effect on the general price level (P) as seen from the quantity theory equation $MV = PY$. This also influences the level of expected inflation rate. As people expect a higher inflation rate, the demand for money curve shifts rightward one more time. The final equilibrium is achieved at point J_3 with interest rate r_3.

In Thomas' terms, "We thus have an initial liquidity effect which tends to reduce interest rates followed by an income effect and a price expectation effect, both of which exert upward pressure upon interest rates." Friedman concludes that the net effect of money supply on the interest rate can be positive (instead of negative as Keynesians firmly believe). Moreover, increased money supply can lead to an increase in the interest rate, with a greater possibility when monetary growth is rapid.

In terms of Figure 11.2, the net effect on interest rates would be decided by the strength of liquidity, income, and price effects. The strengths of income and price effects would decide the extent of the shift of the demand for money curve. If the liquidity effect is greater than income and expected price effects are taken together, then an increase in money supply would lead to a reduced interest rate.

However, if price and income effects are greater than the liquidity effect, then an increase in the money supply may lead to an increase in the interest rate. One thing is clear. Depending upon the state of the economy, there are time lags involved in completing the three effects discussed above. Even though the start is taking place when money supply is increased, they may or may not be finished at the same time.

Obviously, these time lags can determine the net effect on the interest rate of the money supply. The experience of the 1970s in several industrialized countries has proved this theoretical explanation to be valid, so that when money supply changes were rapid, they in fact led to higher interest rates.

Thus, we can easily see that in comparison to Keynesian theory, Friedman's explanation is much broader. While Keynes could see only the liquidity effect, Friedman's theory was the first celebrated attempt to recognize all three effects simultaneously.

11.4 Policy Implications of the New Quantity Theory

One of the main reasons why the monetarists' theory had become extremely popular is its applicability to the experiences of several economies in the 1970s. That was the decade in which economies experienced an increase in money supply simultaneous to the increase (not decrease) in interest rates.

The Keynesian explanation was too naive to analyze a phenomenon such as this, because Keynes could not recognize how an increase in money supply could lead to an increase in interest rates. Obviously, in Friedman's terms, the strengths of income and price expectation effect were greater than the liquidity effect, which lead to higher, not lower, interest rates. The possibility that higher money supply can lead to higher interest rates, and the certainty that it would lead to inflation, especially when the economy has used most of its resources (and output level is inflexible), have led to monetarists' recommendation of following a monetary rule in the performance of the monetary policy.

The recommendation of a monetary rule has basically emerged from Friedman's 1948 article and 1960 book on this topic. Even if the exact percentage of increase in money supply that is expected is of little importance even to the monetarist, Friedman, by analyzing the case of the U.S. economy, has come up with 4 percent as the answer.

He arrived at the monetary rule of an annual 4 percent increase in money supply as the most optimal solution (by monetary policy) by making some assumptions and some arguments concerning the behavior of four variables that form the equation of exchange ($MV = PY$). He assumed that the velocity of money is expected to go down in the future because of his "luxury goods" thesis.

The luxury goods thesis claims that demand for money is like a demand for a luxury good, which means an increase in income would make an increase in its demand, and also it has an income elasticity greater than one. Hence, as real GDP increases, the demand for money increases, and then velocity of money (V) is expected to decrease. Moreover, Friedman pointed out that the United States' real GDP historically has been growing at a 3% rate, which would lead to higher money demand and lower velocity of money. Hence, he expected velocity of money to decline at an average annual rate of 1 percent. Therefore, to have a non-inflationary U.S. economy (that is, P being constant), the money supply (M) must go up with an annual average rate of 4 percent. Hence, the magic figure of "4 percent" growth in money supply is an ideal monetary policy to follow.

After Friedman wrote his article in 1948 about this monetary rule, unfortunately for monetarists the velocity of money measured by using M1 (or even M2) money supply definitions in the U.S. has not shown the expected decline. In recent times, several monetarists, including Friedman, agree that an adjustment in the strict "4 percent" rule is desirable.

Nonetheless, to support the recommendation of the monetary rule, monetarists have put forward several important benefits. First, they argue that an adoption of some kind of monetary rule may end the drastic and severe business fluctuations that are caused by the actual and expected monetary instability. The actual dramatic changes in the growth rates of money supply alter the spending behavior of the public. Also, the instability in the money supply growth rate causes people to expect future instability in the money supply, and business fluctuations are the obvious result. Friedman believes that if a constant money supply growth rule had been used by the Federal Reserve since its inception in 1914, the U.S. economy would have been spared all of the major inflations and depressions and some of the less severe fluctuations.

It is alleged by monetarists that the Federal Reserve on the balance has destabilized the U.S. economy and has thus been a disturbing factor in post-World War I U.S. economic history. Thus, according to monetarists, the number of business cycles would be drastically reduced (and less severe) if a monetary rule was obeyed.

Second, monetary policy of an economy has only one objective to achieve, and that is to stabilize the aggregate demand level of an economy. By implementing the monetary rule, the monetary policy would certainly be able to achieve that. However, in practice, monetary authorities of several countries try to achieve many more objectives than they can handle. For example, authorities assume that stabilization of interest rates, stabilization of business fluctuation, controlling the value of domestic currency (exchange rate stabilization), and achievement of economic growth are all their responsibilities. With these optimistic views, the monetary authorities let the money supply grow at a varied rate.

Strictly speaking, they should concentrate on only one objective of stabilizing aggregate demand, and if they do, then monetary rule is the best policy option. Hence, according to monetarists, another main benefit of adopting monetary rule is to reduce the overall (unnecessary) activism of monetary policy.

Third, by adopting the monetary rule, the monetary authorities would interfere less in economic affairs. This would reduce the pressure on executive and legislative branches of government. Several governmental institutions could be wiped out in this fashion, reducing the tremendous administrative costs. For example, an adoption of a 4 percent rule in the United States would make it unnecessary to have a wage and price control board, or the Federal Reserve Board or the Federal Open Market Committee (FOMC).

With added stability in economic performance, too much activism on fiscal policy would also seem to be unnecessary, and the number of bank failures would be reduced. In general, the proponents of monetary rule assert that there would be an overall stability in an economy with less government intervention. Therefore, the saving of administrative costs would result by following the monetary rule.

It appears from the above discussion that monetarists have a valid point in proposing the monetary rule as the desirable policy path for monetary authorities. However, there are several points that can be made that may explain why monetary authorities of several countries were quite reluctant in accepting any kind of monetary rule as a policy guideline. One such problem in adopting a monetary rule has already been pointed out. It originates from the inability of correctly estimating the behavior of the income velocity of money (V in the quantity theory equation). As was shown later, Friedman incorrectly assumed velocity to decline by a 1 percent annual rate in the future. The experience has evidenced that no consistent reduction rate in velocity of money was observed. Moreover, the velocity of money did show several inconsistent cyclical fluctuations, making it difficult to envision any constant growth rate of money supply desirable for policy.

Hence, even monetarists have modified their demand for adopting a monetary rule. Their recent inclination for optimum monetary policy suggests a "moderate" rather than "constant" growth rate of money supply. But, even if we accept this new meaning of monetary rule, there are practical problems in its complete adoption. This leads us to the second point against the adoption of a monetary rule, which recognizes the difficulty in defining (and measuring) money supply itself. As we saw in Chapter 7, there is just not one acceptable definition of money supply. The inability to arrive at a clear consensus regarding the proper definition of money supply raises severe problems. In the words of Tobin, "Sometimes Friedman and his followers seem to by saying: We don't know what money is, but whatever it is, its stock should grow steadily at 3 to 4 percent."

Another point the neo-Keynesians put forward is that in modern times monetary policy should be responsible for a series of objectives. These objectives include the stability of price level, interest rate, bond market fluctuations, and exchange rate fluctuations. In order to achieve all these objectives, monetary authorities need more, not less, discretion while changing money supply. The monetary rule does not allow monetary authorities to change money supply according to their discretion, and hence, is undesirable.

Also, modern developments in research techniques, use of computers, more information, and better forecasting methods have created a strong justification for a discretionary monetary policy, rather than the one that simply applies the rule. Because of all the above reasons, even if monetary policies have failed in the past, there is ample evidence to expect they could do a better job in the future.

Lastly, several economists were eager to point out that the adoption of a monetary rule by itself did not mean the end of the inflation era. This is because monetary rule can cure only one type of inflation, namely the demand-pull inflation. There is still another type of inflation, referred to as cost-push inflation, which occurs due to a decline in the aggregate supply of the economy that can be cured only by technological advancement, higher labor productivity, and renewed availability of resources.

Thus, the monetary rule, even if adopted, is not going to end all inflation. The recognition of different types of inflation seriously questions the desirability and sufficiency of the monetary rule adoption. Taking all of the above points together makes a very strong case for rejection of the proposal of the constancy of money supply growth rate. In practice, no country has clearly adopted the monetary rule, but in the United States, when inflation seemed out of hand in October 1979, the Federal Reserve did make a shift in its objectives from the stability of the interest rate to the stability of monetary aggregates.

11.5 Crowding Out Hypothesis and Effectiveness (Ineffectiveness) of Fiscal Policy

In the earlier section, we have seen the monetarist views about monetary policy effectiveness and their proposal of monetary rule. In this section we shall try to analyze the monetarist hypothesis about the effectiveness of fiscal policy. As mentioned before, fiscal policy concerns itself with tax and government expenditure changes. Moreover, a pure fiscal policy is the one that carries out tax and government expenditure changes without changes in the money supply of an economy. When government expenditure is greater than tax revenues, we say that the government budget is in deficit; if the reverse is the case, the government budget is in surplus; when government expenditure is matched by the tax revenues, the budget is balanced.

As you may recall, Keynes and Keynesians were in favor of expansionary fiscal policy, at least when there were unused resources in the economy. In other words, carrying out a deficit in the government's budget was not only understandable but a desirable action for Keynesians. Monetarists, on the other hand, hold the view that pure fiscal policy in the long run is unable to increase GDP in the economy. National debt is created when governments sell bonds to the public to finance the expenditure that is incurred over and above tax revenues. As the bonds are sold to the public, the supply of bonds increases, which reduces the price and increases the interest rate. An increase in the interest rate becomes responsible for lower investment, especially when the interest rate is higher than the expected profit rate (MEC).

The events that have been explained in the above chain are the main ingredients of an argument called the "crowding out hypothesis." In Carlson and Spencer's words, "If an increase in government demand, financed by either taxes or debt issuance to the public, fails to stimulate total economic activity, the private sector is said to have been crowded out by the government action."

Crowding out initially was put forward by Anderson and Jordon (1968), who indicated that an initial positive effect of expansionary fiscal policy is compensated by negative effects in the later quarters so that in the long run, an increase in government expenditure has almost zero effect on an economy's output.

There are several explanations for such crowding out to take place on a theoretical basis. First, Friedman and others explain crowding out by stressing that "expansionary" fiscal action might first be reflected in a rise in output, but the financing of the deficit would set in motion contradictory forces that would eventually offset the initial stimulation effect. One of the main reasons why an offsetting effect can take place is the increased interest rate due to added supply of bonds that the government generates to finance the deficit.

One other interesting explanation of the possible crowding out phenomenon is found in Keynes' *General Theory* itself. While Keynes was anxious to point out the expectations and confidence of the producers in determining investment, he was cautious enough to see the possibility that government spending could adversely affect the confidence of the private sector. More specifically, as stated in *General Theory*, "With the confused psychology which often prevails, the government program may through its effect on 'confidence' increase liquidity preference or diminish the marginal efficiency of capital, which, again may retard other investment unless measures are taken to offset it."

Appealing to Denison's law, which says that the ratio of private saving to national income is stable, David and Scadding assert that increased bond sales by government necessarily displaces private bond sales. Hence, the domestic investment is reduced by an equal amount of deficit spending. If the ultra-rationality assumption is really correct, then a complete crowding out effect is inevitable. A complete crowding out is said to have occurred when an increase in government expenditure is completely offset by a decline in domestic investment.

From the above, one can see that monetarists regard monetary policy to be more direct in its effectiveness and fiscal policy to be of less importance because of the crowding out. To summarize this chapter, we can make the case for monetarism by noting the following important points:

1. Monetarists believe that demand for money is a stable function of the permanent level of income and is predictable; hence, velocity of money is stable and predictable.

2. As a corollary of point 1, since velocity of money is stable, any excessive increase in money supply leads to an increase in price level and, therefore, inflation.

3. Monetary policy has direct effects on the economy; hence, it should be carried out with extreme caution. More specifically, monetary authorities should obey the constant money supply growth rate rule, called "monetary rule," for the stability of the inflation rate.

4. Fiscal policy has a limited (or no) effect on the GDP of an economy because of the crowding out hypothesis.

Monetarism, thus, evolves from a strong belief in the above propositions. In modern times, economists, including monetarists, are more worried about the phenomenon of inflation and/or stagflation. In the next chapter we intend to analyze this chronic phenomenon of a consistent increase in the price level and its effects.

Suggested Further Reading

Anderson, L. C. and J. L. Jordon. 1968. Monetary and fiscal actions: A test of their relative importance in economic stabilization. *Federal Reserve Bank of St. Louis Review*, November: 11–24.

Ando, A. and F. Modigliani. 1965. The relative stability of monetary velocity and the investment multiplier. *American Economic Review*, September.

Carlson, K. M. and R. W. Spencer. 1975. Crowding out and its critics. *Federal Reserve Bank of St. Louis Review*. Reprinted in *Current Issues in Monetary Theory and Policy*, by Havrilesky and Boorman, pp. 128–53.

David, P. and J .L. Scadding. 1974. Private savings; ultra-rationality, aggregation and Denison's law. *Journal of Political Economy*, March-April: 225–501.

Friedman, M. 1956. The quantity theory of money: a restatement. In *Studies in Quantity Theory of Money*, ed. M. Friedman. Chicago: Chicago University Press.

Friedman, F. 1968. The role of monetary policy. *American Economic Review*, March.

Friedman, M. 1936. Rules versus authority in monetary policy. *Journal of Political Economy*, February: 1–31.

Friedman, M. and D. Meiselman. 1963. The relative stability of monetary velocity and the investment multiplier in the United States, 1897–1958. In *Commission on Money and Credit Stabilization Policies*. Prentice-Hall.

Friedman, M. and A. Schwartz. 1963. *A Monetary History of the United States 1867-1960*, Princeton University Press.

Goldfeld, S. M. 1973. The demand for money revisited. *Brooking Papers on Economic Activity*, Vol. 3.

Peterson, W. C. 1984. *Income, Employment and Economic Growth*, 5th ed. New York: W.W. Norton and Company.

Rousseas, S. 1972. *Monetary Theory*, pp. 160-80. New York: Knopf Publishers.

Thomas, L. 1979. *Money, Banking, and Economic Activity*, Prentice-Hall.

Tobin, J. 1981. The monetarist counter-revolution today—An appraisal. *Economic Journal*, March: 29-42.

Tobin, J. 1965. The monetary interpretation of history. *American Economic Review*, June: 647.

Wood, J. H. 1972. Money and output: Keynes and Friedman in historical perspective. *Business Review, Federal Reserve Bank of Philadelphia*, September: 3-12.

Wrightsman, D. 1971. *An Introduction to Monetary Theory and Policy*. New York: Free Press Publications.

Chapter 12

Inflation: Causes, Consequences, and Cures

SUMMARY

This chapter addresses inflation, a most puzzling economic problem. While inflation is defined as a consistent increase in the general price level of an economy, this broad definition glosses over many nuances. For instance, the prices of some goods may fall while the prices of others rise during inflationary periods. To authoritatively discuss this topic, the chapter considers the different types of inflation, their respective causes, and the policy actions that may be taken to cure their dangerous side effects.

There are two different types of inflation: demand-pull inflation and cost-push inflation. Demand-pull inflation arises from factors thrusting the level of aggregate demand for goods and services above their aggregate supply. It may be the result of recurring deficits in the government budget, a rising population, changes in expectations about future inflation, and a decreased tax rate. All of these tend to lead to more purchases of goods and services, thereby increasing current aggregate demand. Cost-push inflation, on the other hand, stems from factors increasing production costs and reducing aggregate supply. Such factors include higher wage demands by employees, an increase in the price of raw materials used in the production process, and natural calamities that create a shortage of goods. It is important to recognize correctly which type of inflation an economy is experiencing at a given point, and an important indicator for doing so is the rate of unemployment. Generally, demand-pull inflation is associated with a lower unemployment rate than cost-push inflation. This is because inflation of the cost-push type affects aggregate supply directly and lowers production levels to levels requiring less employment of the labor force. However, it should be noted that both types of inflation are not mutually exclusive, as the factors causing both of these types often occur simultaneously in an economy.

The chapter then considers the consequences of inflation, both imaginary and real. Non-economists often think that inflation worsens the standard of living of an economy, and it is often thought that inflation by itself creates unemployment. Moreover, a layman may take pride in claiming that inflation is always beneficial for the rich and costly to the poor class of a society. None of these assertions is always or necessarily true. Many economies that have experienced inflation have displayed a consistent increase in their standard of living. Furthermore, unemployment is not necessarily a by-product of inflation, because wage rates can be "sticky," or not automatically adjusted, which results in increased expected profit rates for companies. This has the potential to increase investment, expand output, and reduce unemployment. Finally, despite conventional wisdom, debtors are unequivocal winners and creditors are the losers of inflation.

As for the real consequences of inflation, it does pose a danger of "running away" if left unchecked. Expectations of inflation become destabilized during inflationary periods, and the likelihood of a wage-price spiral occurring increases. Second, inflation lowers the value of monetary assets and increases the value of real assets. Thus, inflation gives rise to a redistribution of resources within an economy. This redistribution is displayed once more by the relocation of income away from unorganized labor in favor of organized labor. Last, inflation can transfer into high rates of unemployment, thereby creating the stagflation problem. Numerous theories have been put forth to explain how this is so. One such theory regards the increased interest rate alongside inflation as the culprit, as this reduces investment and depresses aggregate supply. Another theory contends that inflation breeds higher wage demands from labor, which increases the costs of production. In all, there are some severe costs of very high inflation, but small doses of inflation do not hurt the economy.

The chapter concludes by considering the cures for inflation. These cures include balancing the government budget, tightening monetary policy, and, perhaps, implementing an income policy that includes wage and price controls. The pros and cons of each are weighed. While the rationale for the first two options is clear, their execution is often politically unacceptable. Authorities may pursue income policy as a matter of political expediency, but much attention should be paid to its downside risks. Price controls create an artificial shortage, and they can influence the quality of the product if they are allowed to prevail for a long time. Thus, they should only be implemented on a short-term basis, used only for necessities, and be backed by quantity controls.

12.1 Inflation

Among the most puzzling of economic difficulties is the existence of inflation and/or unemployment in an economy. Historically, it appears that inflation, once started, keeps on increasing until the expectations of its future occurrence considerably subside. Inflation has resisted, or at best, has responded only sluggishly to traditional restrictive policies. Although inflation in the United States and India are not of any drastic proportions, historically, it has caused headaches for policy makers. For example, in the 1970s, the inflation rates were staggering in both countries. Hence, it is thought to be a relevant topic to discuss here.

There are numerous questions to be answered. What is inflation? What accounts for its persistence? Why is it regarded as unfavorable? Is there any silver lining to the black cloud of inflation? To answer the above and other similar questions, we address the problem of inflation in this chapter.

12.2 Inflation and Its Causes

One of the intricate problems is to try to define what is really meant by inflation. In the strictest sense of the term, "inflation" means "a consistent increase in the general price level of an economy." But this creates problems because the general price level is defined in at least three ways when calculating inflation, and all are equally acceptable. The most popular way, however, is by using the consumer price index. Once inflation is measured, one has to mention the method of calculating it.

Second, inflation generally refers to a consistent increase in the price level, which evidently disqualifies one-shot increase in prices. How long a price level has to be increasing to be referred to as inflation is also up to the discretion of the interpreter. This gives another reason for misinterpretation of inflation. In general, an increase in the general price level for one to two years should be taken as an inflationary phenomenon.

The third important point about the incidence of inflation is the realization that since inflation only means a consistent increase in the general average price level of all goods, it is perfectly possible that some goods have increased in their price much more than others. Also, it is perfectly possible to pinpoint certain goods that experience a decrease rather than an increase in their prices in inflation. Hence, it is not surprising to see certain goods which, in spite of inflation, are experiencing a decrease in pricing.

Another way to look at an inflationary situation is to define it by the stage of an economy where there is excess aggregate demand for goods and services in relation to their supply. Any time aggregate demand happens to be higher than aggregate supply, irrespective of their absolute levels, the tendency of the general price level is to go up. Hence, if the situation of excess aggregate demand occurs for a long time, inflation may result.

There are basically two sets of causes for inflation if inflation is seen as a stage of excess aggregate demand. The first set are the causes that raise the level of aggregate demand and make it greater than aggregate supply. These causes are called *demand-pull factors*. By its very nature, a demand-pull factor creates a demand-pull inflation. To name a few demand-pull factors, look to the excessive increase in money supply, the government budget deficits, and the increase in export earnings.

The other set of causes for inflation include the *cost-push factors*. These factors are responsible for an increase in the cost of production, and therefore, reduction in the aggregate supply of an economy. The reduced aggregate supply, if aggregate demand is constant, can cause inflation of the cost-push nature. Then, of course, the crucial question is how to differentiate and correctly identify what type of inflation an economy is experiencing at any given point. An important indicator that aids in this is the rate of unemployment. Generally speaking, demand-pull inflation is associated with lower unemployment rates than cost-push inflation. This is logical because the cost-push type of inflation affects the aggregate supply of the economy, while demand-pull does not. A lower aggregate production would not need as much employment of the labor force in the economy; hence, cost-push inflation arrives simultaneously with labor unemployment.

The increase in aggregate demand that causes inflation in the economy can occur because of several reasons. It is important to note that this increase in aggregate demand almost never occurs in the private sector, as it is not capable of generating autonomous shocks to aggregate demand. As we have seen before, consumption cannot, and does not, change vehemently unless there is a change in GDP. Also, private investment, which constitutes a small part of aggregate demand, and whose growth is self limiting, probably produces only a minor increase in demand. That leaves only the public sector to generate any consistent increase in aggregate demand. Indeed, government does possess the power to tax the public, increase money supply infinitely, finance wards, and run deficits in its budget. For this control, and for the use and abuse of its power, government is seen as the sole creator of the demand-pull type of inflation.

A government that runs a deficit in its budget adds to (C + I + G) of an economy at two levels: direct and indirect. The direct impact of increased government expenditure is obvious. As G increases by a certain amount, so does (C + I + G), because G is a part of aggregate demand. The indirect effect occurs with varying degrees of impact, depending upon the way in which the deficit is financed.

There are basically two ways in which the deficit is financed. First, the government can sell bonds to the Central Bank and receive money in exchange. This is no different than asking the Central Bank to print more money to finance the deficit. This process of monetization (due to an increased money supply) has maximum effect on the price level. As mentioned in Chapter 11, monetarists believe that this is the basic cause of inflation.

The second way of financing the deficit is by selling bonds to the public. This creates national debt and hence, the current burden of excessive expenditure by the government is transferred to future generations. Nonetheless, if a creation of national debt does not raise the interest rates excessively, and if the monetary policy, as carried out by the Central Bank of the country, does not increase the money supply to cure the increased interest rates, then this way of financing the deficit has a smaller impact on the general price level of an economy. This process has been discussed earlier. The basic cause of demand-pull inflation is therefore, a consistently occurring deficit in the government's budget.

The second basic cause of demand-pull inflation is an increase in population either because of a high birth-rate, or because of immigration, legal or illegal. Obviously, increased population broadens the list of needs of an economy, and if these needs are backed by increased purchasing power, they appear in increased aggregate demand. Thirdly, the changes in expectations about future inflation can also cause inflation to actually take place. Consider, for example, that policy makers are only discussing a policy of increasing money supply in the future. When the information is widely available, and when the general public knows that an actual implementation of an expansionary monetary policy leads to inflation in the economy, they expect prices to go up in the future. In order to beat the increasing prices, individuals would rush to the supermarkets and start buying goods and services as early as they could. In this case, there is an increase in aggregate demand, despite the fact that no policy action has actually taken place. Thus, expectations play a vital role in the behavior of the price level, and economists have been paying greater attention to this issue since the mid-sixties. We will discuss more about this a little later.

Lastly, a decreased tax rate that is able to generate higher disposable income, can create a demand-pull inflation. As the tax rate decreases, people realize a higher income to use for purchases of goods and services. As the aggregate demand increases, the demand-pull type of inflation may occur. Turning to the cost-push type of inflation, one can point out that it occurs due to increased cost of production, and/or decreased aggregate supply of the economy. The cost of production can increase for several reasons. An evident scapegoat is activity among unions, which demand higher wages. When producers are forced to pay higher wages, they interpret that as an increased cost, and pass it on to the consumers by raising the price of the product.

Second, the prices of raw materials used in production and the depleting stock of natural resources can also be responsible for the increased cost of production. The OPEC price increases of 1973 and 1978 were two examples of increases in the price of raw materials, namely oil, used extensively in the aggregate supply of an economy. In the case of United States, oil is an important input in almost all productive activities. The impact felt by the U.S. economy in terms of decreased aggregate supply was the greatest.

Third, cost-push inflation can also arise because of natural calamities like heat waves, floods, tornadoes, diseases, and several others. All of these natural events are responsible for a decreased supply in the economy, and therefore, a shortage of goods and services. Thus, inflation can be caused by several demand-pull and several cost-push factors. In reality, most of the inflationary phenomena arise because of some factors happening from both types we mentioned. It is, therefore, hard to pinpoint any inflation as being completely a demand-pull, or completely a cost-push type. In other words, factors causing both of these types of inflation occur simultaneously.

12.3 Consequences of Inflation

Before we can find out the real costs of inflation, we have to see some of the imaginary costs. These costs come from the misconceptions held by the general public about inflation. For example, non-economists often think that inflation worsens the standard of living of an economy. From the historical review of the data, this contention is just not true. Many economies that have experienced inflations have shown a consistent increase, rather than decrease, in their standard of living.

Second, it is also incorrectly thought that inflation by itself creates unemployment. Actually, when inflation rises and producers are not initially forced to pay higher wages to compensate for such inflation, the expected profit rate becomes high. As expected, when the profit rate, or Marginal Efficiency of Investment (MEI), increases and becomes greater than the interest rate, producers find out that it is profitable to undertake additional investment. As investment increases, the multiplier theory from Chapter 6 tells us that the GDP of an economy would increase by a larger amount. Assuming that higher GDP needs a greater number of employees to be employed, the increase in GDP leads to an increase (rather than a decrease) in the total employment of our economy. This is the theoretical background of a special theory called the Phillips Curve Hypothesis, which we will discuss in future chapters. The very analysis of the Phillips Curve holds that inflation and unemployment over the long-run have shown a permanent trade-off with each other, as one increases the other decreases. Hence, that conception that higher inflation creates unemployment in the economy is baseless.

Third, a layman may take pride in claiming that inflation is always beneficial for the upper-class, and costly to families that reside in the middle and poverty classes of society. This is not always true. Assuming that the upper-class is the one that holds a lot of stock, bonds, and equities, one should not waste any time in pointing out that in inflation, the real value of all of these financial assets would decline. The creditors, because of the declining value of money in inflation, are the losers, while debtors, or those who have borrowed money from others, are the gainers in inflation. If we think in this aspect, then the general belief that the upper-class is a beneficiary of inflation is untrue. Observing, however, that the government sector is the biggest debtor, in reality there is no doubt that government gains during inflation, in terms of the reduced burden it has to pay to the private sector.

The next logical question is: what are the real costs of inflation? Let us observe the real costs one by one. First, any inflation, if left unchecked, exhibits a danger of running away. This is because in inflationary situations, the expectations of future inflation becomes destabilized. Everyone makes guesses in their own way about future inflation. If further inflation is expected, people then increase the present demand for goods and services. As the aggregate demand increases, the prices tend to rise even further, and inflation worsens. Also, during inflation, to compensate for the declining value of real wages, the employees, either organized or unorganized, fight for higher wages. If their demands are satisfied by the employers, the recipients get higher purchasing power, and the general price level of goods and services increases. Therefore, once inflation begins, it continues to increase.

A high level of inflation undoubtedly is worse for the economy in terms of real costs, than inflation in small doses. This is because as inflation increases to a greater degree, expectations are more destabilized, and runaway inflation is more probable. Runaway inflations, as recently experienced by Argentina, Israel, Mexico, and Brazil, are catastrophic to the economy. In these cases, the economic policy makers cannot visualize the correct solutions for the situation. Thus, in the words of Heilbroner and Thurow, ". . . inflation holds the threat of 'running away'-of quickening its pace until finally the value of money drops to zero, and we have a complete social and economic collapse. Even though actual runaway inflation (or hyperinflation) have been very rare, and in all cases, the consequence of previous military or social disasters, the specter of such a possibility is profoundly unsettling. This is probably the main reason we perceive inflation to be a danger: It is not so much for what it is, but for what it might become."

Second, as briefly mentioned before, inflation lowers the value of monetary assets. The money kept in bank accounts, bonds, insurance policies, stock, etc. lose their value and the families holding these assets are in danger of losing their savings in real terms. Nonetheless, one has to point out the increase in the value of real assets, because of inflation. Anyone who likes to use uncertainty to make profits, would switch from financial investment to real investment for using his/her wealth. This gives us a consequence of inflation, in terms of redistribution of resources.

From the social point of view, inflation is seen as an evil because in it, the value of money declines, and even if employees make the same amount of money, their wages in real terms go down. Now, consider two classes of wage earners: (1) organized labor, who is aggressive via trade unions and similar organizations, and (2) non-organized labor who has no one to represent them in wage negotiations. In case of inflation, the organized labor always gets compensated for the cost of living index, or by going on strike, they make employers pay them more. Non-organized labor, on the other hand, has no one to represent it; hence, it is more difficult for this group to obtain an increase in wages. Thus, inflation transfers income from non-organized labor which is basically poor and socially repressed, to the organized labor. In this regard, there is no doubt about the evil cost of inflation because it benefits only organized labor at the cost of non-organized labor.

Last, as modern day inflations have shown us, there is a danger of inflation being accompanied by a high rate of unemployment, creating what is popularly called the "stagflation" problem. How inflation transfers to high unemployment is somewhat unclear. There are several explanations for stagflation though. One view perceives that high inflation creates high interest rates because the demand for loans from the banks is very high when the price level is rising. As interest rates become higher, there is a possibility that in spite of higher expected profit rate, they become greater than the Marginal Efficiency of Investment. In this situation, as we have learned in earlier chapters, the volume of investment will be lowered, creating a lower real GDP growth rate. A lower GDP growth rate necessitates lay-offs by employers, giving rise to the high unemployment in the economy. This is probably a situation where inflation is the reason for high unemployment.

Second, some people also believe that the foresight of employees to ask for higher wages as soon as they envision a possible inflation, can cause stagflation. More specifically, high inflation leads to high wage demands, which increase the cost of production. When the cost of production goes up, the aggregate supply of the economy declines, and less is being produced with the increased cost. A lower aggregate supply of the economy can create unemployment, thus, inflation can cause higher unemployment in the economy.

Lastly, some economists may seem to hold inflation responsible for policy makers creating unemployment, in order to cure the inflation. Hence, the policy makers who would believe in restrictive stabilization policies as a cure for inflation problems, would be ready to accept the high unemployment. If their policies are unable to be effective on inflation and unemployment, then both can exist simultaneously. Thus, inflation which inherits the imaginary as well as real cost, can have some undesirable consequences on other economic variables like GDP and employment. Let us conclude this discussion by emphasizing that there are some severe costs of a very high inflation, but small doses of inflation do not hurt the economy and instead are desirable and beneficial. Also, one has to remember that just as there are some real costs of inflation, there are some imaginary costs as well. In the next section, we will consider some points about cures for inflation.

Cures for Inflation 12.4

Just like economists differ in their view about what causes inflation, they also differ about what cures it. No one, however, doubts that a severe depression stops any severe inflation. Therefore, the problem becomes not just combatting inflation, but returning to economic growth without creating a severe price increase. The first solution comes from the concept that because deficit financing by the government creates basic inflationary pressure, the cure lies in balancing the government budget. Hence, a balanced budget is a good remedy for inflation, if the government is able to balance the budget. But balancing the budget necessitates either an increase in taxes, a reduction in government expenditure, or both. All of these solutions are politically unacceptable, therefore, the balanced budget solution, even if it seems plausible, has limited applicability and acceptance by government authorities.

The second solution for inflation comes from the monetarists idea of monetary rule, or adopting a tighter monetary policy. Since monetarists believe that too much money chasing too few goods is the only probable way to describe inflation, the solution for inflation lies in putting the brakes on the flow of money supply generated by the monetary policy. The policy of tight money can be a very effective anti-inflationary policy if it is carried out with relentless persistence. Many times, as the price level comes down because of the reduced growth rate of the money supply, monetary authorities celebrate the success by pumping more money into the system. This overly ambitious response can adversely affect the expectation of the public and may discredit the success already achieved.

Moreover, when the government sector is incurring a debt because of its deficit financing, the money supply cannot be held in check for a long time. As we described earlier, a non-monetized debt only leads to an increased interest rate, as the government competes with the private sector for borrowing money. As the interest rate increases, there is more pressure on the monetary policy to ease up on the money supply of the economy. Nonetheless, tight monetary policy as a tool to solve the inflationary problem is widely accepted, and several countries have paid the price of a recession to solve the problem of excessive price increase.

The third solution for inflation is seen in terms of what is popularly referred to as income policy. This involves either voluntary or mandatory price and wage controls. In case of voluntary wage and price controls, the government announces guidelines for employers to voluntarily check the wage-price spiral. The wage-price spiral forms a vicious circle which increases aggregate demand and the cost of production, making it necessary for producers to charge higher prices. As prices go up, there is more of a demand for increased wages. Income policy that requests producers to voluntarily control wages and prices is effective if all employees agree to it. Obviously, when inflation is of a high degree, income policy's effectiveness is limited. When inflation is out of hand, and governments do not have any other option, they tend to consider mandatory price controls which involve an announcement of prices of certain goods, and an implementation of administrative machinery to oversee the implementation of the announced prices. Price control, in fact, can solve the problem of inflation instantly. If governments take charge, and compulsorily ask producers to obey the guidelines, then inflation should come under control. However, as Arthur Lewis puts it, "price control is a delicate instrument, easily misused."

To justify his statement, there are several points. First, price controls cannot be a long-run phenomenon because if they tend to be so, then there is a "resource allocation effect." One must be aware that price controls are not needed for luxury goods as opposed to necessary goods. The prices of luxury goods should go up, because as prices increase, the quantity demanded goes down, and considering that luxuries are not a necessity, this is desirable for an economy. Hence, when price controls are adopted, they should only be used for the necessities. If price controls tend to be of a long-run nature, producers of luxuries would make profits at a higher rate than those of necessities. There would obviously be an incentive for producers to switch their resources from the production of necessities to the production of luxuries; in the long-run, this is certainly not beneficial for the economy.

Secondly, if price controls are to be implemented in the short run, there is a bubble-effect on the prices. The producers, in order to cover the losses, would increase the prices in a more extreme nature when price control policy is discussed by the policy makers. Also, a short-run price control would encourage hoarding of goods and services, creating an artificial shortage, leading to an increase in price and adding to the bubble-effect. Therefore, the government has to decide beforehand the length of time price controls are to be implemented.

Third, since price controls are always used to reduce prices, they mandatorily lower the prices of goods and services from their natural levels. At any price below the natural price, there is a higher quantity demanded by the consumers and a lower quantity supplied by the producers. To adopt the policy of price control is to create a deliberate shortage. Obviously, there would be individuals who would like to buy more at the lowered price, which can create supply problems. Hence, price controls should always be backed by quantity controls. Quantity controls (or rationing) have an administrative cost, because they require responsible and efficient administration; many countries lack this type of administration.

Fourth, there are some individuals who would need the commodity more than others. For example, gasoline is a commodity consumed and needed more by those who commute to their work place, than by those who do not. Hence, it is possible that some people would be ready to absorb an increase in the cost of fuel, while other commuters may not. This creates an illegal market for that commodity, which puts even further burden on the administrative machinery.

Last, price controls can influence the quality of the product if they are allowed to prevail for a long time. This is especially true for food items, where quality of the product is hard to measure. When producers are told that they cannot charge more than the specified amount for certain food items, the easiest way for them to cut costs is to reduce the quality of the product. Hence, price controls need to be backed up not only by quantity controls, but also by quality controls. In general terms, we may conclude by stating that even if price controls are an attractive weapon to be used, they require tremendous administration and they cannot be sustained for a long duration of time. One has to be very cautious in using this delicate instrument.

Having said so much about the cures of inflation, we have come close to an end of this chapter. To recall, we discussed the causes of inflation and categorized the demand-pull and cost- push types; we talked about the imaginary and real costs of inflation, and we summarized the most popular solutions to this phenomenon. In the next chapter, our aim is to analyze the inflationary and recessionary rounds the economy occasionally has to suffer. The cycles are called business fluctuations, and they create a constant headache for policy makers who presume that solving these fluctuations is their responsibility.

Suggested Further Reading

Birch, D. E., A. A. Rabin, and L. B. Yeager. 1982. Inflation, output and employment: Some clarifications. *Economic Inquiry,* Vol. 20: 209-21.

Federal Reserve Readings on Inflation. 1979. Federal Reserve Bank of New York.

Frisch, H. 1977. Inflation theory 1963-1975: A second generation survey. *Journal of Economic Literature,* December.

Glahe, F. R. 1985. *Macroeconomics,* 3rd ed., Chapter 13. Harcourt, Brace and Jovanovich.

Gordon, R. 1984. *Macroeconomics,* 3rd ed., Chapters 8, 9, and 10. Little Brown Publishers

Gordon, R. 1977. The theory of domestic inflation. *American Economic Review,* Vol. 67, February: 128-34.

Heilbroner and Thurow. 1984. *The Economic Problem,* 7th ed., Chapter 32. Prentice-Hall.

Harris, C. L. (ed.). 1975. *Inflation: Long-Term Problems.* New York: Praeger Publishers.

Lewis, A. 1968. *Principles of Economic Planning.*

Chapter 13

Business Fluctuations, Business Cycles, and Their Theoretical Explanations

SUMMARY

Capitalistic countries have always experienced fluctuations in their economic activity. To better understand these fluctuations, this chapter presents a business cycle model and surveys its separate stages. Likewise, some explanations for business cycle occurrence are investigated. This leads into an exploration of the long-standing debate between interventionists and non-interventionists regarding the desirability of government action during downturns in the business cycle.

The four broad stages of the business cycle are recession, depression, recovery, and prosperity. A recession is characterized as a downward movement in the business cycle, which represents a decline in the growth rate, decreased productivity, increased unemployment, but stable or declining prices. Eventually, a recession leads into a depression, depicted by the trough in the business cycle model. This is the lowest point in the business cycle, because the real GNP growth rate is lowest and the overall economic condition is worst. From there, the economy enters into a recovery stage, with growth rates increasing but still lower than the constant growth rate of real GNP. The prosperity phase comes next, characterized by a growth rate exceeding the constant real GNP growth rate. Eventually, the economy reaches a peak point, at which the economy grows at its highest rate and tends to employ all available resources. In reality, these movements in economic activity are irregular. No economy is expected to experience such a systematic cyclical path, as the business cycle is not necessarily rooted in historical experience but rather is a model created for analytical convenience. Moreover, the duration of each stage is unknowable, and it changes according to the case under consideration.

Several theories exist to explain the occurrence of business fluctuations. Among the first to be offered was William Jevons' "sunspots theory." In Jevons' era, the agricultural sector was the main sector of production in the economy. When the weather favored the agricultural sector, the economy prospered with great speed. However, when the weather was not as cooperative, the economy suffered from recession and depression. Thus, the sunspots theory asserts that Mother Nature is the main reason for business cycle occurrence. Compared to Jevons, Joseph Schumpeter gives a great deal of credit to the industrial sector of the economy, reflecting the shifting locus of economic importance in modern times. Schumpeter saw business fluctuations as a result of the changing psychology of a class of innovators, whose activities are key to the growth of the economy. Another popular theory of the business cycle is the *secular stagnation hypothesis*, which proclaims that business fluctuations are the natural by-product of the growth process. As an economy expands, its marginal propensity to consume declines, which leads to a smaller multiplier value and smaller growth in the next round. Paul Samuelson's accelerator-multiplier theory formally codifies the secular stagnation hypothesis, and its equations are explained in detail. Finally, political changes are also a potential cause of business fluctuations. The short-term prosperity created by increased government spending at times of re-election is followed after the election by recession and inflation. Thus, business fluctuations can be man-made.

The proper role of government during downturns in the business cycle is by no means clearly defined. Non-interventionists, consisting of the monetarists, argue that the stability of the private sector is ensured in the long run because of the higher flexibility of prices in the long run compared to the short run. To support their view, the non-interventionists also point to the permanent income hypothesis, which asserts that consumption spending is a stable function of an economy's permanent level of GNP. Also, policy changes involve several types of time lags—including a recognition lag, an implementation lag, and an impact lag—so government policy is not as effective or as timely as the interventionists would like to believe. Among the many arguments of the interventionists, consisting primarily of Keynesians and neo-Keynesians, is the belief that stabilization policies have helped economies more than they have hurt them, and that time lags are likely to be much shorter in modern times because of increased forecasting abilities. Finally, interventionists do not accept the notion that markets are basically stable, because everyone cannot be expected, as the belief in market stability assumes, to have access to all the necessary information.

Introduction 13.1

Any capitalistic economy shows some duration of prosperity, and other periods of recession and even depression. These cyclical fluctuations in the economic activity are referred to as business fluctuations, or business cycles.

Theoretically, one can term each segment of the business cycle separately as recovery, prosperity, recession, and depression. In this chapter, we intend to survey these stages of a business cycle, and investigate some of the explanations of their occurrence. Starting with William Jevons in the nineteenth century, there have been several economists who attempted to explain the causes of business cycles. In modern times, governmental authorities are more aware of the adverse effects a recession or depression can have on the economy.

The policies designed to solve the problems of business cycles are called stabilization policies. The big question discussed quite often in economic literature is whether the government should intervene in the economic affairs and try to adjust the economy, or not.

Those who believe in the intervention are called interventionists who basically consist of Keynesians and neo-Keynesians. Those who claim that government intervention is unnecessary and undesirable are called non-interventionists, and they consist of monetarists and new classical economists. In this chapter we also intend to review the controversial arguments of these groups.

What Are Business Cycles? 13.2

In order to explain the meaning of a business cycle, let us assume for simplicity that a systematic cycle appears as shown in Figure 13.1, in the given duration of time. Also assume that without cyclical fluctuations, the real GDP of an economy would grow at a constant percentage as shown by the horizontal line. Real GDP is the primary measure of economic activity—the final goods and services transactions. Hence, fluctuations in real GDP are a reliable proxy for measuring the business fluctuations.

One can observe that assuming a cyclical growth of actual real GDP of an economy, in Figure 13.1 during time period t_0 to t_1, the growth rate is declining. This means that the economy is suffering the loss of resources, decreased productivity, increased unemployment, but stable or declining prices in this period. The segment of the business cycle in this time period, AB, is referred to as the "depression." Point B is called the "trough," because at that point, the growth rate of real GDP is

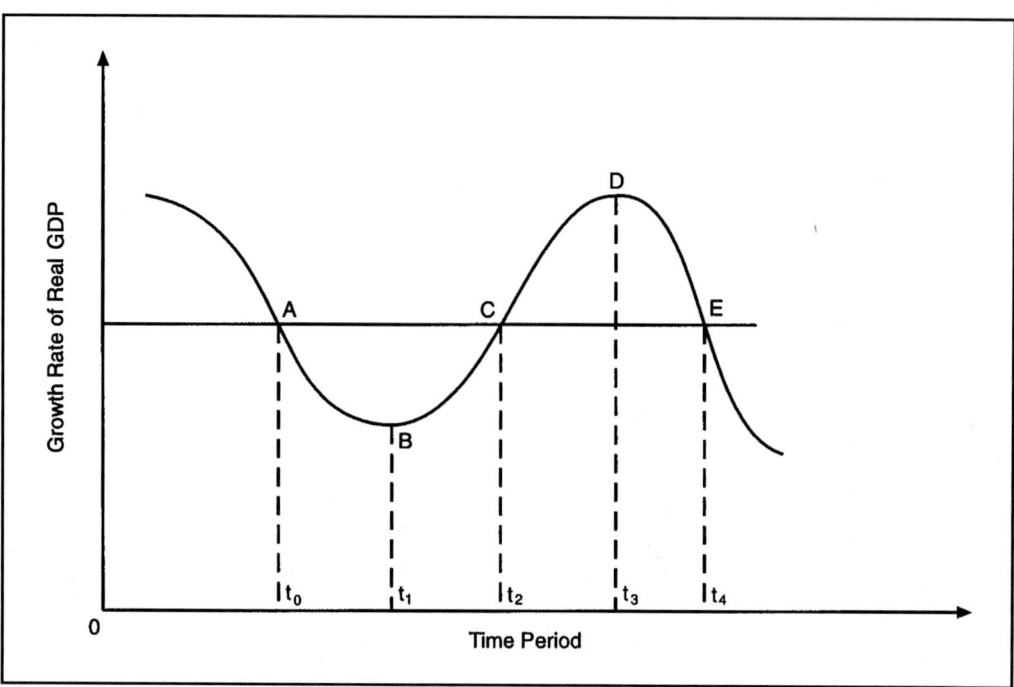

FIGURE 13.1 ■ Business Fluctuations

the lowest. This is obviously the worst situation an economy can experience in terms of employment opportunities, social disorder, and the general performance.

After point B however, the economy starts picking up its growth path as more jobs are offered. The growth rate of real GDP increases and from time t_1 to t_2, a "recovery" stage of the business cycle prevails. In this stage, the economy recovers from the lowest point of growth; still, the growth rate of actual real GDP is not as high as the growth rate that would have prevailed without the existence of the business cycle.

After the recovery stage has been completed, the economy experiences an increase in real GDP at a faster rate than the constant real GDP growth rate. In the economy, a faster growth of real GDP means more jobs are opened, more transactions are done, and the economy is using its capacity at the highest rate. This can also mean that the prices are increasing in certain sectors of the economy. This is likely to happen because some sectors would use their resources earlier than others, and if the demand for the products produced in these sectors keep increasing, then the prices in those sectors would rise faster. Using all the available resources, and increasing the production at the highest rate, means the economy is experiencing "prosperity." This stage is shown by time period from t_2 to t_3 in Figure 13.1. After some time of prosperity, the economy approaches the "peak" point of the cycle. At the peak point, growth of the economy occurs at the highest rate, and the economy tends to employ all the resources available.

For the reasons that we are going to discuss later, after the peak point, the economy starts growing at a slower rate. The productivity is high, but declining, in this time period. This stage is depicted in Figure 13.1 by the time period t_3 to t_4, and is called "recession." The recession stage is similar to depression except that in it, the actual real GDP growth rate is higher than that of the GDP, which increases at the constant rate. The prices tend to be stable in this time period, and the unemployment is increasing.

Two points should be clarified about the definition of the stages of the business cycle. First, even if Figure 13.1 shows a systematic cyclical path of the growth of real GDP of an imaginary economy, in practice, no country is expected to, or has experienced, such a systematic cyclical path. The durations of each stage are likely to change according to the case under consideration. Second, the very fact that the business cycles do not appear as shown in the Figure 13.1, makes it necessary to correctly predict the future path an economy is likely to take, and apply the policy options to adjust for the stabilization. These jobs are performed by the forecasters and the policy makers, respectively.

The Causes of Business Fluctuations 13.3

Among the theoretical explanations available, the foremost is the one given by an economist of the nineteenth century, William Jevons. According to Jevons, the business fluctuations can occur because of the natural condition that can change because of the kind and (sometimes unkind) weather. Obviously, when Jevons was writing, the main sector of production in the economy was the agricultural sector. As the weather favored the production in the agricultural sector, the economy prospered with great speed, and there was visible prosperity in the economy. When the weather was not that cooperative, the prosperity was not as evident, and the economy suffered from the recession and depression. Hence, the basic cause of business fluctuations according to this theory was Mother Nature, or the sunspots. As a result, this theory of Jevons' is called, the "sunspots theory."

The second explanation of the reasons of business cycle occurrence can be found in the celebrated theory of Joseph Schumpeter. In his mind, Schumpeter visualized that the growth of an economy basically takes place because of the work of some important class of people, whom he refers to as innovators. Innovators are the persons who are responsible for the improvement in technology, carry out research and development activities, are production oriented, and whose activities are the key for the growth of an economy. The main reason for the business cycles in the economy, according to Schumpeter, is the psychology of the innovators. If innovators expect the economy to prosper in the future with good speed, they work hard and carry out the inventions with the energy and intensity that are higher than what they would if they had no expectations about the prosperity of the future. As the innovator decides to carry out investment activity, he borrows money from the bank, and the process of the money multiplier takes place. Other innovators are offered similar loans, and the economic activity is enhanced. This is the reason prosperity occurs in the economy.

When the innovators do not expect a bright future, then the borrowing is not carried out with the same speed, as before and the stage of recession begins. Hence, it is the expectation level of the innovators that gives the main impetus to the economy for the growth in the future. The idea of the class of innovators in Schumpeter's theory puts a great amount of credit to the producer's class as compared to the agriculturist class in the Jevons' theory. Nonetheless, in modern times, with an increase in the industrial sector to the degree of prime importance, what Schumpeter advocated seems logical. It is undoubtedly true that the main source of modern growth in the economy is the innovation in that economy. It is no wonder that Schumpeter's theory of business cycles is considered to be the major convincing explanation of the fluctuations in the economic activity.

Another popular theory of the business cycle is offered from the *Secular Stagnation Hypothesis* by Alvin Hansen of Harvard University. The idea used in this hypothesis is strictly Keynesian in a sense that it perceives the decline in the marginal propensity to consume of an economy, when the economy becomes richer. As Keynes had argued before Hansen, when the economy prospers and becomes richer, the propensity to consume becomes less; which as you may recall, affects the value of the multiplier process. This increases the GDP of an economy and there is a growth of the country.

As this process of growth continues for a while, the economy becomes rich, and the rich economy has a lower propensity to consume than a poor economy. Obviously, this means the value of the multiplier (the investment multiplier, of K in Chapter 7) goes down because of this. Any increase in investment would not create as much increase in the equilibrium GDP if the multiplier is smaller than before. Naturally, this would cause a smaller growth of the economy in the next round. Thus, the propensity itself is responsible for a slower growth of an economy according to the *secular stagnation hypothesis*.

When the economy is in the downturn of the business cycle, opposite changes would take place. As the economy progresses with a negative growth, it becomes poorer, and the poor economies would experience an increase in the value of the marginal propensity to consume. Thus, the business cycle may occur because of the natural tendencies of the MPC value to change, as the economy becomes prosperous or poorer.

The third explanation of the business cycle fluctuation is obtained in the theory of another great economist, Paul Samuelson. Samuelson's theory is based on the same idea as the *secular stagnation hypothesis,* but it goes one step further in recognizing another important concept called an accelerator. The accelerator shows us the effect of an increase in GDP on the investment level of an economy. To obtain the value of the accelerator in notational form, let us suppose that the total stock of capital in the economy is K, and the output of the economy is Y, so that K/Y represents the capital including all physical capital including buildings, furniture, land, forests, real estate, and other property. The value of the capital output ratio is much greater than one. Let us denote this ratio by "a."

$$\text{Therefore, } a = K/Y \text{ or } K = a \cdot y$$

Assuming that "a" is constant, any change in the capital stock is caused by a change in the output level, Y. Hence, $\Delta K = a \cdot Y$, but a change in the capital stock of an economy is no different than the investment undertaken in that economy at any given time. Therefore, the left hand side of the above equation can be replaced by investment, "I"; this gives us $\Delta I = a \cdot \Delta Y$.

We now have a relationship between the investment of an economy and the GDP of that economy. Comparing this with the multiplier equation of Chapter 6, which shows GNP, "Y," to be dependent of the investment, "I," we can get the basic two equations of the accelerator-multiplier theory of Samuelson as follows:

$$\Delta I = a \cdot \Delta Y \quad \text{(accelerator equation)}$$
$$\Delta Y = k \cdot \Delta I \quad \text{(multiplier equation)}$$

Now, let us suppose that there is an initial increase in the investment of an economy, this would create an increase in the GDP via the multiplier process, as shown in the multiplier equation. As the level of GDP increases, it creates a further increase in the investment of the economy. This again increases the investment and the chain continues. This is obviously the explanation of the stage of prosperity of the business cycle in that economy. The big question then becomes, "why does this process of an increase in investment and output of the economy slow down?"

To answer that question, consider an application of the *secular stagnation hypothesis.* As the economy becomes prosperous, the value of MPC declines, and the multiplier becomes smaller. In that case, an increase in investment does not cause a great change in output. Because the output does not cause a large change, the investment does not increase by a large amount either. Leading to the same process as before, there is no growth in the economy. This is an explanation of the recession or depression in the economy. Considering the natural tendencies of the economy of the multiplier and accelerator processes, this theory does sound very convincing.

Another explanation of the business cycle is seen in the political steps taken by the administration in an election cycle. In other words, a change in an administration cycle makes it necessary that a business cycle occurs. For example, let us suppose that a new administration has been elected and the policies are not exuberant, so that the process of the multiplier and accelerator discussed above are not underway very vigorously. But when the time of re-election comes, the concern is to stimulate the economy so that adventurous projects are undertaken, money supply is high, infrastructure is built, and unemployment is low.

Such policies tend to affect the level of output and employment first, and the price level with a somewhat longer lag. If the timing is right, the inflation will not show up until after the election is safely decided. Again, when the inflation does appear after the re-election, it can be solved by paying the price of a recession. Thus, the political changes themselves cause the business fluctuations, and the government is the most responsible party for it. The last explanation of the business cycle points out that those man-made causes such as wars, revolutions, strikes, and lockouts are the basic cause of the fluctuating supply of the economy. Obviously, when one accepts the reality of the man-made disturbances in the economy, one does not need any other explanation for a business cycle.

The next point we want to consider is the relevance of the responsibility of the government sector to adopt the policies that can cure business fluctuations. There are believers of the explanation that business cycles are caused by the government; hence, it has no control, authority, or capability to cure them. The class of economists, namely the monetarists, strongly advocates that the government should not try controlling the business cycles of the economy.

However, monetarists form only the vocal minority and many economists and politicians alike have, for a long time, argued that the government should, and could, try to stabilize the economy from the business fluctuations. This, therefore, sets a stage for a controversy that has been debated in the economic literature very strongly by both sides. Those who argue that government intervention is desirable are referred to as interventionists, and those who object to the increased role of the government sector are called non-interventionists. In the next section we will consider both sides briefly.

13.4 Is the Government Interference Desirable?

To consider the controversy, let us first analyze the point mentioned by the non-interventionist. As mentioned before, non-interventionists claim that interference by the government sector is unnecessary and undesirable. To support their belief, they put forward the permanent income hypothesis constructed by Professor Milton Friedman, which states that consumption spending, which is the largest part of the aggregate demand, is the stable function of the permanent level of GDP of an economy. As a consequence, this means that the level of spending, excluding the minor changes in the investment, is basically a stable concept. Another basic stabilizing factor according to non-interventionists is the flatness of the IS curve due to a special reason as follows: monetarists claim that investment is just a part of the total demand that depends on the interest rate; if it is so, investment is more interest sensitive than Keynesians claim. This creates a flatter IS curve, because as we will see in Chapter 16, the slope of the IS curve depends upon the interest sensitivity of the investment function.

The second point non-interventionists put forward is the fact that the price level is flexible, and before the government could correct output from the drastic fluctuation, the price level would have come to an equilibrium level. Therefore, the policy in this case would have been unnecessarily too late. In other words, the stabilization policies need some time to be effective, and the price level is not rigid enough to stay at this increased level for a long period of time.

There are at least three time lags recognized by the non-interventionist. The first one is called the "recognition" lag, which is the time needed for a policy authority to recognize the need for a policy change after a disturbance in the economy has taken place. Let us suppose for example, a natural disaster like a flood occurs in a part of the economy. This can create a supply shock for the economy and therefore, can be considered as a disturbance that needs a correction from the government. It would still take about a week for governmental authorities to realize the situation is serious enough to take an action of correction. This one week is the recognition lag in this case.

Secondly, even after the need for a policy action is recognized, policy authorities take time to implement the policy change. This time is called the "implementation" lag. Generally speaking, monetary policy has a brief implementation lag as compared to the one needed for fiscal policy. Nonetheless, both the above mentioned lags are under the control of the governmental authorities. Hence, together they are called "inside lags."

The third lag is outside the control of the government, hence, is referred to as the "outside lag." This is the time needed for the policy action to show its effects on the economy. Effectiveness of any policy action is measured by the increase in the GDP level it can cause. The higher is the increase in the GDP, the more is the effectiveness of the policy.

Every policy change needs certain time to show its impact on the economy. Moreover, monetarists, as we saw before, believe that the impact lag for the fiscal policy is infinite because of the complete crowding out, and the impact lag for the monetary policy can be infinite if the economy is very close to the full employment stage. In Chapter 15 we discuss these lags in greater detail.

The third point that is made by the non-interventionist relates to the harm that the policy action can do to the economy, in spite of the fact that the price level and aggregate demand are inflexible. They claim that the forecasting ability of the economists is too limited, so that they cannot correctly perceive what change has to be made for a permanent solution to the instability. Further, uncertainty in the policy effectiveness adds an additional source of disturbance that makes the economy less stable than would occur without any changes in the policy decision.

Lastly, non-interventionists also proclaim that in the long-run, the stability of the private sector is more guaranteed than in the short-run, because of the higher price flexibility in the long-run than in the short-run. Therefore, they advocate that the monetary policy follow a monetary rule, and the fiscal policy be conservative and carry out only very necessary services such as maintenance of law and order.

Interventionists, on the other hand, have several points that they put forward in support of government intervention in economic affairs. First, they claim that the forecasting ability and the theoretical underpinning are at a higher level in modern times than in the past. Economists can have more information, they can use better econometric techniques and they have more experience with policy activism than before, which gives us a strong reason to continue government intervention rather than curtail it. This increased forecasting ability has been emphasized by several neo-Keynesians including Modigliani, Tobin, and Gordon. Moreover, they make an observation that stabilization activism has taken the economy out of trouble more than it has gotten it into disorder. Also, the time lags mentioned before are likely to be shorter in the modern time than in the past, because of the increased predictive power.

Secondly, the interventionists do not agree with the monetarists' belief that the markets are basically stable. Due to a lack of information everywhere and due to the lack of capability of the individuals to use the available information, it is inconceivable that the market would be perfectly stable by itself. It is therefore not appropriate that the government stop its stabilizing efforts.

Lastly, but most importantly, many economists just do not agree with the non-interventionists on the grounds that government passivism is an impractical thing in modern times. In most of the free world, the government sector has become so widespread that anywhere we go there is some kind of government action. The public sector offers several thousand jobs, it owns huge amounts of capital, it controls the day-to-day transactions of several businesses, and therefore, in general, it is just not possible to get rid of the government presence in the next few years. Hence, several economists look at government interference as a fixture of the permanent existence and therefore, do not agree with the non-interventionists that there should be no active role by the government in the economy. Then the question still remains, "Why is it that government intervention of any degree has not eliminated business fluctuations from the modern free economies?" One reason for this is the failure of forecasters.

There are several reasons for the forecasting errors. Forecasters make their forecasts by assuming several policy instrument settings. Often, this assumption proves to be unrealistic. Also, there are many non-policy exogenous changes that occur, and the forecasts about the future economic events have to be revised. For example, the OPEC nations' increase in the price of gasoline in 1973 (and 1979) was pretty much unexpected. Hence, forecasters at that time failed to correctly forecast any of the economic events past 1973. Obviously, the government policy actions that were based on the forecasts that did not recognize the exogenous event like the increase in the price of gasoline, were liable to fail in achieving their desired target. To solve this problem in modern times, forecasters and others have started making forecasts for different scenarios. Secondly, the econometric models used for forecasting have become comprehensive in their nature, only in the recent past. Use of computer technology has greatly increased the reliability of these models; hence, the interventionists see much hope for future success in government activism.

Lastly, as a compromise to the debate of the desirability of the government activism, we may state an obvious fact about the popular rule called "Effective Market Classification" rule. This rule states that the number of policy instruments must be matched by the number of targets a policy is trying to achieve. For example, if we want to move to another place by bus, then the bus engine is the instrument to move in one direction, and the bus driver's wheel is the instrument to move in another direction. Therefore, any place on the map can be accessible by rotating these two instruments. Hence, the target of moving in two directions can only be satisfied by having two instruments to get to those targets.

Moreover, EMC rule claims that the instruments should be used for that target on which they have the maximum effect. If monetary policy has an effect on the price level and also on the exchange rate of the domestic currency, then it should be used to control only price level if it is more effective for making changes in the prices, rather than the exchange rate. In more general terms, there are two things government authorities have to keep in mind. First, they should not try to achieve more targets than the available number of instruments. Second, they should assign the policy instrument for that target on which it has the maximum effect to satisfy the condition of the Effective Market Classification rule.

After having said so much about the controversy between two groups of economists, our next concern is to find out more about a theory that is the cornerstone of our time—the increased role of the government sector in the free economies. That theory is the product of a hypothesis put forward by an economist named Arthur W. Phillips. We will discuss the Phillips Curve Hypothesis in the next chapter.

Suggested Further Reading

Clark, J. M. 1917. Business fluctuations and the law of demand. *Journal of Political Economy*, March: 217–35.

Ekeland, R. B. Jr. and R. Tollison. *Macroeconomics*, Chapter 17. Boston: Little Brown and Company.

Hayek, F. A. 1932. *Monetary Theory and the Trade Cycle*. New York: Harcourt Brace and Jovanovich Publishers.

Heilbroner and Thurow. *The Economic Problem*, 7th ed., Chapter 18. New Jersey: Prentice-Hall.

Hicks, J. R. 1950. *A Contribution to the Theory of the Trade Cycle*. Oxford: Oxford University Press.

McConnell, C. R. 1984. *Economics*, 9th ed., Chapter 10. McGraw-Hill Publishers.

Schumpeter, J. 1950. *Capitalism, Socialism, and Democracy*, 3rd ed., pp. 81–86. New York: Harper and Row.

Chapter 14

Phillips Curve Hypothesis: Old and New and Effectiveness of Macro Policies

SUMMARY

The Phillips Curve Hypothesis asserts an inverse relationship between inflation and unemployment. This became a very dominant philosophy in policymaking circles in the 1960s, but its Keynesian foundations were quickly attacked by monetarists who thought its implications for excessive government intervention in the economy led to high inflation. This chapter reviews the Phillips Curve Hypothesis, analyzes the controversy surrounding it, and investigates recent developments in the theory.

The Phillips Curve Hypothesis suggests that as money wages increase, the unemployment rate declines. Arthur Phillips, the economist whose name the hypothesis bears, argues that there are two possible economic reasons for this trade off. First, labor surplus declines as the wage rate decreases, creating lower levels of unemployment. Second, aggregate demand rises as the wage rate goes up, which increases both the price level and the expected profit rate of companies. This improved expected profit rate stimulates greater investment in the economy, which works via the multiplier process to create higher output and employment. After presenting these explanations, the chapter uses a series of differentiated equations to prove that, indeed, the percentage increase in the wage rate is exactly equal to the percentage increase in the price level. This finding confirms a negative relationship between the inflation rate and the unemployment rate.

Although the Phillips Curve Hypothesis was made popular by numerous empirical studies carried out in the early and mid 1960s, the onset of stagflation later in the decade fomented serious doubts about the shape of the Phillips Curve. The expectation that the increasing inflation rate of the late 1960s ought to be accompanied by a declining unemployment rate was not born out in reality. Moreover, economists later found a large degree of dispersion when fitting the inverse relationship empirically, suggesting that the relationship depicted by the Phillips Curve might not be as stable or as consistent as was commonly believed. Thus, economists eventually questioned the uniqueness and stability of the short-run Phillips Curve.

In addition to these empirical setbacks, the Phillips Curve Hypothesis was assaulted on theoretical grounds by the monetarists. This group crafted the Accelerationist Theory, which argues that inflation leads to greater, not lesser, unemployment because of expectations about future inflation. That is, while policymakers may be willing to reduce unemployment at the expense of inflation, people will demand higher money wages to compensate for their loss of real income. If the employers do not agree to these demands, widespread layoffs can result. Even if employees do not ask for higher wages, they would seek another job that would pay them more. As additional persons begin to search for new jobs, unemployment in the economy would increase. Hence, there is no trade off between inflation and unemployment.

In response to the changed nature of the relationship between inflation and unemployment, a modified Phillips Curve now incorporates these expectations of the presence of inflation. The chapter presents the equation for the Expectation Augmented Phillips Curve, and it concludes by explaining how its dynamism allows it to reflect the change in the inflation rate and unemployment rate when workers have high expectations of inflation more adequately than the traditional Phillips Curve.

14.1 Introduction

No other theory about policy activism in the 1960s was more influential than that of Arthur William Housego Phillips, originally of the London School of Economics. He wrote a celebrated article from a visiting position at the Australian National University in 1958 about the empirical observations he made of the economy in the United Kingdom. His theory developed into what is popularly referred to as the Phillips Curve Hypothesis.

Many economists and politicians around the world held views for or against the advocacy of the Phillips curve, and it became a very dominant philosophy in the making of policy in the 1960s. In the United States, the Kennedy and Johnson administrations were clearly influenced by this way of thinking, and in general, governments of the free world engaged in adventurous activism because of the impetus offered by the Phillips curve theory.

By the late 1960s however, the monetarists school vehemently attacked the recommendations of the Phillips curve, insisting that too much government intervention led to high inflation all around the world. There remained several faithful Neo-Keynesians who still supported the message offered by the Phillips Curve Hypothesis. By 1970, this issue emerged as yet another reason for controversy between the two groups of economists: Monetarists and neo-Keynesians.

Our main purpose in this chapter is to review the Phillips Curve Hypothesis, and investigate the recent developments in this theory. Naturally, we also intend to analyze the controversy that surrounds the hypothesis.

14.2 What Is the Phillips Curve Hypothesis?

Phillips observed data of the U.K. economy for the 96-year period from 1861 to 1957 with special attention to the percentage increase in the wage rate and the unemployment rate (unemployment rate was taken as an index of the degree of excess demand of "labor shortage" in the labor market). He found that there had been a trade off between these two variables in the long run. This meant that whenever money wages increased faster, the unemployment rate declined. Hence, at the outset, the Phillips Curve Hypothesis is just an observation that the money wage rate and the unemployment rate of the economy have an inverse relationship. This relationship is shown in Figure 14.1. There was obviously nothing revolutionary about finding a relationship like this, but what was clearly significant was Phillips explanation of this relationship. He argued the there can be two economic reasons responsible for the trade-off.

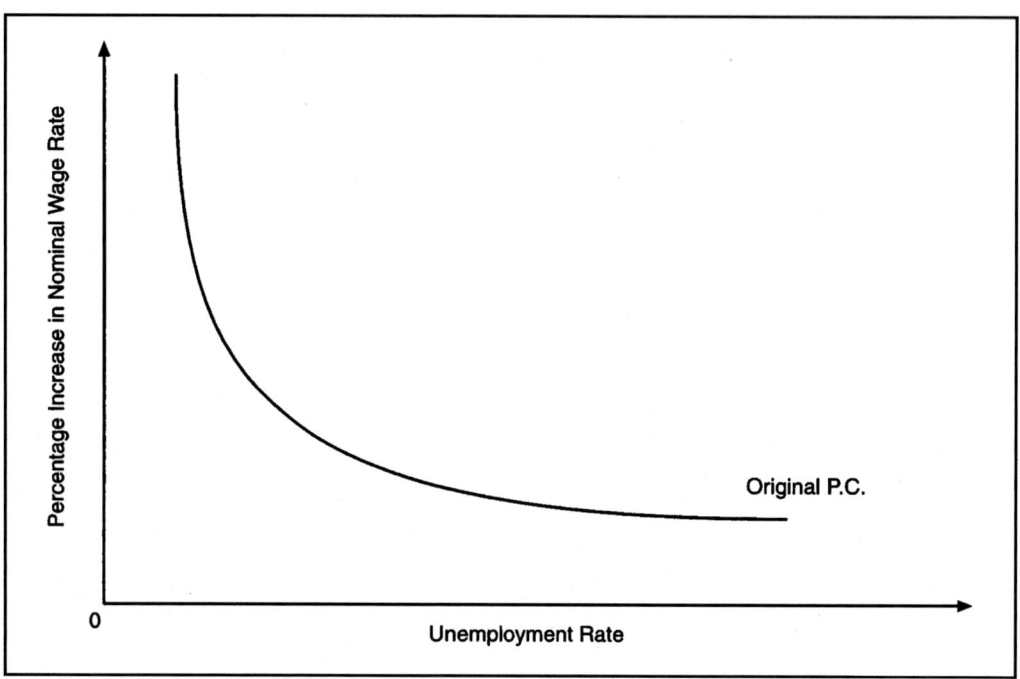

FIGURE 14.1 ■ Original Phillips Curve

First, unemployment is seen as a surplus of labor created by a rapid declining wage rate, and the decline of the labor surplus would create lower unemployment. Hence, the first reason for the Phillips Curve to be downward sloping from left to right is the clear-cut labor market explanation.

Secondly, as the wage rate went up, higher purchasing power was created, which led to a higher aggregate demand. This higher aggregate demand was thought to be responsible for the increased price level and the improved expected profit rate. This higher expected profit rate must have caused higher investment in the economy. Increased investment via the multiplier process creates higher output and employment. Hence, to Phillips, it did not seem completely illogical to post an inverse relationship between the increase in the money wage rate and the unemployment rate.

After Phillips produced his result for the U.K. economy, there happened to be a string of other studies, some of which clearly supported the observations of the Phillips trade off and others that disputed them. Developments and repetition were also accompanied by modifications. In recent years, economists began to interpret the original Phillips relationship in terms of inflation and unemployment rate, as Phillips did. The substitution of inflation rate for the percentage increase in wage rate was logical, because the inflation rate is proportionately related to increase in the wage rate. In order to show this mathematically, let us assume that the wage rate is determined by the value of the marginal product of labor. As you may recall, the total product of labor is the increase in the total product, and the marginal product of labor is the increase in the total product due to employment of the last labor unit. The value of the marginal product is the result of the price of, and the marginal product of, labor; obviously, a producer would be willing to employ labor up to that point at which the value of the marginal product of labor is equal to the wage rate the labor is earning. In mathematical notations, we can write:

$$\text{Wage rate} = \text{Price of the product} \times \text{Marginal product of labor}$$

or,

$$W = P * MP$$

where W = money wage rate,
P = price level, and
MP = marginal product of labor.

Assuming that the marginal product of labor is constant, and totally differentiating the above equation,

$$\Delta W = \Delta P * MP + \Delta MP * + P$$

Because MP is constant, MP is zero. Therefore, we have:

$$\Delta W = \Delta P * MP$$

Dividing both sides of this equation by W, we get the desired result:

$$\frac{\Delta W}{W} = \frac{\Delta P * MP}{P * MP} = \frac{\Delta P}{P}$$

Hence, a percentage increase in the wage rate is exactly equal to the percentage increase in the price level. Therefore, it is possible to view the Phillips curve relationship in terms of a trade off between inflation rate and the unemployment rate. Figure 14.2 shows such a trade off about which we can say the following things.

The Phillips Curve was made popular by several empirical studies performed in the early and mid-1960s to prove the point that there is a trade off between inflation and unemployment of the economy. By itself, a trade off of this sort means that the governmental policies cannot solve both of the problems of the economy simultaneously. The policy makers have to be ready to pay the price of inflation to solve unemployment, and vice versa. The position of this curve determines the available combinations of inflation and unemployment. Any combination to the right of this curve is unfavorable for policy makers, as they represent worsening of both evils in the economy. Any combination to the left of this curve is preferable to the one on the right of it, but it is unattainable by any policy change. Hence, the combinations on the left would be socially acceptable, but

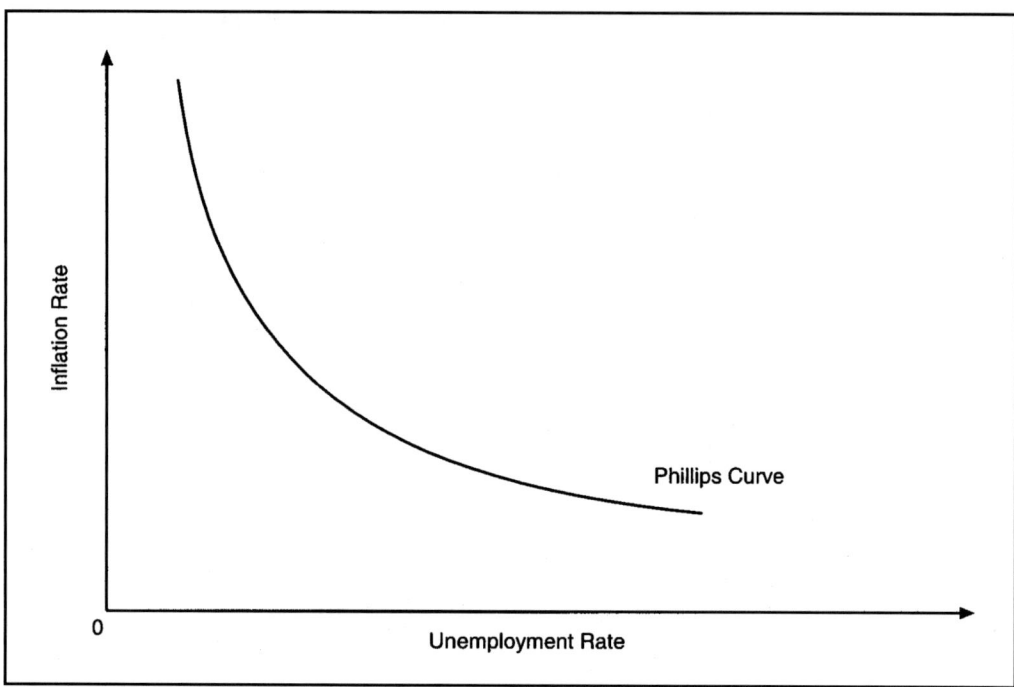

FIGURE 14.2 ■ Modern Times Phillips Curve

practically impossible, for the policy makers to arrive at. Nonetheless, policy makers have an option to select any combination on the curve that they find socially bearable. This type of thinking, based upon assistance offered by the Phillips curve, was dominant in the industrialized countries in the 1960s. Policy makers did not hesitate to adopt expansionary policies when they thought unemployment in the economy was too high. The readiness for paying the price of inflation to solve the problem of unemployment was widespread and at least in the short run, we did witness significant growth in these economies. The Phillips Curve Hypothesis looked very impressive and extremely practical.

The experiences of the late 1960s and early 1970s, however, did not repeat the success achieved by the earlier policy changes, and the economies of most of the industrialized world were beset by the simultaneous existence of inflation and unemployment, popularly labeled the stagflation phenomenon. Besides claiming that the stagflation implied points off the Phillips curve to the right side, there was no theoretical explanation for its existence. Some economists argued in favor of even more policy activism by pointing out the Phillips curve had shifted to the right, and an economy in modern times must be ready to pay the higher price of inflation to solve the problem of unemployment, even if the unemployment is at the same rate as before. They believed that the main reason for this increased sacrifice was the closeness of the economy to the full employment level. As the economy uses most of its available resources, it becomes difficult to employ further labor; this is the reason for higher prices in terms of inflation as related to decreasing unemployment rates. This explanation however, did not convince many other economists, especially the monetarists. However, before we examine the monetarist analysis, let us consider the shape of the Phillips curve under special classical and Keynesian beliefs.

At the theoretical level, the shape of the Phillips curve can be significantly different when we consider these special thoughts of the classical economists and the Keynesians. The classical economists believed that there is always full employment in the economy because of the complete flexibility of the price level, the wage rate, and the interest rate, as we have seen in earlier chapters. Given this belief, no amount of unemployment can be reduced by any amount of inflation. Therefore, in classical analysis, the shape of the Phillips curve would be vertical at the full employment GDP level. In the short run, the Keynesian analysis allows for complete flexibility in the aggregate supply of the economy. Keynes did not see any price and wage flexibility because of his observations of the trade union activity. This belief could lead to a horizontal aggregate supply curve and a horizontal Phillips curve in the Keynesian analysis. Disregarding these extreme cases, up to this point we have considered the Phillips curve of a downward slope from left to right, and discussed its policy options. Now, we must consider the facts of the late 1960s and the early 1970s concerning the simultaneous existence of inflation and unemployment in several developed economies.

The existence of stagflation created doubts about the shape of the Phillips curve. According to the standard Phillips curve analysis of the 1960s, one would have expected the increasing inflation rate of the late 1960s to accompany a declining unemployment rate. In actuality, none of these things happened. Far from purchasing lower unemployment, escalated inflation evidently was required to keep the unemployment rate fixed.

The second reason for increased skepticism of the Phillips curve trade off, according to Humphrey (1973), was the increased evidence that the relationship shown by the Phillips curve might not be as stable or as consistent as was commonly believed. In fitting the Phillips relationship empirically, there was a large degree of dispersion, or variance, of the actual inflation-unemployment about the "fitted" values. In Humphrey's words, ". . . two-variable Phillips relationship was shown to be very loose and inexact." These findings ultimately led an increasing number of economists to question the consistence, uniqueness, and stability of the short-run Phillips curve. However, questioning the logic of the Phillips Curve Hypothesis was not made on the empirical basis alone.

On the theoretical side, Milton Friedman, who was in the University of Chicago in the 1950s, and Edmond Phelps, of the University of Pennsylvania, established the Accelerationist Theory, or what is popularly referred to as the

Natural Rate Hypothesis. This hypothesis claims that expectations about future inflation are the basic cause of non-existence of the trade off between inflation and unemployment, at least in the long run. In a nutshell, their view holds that the policy makers cannot solve the problem of unemployment in the long run, no matter how much inflation they are ready to offer as price. This implies a vertical shape for the long-run Phillips curve.

In order to understand the Accelerationist Hypothesis, consider the chain of events that would take place in terms of Figure 14.3. Let us assume that the economy is initially at point A, where there is large unemployment and relatively low inflation. Looking at the possibility of reducing unemployment at the cost of inflation, the policy makers should be tempted to implement expansionary policies. The situation in the economy can be explained by movement on the Phillips curve from point A to point B. Point B shows a reduction of unemployment at the cost of additional inflation in the economy. Accelerationists claim that people would, in the long run, at point B, realize that their real income is less than at point A because of the inflation. When the price level goes up, the real wage, defined as the ratio of nominal wage and the price level, would go down. As people realize the loss of their real income, they could react in at least two ways. First, they could ask for higher money wages to compensate for their loss of real wage, and if the employers do not agree to their demands, this could lead to widespread lay-offs. Second, if they do not ask for higher wages, the employees could start looking for another job that would pay them more. As additional persons begin to search for new jobs, unemployment in the economy would increase. The situation in the long run would be expressed by a horizontal movement from point B in Figure 14.3. Notice that there is no reduction in inflation when this increase in unemployment is occurring.

Obviously, the job search of the people who realized the loss of their real income continues, as long as there is the same wage rate, and the same amount of unemployment, as before. Hence, the economy would be in a stable situation only at point C. Again, noticing that there is an increase in the unemployment in the economy, the policy makers would be anxious to take the economy to point D, by carrying out another round of expansionary fiscal and monetary policies. This type of reaction by the policy makers would be explained by the movement from point C to D in Figure 14.3. Again, at point D in the long run, people would realize the loss of real income, and their response to that realization would be the same as before. This creates the movement from point D to point E on the horizontal plane. When we consider long-run equilibrium, then only points A, C, and E would be observed, resulting in a vertical shape for the Phillips curve. Hence, the accelerationists argue that in the long run, no government action can be successful

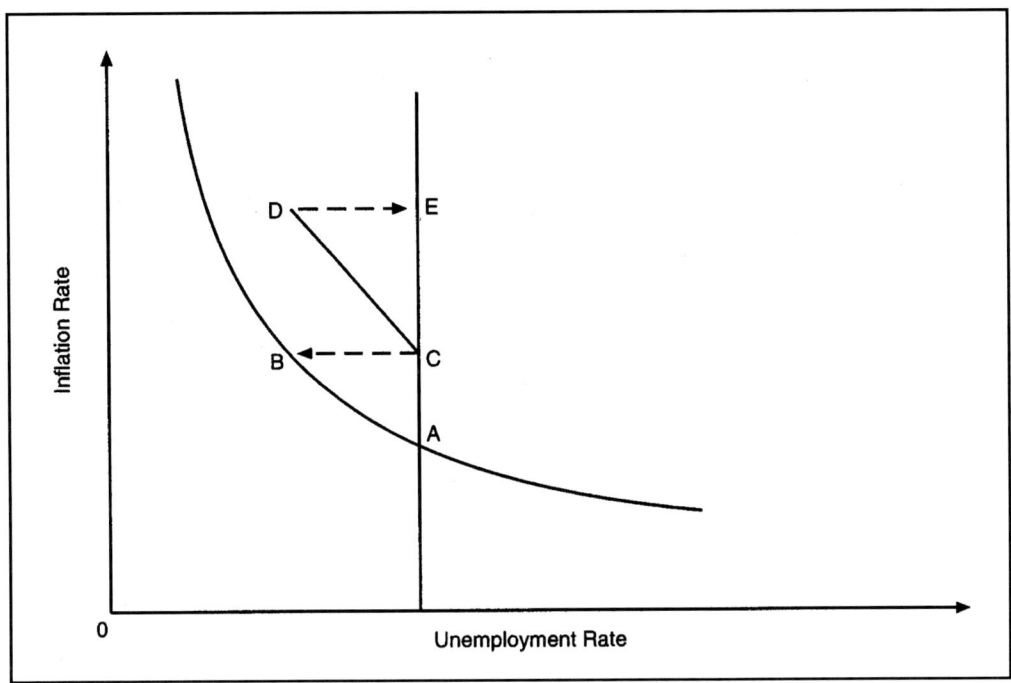

Accelerationists' Phillips Curve ■ FIGURE 14.3

in creating a permanent decline in the unemployment of the economy. In the long run, there is no trade off between inflation and unemployment that tends to persist in the economy, and one that cannot be cured by any payment of inflation, is called the *natural rate of unemployment*. The Accelerationists Hypothesis that claims the existence of a natural rate of unemployment is called the Natural Rate Hypothesis (NRH). In terms of policy consequences, the monetarists and the accelerationists would prefer to see no activism on the part of the government, because no amount of activism is going to permanently cure any amount of unemployment.

However, not all economists agree with the position taken by the accelerationists. Basically, they differ on the shape of the long-run Phillips curve. While accelerationists argue for a vertical shape, the non-accelerationists insist that the long-run shape of the Phillips curve is only steeper than the shape of the short-run Phillips curve. As long as there is a downward slope to the curve in question, there are trade off opportunities for policy makers. Moreover, for the long-run policy options, a steeper Phillips curve only means that the policy makers should be ready to pay a higher price in terms of the inflation to solve the problem of unemployment. In terms of Figure 14.4, there is a clockwise movement in the horizontal direction, but the movement is not as complete, even in the long run, as the accelerationists claim.

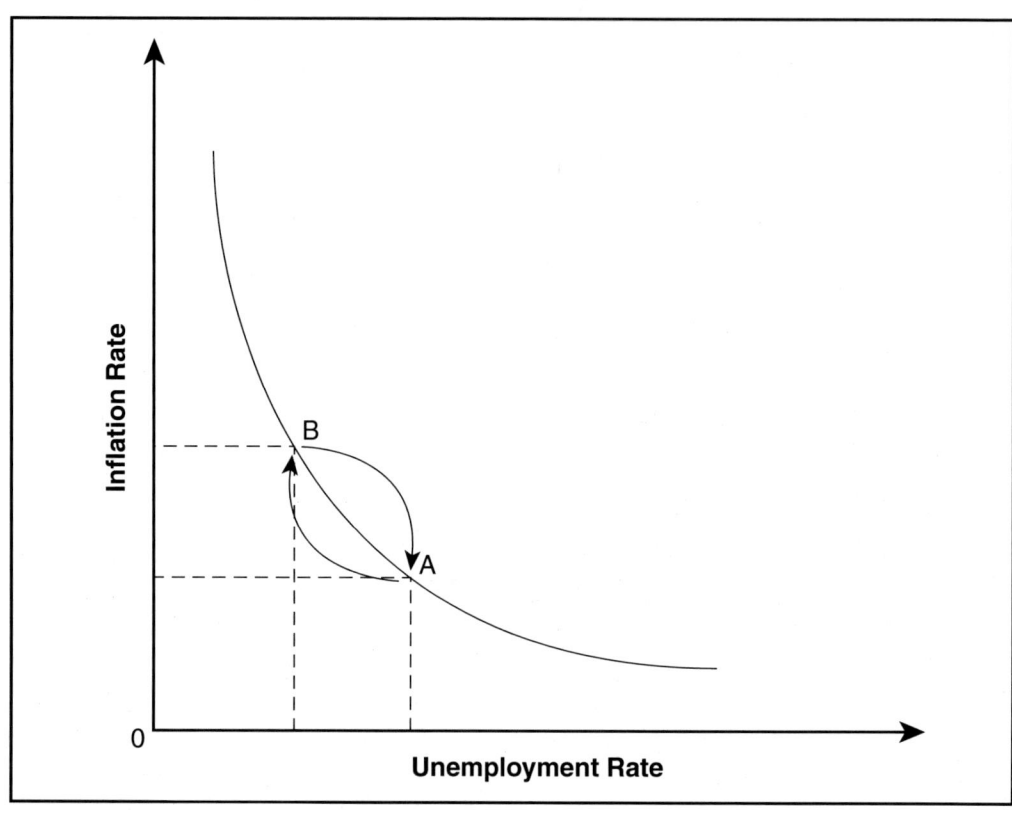

FIGURE 14.4 ▪ Clockwise Movement: Non-Accelerationists' Hypothesis

Obviously, the accelerationists disagree with the charge made against them. More specifically, they put forward the argument about the natural tendency of the market forces to cure its own problem and therefore, believe there is no need for changes in governmental actions. Nonetheless, the controversy between the monetarists and the non-monetarists is as intense as ever about the desirability of the policy options and actions from the government sector. As we are going to concentrate on this topic in future chapters, suffice it to say here that the detailed analysis of the thought of these economists on this particular issue is very important. Also, the simultaneous existence of inflation and unemployment in the industrialized economies in modern times needs additional tools of economic theory called the aggregate demand and the aggregate supply schedules. There is also a basic hypothesis about the behavior of the labor market of the economy, which we have omitted so far.

14.3 Expectation Augmented Phillips Curve

One of the reasons why the traditional Phillips curve relationship vanished was because of the change in the way workers and employees formed their expectations of future inflation. Existence of high current inflation made workers expect the same in the future. Thus, as inflation became consistently positive and more persistent, expectations started to incorporate the presence of inflation. This change in expectations changed the nature of the relationship between inflation and unemployment in the 1970s (the shape of the Phillips curve also had to be revised).

To incorporate this expectation formation in the Phillips curve analysis, consider that π_t^e represents expected inflation in time period "t," and the relationship between last period's actual inflation and the current period's expected inflation is estimated as:

$$\pi_t^e = \int \pi_{t-1} \tag{1}$$

Thus, the value of "∫" captures the effect of last year's inflation rate on this year's expected inflation rate. Obviously, a higher value of "∫," means workers (and firms) can expect higher inflation this year, just because inflation was high last year. It is also imaginable that the value of "∫" increases over the period of time. In the 1950s, when "∫" was small and inflation was low (and non-persistent), it was reasonable to ignore past inflation, and it was logical to expect that this time period's inflation was not very different from last time period's inflation. Hence, if ∫ = 0, π = 0, the Phillips curve relationship was the same as projected by the traditional Phillips curve.

However, as inflation seemed more persistent, workers started assuming that if inflation had been high last year, it was likely to be high this year as well. Hence, the value of "∫" increased steadily. To incorporate the changing value of "∫" in the Phillips curve relationship, we can set an equation as:

$$\pi_1 = \int (\pi_{t-1} - \int \mu_t) \tag{2}$$

Where is the effect of unemployment (μ) on inflation rate (π_t)? Depending upon the value of ∫ one can easily show the effect of expected inflation on the unemployment rate, and vice versa. More specifically if ∫ = 0, then there is no change in the Phillips curve relationship. However, if ∫ = 1, then Equation (2) becomes

$$\pi_t = \pi_{t-1} - \int \mu_t \tag{3}$$

According to Equation (3), if ∫ = 1, then the effect of the unemployment rate is on "change" in the inflation rate. In essence, Equation (3) derives the expectation augmented Phillips curve. When workers have high expectations of inflation, the relationship between "change" in inflation rate and unemployment rate is more relevant than the traditional Phillips curve. We shall consider the exact process of expectations formation in Chapter 15.

Suggested Further Reading

Friedman, M. 1968. The role of monetary policy. *American Economic Review,* March: 1–17.

Gegg, D. 1982. *The Rational Expectation Hypothesis in Macroeconomics.* Baltimore: John Hopkins University Press.

Humphrey, T. 1973. Changing views of the Phillips curve. *Federal Reserve Bank of Richmond Monthly Review,* July: 1–13.

Lahiri, K. 1977. A joint study of expectations formation and the shifting Phillips curve. *Journal of Monetary Economics,* No. 3: 347–57.

Lipsey, R. 1960. The relation between unemployment and the rate of change of money wage rates in the United Kingdom, 1891–1957: A further analysis. *Economics,* February: 1–13.

Phelps, E. 1972. *Inflation Policy and Unemployment Theory.* New York: W.W. Norton.

Phillips, A. W. 1958. The relation between unemployment and the rate of change of money wages in the United Kingdom, 1861–1957. *Economica,* November: 283–99.

Rees, A. 1970. The Phillips curve as a menu for a policy choice. *Economica,* August: 227–38.

Solow, R. 1976. Down the Phillips curve with gun and camera. In *Inflation. Trade and Taxes,* D. Beaseley (ed.). Ohio University Press.

Chapter 15

Expectations Hypotheses and Time Lags Involved in Policy Effectiveness

SUMMARY

The extent to which actions taken by a monetary authority in a period of downturn can stabilize the economy is befuddled by a host of problems. Among the most noteworthy obstacles are time lags involved in the operation of fiscal or monetary policy, and expectations generated among the general public of the inflationary effects of stabilization policies. This chapter examines each of these obstacles and their consequences for the effectiveness of government policies.

An expectation about future inflation is just as effective as an actual increase in the general price level in creating a detrimental effect on the economy. When analyzing inflationary expectations, it is important to understand how people form these expectations of future prices. Two hypotheses that help us understand the process of expectation creation are the *adaptive expectation theory* and the *rational expectation theory*. The adaptive expectation theory claims that people learn, at least partially, from previous experiences when forming an expectation of the future inflation rate. If people have learned from past experience that an expansionary policy causes inflation in the economy, then an expansionary policy in the current time period would dictate them to expect at least some inflation in the future. The amount of time it takes for a person to adjust their expectation is known as the speed of adjustment, and this determines the effectiveness of the policy action. The smaller this time period, the less effective the policy action. A crucial implication of this theory is that the variable, the inflation rate, must actually change before individuals begin to anticipate future changes.

The rational expectation theory, on the other hand, assumes that people are bombarded with such a large amount of information that they form mental models to analyze economic changes. This implies that people can correctly anticipate the effects of an expansionary policy as soon as, or even before, the policy is enacted. The inflation rate need not change before people formulate their expectations about future inflation. They immediately demand higher wages, resulting in decreased output and inflation of the cost-push type. Thus, no expansionary policy is effective, and there is no incentive for policy activism. Upon closer scrutiny, however, the rational expectation theory makes some haughty assumptions. Even when information is abundantly available, people do not always use it to make expectations about future prices. This is because very few people are actually interested in following every policy change. Given this, we cannot assume that people's expectations are rational. There is scope in reality, therefore, for expansionary policies to have at least limited effectiveness.

For any policy change there are several time lags that can create delays in the effectiveness of the policy action. Those lags within the control of the government are known as *inside lags.* These consist of the *data lag,* the time involved in getting information about an economic disturbance once it has occurred; the *recognition lag,* the time interval between the assessment of an economic disturbance and the decision by monetary authorities that a corrective policy is needed; and the *implementation lag,* the time involved in implementing a policy change once the need for it has been realized. *Outside lags* are beyond the control of government. These include the *transmission lag,* the time interval between the policy decision and the actual implementation of the policy change; and the *impact lag,* the amount of time needed for the policy change to show its effects once it has been implemented.

The chapter rehashes the debate between the monetarists and Keynesians over the merits of fiscal and monetary policy with a brief summary of their respective arguments. It concludes, nonetheless, by noting that both pose problems when used in an expansionary manner. Policy makers must remain cautious of the folly of over-activism resulting from the pursuit of unattainable objectives.

Introduction 15.1

We concluded the last chapter by saying that government stabilization policies will be ineffective if the public correctly perceives their inflationary effects. That is not the only problem a monetary authority faces. Non-interventionists are eager to point out the time lags involved in the operation of the monetary or fiscal policy. There are also the critics who believe in the adaptive expectation hypothesis and in rational expectation theory in the simplest forms, who then examine the consequences thereof for the effectiveness of the governmental policies.

Effectiveness of the Policy 15.2

To recollect, let us briefly summarize the economic events that normally would take place due to an expansionary monetary or fiscal policy. In Figure 15.1, starting with the original equilibrium at point J, let us suppose that the government decides to increase money supply or government expenditure. There will be an increase in the aggregate demand due to these policy actions and a shift of the aggregate demand schedule to the right. The new equilibrium would be attained

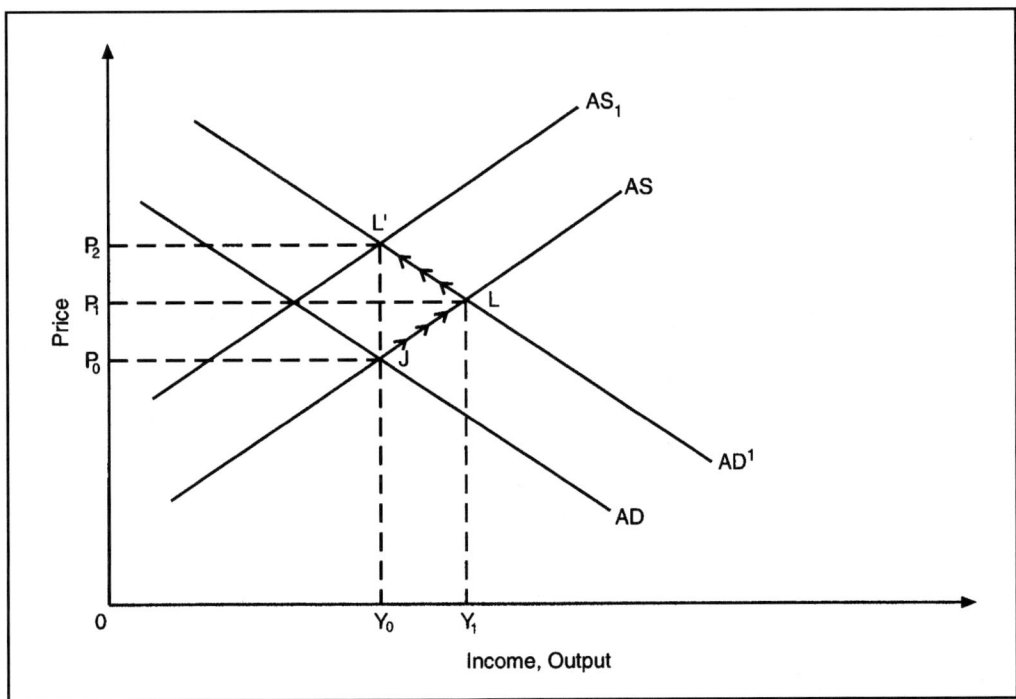

FIGURE 15.1 ■ Effectiveness of the Policy

at point L with a higher GNP and higher price level. Because the GNP level is increased by the policy action, we could conclude that the action was effective. But the effectiveness of the policy action could be short-lived, depending on the speed at which expectations of the public are adjusted to the higher price level at point L.

As we have seen in Chapter 14, the slower the rate of adjustment of the expectations to the future prices, the longer the effectiveness of the policy action. If people become aware of the fact that there is a loss of real income due to a higher price level at point L, and if they set their wage contracts for the short-run durations as opposed to the long-run durations, then they would immediately ask for the higher wages to compensate for the loss of real income. As a result of these demands for higher wages, the cost of production would increase, causing the supply curve in Figure 15.1 to shift to the left. This would obviously nullify the effectiveness of the policy. Moreover, one may note that expectations about future inflation are as effective as the actual increase in price level in creating a leftward shift of the supply curve. Now the big question is: How do people form an expectation of future prices? Also, what are the consequences of the mechanism of expectation formation on the effectiveness of policies? One theory that claims to answer these questions is the adaptive expectation theory.

15.3 Adaptive Expectation Theory

Introduced in writing by John Muth in 1961, but elaborately developed by Phillip Cagan of Columbia University in the 1970s, the adaptive expectation theory claims that people, when they form an expectation of the future inflation rate, learn at least partly from their old mistakes. Hence, if they have learned from their past experience that an expansionary policy causes inflation in the economy, then an expansionary policy of this time period would dictate them to expect at least some inflation in the future. In mathematical terms, it means that when expectations of future inflation are formed, the following equation is used:

$$P_t^e = P_{t-1}^e + \int (P_{t-1} - P_{t-1}^e) \tag{1}$$

where P_t^e = expected inflation rate of the current time period,

P_{t-1} = expected inflation rate of the last time period,

P_{t-1}^e = actual inflation of the last time period, and

$\int$ = coefficient of adjustment with its value between zero and one. $0 < \int < 1$.

Depending on the value of the coefficient "$\int$," we have several scenarios to predict. Let us suppose that the value of "$\int$" happens to be zero. By using the zero value for "∫" in Equation (1), we get $P_t^e = P_{t-1}^e$ (i.e., people do not adjust their expectations at all to the actual value of inflation). Keeping in mind that this type of behavior is unrealistic, in terms of Figure 15.1, there would be no change in the location of the aggregate supply curve in this case. This is because if people expect inflation in this time period in the same way as they expected it last year, they would not ask for any higher wages, the cost of production would remain unchanged, and the aggregate supply curve would stay at the same location as before. The policy would be effective permanently. On the other hand, if "∫" is equal to 1, the expected inflation rate is always set equal to what actually occurred in the last year. If people correctly perceive the actual inflation occurring at point L in Figure 15.1 to form their future expectations, then they would obviously ask for higher wages in the future contract, the cost of production would go up instantly, and the aggregate supply curve would shift to the left, creating lower GDP and higher unemployment in the economy.

Barring these extreme cases, the value of "∫" always remains between zero and 1, and it is referred to as the *speed of adjustment* to the changes in circumstances. The speed of adjustment determines the effectiveness of the policy action. The closer the value of "∫" to unity, the lower the effectiveness of the policy action. In general, the adaptive expectation theory claims that depending on the value of the coefficient "∫," the effectiveness of policy action is decided. It is perfectly possible that the policy is effective at one time period, and is completely ineffective in the other, because the value of "∫" is liable to change. In terms of empirical evidence, the policy actions were more effective in the initial stages when the government started becoming ambitiously active in the 1940s and 1950s. However, as people learned from their old experiences, the policy actions in the 1960s and 1970s were much less effective.

Hence, the adjustment process for the future expectations of the inflation rate does create a problem for monetary policy effectiveness. There are, however, other economists who claimed, in the late 1960s, that the effectiveness of the policies is essentially zero, especially when people have what they call "rational" expectations.

15.4 Rational Expectation Theory

A crucial implication of the adaptive expectation formation was that the variable must change before individuals begin to anticipate further changes. For example, the public must observe an actual decline in the inflation rate in this period to expect a reduced inflation in the next period. The rational expectation theory goes one step further. This theory was propounded by Thomas Sargent and Neil

Wallace of the University of Minnesota, and was further extended by Robert Lucas of the University of Chicago. It claims that the public in modern times is exposed to more information via television, radio, newspaper, etc. This free information enables every economic agent to form a special model of his/her own to analyze the economic changes. Moreover, as the information in the future changes, everyone feeds that information into his/her forecasting model, so that any policy announcement immediately affects the expectations about future changes in the economy. Hence, in the case of rational expectations, people already know what would be the effect of an expansionary policy. Also, if people have observed in the past the inflationary consequences of an increase in money supply, then in the current times, even when the policy makers are discussing an adoption of an expansionary monetary policy, the public, by looking at their rationally built model, correctly anticipates the upcoming inflation.

This obviously causes a severe problem for the effectiveness of the policy. As people correctly anticipate the inflation, they ask for higher wages as soon as the policy is enacted (or sometimes even before enactment of the policy). Their demands for higher wages create a shift of the supply of the labor curve, reducing employment and output, and the effectiveness of the policy is nil. As Johnson and Roberts put it:

> The implication of the rational expectations is that expectation would be reformulated sooner than under adaptive expectations based on observations of actual changes in the variable alone. For example, the rate of increase in prices would not necessarily have to decrease before individuals anticipated that prices would be rising at a slower rate. All that would be necessary for the reformulation of expectations is the realization of a change in monetary or fiscal policy that would lead to a reduction in the rate of increase in prices. (p. 432) (2003)

Thus, the rational expectation theory succeeds in putting a serious question in front of the policy makers. As opposed to the Phillips Curve Hypothesis that claimed, at least, partial success in solving the two main problems of the economy, viz. inflation and unemployment, the rational expectations hypothesis offers no incentive for policy activism. From the policy makers' point of view, several lessons can be learned from the rational expectation theory. First, never announce the policy beforehand, because if it is announced previous to its enactment, then people already expect what is coming and change their actions to compensate for the anticipated change. Second, do not be honest in accepting the fact that you are trying to trade off inflation for unemployment and vice versa, because if people know it for a fact, then they would anticipate an expansionary policy in the case of high unemployment, and a restrictive policy in the case of severe inflation. Policies lose their effectiveness if people are able to anticipate the actions in advance. Third, the key for the success of policy activism is in the ability to not let people know what the future changes in the policy will be.

In terms of Figure 15.2, expansionary policy effectiveness can be seen when people have adaptive and rational expectations. The movement from point A to B is very quick when people possess rational expectations, giving zero effectiveness to the policy change. The next question naturally is, do people in fact possess rational expectations? The answer is obviously "no," not at least when we are considering the general public in the whole economy. Even when information is abundantly available, people do not always use it for making the expectation of the future prices. How many people in reality are interested in building an economic model and watching every policy change? Very few. People hardly even realize the meaning of the policy changes, let alone the working of them. Hence, in a complex world with many individuals of different attitudes and tastes, it is irrational to expect that people have rational expectations. This means that a policy activity can have at least limited effectiveness in reality. These practical limitations give a ray of hope for policy activism. However, the rational expectation hypothesis cannot be completely ignored. Also, on the microeconomic basis, rational expectations can have application in certain areas like the stock market, where the dealers are very attentive to everyday changes in policy activity and they, in fact, use certain rationality in their expectations of the future variables.

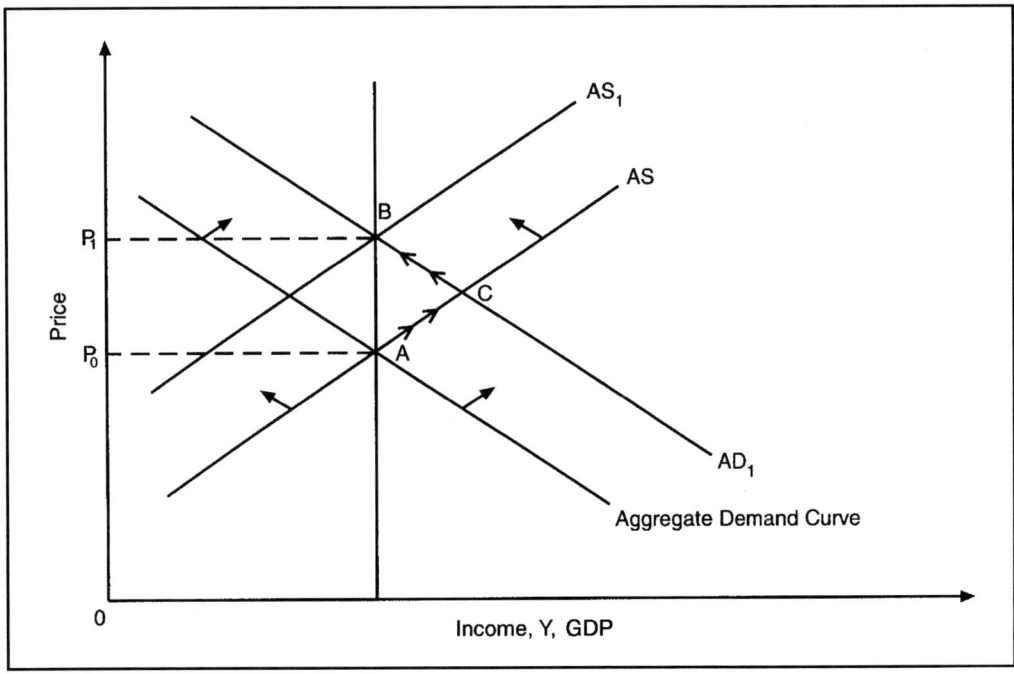

Expectation Hypothesis and Policy Effectiveness ■ **FIGURE 15.2**

As far as the problems for the monetary policy are concerned, the expectations hypothesis makes it clear that policy effectiveness is hampered by the information available to the public, and the rationality of their expectations. Policy makers have to keep a close check on these expectation formation processes if they are to succeed in their actions.

15.5 Lags in the Operations of the Policy

The second set of problems for the monetary policy are created by the time lags involved in the operation of it. For any policy change, there are several time lags, like the time involved in implementation, recognition, etc., which can create delays in the effectiveness of the policy action. In the early 1960s, economists started paying special attention to these time lags because they happened to be another point on which the non-interventionists could rest their case for non-activism on the part of the government.

There are basically two major types of lags. The wages, which naturally occur, but are under the control of the government, are called inside lags, and those which are outside the control of the policy makers are called outside lags. In turn, there are three inside lags and two outside lags.

The first inside lag is called "data lag." It is the time involved in getting information about an economic disturbance once it has occurred. For example, let us suppose there is an occurrence of a disturbance in the economy like a heat wave in a certain part of the country. Obviously, it would take time to correctly analyze the severity of the heat wave, and the loss that would be incurred because of it. This time involved is known as the data lag. Secondly, even when government has obtained the information about the heat wave, policy makers may think of it as a short-run disturbance, and one that does not call for any policy action. If governmental authorities take a certain amount of time to make up their mind about the need for a policy change to correct the disturbance, then that time is called the "recognition lag."

The third lag is called the "implementation lag." It is the time involved in implementing the policy change once the need for it has been realized. For example, the fiscal policy change has to be approved by several committees in the governmental structure once it is decided a change should be made. In this respect, monetary policy is in a better situation because generally, monetary policy actions are implemented more quickly than fiscal policy changes. Note that all of the above lags are under the control of the policy makers. If they have to, in the case of emergencies, they can reduce the length of these time lags very easily. For example, the recognition lag can even be negative, if the government correctly anticipates the disturbance well ahead of time. For this reason, these lags as mentioned before, are called inside lags.

There are two outside lags: (a) transmission lag, and (b) the impact lag. The transmission lag is the time interval between the policy decision and the actual implementation of the policy change. This again, is more relevant to fiscal policy than to monetary policy. Once it has been determined that a policy change is necessary, monetary policy activation takes less time than fiscal policy change, such as a tax change.

Finally, the most interesting lag is the impact lag. It is the time needed for the policy change to show its effects once it has been activated. The effectiveness of a policy change is measured by the amount of change it can cause in the real GDP of the economy. If there is no change in the real GDP, then the policy is termed ineffective. What is the impact lag for the fiscal policy? The answer to this question would depend on whom you are asking the question. For example, the monetarists would point out the complete crowding out phenomenon, and would conclude that the impact lag for the fiscal policy is infinite. On the other hand, Keynesians would explain the multiplier process, and would conclude that the impact lag is the time involved in finishing the chain of multiplier that we discussed in earlier chapters. This, they would assert, is a shorter lag than the impact lag of the monetary policy.

The effectiveness of the monetary policy, according to the Keynesians, occurs only via the Keynesian chain that we discussed before. Remember that the Keynesian chain is the only way in which Keynes and the Keynesians claim the monetary policy can be effective. Hence, according to their thinking, it takes longer for monetary policy to be effective, than for fiscal policy. This gives them another reason to believe that fiscal policy is superior or stronger than monetary policy. Monetarists, on the other hand, insist that the monetary change does not need the Keynesian chain to be effective. Its impact is more direct via the quantity theory of money. According to the monetarist, and especially Friedman, it takes about sixteen months for any monetary policy action to show its effects on the economy. Sixteen months is a long time for sure, but in case of fiscal policy change, things are even worse because the impact lag (because of the crowding out) is infinite.

To summarize, we can show a hypothetical movement of the real GDP of an economy in Figure 15.3, and specify the time "∫" periods, for each lag we mentioned above. The main contention of all the above discussion is that policy effectiveness does not involve several lags, and policy makers should be aware of those.

Besides the time lags and the expectation hypothesis, there are also some other beliefs which claim that policy activism has problems. One such theory is called

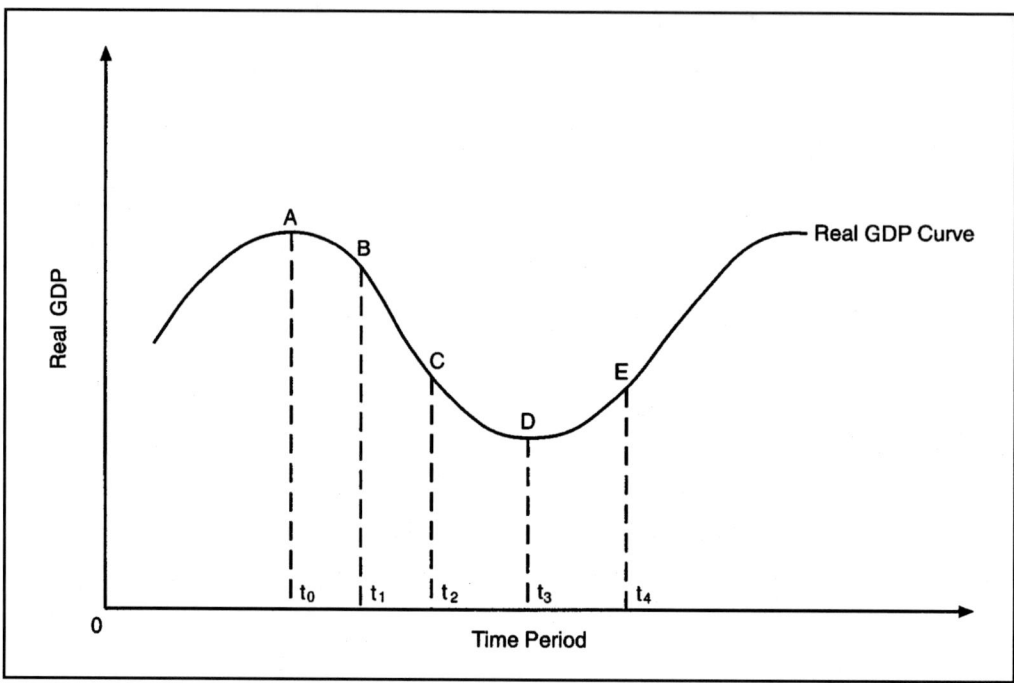

FIGURE 15.3 ■ Time Lags in Policy Action

the Credibility Hypothesis, as given by William Fellner, a former Yale University Professor, but now with the American Enterprise Institute. According to Prof. Fellner, when the public has come to believe that the governmental policy makers have a tendency to adopt only expansionary policies, then adopting a restrictive policy does not easily generate desirable results. In other words, a restrictive policy with an objective of controlling inflation would not do so, if the public knows or expects that the government has a usual tendency to adopt expansionary policy. The government, therefore, has limited credibility with the public and as a result, the policy effectiveness can be restricted. The credibility hypothesis puts policy makers in a difficult situation, as they would find it hard to make changes in the direction of policy activism.

We have, in this chapter, discovered the problems involved in the policy making of monetary or fiscal changes. Because these problems exist, policy makers should be cautious about over-activism and unattainable objectives. Moreover, there are international effects of any policy change, fiscal or monetary, that we have not considered so far. We will devote our next chapter to that purpose.

Suggested Further Reading

Anderson, L. C. 1969. *An Evaluation of the Impacts of Monetary and Fiscal Policy on Economic Activity,* pp. 223–40. Proceeding of the Business and Economic Statistics Section, District of Columbia, American Statistical Association.

Ando Brown, A. E. C., R. Solow, and I. Karekan. 1963. *Lags in Fiscal and Monetary Policy.* Commission on Money and Credit, Stabilization Policies, Prentice Hall.

Cumbertson, J. M. 1960. Friedman on the Lag in Effect of Monetary Policy. *Journal of Political Economy,* December: 617–21.

Friedman, M. 1960. *A Program for Monetary Stability,* pp. 87–89. New York: Fordham University Press

Hamberger, M. J. 1969. The impact of monetary variables: a survey of recent econometric literature, pp. 37–49. *Essays in Domestic and International Finance.* Federal Reserve Bank of New York.

Mayer, T., J. Duesenberry, and R. Aliber. *Money, Banking and the Economy.* Norton and Norton.

Mayer, T. 1967. The lag in effect of monetary policy: Some criticisms. *Western Economic Journal,* September: 324–42.

Smith, W. L. 1956. On the effectiveness of monetary policy. *American Economic Review,* September: 588–606.

Thomas, L. 1985. *Money, Banking and Economic Activity,* 3rd ed., Chapter 22. Prentice Hall.

Warburton, C. 1971. Variability of the lag in the effect of monetary policy, 1919-1965. *Western Economic Journal,* June: 113–15.

Chapter 16

Macro-Monetary Theory in Open Economy Setting
IS-LM and BB Curve Derivations and Mundell-Fleming Model

SUMMARY

Lessons concentrating on the commodity and money markets would be incomplete without a detailed overview of how they interact to establish general equilibrium in an open economy setting. The IS-LM framework introduced in this chapter allows us to analyze both markets simultaneously as well as determine the effects of stabilization policies on an economy's general equilibrium combinations of interest rate and real output.

Our discussion of the IS-LM framework begins by deriving the IS and LM curves and explaining the reasons for their shifts. The IS curve is the locus of combinations of interest rate and income at which the commodity market is in equilibrium. Investment and savings are the main components of aggregate demand and aggregate supply, respectively, and they comprise the IS curve. A shift of the IS curve is precipitated by anything responsible for altering investment and/or saving behavior, including increases in business or consumer confidence and/or an expansionary fiscal policy. Moreover, the slope of the IS curve is determined by the economic multiplier and the elasticity of investment with regard to changes in the interest rate. The slope of this curve is downward sloping from left to right because investment rises as the interest rate decreases, which forces us to consider higher levels of income at lower interest rates in order for savings to remain on par with investment.

The LM curve is defined as the locus of combinations of interest rate and income at which the money market is in equilibrium. Consisting of money supply and money demand, the LM curve has a slope that depends on the elasticity of money demand to changes in the interest rate. There is a direct relationship between income and the interest rate levels which maintain money market equilibrium, meaning the LM curve is upward sloping from left to right. Shifts in the LM curve, meanwhile, are caused by changes in money supply and/or modified expectations of the future rate of inflation. For example, an expansionary monetary policy would introduce an excess supply of money into the money market, causing the LM curve to shift to the right and resulting in a lower interest rate and a higher GDP level. Obviously, the link between these two markets is the real interest rate, and the intersection of the IS and LM curves represents the special levels of GDP and interest rate at which equilibrium of both the commodity and money markets is achieved.

The chapter then discusses the "third" market of a macro-economy, represented by the balance of payments (BOP). The BOP is a record of an economy's transactions with the rest of the world, and some procedural points must be considered in order to understand its function. For example, double-entry accounting is used when recording each transaction. Also, the BOP is actually comprised of four smaller balances, including the balance of goods and services, the current account balance, the capital account balance, and the official reserve settlement balance.

The BB curve, which by definition is the locus of combinations of the interest rate and income levels at which the BOP is in equilibrium, is then considered. The slope of the BB curve is determined by the degree of mobility of financial capital internationally and shifts of this curve are caused by changes in the exchange rate. By applying Walras' Law—which states that the final nth market must also be in equilibrium if a system of n markets has n – 1 of them in equilibrium—we know that when the BB curve is superimposed on the aforementioned LM and IS curves, their meeting point establishes the long-run general equilibrium point of the macro-economy. Besides yielding the unique combinations of interest rate and income that achieve long-run general equilibrium, the IS-LM framework also allows us to analyze the effects of fiscal and monetary policy changes in the monetary and real sectors of the economy. An expansionary monetary policy, for instance, yields a lower interest rate and leads to a capital inflow, while expansionary fiscal policy increases the interest rate and leads to a capital outflow.

The chapter concludes by surveying the three principal approaches of measuring the BOP. These include the Marshall-Lerner condition, which considers the overall effect of real exchange rate devaluation on a country's balance of trade; the Absorption approach, which states that a currency devaluation must be associated with an action that leads to lower absorption in order for it to create a surplus in the Balance of Payments; and the Monetary approach, which asserts that changes in the Balance of Payments are caused by capital inflows and outflows, such that excess demand for (and excess supply of) money is responsible for a deficit (or surplus) in a country's Balance of Payments.

16.1 Introduction: Derivation of IS-LM Curves: Basic Concepts

Chapter 6 concentrated on commodity market transactions and its equilibrium, while Chapter 12 went through the discussion of the money market in Keynesian terms. The analysis of the commodity market can be carried out in real terms, without much regard to monetary variables. In Chapter 12, we dealt with the money market equilibrium and transactions in purely monetary or nominal terms. The link between the commodity market and money market is observed to be the real interest rate. The interest rate affects investment in the commodity market and the demand for money in the money market. Also, national income, or aggregate supply of an economy, influences the consumption in the commodity market and the demand for money in the money market. With this in mind, one can imagine some special levels of GDP and interest rate at which both markets can have equilibrium.

Sir John R. Hicks of Cambridge University developed a special technique called the IS-LM framework in the late 1930s to analyze the equilibrium of both markets simultaneously by locating the equilibrium combination of the interest rate and income. In this chapter, we will develop the same IS-LM framework and use it to analyze the effects of the stabilization policies of an economy. Stabilization policies are defined as any actions of the government to stabilize the economy from business fluctuations, which supposedly take place in a free capitalistic economy.

There are two basic stabilization (or demand management) policies, namely *fiscal policy* (dealing with government expenditure and taxes) and *monetary policy* (dealing with money supply and interest rate). In this chapter, we will analyze the effects of these policies in terms of the IS-LM framework.

16.2 The Commodity Market Equilibrium and IS Curve

The commodity market, analyzed in Chapter 6, is said to be in equilibrium when aggregate demand in an economy is equal to aggregate supply. This is the same condition required to define the equilibrium level of income. If aggregate demand is greater than aggregate supply, the economy experiences inflation, and if aggregate supply is greater than aggregate demand, the economy suffers from a recession (or deflation). It is only when they are equal that there is neither inflationary nor deflationary pressure on the price level of an economy.

Assuming two simplifying things—namely an idle government sector, so that G = 0, Tx = 0, and a closed economy so that X = 0 and M = 0—the aggregate demand of an economy is defined as consumption (C) plus investment (I). The aggregate supply is total income, which is equal to consumption (C) plus saving (S). Hence, commodity market equilibrium is defined as follows:

For commodity market equilibrium we need

Aggregate demand (or total expenditure) = Aggregate supply (or total income)

or with the simplifying assumptions above, we need,

$$C + I = C + S$$

or we need

$$I = S.$$

Hence, if total investment in the economy is equally matched by the total saving in the economy, we say that commodity market equilibrium is established. Obviously, this condition is exactly the same as defining the equilibrium level of income. Thus, the IS curve is defined as the locus of combinations of interest rate and income (Y) at which the commodity market is in equilibrium.

Investment, as we have seen in Chapter 6, is decided by the MEC and interest rate level. The lower the interest rate, the higher the investment level will be, and the higher the equilibrium level of income. Hence, as the interest rate goes down in the commodity market, investment increases, and if we want saving to be equal to investment (i.e., re-define commodity market equilibrium), then we must consider a higher level of income. Only at a higher level of income do people tend to save more. Thus, the locus of interest rates and income levels that keep the commodity market in equilibrium is seen by the downward sloping line from left to right.

In terms of a numerical example, let us suppose that the interest rate is 12 percent, and at that interest rate investors decide to invest $100. The level of income that generates a saving of $100 (supposing MPS = .2) is $500. Hence, at an interest rate of 12 percent, $500 is the income level that keeps the commodity market in equilibrium. In Figure 16.1, the combination of interest rate of 12 percent and income of $500 is plotted by point K. Now let us assume that the interest rate goes down to 10 percent so that the MEC becomes greater than interest rate (r). When the MEC is greater than r, investors decide to invest more than $100, perhaps $150. In order to consider saving to be $150 (so that the commodity market will again be in equilibrium), we must consider an income level of $750 (with assumed MPS = .2).

Initially, with the interest rate of 12 percent, MEC must have been 12 percent, because for optimum investment determination as we saw in Chapter 5, we need equality of MEC and r. Hence, as interest rate declines to 10 percent we find that MEC > r, so investment begins to increase.

Thus, the combination shown by point S in Figure 16.1 also establishes commodity market equilibrium. By repeating this procedure, we can plot a few other points on the graph, and by joining these points, the resulting curve is known as the IS curve. At each point on the IS curve, we have equality of investment and saving (therefore, the name IS). If we relax the simplifying assumption that we made earlier, the IS curve might change its location, but the inverse relationship that it shows would stay the same. An active government, for example, adds government expenditure (G) as another expenditure item to aggregate demand, and taxes (T) as another income item to the income side. Hence, commodity market equilibrium requires:

$$C + I + G = C + S + T$$

or

$$I + G = S + T$$

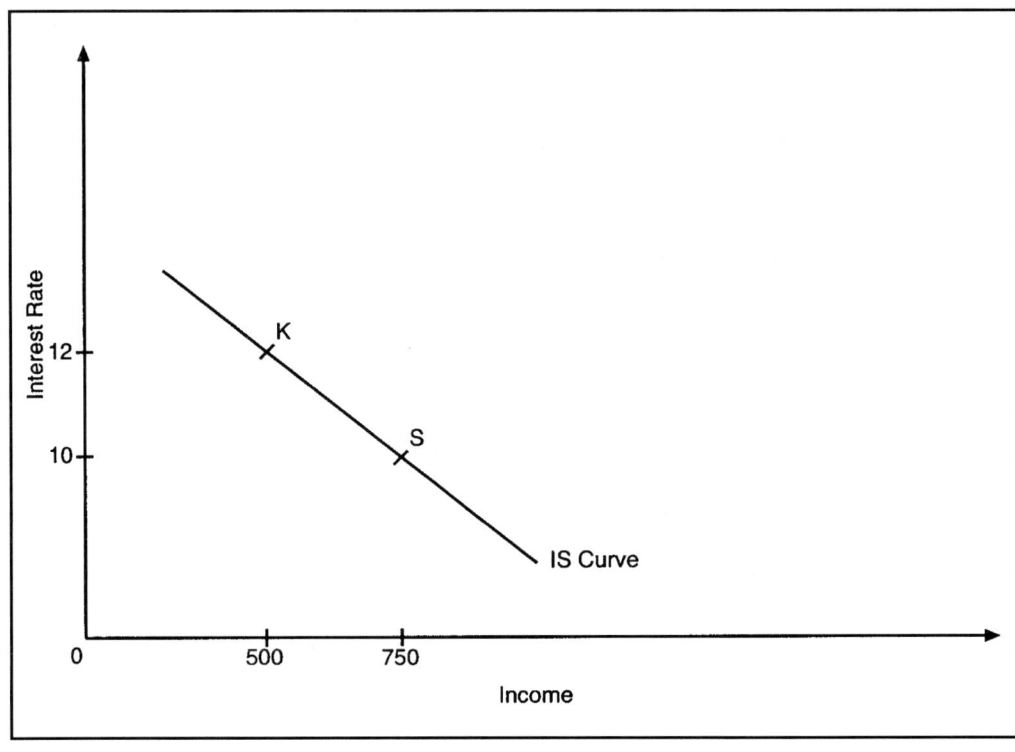

Derivation of IS Curve ■ FIGURE 16.1

Any factor that is responsible for changing investment (besides the interest rate, of course) causes a shift in the IS curve. For instance, if there is an increase of business confidence, there will be an increase in MEC, and an increase in investment expenditure. At the same interest rate, we would get higher level of equilibrium income; hence, all points of the IS curve would shift to the right. An improvement in business confidence, thus, can shift the IS curve to the right.

If government decides to carry out an expansionary fiscal policy (an increase in G), then we would also have an increase in equilibrium level of income, and so, all the points in the IS curve would be achieved to the right of the old IS curve. An increase in G will shift the IS curve to the right, and a decrease in it will shift the IS curve to the left. The value of the multiplier (K), which depends upon MPS, is capable of shifting the IS curve as well. A lower value of MPS (that means higher value of multiplier) can shift the IS curve to the right; the value of the multiplier also changes the slope of the IS curve. The higher value of K creates a flatter IS curve.

Another factor that determines the slope of the IS curve is the responsiveness of investment to the changes in interest rate. This responsiveness is also referred to as *elasticity*. A higher elasticity means that, with a small decrease in interest rate, there is greater increase in investment; this creates a flatter IS curve. (For mathematical treatment of this, please see Gordon in Suggested Further Reading.)

Any factor that influences the saving behavior of the public can also cause a shift in the IS curve. Suppose an improvement in consumer confidence induces a reduction in the marginal propensity to save. Saving would decrease in this case, and the IS curve should shift to the right because we have higher consumption. To summarize in Thomas' words, "an event which shifts I + G rightward (upward) or S + T leftward (downward) will shift the IS schedule rightward (upward) and thus exert an expansionary effect on GDP. Any event which shifts I + G leftward (downward) or S + T rightward (upward) will shift the IS schedule leftward (downward) and thereby exert a contradictory influence on GDP."

16.3 Money Market Equilibrium and Derivation of the LM Curve

Money market, as introduced in Chapter 6, consists of the money supply (MS) and the demand for money forces. The money supply, in general, consists of coins, currency, and demand deposits, and is controllable by the central bank of the economy. Money supply is therefore regarded as an autonomous or exogenous variable.

Demand for money is hypothesized in Chapter 6 to be a function of interest rate and income levels of an economy. It is positively related to income and negatively related to the interest rate, as depicted in Figure 16.2. The money market is said to be in equilibrium when the demand for money is equal to the supply of money, as is the case with point J in Figure 16.2. However, note that when we drew the curve in Figure 16.2 representing the demand for money (which shows the inverse relationship between interest rate and money demand), we had implicitly assumed a constant income level. Otherwise, as income changes the demand curve for money, it is likely to shift from one location to another. At higher incomes with the given interest rate, people tend to demand more money, hence, there would be a rightward shift in the demand for money curve.

The LM curve is defined as the locus of combinations of interest rate and income, at which the money market is in equilibrium. As income increases, the demand curve for money in Figure 16.2 shifts to the right, and with a constant money supply the interest rate needed to achieve money market equilibrium is higher. Hence, there is a direct, or positive, relationship between income and interest rate levels that keep the money market in equilibrium.

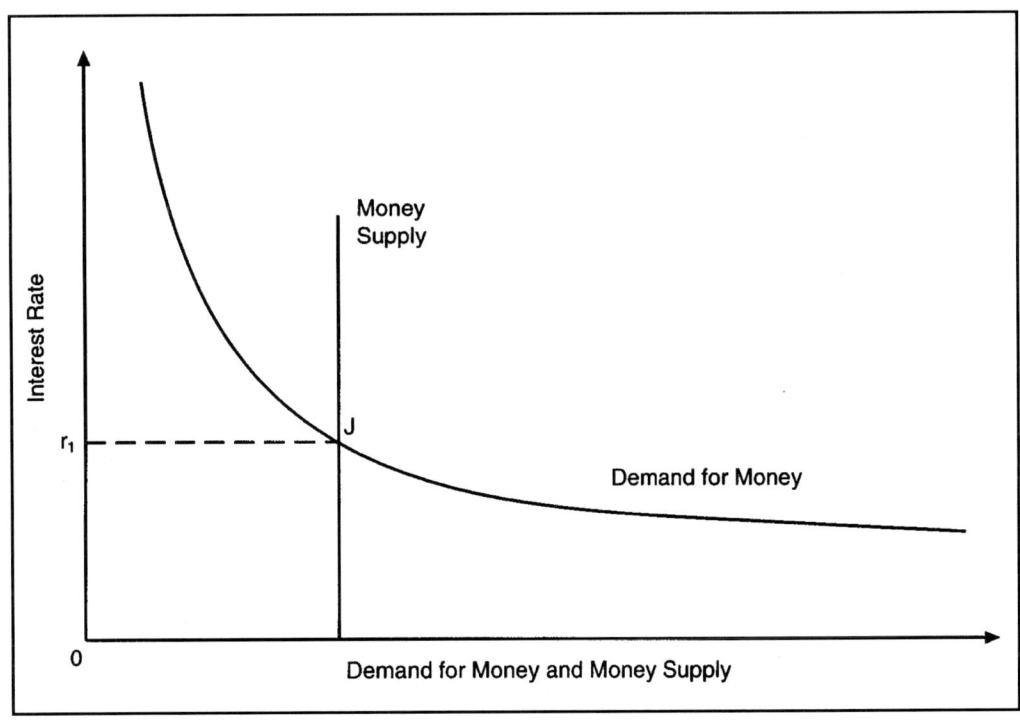

Money Market Equilibrium ■ FIGURE 16.2

Let us suppose that at an income of $100 and an interest rate of 6 percent, the demand for money is equal to 60. Let us suppose, too, that the money supply as determined by the central bank of the economy is equal to 60. Hence, the given combination of interest rate and income is on the LM curve. In Figure 16.3, that combination is shown by point A. As we consider an increase in income from $100 to $150, demand for money would increase from 60 to a higher level (say, 85). Now if we desire to bring the demand for money back to be equal to the supply of money, we must consider an interest rate higher than 6 percent (say 9 percent). Hence, the new combination of interest rate (9 percent) and income (150) would also keep the money market in equilibrium. Obviously, there are infinite combinations of income and interest rates that can be found in this manner. The curve joining these combinations is called the LM curve.

The points on the lower left portion of the LM curve have a low level of income, and, therefore, a lower demand for money than that needed for money market equilibrium. These points are characterized by an excess supply of money. Similarly, points on the right side of the LM curve show higher income, and a higher demand for money needed for money market equilibrium. These points show an excess demand for money in the money market. The slope of the LM curve clearly depends upon the responsiveness (or elasticity) of demand for money to the changes in the interest rates. If this responsiveness is very high, then even

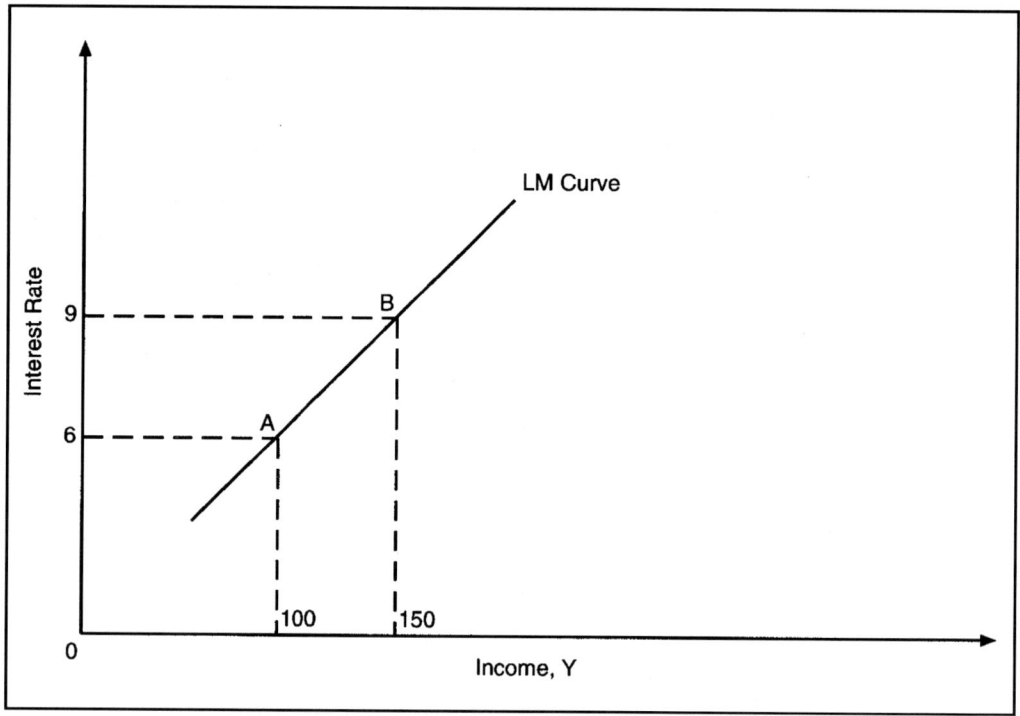

FIGURE 16.3 ■ LM Curve

a small change in the interest rate will bring about a large change in the demand for money, while a large increase in interest market rate would create money market equilibrium, giving a flatter shape to the LM curve. Obviously, in the reverse case, when demand for money is inelastic with respect to the interest rate, the LM takes a steeper shape. In extreme cases when demand for money is completely elastic with respect to the interest rate, the LM curve would be horizontal. When the demand for money is completely inelastic (absolutely non-responsive to interest rate changes) then the LM curve would be vertical.

Shifts in the LM curve may be caused by the actions of monetary authorities. An increase in the money supply, for example, would shift the vertical money supply curve to the right in Figure 16.3, and the interest rate required for equilibrium in the money market would decline. In Figure 16.3, the LM curve would shift to the right. Similarly, a decrease in money supply would create a leftward shift of the LM curve.

Another variable that causes shifts in the LM curve is the expected rate of inflation. If people expect higher inflation in the future (this can happen for many different reasons, for example, an announcement from monetary authority to increase money supply in the future), then people would sell many of their securities (bonds) and get ready to beat the inflation by holding more money in cash. The demand for money would increase, and the demand curve for money would shift rightward. At any given income level then, we would observe a higher interest rate that would keep the money market in equilibrium. This causes a shift of all points on the LM curve to the left. Thus, an expectation of higher inflation rate causes a leftward shift in the LM curve, and expectations of declining inflation in the future make the LM curve shift to the right. Having seen the derivations of IS and LM curves and the reasons for their shifts, we are in a position to use them for defining the general equilibrium of an economy.

General Equilibrium of a Macro-Economy 16.4

At all points on the IS curve we have shown the existence of commodity market equilibrium. At all points on the LM curve, the money market of an economy is in equilibrium. The intersection point of the IS and LM curves would therefore establish the equilibrium of the entire economy if we assume that there are only three markets.

At any point to the left of the LM curve, we have excess money supply in the money market, and at any point to the right of the LM curve we may observe an excess demand for money. This is because at all points to the left of the LM curve, the interest rate is higher than that required for money market equilibrium. Hence, quantity of money demanded is lower than quantity of money supplied.

Similarly, at any point to the left of the IS curve, we have excess supply of commodities. At all points to the left of the IS curve, the interest rate is lower than that required for commodity market equilibrium (or for making investment = saving), leading to higher aggregate demand (C + I) than aggregate supply (C + S).

This can be further explained as follows: Consider point J in Figure 16.4, where the interest rate is r_2 and income is Y_2. However, for commodity market equilibrium (or for point L on the IS curve), one needs Y_2 income and r_1 interest rate. Hence, the interest rate at point J is lower than that required for commodity market equilibrium. Therefore, investment at point J is higher than that required for commodity market equilibrium, leading to higher aggregate demand than aggregate supply.

The same logic can be used to determine excess demand (or excess supply) in the commodity or money markets at any other point that is outside the IS or LM curves.

At the intersection point of the IS and LM curves, the economy has equilibrium in the commodity as well as the money market. Point E in Figure 16.4 is called the "general equilibrium" point. Thus, the IS-LM framework yields the unique combination of interest rate and income that achieves the general equilibrium. This is probably the biggest advantage of constructing the IS-LM framework. Another

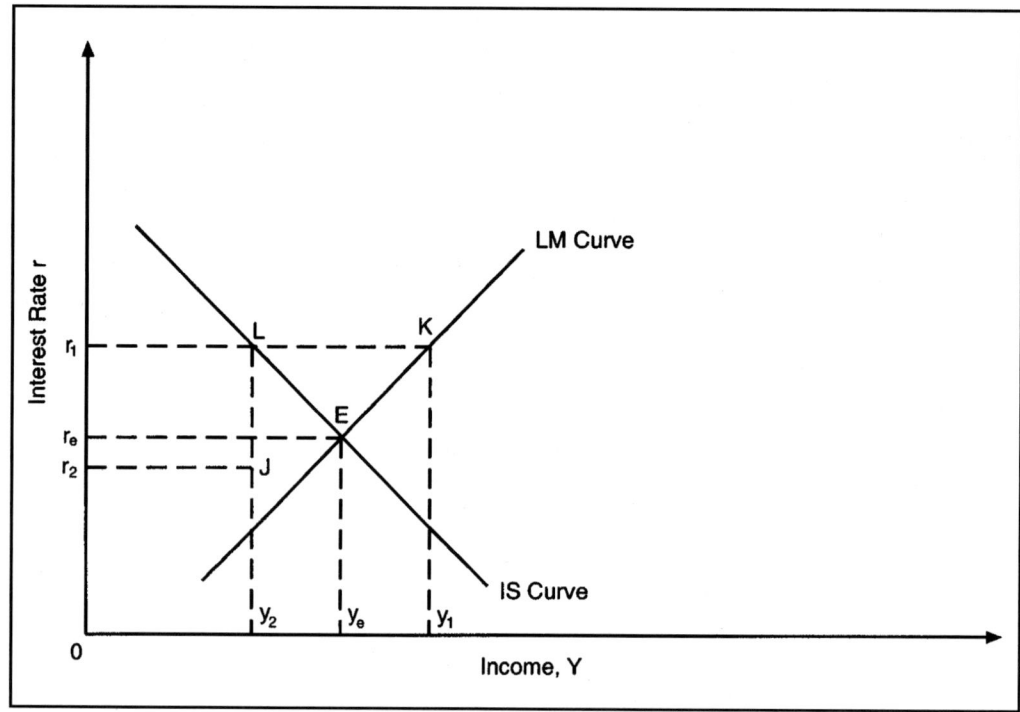

FIGURE 16.4 ▪ General Equilibrium and IS-LM

important benefit of this framework explains how an economy possesses a built-in mechanism, by which point E would always be attained in the long run. Suppose the economy is experiencing Y_1 income level, r_1 interest rate, and is at point K. With these levels of income and interest rate, there would be equilibrium in the money market (K is on the LM curve), but excess supply of commodities in the goods market. Due to the lack of sufficient demand, inventories would accumulate, interest rate would start going down, and income would start declining. As GDP declines, demand for money decreases and interest rate drops further. The economy achieves lower levels of interest rates and income in this manner. This process is expected to continue as long as there is disequilibrium in the commodity market.

In the long run, the combination of interest rate and income, shown by point E, is established.

Monetary Disturbances and the IS-LM Framework 16.5

Another advantage of the IS-LM framework is its ability to analyze the effects of disturbances in the monetary as well as the real sectors of an economy.

To analyze the effect of an expansionary monetary policy on general equilibrium, we will begin with a situation at point E_1 in Figure 16.5, with interest rate r_1 and income Y_1. With an increase in money supply, there happens to be an excess supply of money in the money market, and the LM curve shifts to the right. The increase in money supply created by buying government securities from the public increases the demand for securities and increases its price, lowering its yield. The interest rate, therefore, is expected to go down due to the expansionary monetary policy. This reduced interest rate is responsible for an increase in investment in the commodity market. The increased investment, due to multiple processes, raises the level of GDP of an economy. Hence, with the LM curve shifting to the right, the economy attains a new equilibrium at point E_2, with interest rate r_2 lower than before and an income level higher than before.

Similarly, if people expect an increase in interest rates in the future (for whatever reason), then the demand for money may increase causing excess demand for money in the money market. This would shift the LM curve to the left because, at the same level of income, there would be a higher interest rate that would achieve the money market equilibrium. With the LM curve shifting to the left, the economy may end up with lower income and higher interest rates in this case. In general, any event that increases (decreases) demand for money (money supply) causes an excess demand for money, and becomes responsible for shifting the LM curve to the left. This event leads to higher interest rates and lower income in the economy. On the other hand, any event that decreases (increases) demand for

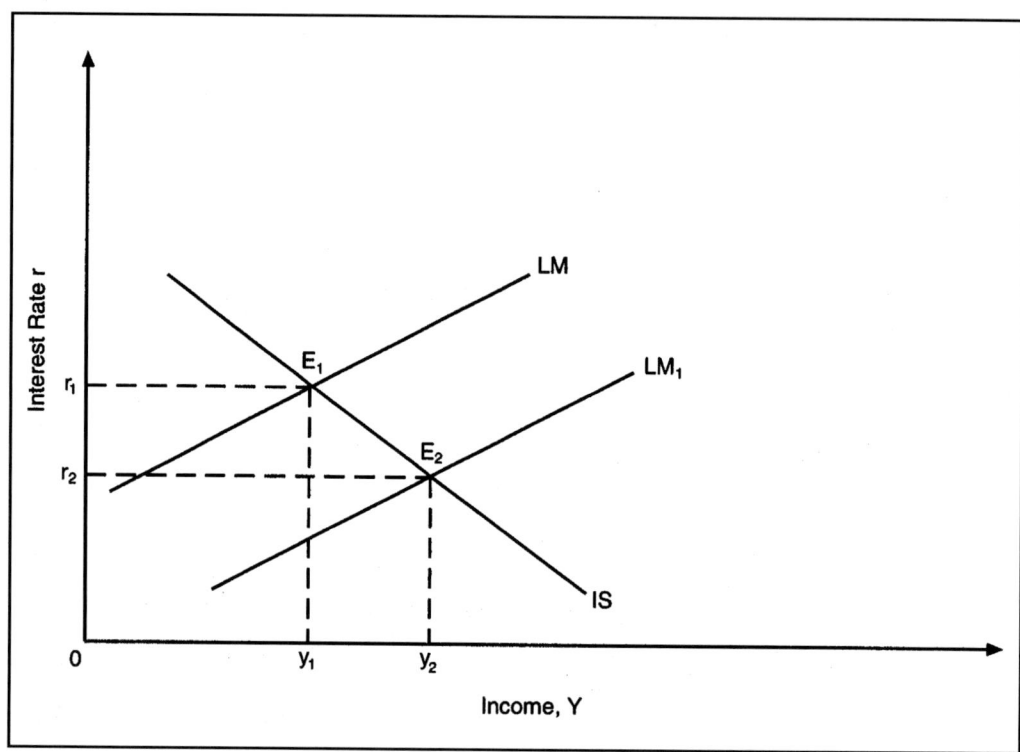

FIGURE 16.5 ■ Monetary Policy and IS-LM

money (money supply) causes an excess supply in the money market, and thereby shifts the LM curve to the right. This event leads to lower interest rates and a higher income in the economy. Thus, the effectiveness of monetary policy can be observed by using the IS-LM framework.

16.6 Disturbances in the Real Sector and IS-LM Framework

The real sector disturbances are basically generated by the government making changes in fiscal policy. As mentioned before, changes in taxes, as well as changes in government expenditures, are responsible for shifting the IS curve from one location to another. Suppose the government decides to increase the income tax rate. This would create lower consumption because the disposable income of the economy would be reduced by higher taxes. An increase in income taxes, therefore, would lead to lower aggregate demand, and would shift the IS curve to the left. Similarly, an increase in corporate tax would create a lower expected profit rate for corporations. This may lead to lower investment, and may also cause a leftward shift of the IS curve.

An increase in government expenditure (an expansionary fiscal policy action, to be more general) can have an effect on the aggregate demand of an economy. An increase in government expenditure, due to the multiplier process, causes an increased expenditure that is financed by selling bonds to the public. This creates an excess supply of bonds in the market, which reduces the price of bonds and increases the interest rate needed to be offered on it. Nonetheless, in this case, fiscal policy action is said to be effective because it leads to a higher level of GDP. The difference between the effectiveness of expansionary fiscal and monetary policies is that the former leads to a higher interest rate, while the latter leads to a lower interest rate. According to Keynes, if both policies are pursued simultaneously, then a constant lower interest rate is possible together with economic growth and higher employment.

In an extreme (special) case of the existence of the liquidity trap, the ineffectiveness of monetary policy can be analyzed by simple modification in the IS-LM framework. When the liquidity trap exists, the shape of the demand curve for money becomes horizontal and it has repercussions on the shape of the LM curve. As long as the interest rate is very low, the demand curve for money is horizontal and therefore the LM curve is horizontal. When the interest rate is higher than the lowest possible level, the demand curve for money has a normal downward sloping curve.

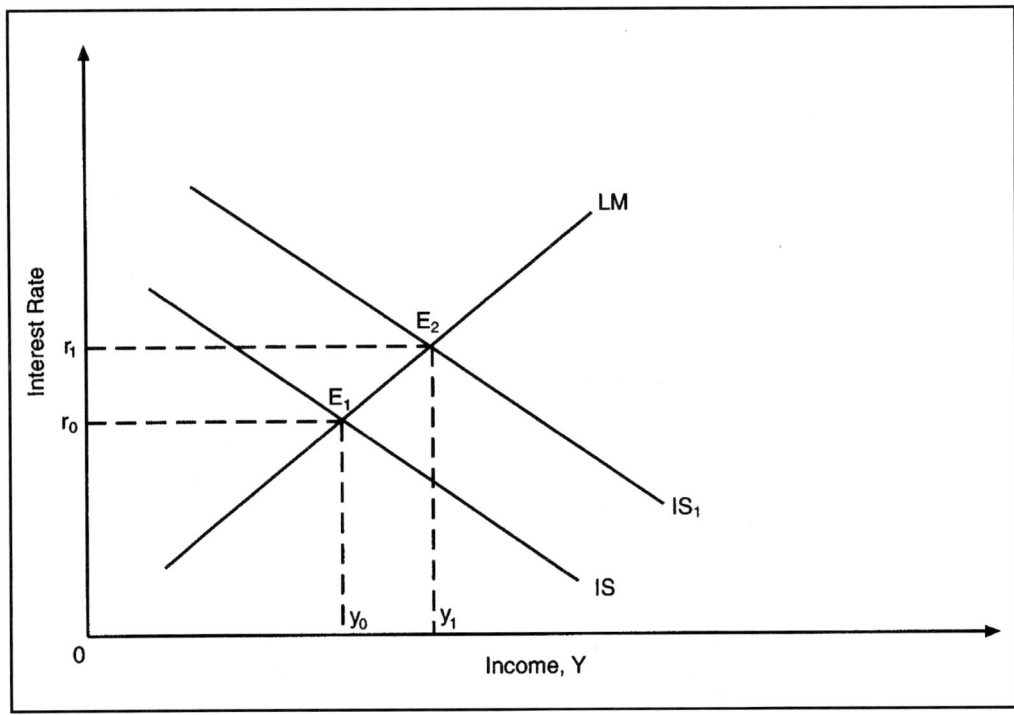

Effectiveness of Fiscal Policy and IS-LM ■ **FIGURE 16.6**

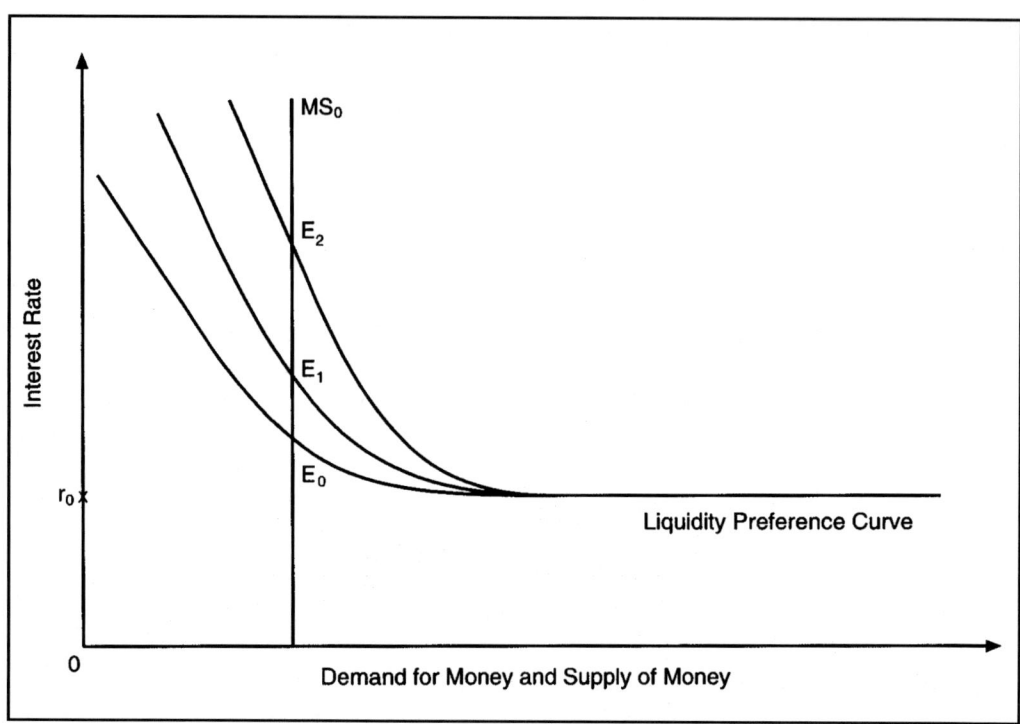

FIGURE 16.7 ■ Liquidity Trap and Demand for Money Curve

Hence, at r_0 interest rate, the LM curve is horizontal. If the interest rate happens to be higher than r_0, the demand for money would have the usual shape, and the LM curve is upward sloping as usual for all interest rates, except the minimum level. Any expansionary monetary policy in this case would be unable to shift the horizontal part of the LM curve. (This is because there would always be a liquidity trap at the r_0 level of interest rate.) The monetary policy becomes completely ineffective due to the existence of the liquidity trap. Thus, in a liquidity trap, the Keynesian chain breaks down. Given the downward sloping IS curve, however, there is no limit to the effectiveness of fiscal policy, which causes a shift in the IS curve. An expansionary fiscal action, for example, could always make the IS curve shift to the right, and new general equilibrium will be achieved to the right of point J in Figure 16.8. Thus, the IS-LM framework is useful for analyzing the special problem like the liquidity trap. A unique characteristic of the IS-LM framework is that it considers the equilibria of money and commodity markets simultaneously. As we just saw, it can be modified to show limitless effectiveness of fiscal policy and complete ineffectiveness of monetary policy in the case of a liquidity trap.

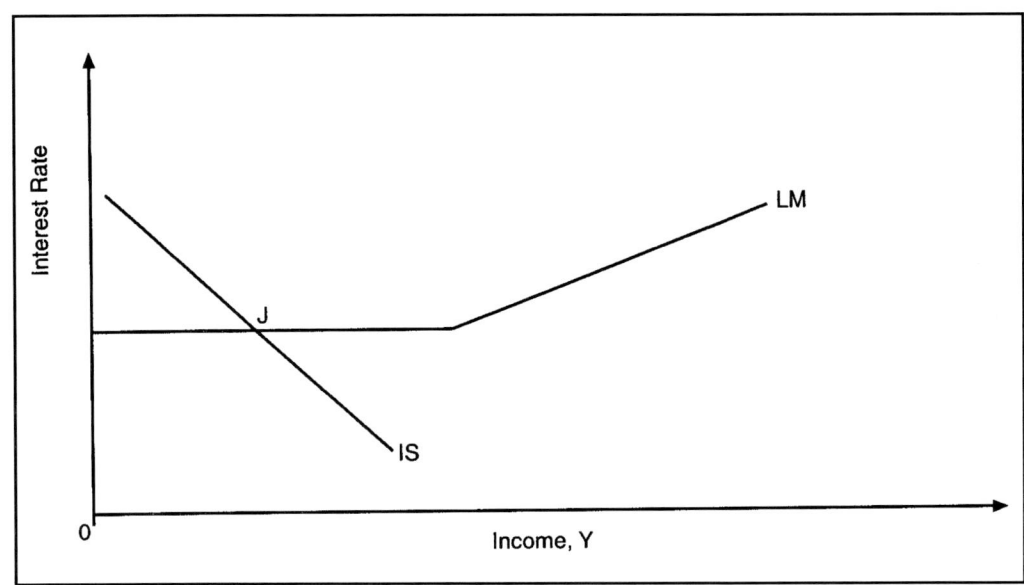

Liquidity Trap and LM Curve ■ **FIGURE 16.8**

We can also analyze the other extreme case of classical economists' belief in the quantity theory of money and its effect on the shape of the LM curve with the use of Figure 16.9. Strictly speaking, the quantity theory equation of Chapter 9 emphasizes only the medium of exchange function of money. The demand for money is either not recognized by the quantity theory, or is assumed to be independent of the interest rate. Hence, the demand for money is assumed to be completely non-responsive (inelastic) with respect to interest rate changes. In this case, the demand for money is shown by a vertical straight line, and there is only one income level that can achieve money market equilibrium. Obviously, given only one income level that keeps the money market in equilibrium, the shape of the LM curve is also vertical.

In this special case of a vertical LM curve, no fiscal policy action (the shifts in IS curve) can be effective to cause changes in income and employment of an economy. The monetary policy, however, is able to shift the LM curve to the right—an expansionary monetary policy would create excess money supply, and to achieve another money market equilibrium by wiping this excess out, we must consider a higher level of income. Hence, as shown in Figure 16.9, the LM curve shifts right due to an expansionary monetary policy and can be effective in creating a higher level of income and employment. To classical economists, these actions were not desirable. They were advocates of the laissez-faire policy, which means letting the economy function by itself and not intervening in the efficient market forces that are supposed to cure any disequilibrium situation.

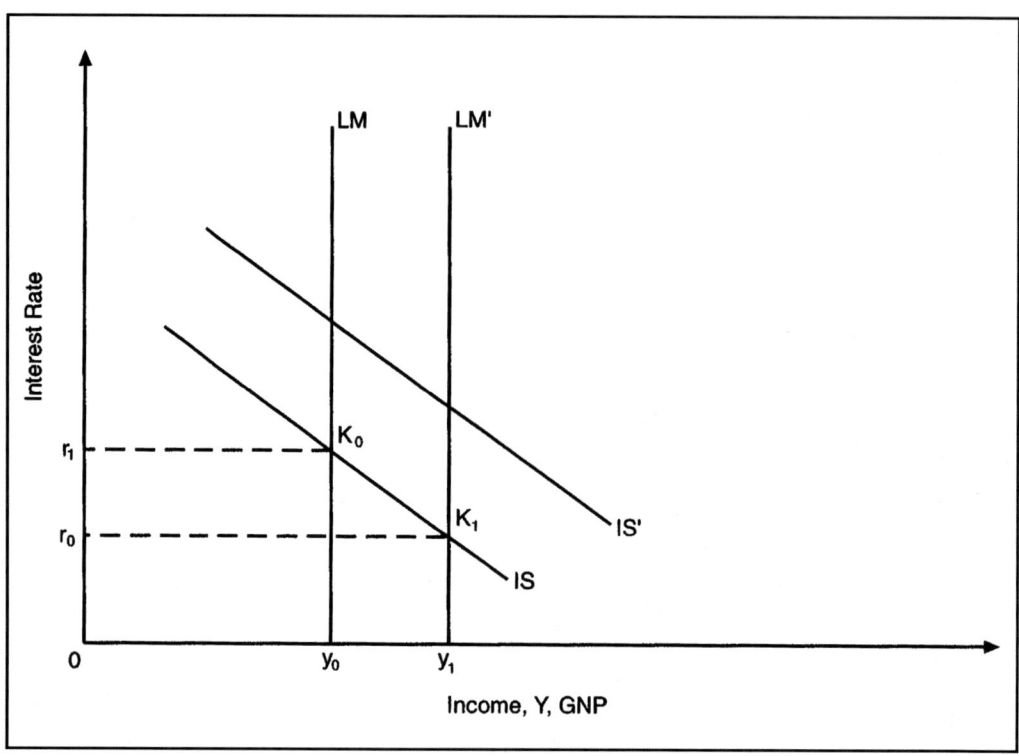

FIGURE 16.9 ■ Classical Model and IS-LM

Proponents of the IS-LM framework use it to analyze several other real world problems. A reader can make up problems of his/her own, and can examine their effects on the IS and LM curves to summarize their consequences on national income and interest rates.

16.7 Macro-Monetary Theory in Open Economy Setting

So far this book has dealt only with the analysis of a closed economy. It is, however, a grave mistake to think that monetary theory does not include concerns about the economy's openness and that there is little to talk about monetary theory in an open economy setting. In fact, in the last few decades, few other areas of economic science have developed faster than the area of open economy's monetary theory. We now present a few important definitions of such concepts as the balance of payments (BOP) of an economy, the foreign exchange market, and equilibrium of the external sector of the economy. By using the external sector's equilibrium one can also discuss the general equilibrium idea with the help of the IS and LM curves.

Balance of Payments (BOP) of an Economy 16.8

Any discussion of the Balance of Payments (BOP) needs clarification of some procedural points. First, BOP in general is defined as a record of international transactions of an economy with the rest of the world. International transactions are of two basic types: (1) transactions of goods and services, and (2) transactions of financial assets such as bonds, stocks, etc. While recording the BOP, entries are divided into different balances that concentrate on the recording of specific exchanges.

Second, for BOP recording, only the permanent residents of a country are considered to be the domestic residents. Hence, such persons as visitors, temporary workers, foreign students, or diplomats are seen as foreign nationals. In fact, the purchases of these individuals are the same as an export from a country. A payment to these individuals is also seen as a capital outflow from the country. Third, any activity that leads to an increase in the purchasing power of the domestic residents is recorded as a credit on the BOP, and any activity that results in a decline in the purchasing power is recorded as a debit.

Fourth, each transaction on the BOP is recorded twice following the "double entry bookkeeping" system. Fifth, contrary to general belief, just like a deficit in the BOP does not necessarily indicate a loss in an economy's welfare, a surplus in the BOP does not necessarily mean an increase in an economy's welfare. Therefore, it is not true that a country that has higher exports than imports is better off than a country that has higher imports than exports. One of the famous and witty economists, Herbert Stein, once made an interesting comment about the BOP deficit and surplus: "Last year I went to Paris, and spent a lot of money on shopping. This essentially created a large deficit on U.S. BOP but, I loved every minute of it!" Hence, one has to recognize that activities that create a deficit in the BOP do not necessarily lower the economy's welfare.

Consider another case of a purchase of domestic property by foreign residents. Clearly, when foreign residents buy domestic properties, one may think that this should lead to lower economic welfare. However, for BOP recording, this only means a capital inflow and, therefore, a credit on the capital balance leading to a surplus in the BOP. In any country's BOP records, there are basically four major balances.

BALANCE OF GOODS AND SERVICES ACCOUNT

This account records the transactions of goods and services as reported by the Department of Customs or Foreign Trade. This balance gets a credit entry when goods leave a country, and transactions that make foreign goods and services enter a country are recorded as debits. Hence, exports are a credit and imports are a debit. Surplus on this account is popularly called Net Exports.

BALANCE ON CURRENT ACCOUNT

This account records all transactions on the goods and services account, adding to it special transactions referred to as unilateral transfers. As the name suggests, unilateral transactions are those that are said to be "one way traffic"—those that leave the country without any expectation of repayment. Hence, such payments as foreign aid, retirement payments to retirees abroad, foreign base payments, and military personnel expenditure, etc., are classic examples of unilateral transactions. Current account therefore records all exports and imports, and adds to it the unilateral transactions.

CAPITAL ACCOUNT BALANCE

This balance is reserved for recording all capital transactions. When foreign residents buy domestic financial assets like bonds, stocks, government securities, etc., there is a capital inflow into the economy. These transactions are recorded as credit on the capital account. When domestic residents purchase foreign financial assets there is a capital outflow, and these transactions are recorded as debit on the balance of payment. Thus, a surplus occurs on the capital account when there is greater capital inflow than outflow.

OFFICIAL RESERVE SETTLEMENT BALANCE

This balance records all transactions that occur at the governmental level, or at the central bank level of a country. Clearly, when the central bank has a greater amount of foreign reserves in its possession, there is a credit on this balance. Of course, all central banks have reserves of foreign currencies, Special Drawing Rights (SDRs), gold stock, and such weighted currencies as European Currency Unit. Special Drawing Rights are issued by the International Monetary Fund, a fund of approximately 144 countries. Each member country is required to contribute to this fund per an accepted formula that depends on the size, population, and GDP of a country. If a particular country wants to contribute more than this formula requires, the IMF issues a Special Drawing Right (SDR). Thus, when a country has a large stock of SDRs, there is a credit on the official reserve balance of the BOP.

Therefore, balance on goods and services, current account balance, capital account balance, and official reserve settlement balance are the four major balances of the BOP. The three main economic variables that influence the BOP changes are: GDP (Y), exchange rate, and interest rate. When there is a higher GDP, there is a higher capacity of the economy to import from the outside world, and imports increase. Thus, there is a positive relationship between GDP and imports (M). An equation that shows this positive relationship is called the import function, and a typical import function is represented as follows:

$$M = m0 + m1Y$$

where m0 is the constant in import function, i.e., the amount of imports when the GDP is zero, or that part of import that is independent of GDP levels (m0 is also called autonomous imports), and m1 represents the slope of the import function, and is measured by the ratio of change in import over change in the GDP. The m1 is also called the marginal propensity to import (mpI).

The effect of an interest rate change is seen more on the capital account than on the current account. As domestic interest rates become higher than the foreign interest rates, foreign residents will tend to purchase domestic financial assets, and there will be a capital inflow creating a surplus on the capital account of the BOP. Similarly, a reduction in the domestic interest rate can create a capital outflow, as domestic residents will tend to buy more foreign financial assets. Exchange rate changes can also have an effect on the BOP by making imports or exports change. When the exchange rate increases (and domestic currency depreciates), then imports become more expensive, and if the import demand is elastic then there is a reduction in import. (Similarly there is an increase in exports with an increase in the exchange rate.)

FOREIGN EXCHANGE MARKET

The foreign exchange represents a number of foreign currencies. In fact, unless one has a common unit of measuring foreign currencies, one can treat foreign exchange only as a theoretical concept rather than a practically measurable item. But we can talk about only one foreign currency when we treat an exchange rate of domestic currency in terms of one foreign currency, and analyze the foreign exchange changes. Thus, in the foreign exchange market, consumers purchase foreign currencies and suppliers supply them. When the prices of foreign currencies are expressed in terms of domestic currency they are called *exchange rates*. There is a separate exchange rate for each foreign currency, but all the exchange rates are determined by supply and demand forces of the foreign exchange.

In practice, foreign exchange transactions can occur on the streets of Mumbai or Mombasa, or they can take place in a plush bank in Singapore. Nonetheless, the volume of foreign currencies bought and sold on a daily basis is as high as US$1 trillion. Clearly, the foreign exchange market is the largest market, and is the one that never closes. Traders can be individuals, banks, other financial institutions such as investment companies, multinational corporations (MNC), and governments.

EQUILIBRIUM OF FOREIGN EXCHANGE MARKET

In the foreign exchange market, there is a force of demand for foreign exchange and a force of supply of it. These two forces decide the exchange rate of a currency. The demand for foreign exchange is created by domestic residents when they want to import more from outside an economy. On the other hand, a supply of foreign exchange is created by foreign residents when they desire to import from us, leading to a higher quantity of our exports. For our analysis, let us define an exchange rate as the ratio of number of domestic currency units per foreign currency unit. Hence, as the exchange rate goes up, more domestic currency is available for foreign currency, so that there is a devaluation of the former.

On the other hand, as the exchange rate goes down, more foreign currency is available for the same amount of domestic currency, so there is revaluation of the domestic currency. In terms of the demand and supply of foreign exchange at a higher exchange rate, when the value of domestic currency is lower with respect to foreign currency, there is higher demand for our products from the foreign residents, which creates a higher supply of foreign exchange. In terms of Figure 16.10, there is a direct relationship between the exchange rate and the supply of foreign exchange. (This is a simplified explanation of the real derivation of the curve. An advanced textbook would make it clear that depending upon the value of elasticity it is possible to have a backward bending supply curve for foreign exchange.)

When an exchange rate is higher, and when the value of domestic currency in terms of foreign currency is lower, domestic residents reduce their demand for foreign products. This is because with the new lower value of domestic currency, the foreign products are more expensive. Hence, our imports go down, leading to a lower demand for foreign exchange. In Figure 16.10, the demand for foreign exchange curve slopes downward from left to right because of this inverse relationship between the exchange rate and the quantity demanded of the foreign exchange.

At a point where demand and supply of foreign exchange curves meet, the equilibrium of the foreign exchange market is established. The exchange rate at which these demand and supply forces are equal is called the *equilibrium exchange rate.*

At any exchange rate above the equilibrium exchange rate, there is a higher quantity of foreign exchange supplied than demanded, leading to a surplus in the BOP. At a lower exchange rate there is a deficit in the BOP. Balance of payments

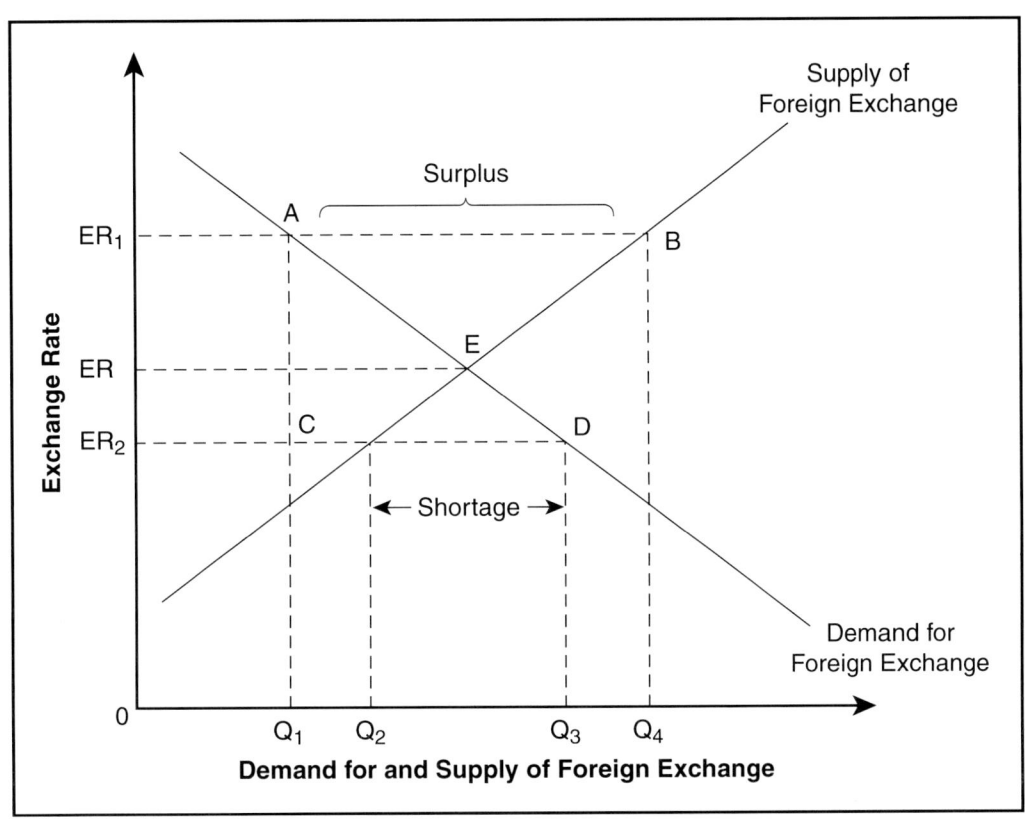

Demand for and Supply of Foreign Exchange ■ **FIGURE 16.10**

is in equilibrium at the point where the demand for and supply of foreign exchange curves intersect.

Now let us examine an effect of interest rate change on the equilibrium of the foreign exchange market. As mentioned before, at a higher interest rate there is an increase in the capital inflow as more and more financial capital would be allocated to the domestic economy from abroad to gain from the higher interest rate. This increased inflow of foreign capital would create a surplus in the BOP of the economy. Therefore, an increase in the interest rate creates a surplus in the BOP. On the other hand, as mentioned in the import function, an increase in the GDP of an economy would influence the amount of imports of that economy. A higher GDP would create a higher quantity of imports and, therefore, a deficit in the BOP of an economy. If we try to find out combinations of interest rates and income levels that keep the BOP in equilibrium, then they would be shown by an upward sloping curve from left to right. These combinations are shown in Figure 16.11 and are joined by a curve called the *BB curve*. The BB curve by definition is the locus of combinations of interest rates and incomes at which the BOP of an economy is in

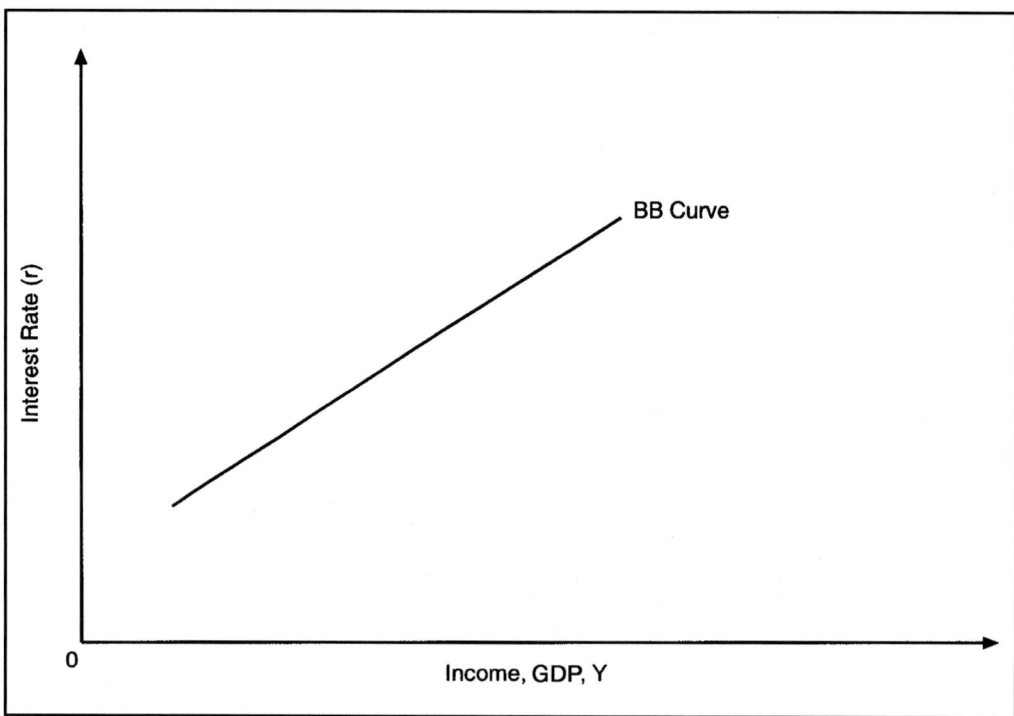

FIGURE 16.11 ■ The BB Curve

equilibrium. The slope of the BB curve depends on the international mobility of financial capital. If the capital is very mobile internationally, then a small change in interest rates creates a large inflow and outflow of capital. This makes a large disequilibrium in the BOP. To have another point of equilibrium, we need a large change in GDP to be associated with a small change rate. Hence, the BB curve is flatter when the international capital mobility is higher. In fact, in an extreme case of perfectly mobile capital, the BB curve is horizontal. When the capital is perfectly immobile, the slope of the BB curve is vertical.

Shift of the BB curve is created by changes in the exchange rate. If the exchange rate increases (and domestic currency depreciates), then at the same interest rate we need a higher GNP level to have equilibrium in the BOP. This is because increases in exchange rates create higher exports and lower imports. Therefore, to have BOP = 0, we need to have higher Y with any given interest rate; hence, the BB curve shifts to right.

Together with the IS and LM curves, we now have the BB curve that can be used to redefine the general equilibrium in an economy. In Figure 16.12, the money market, the commodity market, and the BOP of the economy are in equilibrium at point E, and the general equilibrium is said to be established at that point.

There is a special reason why the BB curve will have to pass through the intersection point of the IS and LM curves, which is given by Walras' Law that states:

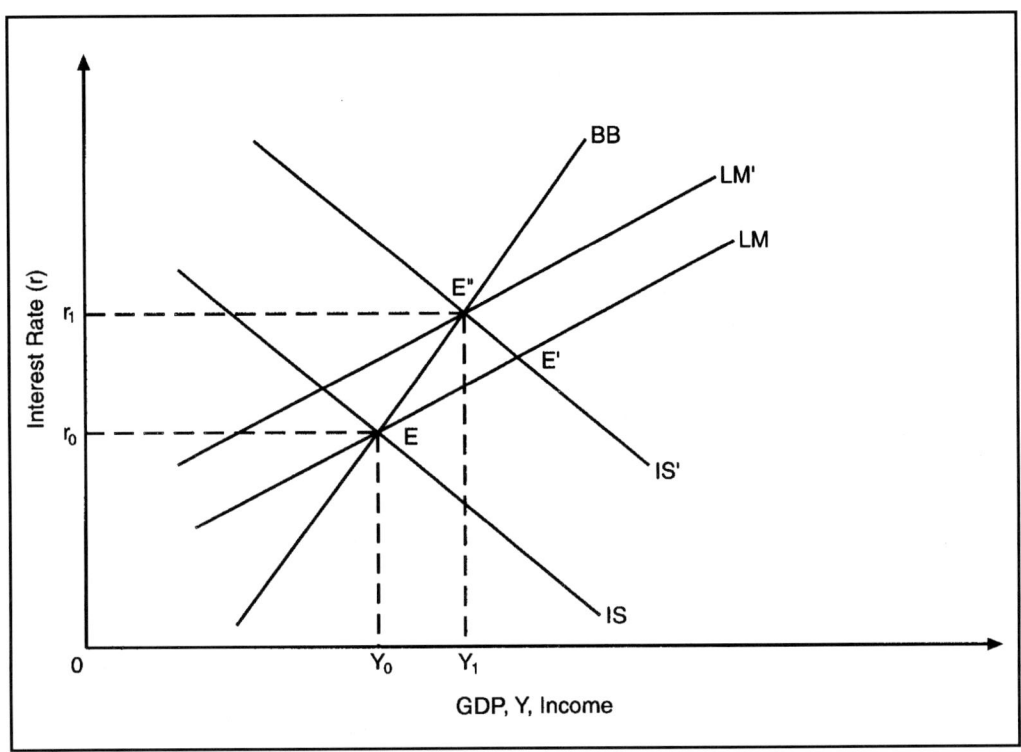

General Equilibrium Using BB Curve ■ **FIGURE 16.12**

If there are "n" markets in the economy, and if n − 1 markets are in equilibrium, then the nth market is also in equilibrium. When we consider only three markets in the economy—namely money, commodity, and international trade—then by using Walras' Law, it is obvious that the BB curve must pass through the point at which the commodity and money markets are simultaneously in equilibrium (i.e., through the intersection point of the IS and LM curves).

Now let us analyze the changes in the equilibrium combinations of interest rates and income due to fiscal and monetary policy activities in an open economy setting. Let us suppose initially that the fiscal policy action happens to be expansionary (i.e., there is either an increase in government expenditure, and/or a reduction in taxes, and/or both). Due to this, the IS curve would shift to the right. As government expenditure is financed by selling bonds to the public, the supply of bonds would go up and the price of bonds would go down, leading to a higher interest rate. But a higher interest rate can have two types of effects on money and the international market. In the money market, there is a decrease in demand and, therefore, a movement on the demand for money curve to the left.

In terms of the IS-LM-BB analysis, there is a shift of the LM curve to the left. Also, the higher interest rate is responsible for an inflow of foreign capital into the country. This leads to a surplus in the BOP of the economy. In terms of

Figure 16.12, due to expansionary fiscal policy, the general equilibrium point moves from point E to E' to E". Thus, an expansionary fiscal policy is accompanied by a surplus of BOP, assuming that the higher GDP has no effect on the imports of goods and services. If higher government expenditure is responsible for higher GDP, which in turn causes a higher amount of imports, then there could be a nullifying effect on the BOP.

Similar to the fiscal policy change, we can also use the IS-LM-BB curves to examine the effectiveness of monetary policy in the open economy setting. Let us suppose that monetary authority decides to increase the money supply. In terms of Figure 16.13, as the money supply is increased, there would be an initial change in the money market, leading to a rightward shift of the LM curve to LM_1.

A rightward shift of the LM curve would lead to a decrease in the interest rate of the economy, and increase in the GDP level. A lower interest rate is also responsible for the increase in private domestic investment, leading to a higher GDP level. Hence, the IS curve would shift to the right to IS_1'. Final equilibrium is reached at point K in Figure 16.13. Therefore, in terms of having an open economy equilibrium, it is better that an expansionary monetary policy is carried out.

An expansionary monetary policy, via the lower interest rate created by it, leads to an inflow of capital. An expansionary fiscal policy, on the other hand,

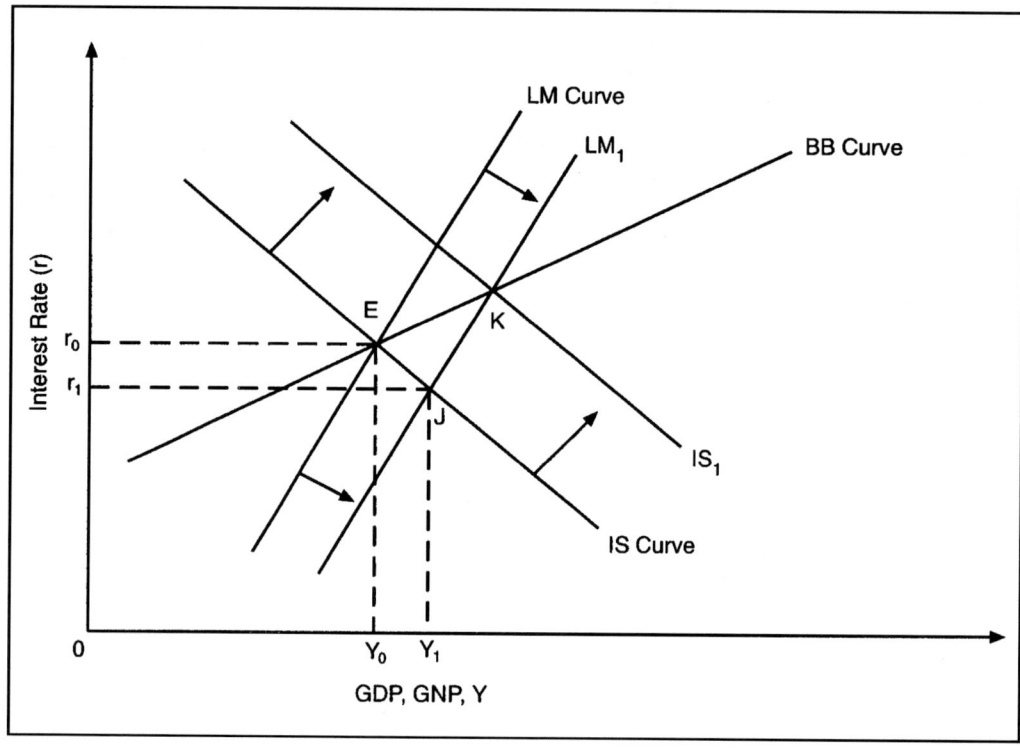

FIGURE 16.13 ■ Expansionary Monetary Policy in Open Economy Setting

leads to higher interest rates and, therefore, outflow of financial capital. Nonetheless, both policies lead to higher GDP levels, which would create a deficit on the current account of an economy's BOP.

A more complicated analysis can determine the effects of capital mobility on the effectiveness of monetary and fiscal policy. It can also derive an international autonomous expenditure multiplier. We shall leave these issues for an advanced textbook and refrain from discussing them here. In the following section, however, we will focus on different approaches to analyzing the behavior of an economy's BOP.

16.9 Behavior of the BOP: A Survey of Approaches

One of the most famous approaches to explain the behavior of the BOP is the Keynesian approach. It concentrates on the values of elasticities of demand for export and import of an economy. With the help of a famous mathematical condition derived by two popular economists, Alfred Marshall and Abba Lerner, called the Marshall-Lerner condition. The Keynesian approach dictates that the BOP behaves in a very special way. More specifically, a decline in the value of a country's currency may not lead to a surplus in the BOP if the sum of elasticities of demand for export and for imports is less than unity, or one. Thus, the Keynesian approach relies on the elasticities and is also referred to as the elasticity approach.

The second approach to the BOP behavior was developed by Sidney Alexander in 1951, and is called the absorption approach. To elaborate the absorption approach's arguments, a simple identity of total expenditure = total income is used. Consider the total expenditure of an economy as $C + I + G + X - M$, and total income as equal to the level of GNP of Y. Moreover, ignore the capital flows by assuming a perfect capital immobility. In this case, the BOP is defined by export and import alone, and therefore $BOP = X - M$. If we denote $C + I + G$ by one letter, A, and call it the domestic part of the total expenditure, or absorption, then $BOP = X - M = Y - A$.

It is clear from the above that for any change to have a surplus in the BOP, one needs to have either a decline in A, or an increase in Y. Therefore, a change in the exchange rate such as a depreciation of the domestic currency, can lead to surplus in the BOP only if it is accompanied by a decline in A or an increase in Y. Considering that an increase in Y is outside the control of the policy members (another word for that is endogenous), then policy makers must have a decline in absorption to have a BOP surplus. Hence, the absorption approach tells us that devaluation of a currency must be associated with an action that leads to lower absorption, such as a decline in government expenditure (G) or restrictive fiscal policy, to have a surplus in the BOP.

The third approach to BOP was developed by a few famous monetarists, but it relies heavily on the works of the late Prof. Harry Johnson of the University of Chicago. Because this approach concentrates on capital (or monetary) flows and treats them as the main source of change in the BOP, it is also referred to as the monetary approach to BOP.

The monetary approach claims that the excess demand for (and supply of) money can be responsible for the deficit or surplus of the BOP. More specifically, they argue that a surplus of money supply over the demand for money in the money market leads to the outflow of financial capital. If the domestic residents do not intend to hold it, it is natural that the capital outflow of the economy would increase, leading to a deficit in the BOP of that economy.

On the other hand, if people demand money in a greater amount than the country's monetary authorities are willing to supply, then there would be an inflow of capital from abroad, leading to a surplus in the BOP of that economy. Monetarists, therefore, believe that the BOP changes of an economy can easily be analyzed by looking at the money market changes in the economy. Moreover, recall that monetarists claim the stability of the demand for money function as mentioned in earlier chapters. In terms of the BOP and the open economy, this may have some interesting repercussions.

For example, suppose that the demand for money is, in fact, stable and the domestic monetary policy is to increase the money supply in the economy. If people do not desire to hold more money than the stable demand for money function dictates, there would be an excess supply of money in that economy. Obviously, this would lead to an outflow of capital from the economy, and a deficit in its BOP. In this manner, the effect of an expansionary monetary policy would only create a deficit in the BOP. Obviously, the effectiveness of the policy change, as measured by the increase in the GDP level it causes, would be zero.

A change in the BOP can occur, according to the monetarists, only when there is either a change in demand for money, or an exogenous change in money supply. The changes in demand for money would not occur unless there are changes in the GNP, real interest rate, and/or the inflation rate—the variables that effect the volume of demand for money. But none of these are exogenously determined; therefore, the demand for money cannot change drastically. You may think that the interest rate can be changed by monetary policy, but do not forget that according to the monetarists, the interest rate elasticity of demand for money is marginal, and there is no big change in the latter variable because of a change in the former.

To conclude the above discussion, we can say that according to the monetary approach to the BOP, expansionary monetary policy leads to an outflow of capital, and in the open economy setting, the effectiveness of the monetary policy is questionable. To continue the argument further, some monetarists claim that the effect of the deficit in the BOP created by an expansionary policy, due to the outflow of capital, is called the *offset effect*. Several monetarists were busy estimating the value of this offset effect in empirical terms. The empirical value of this offset effect is called the *offset coefficient*.

Suppose for a moment that the offset coefficient in reality is, in fact, significant, and there is a great outflow of capital any time a monetary policy undertakes an expansion of money supply. Also consider that the world consists of a few small, and many large economies. Let us assume further that the large economies undertake expansionary monetary policies so that they incur a big outflow of capital. This would naturally create an inflow of capital in the small economies who would find an involuntary increase in the foreign reserves component of their money supply. If the small economies are worried about the value of their domestic currency in terms of the currencies of the large economies, they have only two options to tackle the problem. They can either revalue their currencies, or allow their domestic money supplies to grow with the world money supply. If they are forced to select the second option, then the involuntary increase in their domestic money supply can create a round of inflation in the small economies. Thus, without intent, the small economies would import the inflation of the rest of the world. This is called the monetarist explanation of the importation of inflation.

A number of economists have recently conducted studies to evaluate the validity of the monetarist model of the importation of inflation. Even if there are mixed results, the argument is valid in theory. The application of this model would depend upon several factors. First, the openness of an economy is very important. The higher the openness of the economy, the greater the applicability of this model. Second, the ability of domestic monetary authorities to revalue the domestic currency can determine the effect of international outflow of capital. Third, the effect of the increase in foreign reserves on the domestic money supply will not be high if the domestic monetary policy is to sterilize the increased foreign reserves. The sterilization process involves reducing the domestic component of the money to accommodate the increase in the foreign component. An increased sterilization activity puts additional pressure on the value of domestic currency. Hence, there is a practical limit to the ability of any monetary authority to carry out the sterilization of foreign reserves inflow. The fact remains that an excessive increase in the world money supply would be responsible for inflations in the small economies.

There is another theory on which the monetary approach to BOP relies. It is called *purchasing power parity theory,* and with the help of this theory, monetary economists can draw a law of one price. Both concepts mean that when there is an increase in the price level of one economy by assuming a two-economy world, free trade, and fixed exchange rates, we can show that there is one price that prevails in both economies. As one economy faces an increase in money supply, the excess money flows to the other economy via capital outflow, and the other economy suffers the problem of inflation. Moreover, the increase in price level of one economy creates higher imports of that economy, and higher exports of the other. This again leads to an importation of inflation in the other economy if both allow free trade. In recent times, world trade has consistently been on the rise. The monetary theory of the BOP has, therefore, become even more applicable to the real world today than ever before.

This completes our overview of monetary theory in an open economy setting. Obviously, in international finance classes and textbooks, more attention is paid to the detailed analysis of these concepts. Another important topic to consider is that of the international monetary system. In the next chapter, we present some of the new ideas put forward by economists to revitalize the international monetary system.

Suggested Further Reading

Aghevli, B. and M. Khan. 1977. *The monetary approach to balance of payments determination, an empirical test.* Staff Papers, IMF, pp. 275–90.

Akhtar, M. A., B. Putnam, and W. Sykes. 1977. *Fiscal Constraints, Domestic Credit and International Reserve Flows.* Unpublished manuscript.

Bhatia, S. L. 1982. The monetary theory of balance of payments under fixed exchange rates: An example of India 1951–1973. *The Indian & Economic Journal,* No. 3, January–March: 30–40.

Boyes, W. J. 1984. *Macroeconomics: The Dynamics of Theory and Policy,* Chapter 4. Cincinnati, Ohio: Southwestern Publishing Company.

Chen, H. and N. Sargen. 1975. Central bank policy towards inflation. *Federal Reserve Bank of San Francisco, Business Review.*

Courchene, T. and Singh, K. 1976. The monetary approach to the balance of payment: An empirical analysis of fourteen industrial countries. In *Inflation in the World Economy,* eds. Parkin and Zis. Manchester: Manchester University Press.

Dernberg, T. and D. McDougall. 1976. *Macroeconomics,* Chapters 8 and 9. New York: McGraw-Hill Publishers.

Genberg, H. 1976. Aspects of the monetary approach to the balance of payments theory: An empirical study of Sweden. In *Inflation in the World Economy,* eds. Frenkel and Johnson. Manchester: Manchester University Press.

Gordon, R. 1984. *Macroeconomics,* 3rd ed., Chapter 4. Boston: Little Brown and Company.

Hean, D. L. 1976. International reserve flows and money market equilibrium: The Japanese case. In *The Monetary Approach to the Balance of Payments,* eds. Frenkel and Johnson. Manchester: Manchester University Press.

Hicks, J. 1937. Mr. Keynes and the "classicals": A suggested interpretation. *Econometrica,* April: 147.

Johnson, H. G. 1972. The monetary approach to balance of payments theory. *Journal of Financial and Quantitative Analysis,* Vol. 7: 1555-72.

Kemp, D. S. 1975. Balance of payments concepts—what do they really mean? *Federal Reserve Bank of St. Louis Review,* Vol. 57, July: 14-23.

Kreinin M. and L. Officer. 1978. The monetary approach to the balance of payments: A survey. *Princeton Studies in International Finance,* No. 43. Princeton: University of Princeton.

Kulkarni, K. and S. Dhekane. 1981. The monetarist model of imported inflation in a small open economy. *Economic Affáirs,* Vol. 26, No. 3: 288-505.

Kulkarni, K. 1982. *Stagflation as Caused by Worldwide Inflation in Small Open Economy with Special Reference to the Netherlands.* Unpublished Ph.D. dissertation of University of Pittsburgh.

McGee, R. 1984. A graphical exposition of a more complete Keynesian system. *Journal of Macroeconomics,* Fall: 559-70.

Mishkin, F. S. 1995. *The Economy of Money, Banking and Financial Markets,* 3rd ed., Chapter 23. New York: Harper Collins Publishers.

Mussa, M. 1976. Tariffs and the balance of payments: A monetary approach. In *The Monetary Approach to the Balance of Payments,* eds. Frenkel and Johnson. University of Toronto Press.

Salvatore, D. 1983. *International Economics.* New York: Macmillan.

Swartz, A. and J. Kooyman. 1975. Competition and the international transmission of inflation. *De Economist,* Vol. 123: 723-48.

Thomas, L. 1982. *Money, Banking and Economic Activity.* Prentice-Hall.

Tyson, L. D. and E. Neuberger. 1979. The impact of external economic disturbances on Yugoslavia: Theoretical and empirical explorations. *Journal of Comparative Economics,* Vol. 3: 346-74.

Tsiang, S. C. 1966. The monetary theoretical foundation of the monetary approach to the balance of payments. *Oxford Economic Papers,* Vol. 29: 329-38.

Whitman, M. Y. N. 1977. Global monetarism and the monetary approach to the balance of payments. *Oxford Economic Papers,* Vol. 29: 319-38.

Zecher, R. J. 1976. Monetary equilibrium and international reserve flows in Australia. In *Inflation in the World Economy,* eds. Frenkel and Johnson, pp. 189-215. Manchester: Manchester University Press.

Chapter 17

Recent Developments in Macro-Monetary Theory: A Short Review

SUMMARY

Although earlier chapters detailed the watershed developments in macro-monetary theory accruing since the significant breakthroughs of Sir John Maynard Keynes, including the Monetarist revolution and the formalization of the Expectations hypotheses, even newer contributions have had a profound impact on the thought processes surrounding policymaking. This chapter briefly summarizes these most recent developments in monetary theory and applies some of their lessons to a case study of India.

By the 1990s, the death of the Keynesian Cross and the enhanced suitability of the Aggregate Demand–Aggregate Supply framework had been generally accepted as a foregone conclusion. To its detriment, the Keynesian Cross assumed constant prices, meaning it could not account for the possibility of inflation. The Aggregate Demand–Aggregate Supply framework, on the other hand, was quite capable of dealing with increasing prices as well as the unemployment problem as measured by the reduction in real GDP. Hence, in modern times, policy effectiveness is not determined solely by a policy's ability to reduce unemployment, but also by its ability to keep inflation within reasonable bounds. Accordingly, the chapter recreates the AD and AS curves to review the effectiveness of demand management policies, while also summarizing the Classical, Keynesian, and Monetarist interpretations of the Aggregate Demand–Aggregate Supply model. With the help of this improved monetary analysis tool, the chapter also discusses the phenomenon of cost-push inflation that characterized the stagflation problem of the late 1970s in the United States and India. In short, the oil price shocks during this time period caused the overall cost of production to increase, creating a leftward shift in the AS curve. These leftward shifts not only led to higher price levels, but also lower GDP, which subsequently caused higher unemployment.

The popularity of the Aggregate Demand–Aggregate Supply model is rivaled by that of another, albeit inferior, conceptual development of the 1980s: supply-side economics. This is by no means a complete economic model; rather, it is an idea that government can actually maximize its tax revenue by establishing lower tax rates for producers and consumers. This argument gained credence with the development of the Laffer curve, and its tidy logic won the support of the Reagan administration as it cut taxes in 1981. However, supply-side economics faded away once the U.S. economy ran into a severe recession lasting from 1982 to 1984.

Taylor's rule was another significant development of this period, as it seeks to foretell the behavior of monetary policymakers by asserting that the monetary authority sets its interest rate target based on three readily observable variables: an estimated long-run real interest rate; any current deviation of the actual inflation rate from the monetary authority's inflation rate objective; and the gap between actual real GDP and the measure of "potential" GDP under the full employment of resources. The empirical evidence offers mixed reviews for Taylor's rule, as some like Robert Barro have shown that the Federal Reserve's post-1988 behavior does satisfy this rule, while others like Patrick Minford question whether Taylor's rule actually captures the behavior of monetary policymakers or if it is just an equation that is statistically true. The rapid technological and economic innovations of the 1990s also led to a greater appreciation of the role of technology in the economic growth process. New Growth Theory focuses explicitly on the role of technological innovation, and it suggests that technological progress is determined by three factors: new ideas in the form of profit-seeking research; international openness and trade liberalization; and human capital formation.

The chapter concludes by sketching a broad overview of the implementation of monetary policy in India, and identifying where policy has benefited from these new theoretical insights. In India, there is no independence of monetary policy because the central bank is subservient to the Finance ministry. Nonetheless, its monetary policy was quite capable of pursuing economic growth and controlling inflation throughout not only the 1990s, but also during the early years of the twenty-first century. In this way, we can assert that the Reserve Bank of India successfully executed the lessons of the Aggregate Demand–Aggregate Supply model. In general, then, the economic principles discussed throughout this chapter are quite applicable to Indian circumstances.

Recent Developments in Macro-Monetary Theory with Special Reference to India

17.1

In earlier chapters we discussed the Monetarist revolution (Chapter 11), and the Expectations Hypothesis (Chapter 15) as the theoretical developments of the 1960s and 1970s that guided the policymaking of the 1980s in the United States and in almost all of the free world. However, these were not the only developments that occurred after Keynesian contributions of earlier times. In fact, some notable and significant developments were made as recently as the late 1990s. Our purpose here is to briefly recognize those contributions that had serious consequences for policymaking.

In this chapter, therefore, we summarize only the newest developments in monetary theory by keeping in mind their applicability and suitability for Indian conditions. As it is, given the framework of heavily controlled interest rate structures, most of the theoretical arguments are applied to Indian conditions in a limited way. However, one can also argue that market conditions dictate the movement of all controlled variables, including, of course, interest rates (and exchange rates or any other price levels). In other words, if the market interest rate is higher (or lower) than the controlled interest rate, then policymakers have to bend according to market pressure and adjust the interest rate in that direction sooner or later. For example, if the demand for money is higher than the money supply, then the market interest rates are pushed higher, despite the unwillingness of authorities controlling those interest rates. Hence, the theoretical principles that govern market behavior to some extent also govern the behavior of policymakers, at least in the longer term. Throughout this chapter (as we have implicitly been doing throughout this book), we shall assume that this argument holds; hence, we are not precluded from considering any theoretical principle that governs the policy change.

One of the most significant theoretical improvements that dominated the 1990s was the decline in emphasis on the Keynesian Cross and the growing emphasis on the aggregate demand-aggregate supply model to analyze the inflation and unemployment problem. As discussed in earlier chapters, the Keynesian Cross was supposed to be an excellent tool to define the GDP gap leading to unemployment in the economy. However, it explicitly assumed constant prices and therefore did not allow for changing price levels (or inflation). The aggregate demand-aggregate supply model, on the other hand, was quite capable of dealing with increasing prices, as well as the unemployment problem as measured by reduction in real GDP. Moreover, in modern times, policy effectiveness was seen as not just an ability to reduce unemployment (by increasing GDP), but also an ability to keep inflation under check. In fact, the events of the late 1970s, when stagflation was at a peak all over the world (including in the United States and India), most textbooks of macro theory accepted the contention that the "Keynesian Cross was not as useful as the aggregate demand and aggregate supply model." Then again, a typical policy change (whether fiscal policy or monetary policy) was generally seen as the demand management policy change which could easily be incorporated into the aggregate demand model, but not necessarily into the Keynesian Cross model.

The policy effectiveness can be analyzed by using this model as follows: Consider Figure 17.1, that has original locations of aggregate demand and aggregate supply

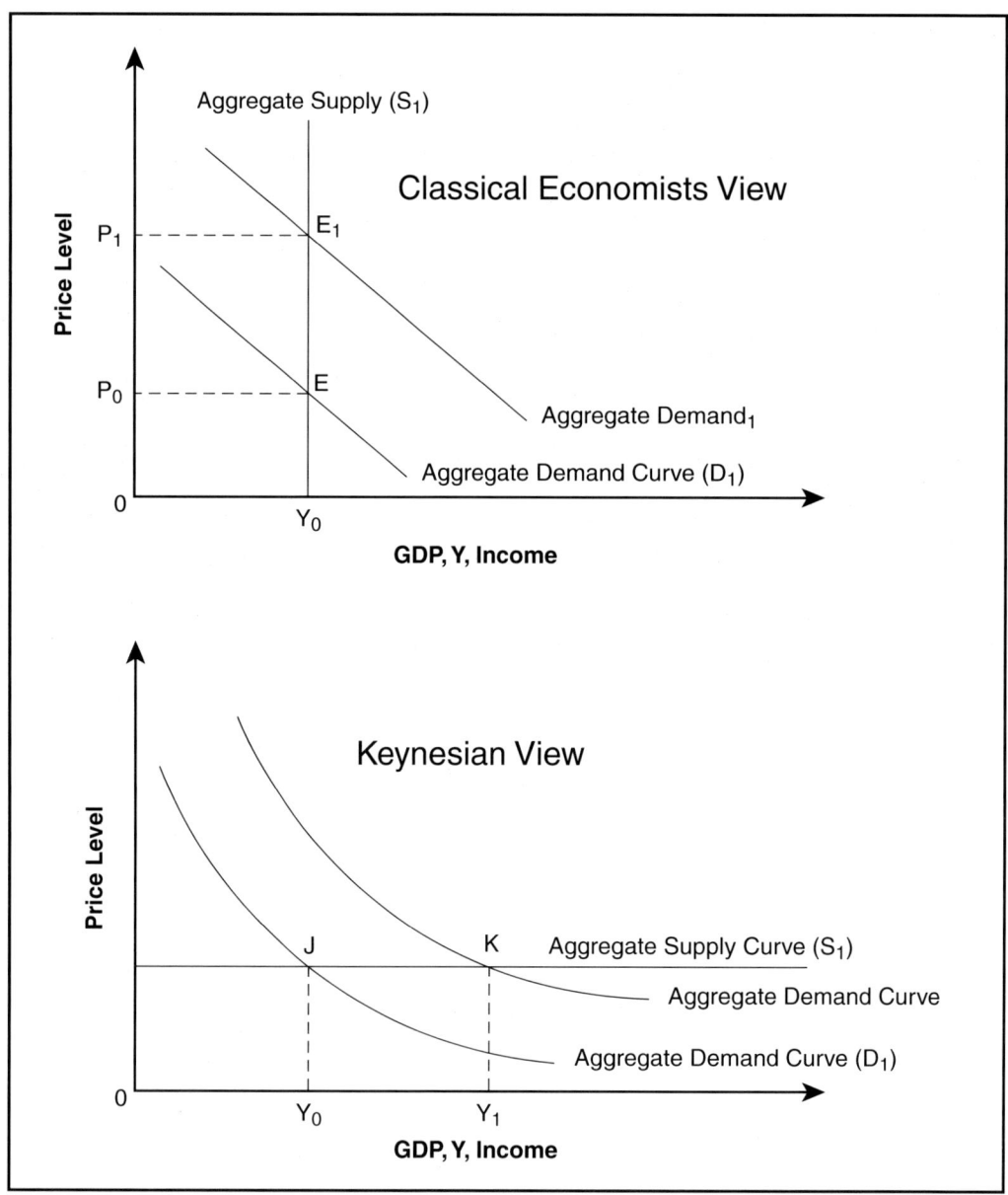

FIGURE 17.1 ■ Aggregate Demand–Aggregate Supply Model: Classical Economists' and Keynesian Views

at D_1 and S_1 levels. Assume that the aggregate demand and aggregate supply curves are derived in the same process as in Chapter 18. Also assume that a downward sloping aggregate demand curve and an upward sloping aggregate supply curve determine the commodity market equilibrium at their intersection point, and that an equilibrium general price level initially exists at that point. Using these assumptions, we can proceed in explaining the policy effectiveness, using this initial market equilibrium stage. (HINT: For more curious students, reading Chapter 18 before this discussion can be useful.)

Using the above model, we can summarize the main arguments of the three schools as follows:

1. **Classical economists:** Recall from our earlier chapters the assertion of Classical economists that there is always full employment in a capitalistic economy, given the flexibility of all prices in all markets. This creates the vertical aggregate supply curve at some (full employment) level of real GDP in Figure 17.1. Hence, in the Classical economists' viewpoint, the equilibrium real GDP is at Y_0 level and the demand management policies only shift the aggregate demand curve to the right, leading to only a higher price level and no change in real GDP or unemployment.

2. **Keynesians:** With assumed rigid price levels, the aggregate supply curve is almost horizontal (perfectly elastic) in the Keynesian case. With the horizontal aggregate supply curve, when demand management policies are expansionary, there is a shift of the aggregate demand curve to the right and the price level almost stays the same while real GDP increases. Fiscal and monetary policies in the Keynesian view are always effective in terms of being able to increase the real GDP. The special case of the liquidity trap makes the aggregate supply curve perfectly vertical and any increase in money supply is unable to raise the real GDP further.

3. **Monetarists:** The aggregate supply curve in the monetarists' case is a special shape: it is horizontal until the economy reaches full employment and becomes vertical at the full employment level of GDP, as shown in Figure 17.2. Hence, in the world described by the monetarists (and as we saw in Chapter 10), demand management policies are effective when the economy is producing less than full employment output and cease to be effective at the full employment level. Hence, "money does matter" as long as the economy is producing at less than full employment level. Also, as we proposed before, if the "crowding out" hypothesis is valid, then fiscal policy can lead to a rightward shift in the aggregate demand curve only temporarily, because when crowding out is complete, there is a backward shift in the aggregate demand curve. Also, when full employment GDP is reached, any increase in the money supply leads to an increase in the general price

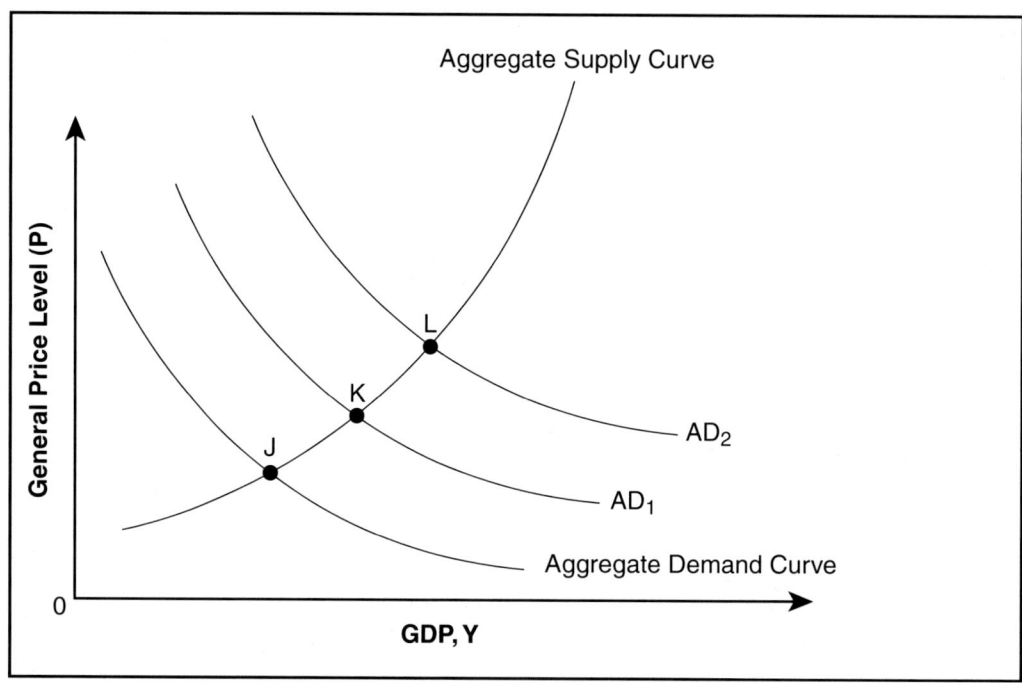

FIGURE 17.2 ■ Monetarist World and Aggregate Demand–Aggregate Supply Model

level alone, a conclusion that was aptly supported by the old quantity theory of money (Chapter 6) and by Classical economists. Thus, the monetarists' prescription of adopting monetary rule becomes relevant when the economy is close to a full employment situation.

The main purpose of this discussion is to show that the "death" of the Keynesian Cross was inevitable, since in the 1990s most macro monetary textbooks thought that a better job was being done by the aggregate demand–aggregate supply model described above. In fact, the Keynesian analysis in many textbooks became confined to consumption function, investment determination, and multiplier analysis. In the 1990s, textbooks also began to put much less emphasis on the use of the Keynesian Cross for policy analysis.

With the help of the aggregate demand–aggregate supply model, one can also investigate the phenomenon of cost-push inflation that characterized the stagflation experience of the late 1970s in the United States, as well as in India. One of the primary reasons for this phenomenon was the tremendous increase in crude oil prices announced by the Organization of Petroleum Exporting Countries (OPEC) in 1979. How can one use this model to show the simultaneous existence of inflation and unemployment? The answer seems to be easy. As oil prices go up, the cost of overall production increases, creating leftward shifts in aggregate supply curves as shown in Figure 17.3. These leftward shifts not only result

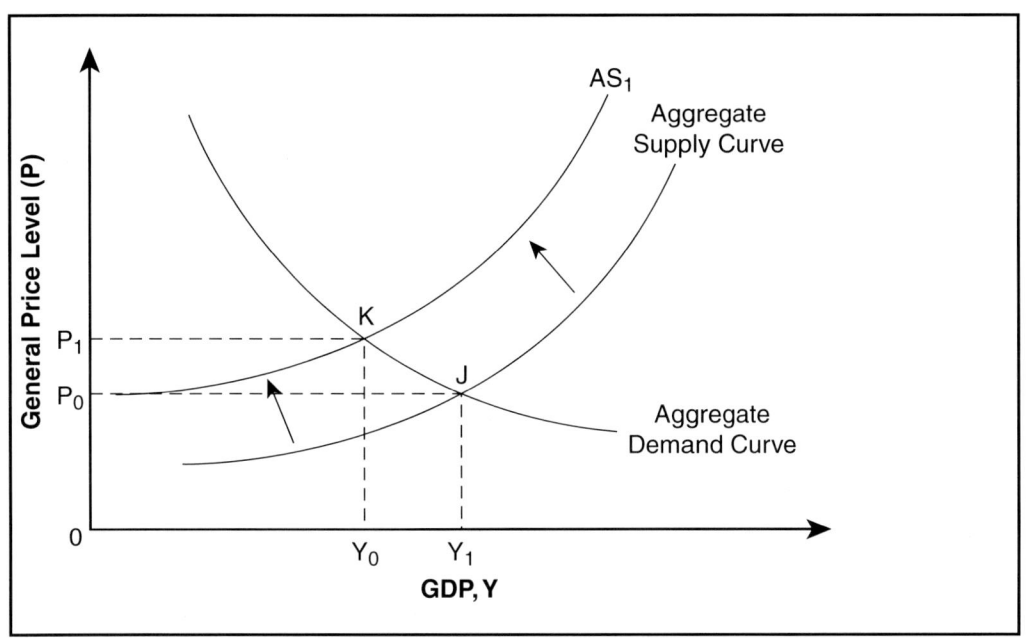

Stagflation and Aggregate Demand–Aggregate Supply Model ■ **FIGURE 17.3**

in higher price levels (inflation), but also become responsible for lower GDP, which leads to higher unemployment. With the aggregate supply curve almost horizontal in their analysis, Keynes' modern time supporters (aptly called Neo-Keynesians) could not explain the reasons for stagflation in their traditional analysis. Thus, another positive feature of the aggregate demand-aggregate supply model was its ability to explain the realistic phenomenon of stagflation.

In a similar way, one can also discuss "supply side" economics (or as some have referred to it, "Reaganomics") with the use of this model. Supply side economics, exemplified by President Reagan's policies in the early 1980s in the United States, and to some extent by the policies of Prime Minister Margaret Thatcher in the United Kingdom, is not a complete economic model. Rather, it is just a belief that when taxes are lowered and returned to consumers, the consumers not only increase their consumption but also increase their savings. Increased savings, in turn, are believed to be a boost for higher lending to businesses, since there are more funds to loan. As the business sector receives more lending, it can carry out more investment activities, which then "trickles down" to a higher GDP and economic growth. Thus, tax cuts can be beneficial to the economy if the above chain of events works completely. Another supportive pillar for supply-siders came from a magnificent work by Arthur Laffer, who drew a bell-shaped tax revenue curve (as in Figure 17.4) to show that a cut in tax rates can in fact increase tax revenues. In Figure 17.4, as the tax rates (horizontal axis) increase up to a certain point (say point K), the tax revenue (vertical axis) will go up. But, as the tax rates

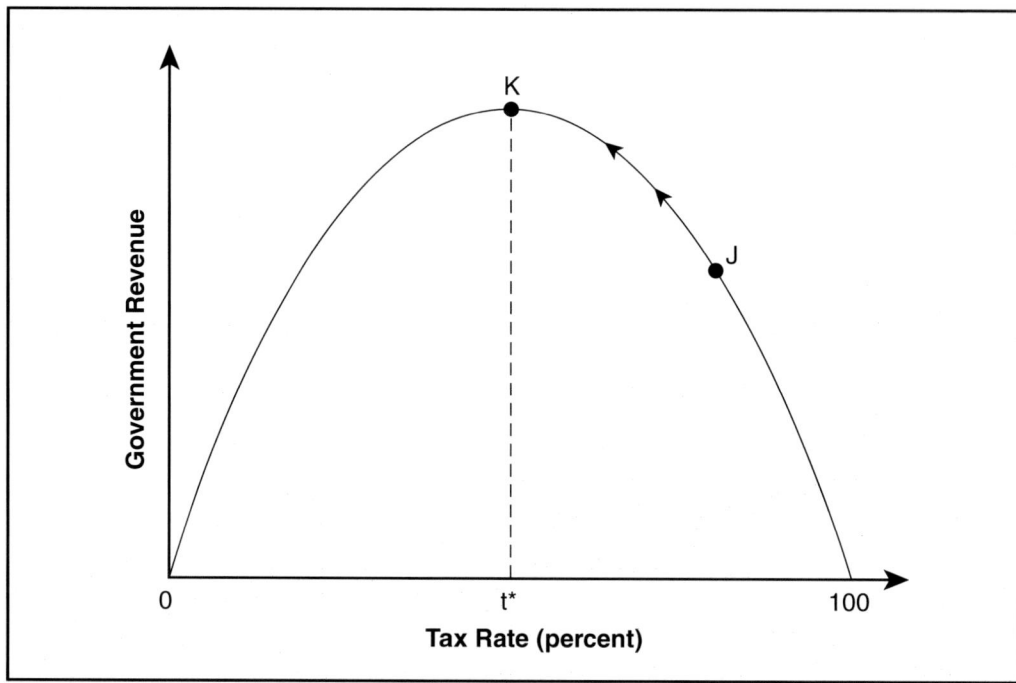

FIGURE 17.4 ■ The Magic of the Laffer Curve

are increased beyond a certain limit (decided differently in each country), the tax revenues decline, as taxpayers at some point have a higher incentive to find more loopholes in the system and avoid paying taxes. Thus, if an economy is already on the declining portion of the tax revenues curve, a prudent policy is to lower tax rates, not raise them.

Equipped by this argument offered by the Laffer Curve, the Reagan administration announced tax cuts in 1981, but the logic apparently did not work. Instead of expanded growth, the U.S. economy ran into a severe recession in the 1982–1984 period. Coupled with the monetarist prescription of keeping the money supply growth rate stable, interest rates increased tremendously and the experiment was seemingly abandoned. Supply side economics faded away as fast as it arrived.

The other significant theoretical development concerned the motives of monetary policymakers. Ever since the experiment by the Federal Reserve to keep U.S. money supply growth stable from 1979 to 1982, there have been continuous attempts by monetary economists to judge the future behavior of policymakers. In fact, in the 1980s, the Federal Reserve gave up its practice of announcing its future intentions concerning policy, and it became a favorite field for economists to theorize on the policymakers' behavior as well as their intentions.

Most relevant in this literature is Professor John Taylor's rule for analyzing the behavior of monetary policymaking. In 1993, Professor Taylor of Stanford

University, proposed a rule asserting that monetary policy sets its interest rate target based on the following variables (the Taylor Rule therefore implicitly assumes that monetary policy's objective is to control the interest rate rather than the money supply): (1) an estimated long run in the real interest rate, (2) any current deviation of the actual inflation rate from the Fed's inflation rate objective, and (3) the gap between actual real GDP and the measure of "potential" GDP under full employment of resources. While some economists questioned whether monetary policy behavior can be explained by one equation, others, such as Robert Barro of Harvard University, have shown that the post-1988 behavior of the Federal Reserve does in fact satisfy the Taylor Rule.

Other economists, such as Patrick Minford, have questioned whether the Taylor Rule actually captures the behavior of monetary policymakers or whether it is just an equation that statistically hold true. The jury is still out on the final verdict on the importance of the Taylor Rule, but one thing is true: it did stimulate the interest of other monetary economists in formulating some arguments for policymakers' behavior.

The 1990s proved to be one of the most exciting decades in the history of many nations, primarily because of technological innovations in computers, communications, and information generation areas. The decade proved to be extraordinary years for U.S. economic growth that transferred into growth for many other economies, including those of China and India. In terms of conducting monetary and fiscal policies, the headache of inflationary pressure was self-contained by a tremendous increase in real GDP prompted by unprecedented technological improvement. On a theoretical basis, economists realized the need to incorporate the role of technological improvement in economic growth. Primary work in this field was done by Paul Romer (1986). In summarizing the economic growth model based on the idea of technological innovation, one notes that macro-monetary theory is also referred to as the "New Growth Theory," primarily because no other theory so far has placed so much importance on technological innovation (with the exception of the Schumpeterian theory of economic development). In fact, in models such as the neo-classical growth model, technological innovation was considered to be an exogenous variable much less important to growth than traditional factors of production such as capital and labor. In the New Growth Theory, technological progress is seen to be determined by three factors: (1) new ideas (profit-seeking research and development), (2) international openness and trade liberalization, and (3) human capital formation, which includes all cultural and psychological factors responsible for higher productivity.

Profit-seeking research is seen to be influential for economic growth because it is responsible for capital accumulation and new products that create markets not only domestically, but also internationally. However, openness is not just exporting ideas; it is also the ability to copy magnificent technological improvements of foreign producers and specialize according to comparative advantage. Hence, the New Growth Theory recognizes the role of international trade in a new dimension. The dynamic positive effects of international trade recognized by Romer's model are increased market size, increased product market competition, access to foreign ideas and capital, and elimination of duplication requirements in innovation. Just as international trade is seen as more beneficial in this model than in traditional models, so are the gains from building the human capital base. To be fair, many other growth theorists have given justified importance to the human capital construction. But improved human capital can lead to faster innovation, and can therefore be responsible for the economic growth emphasized in the New Growth Theory. Since our purpose is not to carry out an extensive survey of all growth theories, we shall limit ourselves only to the brief recognition of this new development.

17.2 Monetary Theory and Policy Developments in India: A Case Study

Main decisions of monetary policy in India are made and announced by the Reserve Bank of India (hereinafter "RBI"), which is under the control of the Finance Ministry. While the independence of monetary policymaking is a subject of much discussion in other countries such as the United States and Germany, there is no such debate in India: monetary policy is totally dependent upon governmental ministerial decisions and is not independent from the government's administration. At its inception in 1934 with the Reserve Bank of India Act, RBI was in fact privately owned by its shareholders, but it was nationalized just after independence in 1949 to carry out all state-mandated functions of monetary policy. As one can imagine, the major functions of RBI are to (1) serve as the Banks' bank by controlling cash reserve ratios (a ratio of required reserves to be kept with RBI by each commercial bank); (2) serve as Bank for the Government of India; RBI provides short-term credit to the government and manages the public debt; (3) issue currency for circulation; and (4) promote rural credit, agricultural finance, export finance, and industrial finance. All of these functions are handled together with bank regulation that is much tougher in India than in developed countries. In general, money supply management is the main responsibility of RBI and is carried out with significant oversight from the Ministry of Finance. Another important point is that in India, money supply management basically needs management of currency in circulation, primarily because even in 2004, roughly 80 percent of the Indian money supply is in cash. Hence, monetary policy involves issuing more currency rather than carrying out bond market transactions as traditionally done in developed countries.

The initial years of RBI were characterized by "controlled expansion." In fact, a brief summary of RBI's objectives can be described as follows: "With the introduction of the Five-Year Plans, the need for appropriate adjustment in monetary and fiscal policies to suit the pace and pattern of planned development became imperative. The monetary policy since 1952 emphasized the twin aims of the economic policy of the Government: (a) speed up economic development to raise standard of living and (b) to control inflationary pressure" (Datta-Sundharam, 2004, p. 858). While credit expansion was essential for economic development, too much credit expansion would have created inflationary pressure which needed to be checked. It appeared that the objective of controlling inflation was not met in the mid-1970s and the monetary policy objective was significantly pointed towards controlling the flow of credit. While inflation rates went down in the 1980s, interest rates reached very high levels (as high as 16 percent to 18 percent). In the 1990s, however, India's monetary policy did a commendable job of controlling inflation and bringing interest rates down. Moreover, the start of the first decade of the twenty-first century has been very remarkable, as in the last four years the Indian economy has seen not only significant growth but also reasonable inflation. One can advance several reasons for such a great showing on the economic front. The theoretical principles that govern the activities of RBI are not very different than the ones that are discussed in developed countries such as the United States and the United Kingdom. In fact, as witnessed by researchers in RBI's Economic Analysis Wing and other famous research institutions funded by RBI (such as the Indira Gandhi Institute of Development Research in Mumbai or the National Institute of Bank Management in Pune), the theoretical arguments follow the same line of reasoning as seen in the United States. Hence, the principles discussed in the early part of this chapter are also quite applicable to Indian circumstances.

Suggestions for Further Reading

Gupta, S. B. 1998. *Monetary Economics: Institutions, Theory and Policy.* New Delhi: Chand and Company Limited.

Miller, L. R. and D. VanHoose. 2004. *Money, Banking and Financial Markets,* 2nd ed. Mason, Ohio: Thomson Learning Company.

Ruddar, D. and K. P. M. Sundharam. 2002. *Indian Economy,* 45th ed. New Delhi: Chand and Company Limited.

Seth, M. L. 1985. *Monetary Economics,* 7th ed. Agra: Rashtriya Art Printers.

Chapter 18
Aggregate Demand and Aggregate Supply Analysis

SUMMARY

The weaknesses of the IS-LM model previously discussed dictate that a more robust monetary tool be used to explore the economic challenges of inflation and unemployment. This chapter lays the foundations of the Aggregate Demand–Aggregate Supply framework by deriving its component parts and analyzing the effects of price level changes on this framework.

Aggregate demand (AD) is composed of consumption, investment, and government expenditure. Its schedule is derived by making a few rational assumptions: we must assume that money illusion is nonexistent, and that money demand is unaffected by changes in the price level. By doing this, and by considering the commodity and money markets underlying the IS-LM analysis, we are able to observe the effects of price level changes on money supply and GDP. The AD curve may then be plotted as a downward-sloping line on a graph juxtaposing price level with GDP, or income. This signifies an inverse relationship between these two variables; hence, the AD curve is the locus of combinations of the price and GDP levels at which the commodity and money markets are in equilibrium. Another important characteristic of the AD curve is that its slope depends upon the slopes of the IS and LM curves, and the chapter explains how the AD curve is affected by the relative flatness or steepness of each. Moreover, shifts of the AD curve are caused by government policy changes, such that an expansionary monetary or fiscal policy initially precipitates an upward shift of the AD curve until the crowding out effect causes the AD curve to shift back down.

Aggregate supply (AS), as its name suggests, is determined by the total product of the economy as produced by the available labor force. In order to determine the behavior of aggregate supply, we must explore how the total product of the economy is determined. This requires analysis of the labor market, as labor is assumed to be the main factor of production. A crucial question thus ensues: How does the economy decide the optimum employment of labor? To answer this question, the chapter considers the production process in detail, concluding that the wage rate essentially decides the willingness of producers to hire more or less workers, thereby giving an inverse relationship between wage rate and quantity of labor demanded. This contrasts with the positive relationship observed between the wage rate and the quantity of labor supplied. The optimum level of employment in the economy can be determined by locating the intersection point of these two curves. Once the optimal employment level is discovered, the total product curve can be deduced, which depicts a direct relationship between price level and total product, or aggregate supply. This then allows us to plot the AS curve alongside the AD curve, yielding the unique combinations of price and income levels at which there is general equilibrium in the economy. This framework is also useful for the analysis of inflation, which can occur when there is either an outward shift of the AD curve or an inward shift of the AS curve.

The chapter concludes by analyzing the shapes of the AD and AS curves according to the special beliefs of Classical and Keynesian economists. According to the Classical economists, the AS curve is a vertical line, because the classical assumption of perfect flexibility of prices and wages ultimately implies that a price level increase will not lead to an increase in employment or GDP, as workers supply less labor than before once they realize their real wage has been reduced. The policy implication of this analysis is that an expansionary policy will only lead to higher prices and no improvement in GDP. Keynesians, however, contend that the AS curve is upward sloping from left to right, because the wage rate is fixed at a certain level because of labor union activity, etc. This shape of the AS curve means that a price level increase will result in increased employment, more total product, and a higher GDP level. In the Keynesian interpretation of aggregate supply and aggregate demand, expansionary policies are beneficial to the economy.

18.1 Introduction to Aggregate Demand and Aggregate Supply as a Tool

In this chapter, we examine another useful tool for monetary analysis of the problems of inflation and unemployment. Such a tool is needed because, as you may recall from earlier chapters, the IS-LM framework is insufficient to deal with the inflationary aspect of the economy. The IS-LM framework is problematic because it expresses all variables in real terms and assumes the price level to be constant. In the 1970s, the phenomenon of stagflation necessitated the introduction of the aggregate demand and aggregate supply approach. Aggregate demand of the economy is made up of consumption, investment, and government expenditure of the economy, and is related inversely to price level. As the price level changes, there are reflections in aggregate demand that we would consider by looking at the equilibrium of the commodity and money markets as given by the IS-LM framework. The relation of the price level and the equilibrium GDP is known as the aggregate demand schedule of that economy. In the initial part of this chapter, we will consider the derivation of this schedule.

The aggregate supply is determined by the total product of the economy as produced by the available labor force. This brings us to another important market, the labor market, that we have ignored so far. There are labor demand and supply forces which are determined by the wage rate of the economy and are used to determine the aggregate supply curve. Having derived the aggregate demand and the aggregate supply curves, we can deal with the price level changes that create inflation in the economy.

18.2 Derivation of the Aggregate Demand Schedule

As mentioned before, one needs to consider the equilibrium of the commodity and the money markets by looking at the IS-LM framework and the effects of price level changes on that framework. Before we do that, however, let us make some simplifying assumptions. Let us assume that the price level change does not have any effect on the commodity market equilibrium, so that a price change does not affect the location of the IS curve. This can be a rational assumption if we consider that the variables in the commodity market are expressed in real terms and they do not change when there are mere price changes. Obviously, due to a price change, the real consumption, the real investment, and the real government expenditure values do not change if there is no "money illusion" existing among the public.

Money illusion is the illusion held by the public that allows real values to be influenced by changes in the nominal variables such as the price level. For example, if a boss guarantees a worker a raise of ten percent in his next paycheck and in the end gives him a raise of only five percent, then the worker may think that he has been cheated. That feeling of the worker is termed a money illusion. An illusion, because in spite of the five percent raise he is getting, he believes he has been cheated. The same thing may happen in a macro sense as well.

When economic agents possess a money illusion, the real variables in the economy are affected by mere price changes. For the derivation of the aggregate demand schedule, assume that there is no money illusion in the commodity market. Second, observe that the demand for money, as it is measured in real terms, in the absence of a money illusion, is unaffected by the changes in the price level. This means that when there is a price level change, in a money illusion-free economy, the only variable that would be affected is the real change inverse to the changes in the price level. As the price level goes up, the real money supply, M/P, would go down and vice versa.

We are now in a position to define what the aggregate demand schedule really stands for. It is the locus of combinations of the price level and the GDP level at which the commodity and money markets are in equilibrium. Given the above assumptions, an increase in the price level would create a shift of the money supply curve in Figure 18.1. Starting with the initial money market equilibrium at

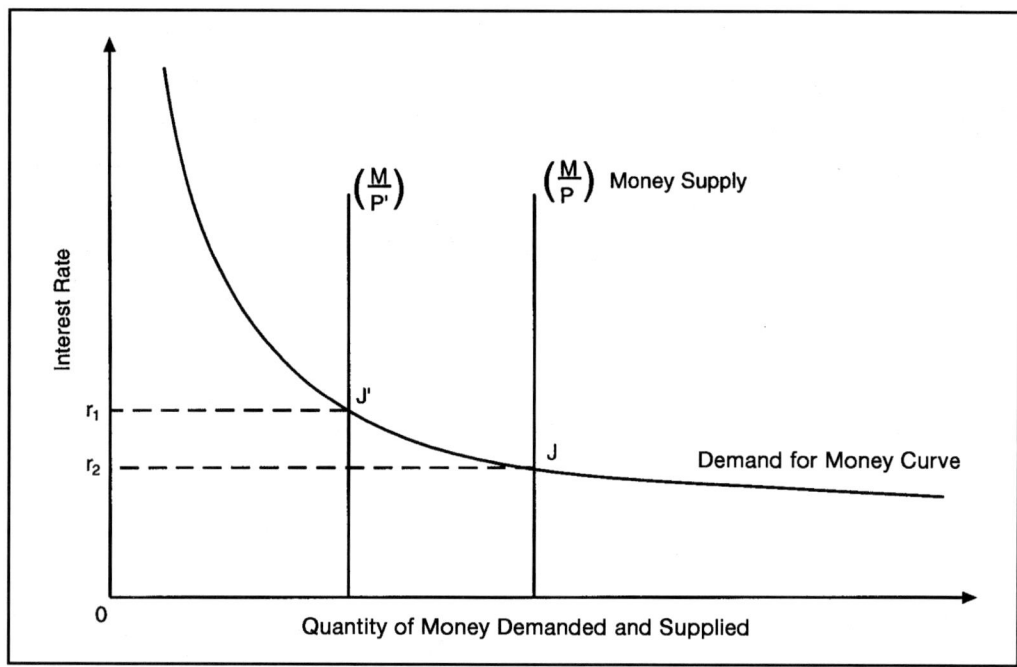

FIGURE 18.1 ■ Money Market Equilibrium and the Price Changes

point J, suppose the price level goes up from P to P'. The new money supply would be lower, and the money supply curve would shift to the left. The new money market equilibrium rate would be higher than before at point J'. In terms of the IS-LM framework, the increase in the price causes a lower real money supply and shifts the LM curve to the left. As discussed in Chapter 8, the decrease in money supply creates a leftward shift in the LM curve.

In terms of Figure 18.2, starting with the original general equilibrium at point E, due to the shift of the LM curve to the left, the new equilibrium is achieved at point E' with a higher interest rate and lower equilibrium GDP. Thus, a higher price level via money market changes and the shift of the LM curve to the left creates a lower level of equilibrium GDP in the economy. When we concentrate on the price levels and the GDP levels in the above discussion, so far we know at least two combinations of price level and GDP where commodity and money markets are in equilibrium. Those combinations are P and Y and P' and Y' where P < P' and Y > Y'.

When we plot these combinations on another graph with the price level on the vertical axis and the GDP, or Y, on the horizontal axis, we can get two points viz. K and K' in Figure 18.3.

Figure 18.3 includes some additional equilibrium combinations that can be obtained in the same fashion. That is, consider another change in the price level, determine the shift in the LM curve, and finally the change in the equilibrium

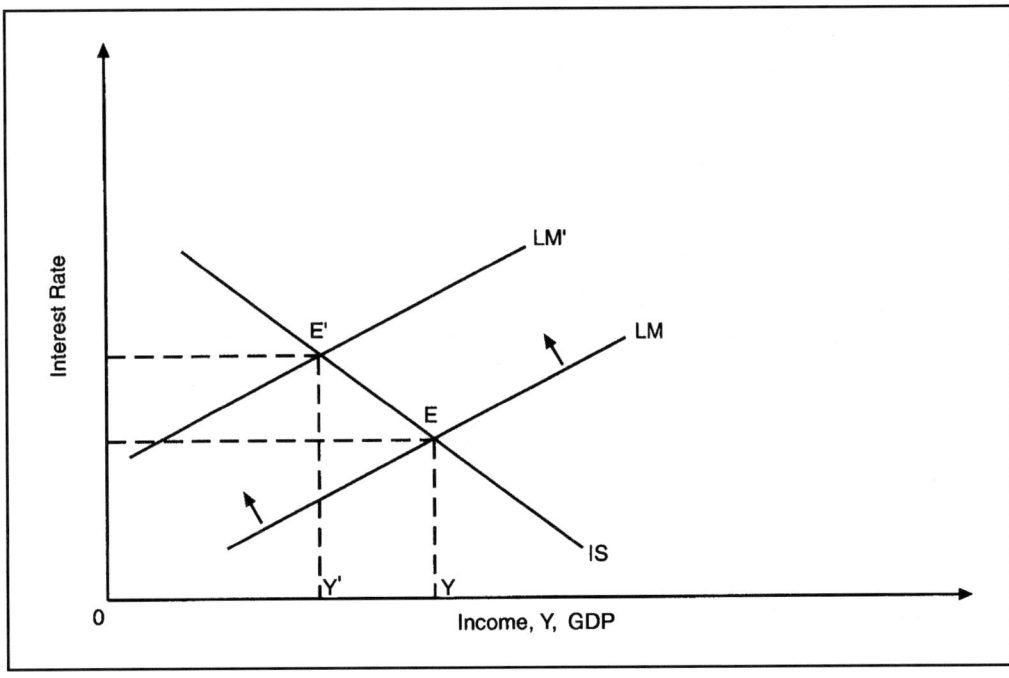

IS-LM Framework and the Price Level Change ■ **FIGURE 18.2**

AGGREGATE DEMAND AND AGGREGATE SUPPLY ANALYSIS **281**

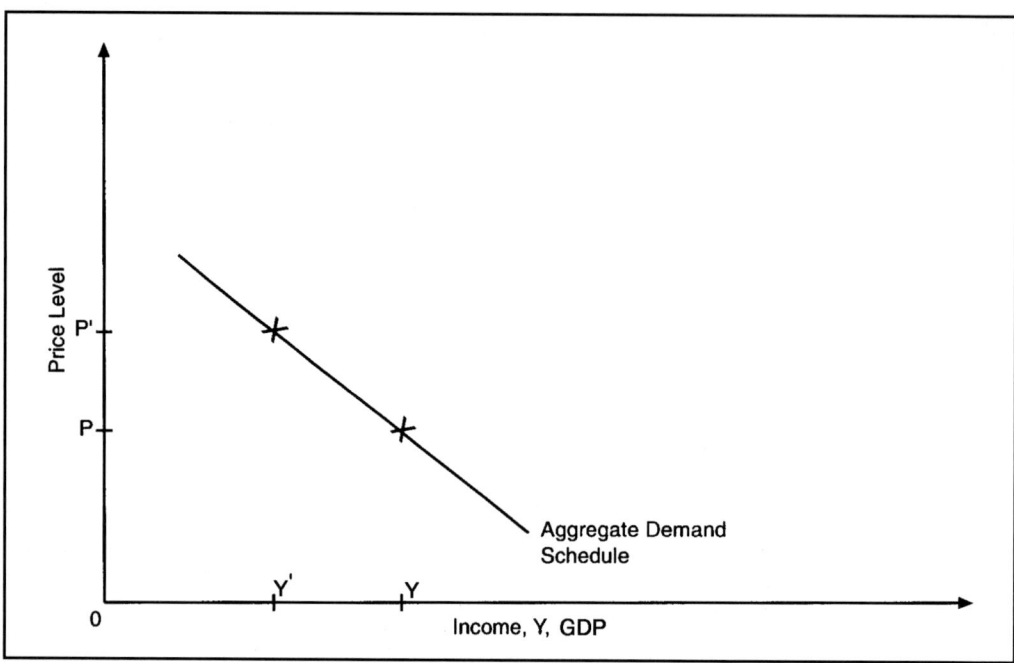

FIGURE 18.3 ■ Derivation of the Aggregate Demand Schedule

GDP. The several points of Figure 18.3 can be joined by a curve sloping downward from left to right. Thus, as the price level goes up, the equilibrium GDP goes down. This inverse relationship between the price level and the GDP level is called the aggregate demand schedule. This is shown in Figure 18.3.

The main characteristics of the aggregate demand schedule are as follows:

1. The curve shows all the possible crossing points of a single commodity market equilibrium and the various money market equilibrium at different price levels. Every point on this curve shows the general equilibrium in the economy.
2. The distance between any point on the aggregate demand schedule and the vertical axis is the value of the total expenditure in the economy. Hence, any change in the values of consumption or investment or government expenditure would make this curve shift.
3. The slope of this curve depends upon the slopes of the IS and LM curves. Hence, the factors responsible for the slope changes in these curves would be the same factors that would cause changes in the slope of the aggregate demand schedule. It should be obvious that the steeper the IS curve, the steeper that the aggregate demand schedule will be. The slope of the IS curve depends upon the responsiveness of the investment to the changes in the interest rate, or specifically, the elasticity of investment with respect to the

interest rate. The higher the value of this elasticity, the flatter the IS curve will be, and the flatter the aggregate demand schedule will be.

For the LM curve, the story is different. A flatter LM curve would create a smaller change in the equilibrium GDP, if it were to shift. This would give a steeper aggregate demand schedule. Hence, the steeper the LM curve, the flatter the aggregate demand schedule will be, and the flatter the LM curve, the steeper the aggregate demand schedule will be. You may recall that the slope of the LM curve depends upon the responsiveness of the demand for money with respect to the interest rate. The higher this elasticity, the flatter the LM curve will be, and the steeper the aggregate demand schedule will be. Also, in the special case of the classical analysis, when it is expected that demand for money is completely inelastic with respect to interest rate changes, the LM curve becomes vertical. In this special case, the aggregate demand curve is also a horizontal straight line. This means that due to price changes, there is no change in the value of the equilibrium GDP and the aggregate demand curve is a vertical straight line.

Shifts in this curve are caused by the policy changes of the government. If the government decides to adopt an expansionary fiscal policy, it initially would create an upward shift in the aggregate demand schedule; but, as there is a decrease in the private sector investment due to the crowding out effect, there is a downward shift in that curve and the effect of the fiscal policy is nullified. The exact shift of the curve would be decided by the degree to which the crowding out takes place.

Derivation of the Aggregate Supply Curve 18.3

Together with the aggregate demand schedule, we must now investigate the behavior of the aggregate supply of the economy. Considering that the aggregate supply of the economy is made up of the total production or the total product in that economy, we should examine how the total product of the economy is determined. Assume that labor is the main factor of production. Higher production needs higher employment of labor, and vice versa. Hence, the total employment of labor in the economy decides the total product produced in the economy. Now the question is, how does the economy decide the optimum employment of labor? Obviously, the producers demand labor and they are the ones who determine how much employment of labor is offered in their firms. Let us suppose that they make their decisions depending upon the wage rate and the productivity of the labor. Thus, in the labor market there are two decisions to be made: (a) how many workers would be demanded at different wage rates as decided by the producers, and (b) how much labor is to be supplied at the wage that is offered by the producers, which will be decided by the labor. Now let us make some simplifying assumptions: (a) let us assume that labor is the homogenous factor of production and is perfectly divisible; (b) let us also assume that producers face the situation where they are offering a constant wage rate to the homogenous labor.

Now let us consider a few things about the production process. When the producers have a choice of deciding their volume of production, and when they enter into a production process, they would initially face increasing marginal returns, then constant marginal returns, and then diminishing marginal returns. This is called the "law of changeable returns" and it has universal applicability, as it is extremely logical. When all other factors of production are constant in their employment and when an employer is adding more units of labor, initially he would experience an excess capacity; therefore, the productivity of labor would also be increased so that the returns of the production would also be increasing. However, as capacity of the plant is utilized more and more, the additional employment of labor does not bring about as much productivity as before so that the returns would become constant and then eventually decline. When all other things are constant, it also makes sense that an employer would continue hiring more labor when the returns are increasing. Hence, the producer would always produce in that stage of production in which there are declining returns (or, to put it in other words, where the marginal productivity of labor is declining). In terms of Figure 18.4, as the labor employment is increased, the marginal product

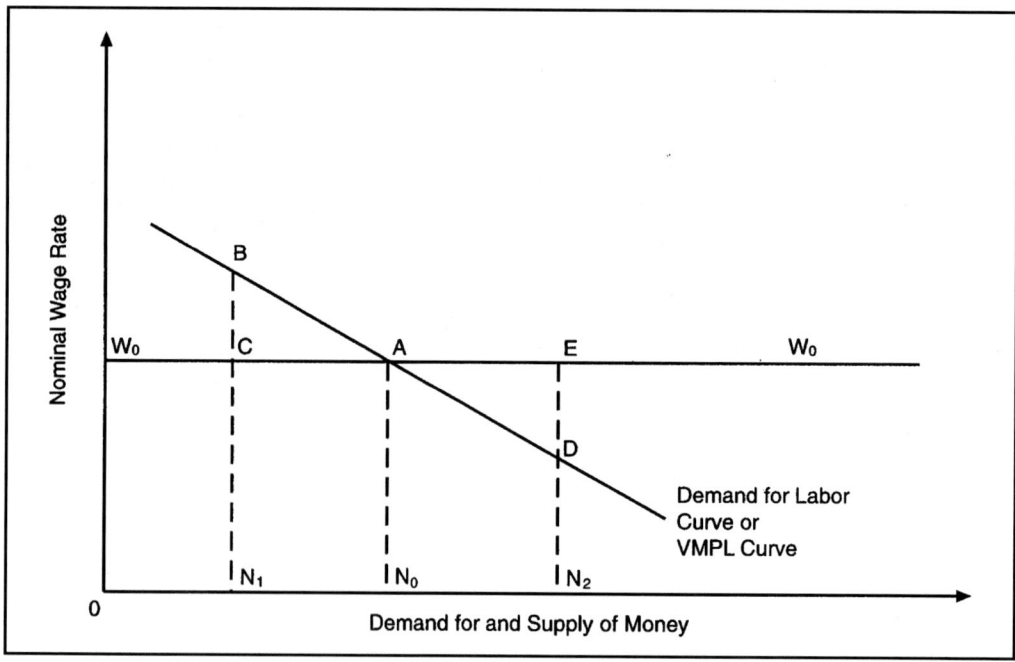

FIGURE 18.4 ■ Labor Market Analysis and the Optimum Employment

of the labor declines; hence, the marginal product curve is downward sloping from left to right.

Now let us define a new concept called the "value of the marginal product of labor," or VMPL. VMPL is nothing but the product of the price of the good and the marginal productivity of labor. If we assume a constant price of the product, then the VMPL curve would also be downward sloping from left to right in Figure 18.4. Producers, if they could have it their way, would like to decide the wage rate that is exactly equal to the VMPL. This is because if VMPL > Wage Rate (W), then producers would know that the value of the marginal product of labor (or the value of change in the total product caused by the last unit of labor) is greater than the wage offered; hence, the producers would be happy to employ more labor. As the producer does that, the VMPL would decline since higher employment brings lower marginal product of labor. Exactly the opposite would happen if VMPL < Wage Rate. In equilibrium, the producers would prefer to offer the wage rate that is exactly matched by the VMPL. Additionally, we should consider that the wage rate in the economy and the supply of labor would have a direct or positive relationship. As the wage rate goes up, there would be a higher number of people ready to work, or the same number of people would be happy to work longer. Hence, the supply of labor curve is sloping upwards from right to left.

The downward sloping demand curve for labor and the upward sloping supply curve of labor are shown in Figure 18.5. The demand curve for labor is also called

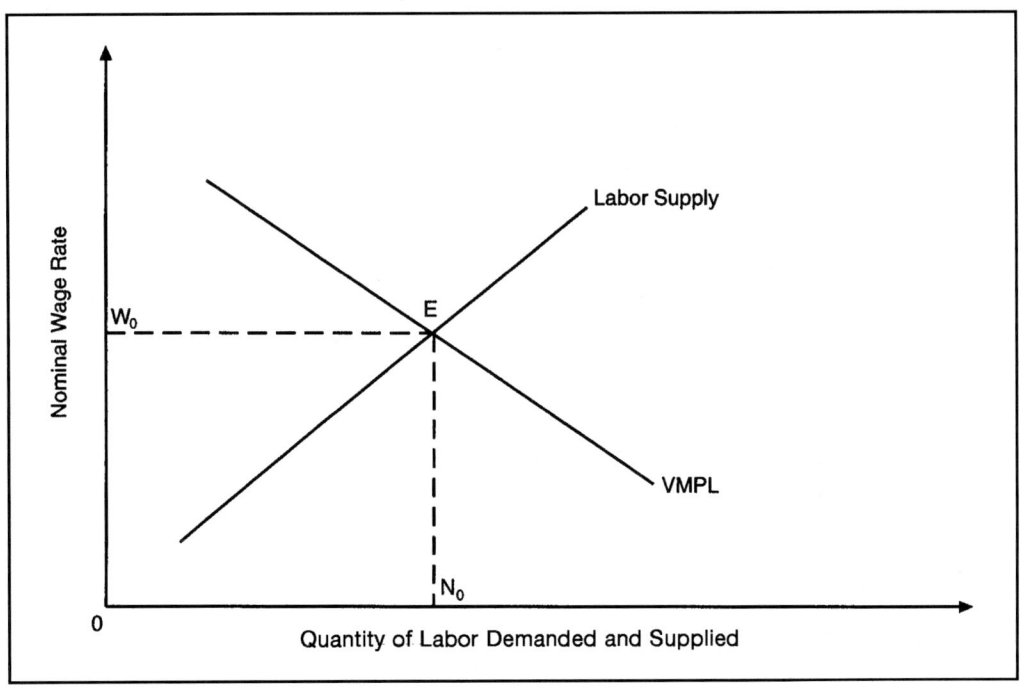

Equilibrium of the Labor Market ■ **FIGURE 18.5**

the VMPL and the wage rate decides the willingness of the producers to hire more or less laborers.

Now, knowing the positions of these two curves we can determine the optimum level of employment in the economy as given by the intersection point of these two curves. The intersection point is called the "point of equilibrium" in the labor market and the wage rate decided by this equilibrium point is the "equilibrium wage rate."

Given the optimal level of employment in the economy from the labor market analysis, we can determine the total product that can be produced by this amount of employment by using the total product curve in Figure 18.6. With labor employment on the horizontal axis and the total product on the vertical axis, Figure 18.6 shows the application of the law of changeable returns. Initially, with an increase in the employment of labor, the marginal product of labor increases, so the total product increases at a faster rate. (Notice that the marginal product is the slope of the total product curve, or the rate of increase in the total product.) When the marginal product of labor becomes constant, the total product curve becomes a straight line, and when the marginal product of labor is declining, the total product curve becomes concave. It is, therefore, important to understand why the total product curve takes the special shape as shown in Figure 18.6. Since the total product is the GDP of the economy, by observing its behavior we can derive the aggregate

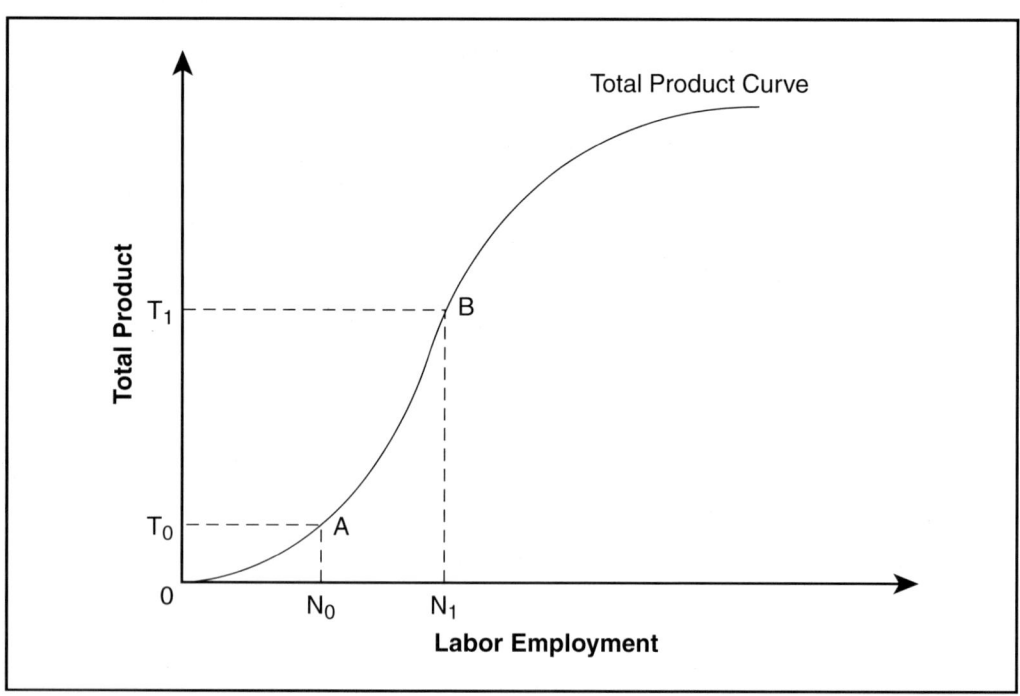

Total Product Curve ■ **FIGURE 18.6**

supply of that economy. Now let us analyze the effect of price changes on the aggregate supply of the economy. As the price level goes up, there is a shift of the VMPL curve in the labor market graph (Figure 18.5), since VMPL stands for the product of the price of the goods and the marginal product of labor. As the VMPL curve shifts to the right, with the upward sloping labor supply curve, we find a new equilibrium in the labor market with higher wages and higher employment. As the employment increases, the total product of the economy increases (which also means an increased aggregate supply in that economy).

Thus, as the price level increases, under normal circumstances, there is an increase in the aggregate supply of the economy. Hence, in Figure 18.7, the relationship between the price level and the aggregate supply is shown by the upward sloping curve from left to right.

We are now in a position to talk about the equilibrium price level of the economy by observing its aggregate demand and aggregate supply curves together. This is done in Figure 18.7. Remember that the aggregate demand schedule shows the combinations of price and income levels at which both money and commodity markets are in equilibrium. The aggregate supply curve, on the other hand, shows how much an economy would be ready to produce at different price levels. Together, these curves would decide the unique combination of the price level and income level at which the money and commodity markets are in equilibrium.

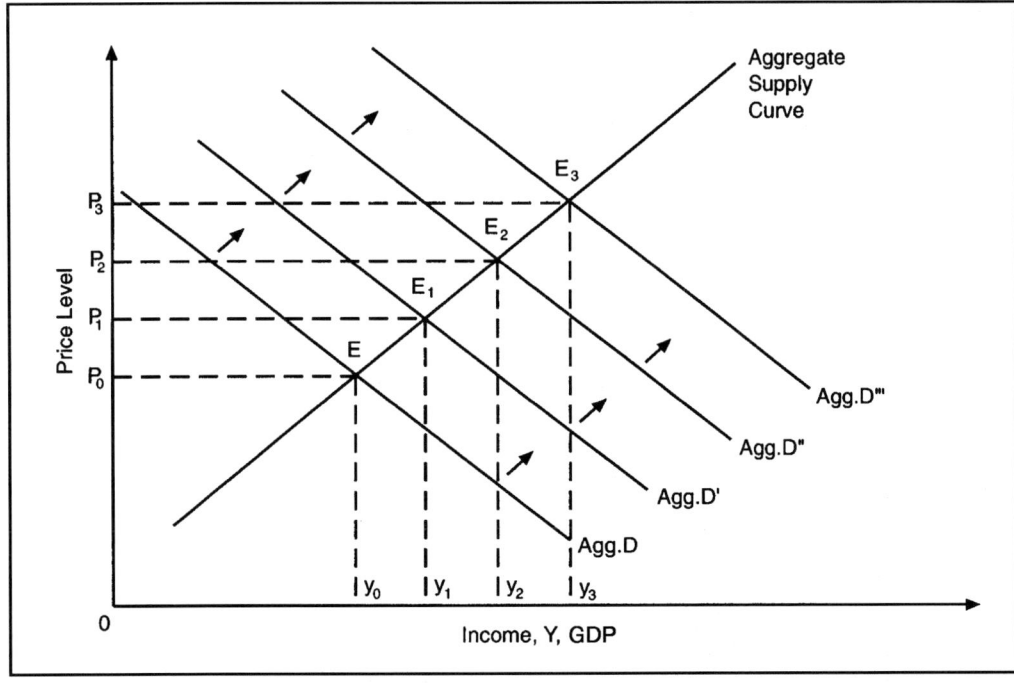

Aggregate Demand and Aggregate Supply Curves ■ **FIGURE 18.7**

Their intersection point, therefore, is called the equilibrium point. Besides defining the equilibrium point in the above manner, this framework is also useful in analyzing the problem of inflation. But before we analyze the inflation problem, let us first define it. As you may recall from an earlier chapter, inflation is a consistent increase in the general price level. In terms of Figure 18.7, it means a continuous increase in the variable on the vertical axis.

Hence, unless we observe an increase in the price level in Figure 18.7, we will not be able to analyze the inflation phenomenon. To do that, let us examine the shifts in the aggregate demand and the aggregate supply curves. Consider, for example, an adoption by the government of an expansionary fiscal or monetary policy on a continuous basis. This would create continuous upward shifts in the aggregate demand curve leading to a continuous increase in the price level and income levels. The policy would be regarded as effective, but inflationary. Thus, inflation can be caused by a continuous increase in the government budget deficit or money supply of the economy. The inflation that takes place due to continuous shifts in the aggregate demand curve is labeled as "demand-pull" inflation. This is, however, not the only way inflation can occur. Consider the increase in the cost of production due to, say, an exogenous increase in the input price. This can create a leftward shift in the aggregate supply curve causing an increase in the price level and decline in the GDP of the economy. A continuous occurrence of this type of phenomenon would lead to an inflation problem in the economy. Also observe that a decline in income of the economy is the same as reduced employment of labor. Hence, a shift in the aggregate supply curve not only causes inflation but also is responsible for unemployment, referred to as "stagflation."

18.4 Analysis of Classical and Keynesian Thoughts

On a theoretical basis, one can analyze the possible changes in the shapes of the aggregate demand and aggregate supply curves according to the special beliefs held by Classical economists and the Keynesians.

CLASSICAL ECONOMISTS AND AGGREGATE DEMAND AND AGGREGATE SUPPLY FRAMEWORK

Recall that the Classical economists believed in the quantity theory of money and perfectly flexible prices, wages, and interest rate levels. Also, they did not recognize the phenomenon of money illusion, believing in perfect foresight on the part of the public. Hence, when the price level goes up and the VMPL curve shifts upwards, Classical economists believed that the public would realize the loss of real income due to the increased price level. When the wage rate is perfectly flexible, they would try to compensate this loss by supplying less labor up to that point at which their real wage rate is the same as before. In terms of Figure 18.8, starting with the original equilibrium in the labor market at point B, when there is an increase in the price level due to the loss of real income, the supply of labor curve shifts to the left. The shift in labor supply would occur up to that point at which the real wage remains the same amount as before and the money wage goes up the same amount as the increase in the price level. The same real wage rate gives the same amount of labor employment in the economy. Hence, the price level increase in the classical model does not lead to an increase in employment. This obviously means that the increase in the price level does not lead to any increase in the total product and, therefore, the GDP of the economy. As a consequence, Classical economists believe that the shape of the aggregate supply curve is perfectly vertical. With a completely vertical aggregate supply curve, the policy of the government has an interesting reflection.

When any expansionary fiscal or monetary policy is undertaken by the government, there is a rightward shift of the aggregate demand curve, as shown in Figure 18.9. But due to a vertical aggregate supply curve, with an expansionary monetary or fiscal policy, there is a higher price level and no change in the GDP level of the economy. Thus, we can use this framework to reach the same conclusion as we have seen several times before, that the classicals believed in complete

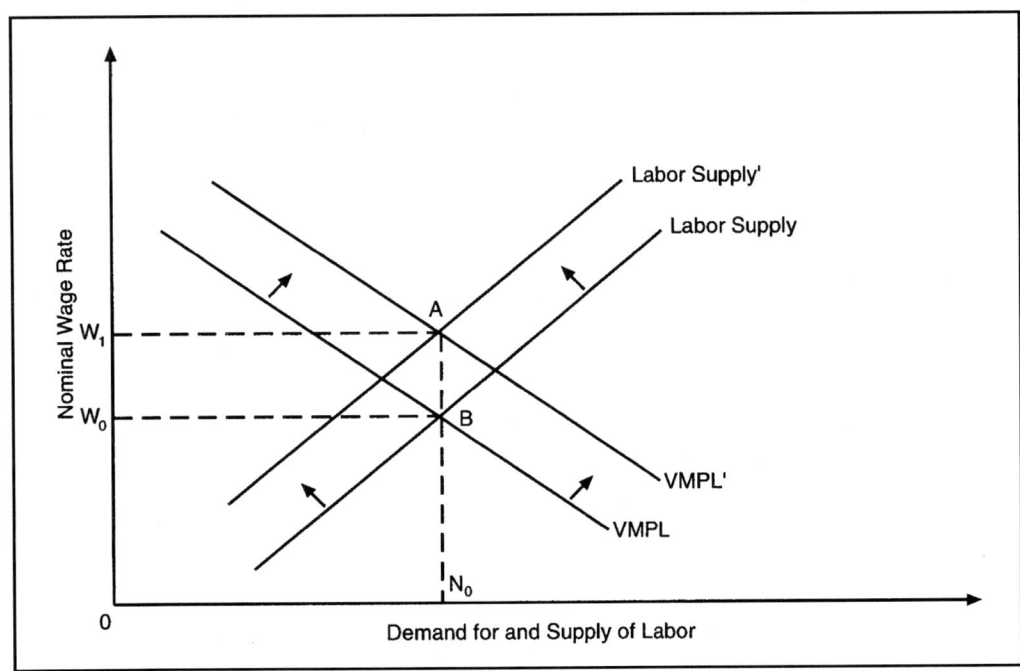

Classical Beliefs in the Labor Market ■ FIGURE 18.8

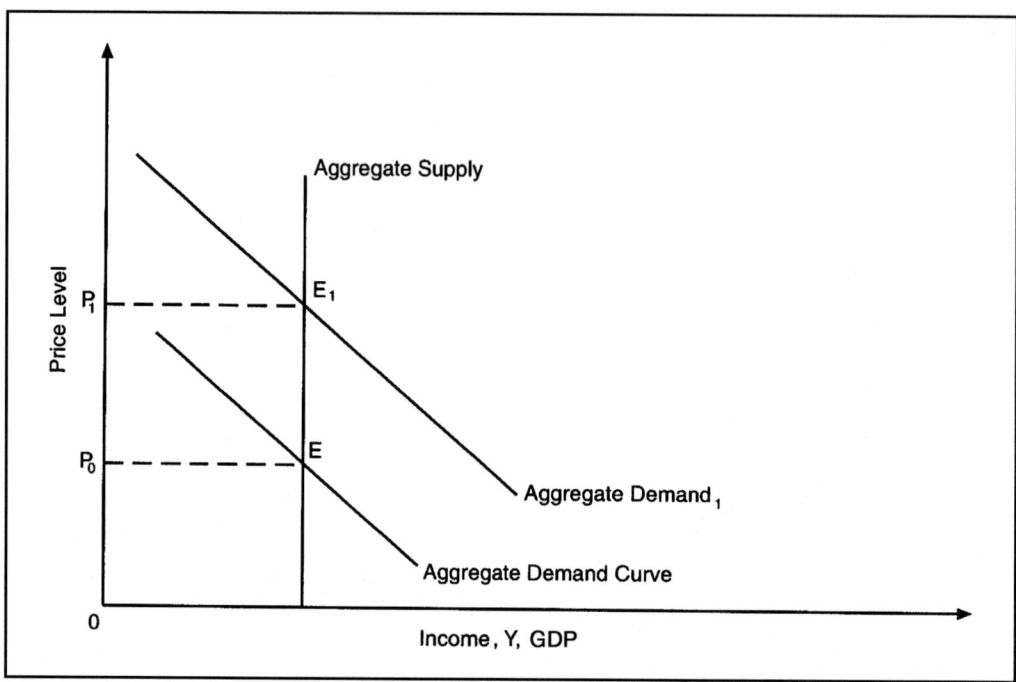

FIGURE 18.9 ■ Classical Beliefs and the Aggregate Demand and Supply Curves

ineffectiveness of government policies. Starting with the initial equilibrium at point E, when the government adopts an expansionary policy, there is a shift of the aggregate demand curve, giving us a new equilibrium point E_1 where there is a higher price level and the same level of income.

KEYNESIAN BELIEFS

In a similar fashion, we can also incorporate the special Keynesian feeling about the shape of the aggregate supply curve and the effectiveness of the policies. As you may recall from earlier chapters, Keynes believed in an active role by the government. In terms of labor market analyses, Keynes observed that in reality, the wage rate is constant at a certain level. This is because Keynes observed that the trade unions do not agree to wage cuts unless they are threatened with loss of jobs. This moves wages in a downward direction. On the other hand, when producers are free to demand any amount of labor at the given wage rate, it is unlikely that they would voluntarily increase the wage rate level. Hence, according to Keynes, the wage rate can be taken as fixed at a certain level. Therefore, as a consequence of his observation of reality, Keynes believed that the wage rate in the economy would be perfectly inflexible. To show this, let us draw a horizontal line in Figure 18.10 at a certain wage rate, say W_1.

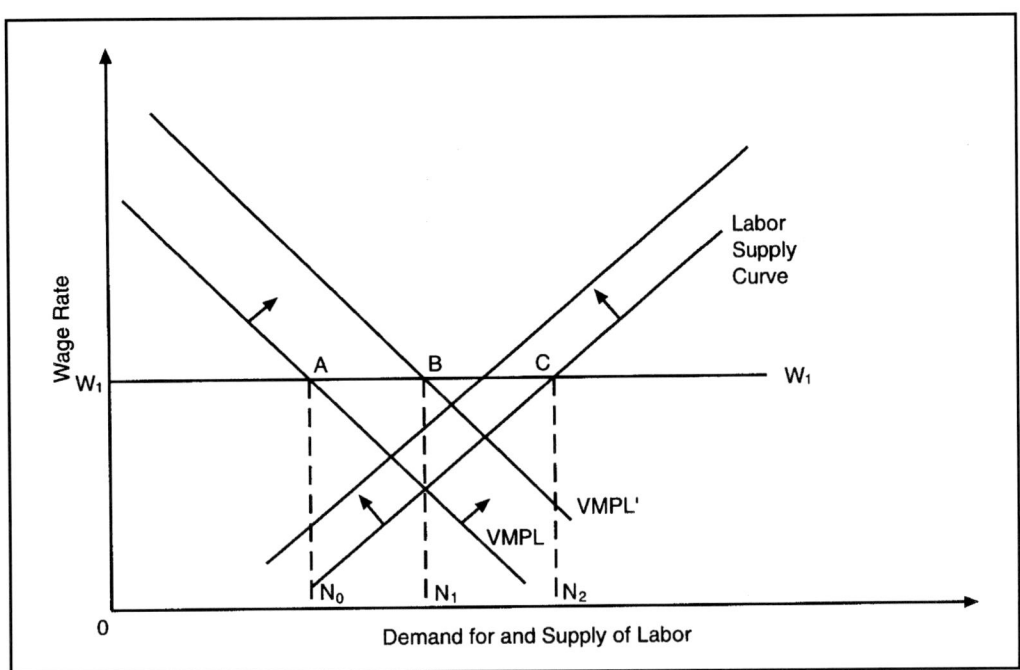

Keynesian Analysis and the Labor Market Equilibrium ■ **FIGURE 18.10**

When there is an increase in the price level under these circumstances, the VMPL curve shifts to the right. Also, if people have the money illusion, they do not supply any less labor than before, and the supply curve stays at the same location. However, if people do not have the money illusion, the supply of labor curve shifts to the left since they realize the loss of real income and start supplying less labor. In either case, with the constant wage rate, the employment of labor increases due to the increase in the initial price level.

Thus, in the Keynesian analysis, the increase in price level leads to an increase in employment in the labor market. This increased employment obviously means more total product from the total product curve and higher GDP level. Hence, the aggregate supply curve in the Keynesian analysis is upward sloping from left to right. The policy consequence of such a shape is obvious. With the increase in government expenditure and/or money supply, there is a rightward shift in the aggregate demand schedule. In terms of Figure 18.11, it means a shift of the original equilibrium to a new point M, where we have higher GDP than before the policy activity. Hence, in the Keynesian analysis, we see that the government policy is effective, but in the case of the Classical analysis the effectiveness of the policies is non-existent. Thus, aggregate demand and aggregate supply curves can be used to show the special assumptions and analysis of Classical economists and those of Keynes.

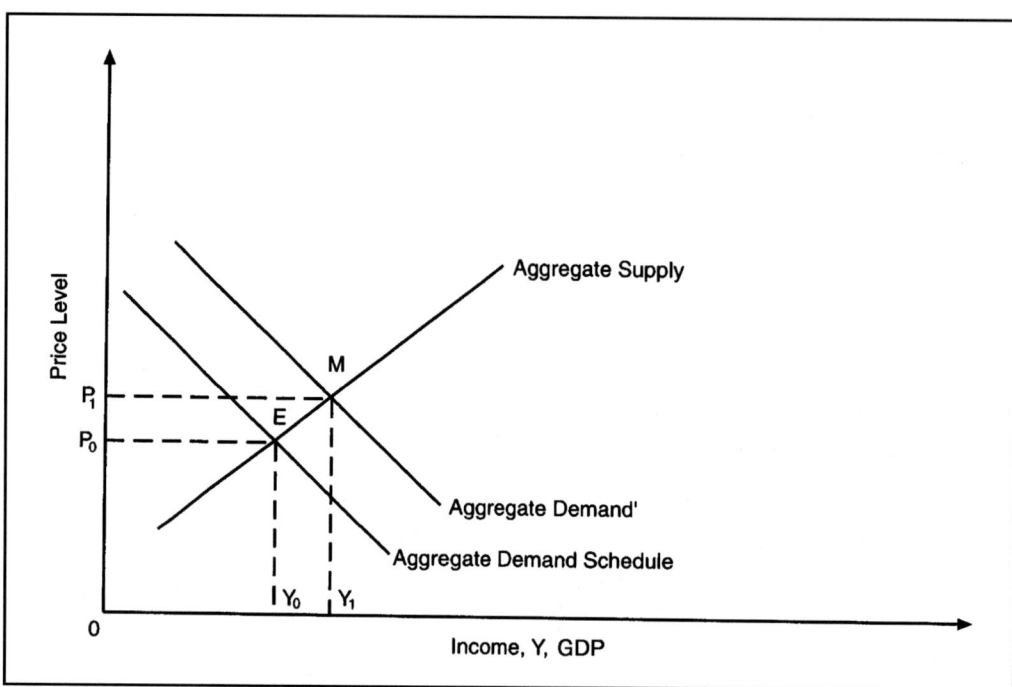

FIGURE 18.11 ■ Keynesian Analysis and the Aggregate Supply Curve

Notwithstanding these opposing views and realizing that, in reality, wages are neither completely flexible nor fully rigid, we can see that policy effectiveness depends upon how quickly people realize the loss of real income due to the inflation caused by expansionary policies, and how long a time they take to supply less labor as a result of this realization. If they are slow in realizing this, the policies can be effective longer. On the other hand, if they are smart enough to realize that the expansionary policies caused higher price levels and, therefore, less income for them, then the policies are not effective for a long time.

Therefore, it essentially comes down to the statement that the policymaker should be clever to fool people into not noticing the inflationary effects of his policies, and if he is successful in doing that, his policies will be effective longer. In this regard, we must also pay attention to the process of people forming expectations of future prices. This is because if people believe that the future price level is going to be higher than the present one, they would supply less labor and the GDP of the economy would be reduced. On the other hand, in spite of an expansionary policy, if people are made to believe that inflation is improbable, then the policy can be effective for a longer time. It is, therefore, almost mandatory that we pay more attention to the formation of expectations by the public.

Suggested Further Reading

Boyes, W. 1984. *Macroeconomics,* Chapter 7. Southwestern Publishers.

Christ, C. F. 1969. A model of monetary and fiscal policy effects on the money stock, price level and real output. *Journal of Money, Credit and Banking,* No. 1.

Clower, R. and A. Leijonhufvud. 1975. The coordination of economic activities: A Keynesian perspective. *American Economic Review,* May.

Froyen, R. T. 1983. *Macroeconomics: Theories and Policies.* New York: Macmillan Publishers.

Gordon, R. 1976. Recent developments in the theory of inflation and unemployment. *Journal of Monetary Economics,* Vol. 2: 185–219.

Gordon, R. 1984. *Macroeconomics,* 3rd ed., Chapter 6. Boston: Little Brown Publications.

Hough, L. 1954. The price level in macroeconomic models. *American Economic Review,* Vol. LXIV, June: 269–86.

Leijonhufvud, A. 1968. *On Keynesian Economics and the Economics of Keynes.* New York: Oxford University Press.

Samuelson, P. and R. Solow. 1960. The problem of achieving and maintaining a stable price level: analytical aspects of anti-inflation policy. *American Economic Review,* May: 177–94.

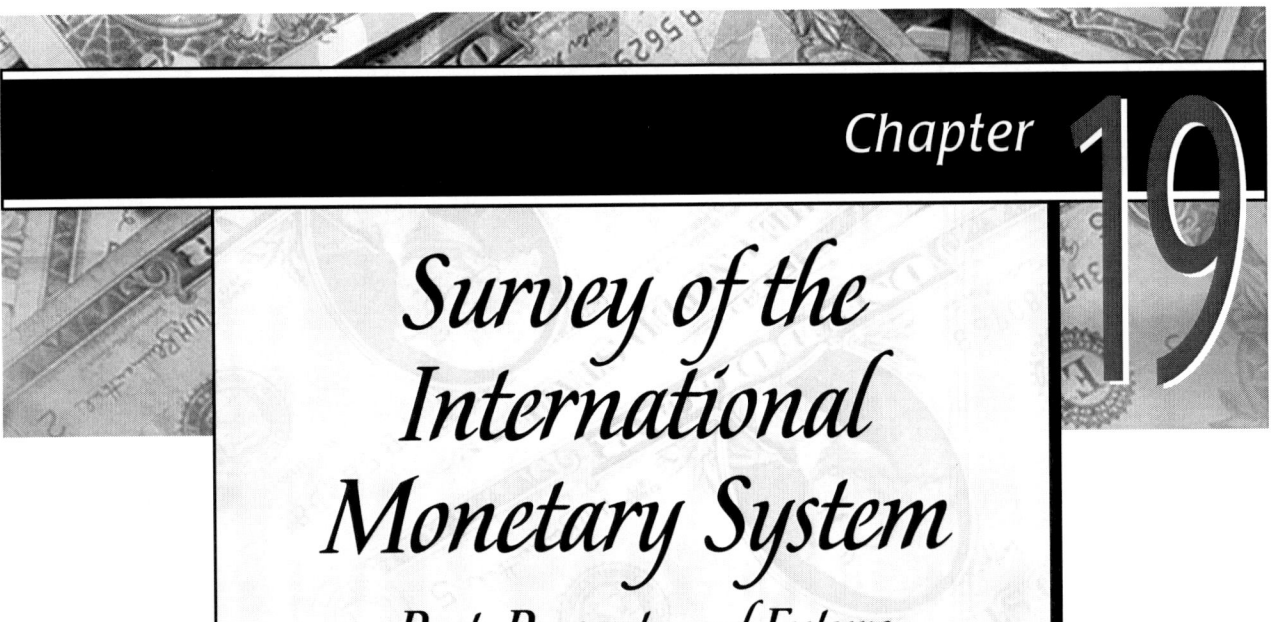

Chapter 19

Survey of the International Monetary System
Past, Present, and Future

SUMMARY

To discuss a topic as broad in scope as the history of the international monetary system risks omitting or circumscribing essential details. Yet, it is a necessary endeavor to better understand what future possibilities may exist for this important structure. This chapter recounts this history, analyzes ideas of the workings of the international monetary and exchange rate system, and proposes practical solutions for the misgivings surrounding its functions.

We must begin with a discussion of the gold standard, which prevailed from 1880 to 1914. As the first truly international monetary system, the gold standard demanded that both the value of a unit of a currency and the quantity of it in circulation be specified in terms of gold. Hence, in this system, the exchange rate between two currencies was the ratio of their "mint" prices. Despite many successes, it was eclipsed by a modified gold standard known as Bretton Woods in 1945. As a convergence of two projects—to promote international cooperation in monetary and foreign exchange policy and to facilitate international loans and aid for post-World War II reconstruction—Bretton Woods sought to use the U.S. dollar as the international reserve currency of choice by anchoring its value to gold via full convertibility of the dollar into gold. This system effectively dissolved in 1973 when the United States blocked full convertibility. The lessons learned from the operations of this system are varied, and the chapter considers each at length. While some analysts believe Bretton Woods failed because of ambiguities inherent in the system itself, others like Oppenheimer argue that its failure is due primarily to the refusal of vital countries to revalue gold.

A brief overview of the European Monetary System (EMS) and the European Monetary Union is then presented, as the process culminating in the introduction of the euro in 1999 represents one of the major developments to take place within the international monetary system. As the chapter highlights, the EMS was launched in March 1979, and it established the initial criteria for monetary integration. The Maastricht Treaty of 1993 bolstered these criteria and laid out three stages for monetary integration: elimination of all restrictions on the movement of capital; establishment of the European Monetary Institute (EMI), which sought to oversee the operation of the EMS and promote use of the European Currency Unit (ECU) and the ECU clearing system; and the introduction of the euro itself. While the euro has made many strides and its future as an international reserve currency looks exceptionally bright, stumbling blocks still remain which prevent it from achieving its full potential.

The chapter concludes by surveying some of the problems of the current monetary and exchange rate systems, proffering possible solutions to the malaise. For example, the exchange rate flexibility that currently dominates is likely to yield unwelcome effects on national economies, and the inability to justify reliance on the U.S. dollar as the principal reserve medium based on many economic indicators poses questions about the prospects of an open trading system. Many analysts have introduced their interpretations of the best way to limit arbitrary movements in real exchange rates, but the proposal of a world central bank is by far the boldest alternative because it eliminates the ever-present threat of short-sighted domestic policies. However, because countries still fear the loss of sovereignty over monetary affairs, this is an impractical solution.

Morse describes a tiered system as an alternate way in which the international monetary system might be organized, whereby governments of the industrialized world would institutionalize relations among themselves and coordinate their actions so as to reduce the ability of each to harm the others and to buffer their own network from outside pressure. This system would be global in scope, so different rules would have to be applied to different types of activities and relationships. Thus, it would be a more pluralistic international order in which no society plays a predominant role. Nonetheless, this system auspiciously assumes that members of the club would be willing to work out an economic truce with one another. As one may conclude, the future of the international monetary system is still much in doubt, and analyses to this effect depend much on interpretation.

19.1 Introduction

While forecasting interest rates and other macroeconomic variables is a dangerous venture, predictions for the future of the international monetary system are even harder. Several prevalent theories try to make predictions, but they all can be incorrect. This chapter intends to analyze the ideas behind the international monetary and exchange rate systems and proposes practical solutions for its problems.

19.2 International Monetary System: Past and Present

By 1880, the majority of the countries in the world were on some form of a gold standard. Connolly helps us in reviewing lessons learned from the past. The classical gold standard prevailed from around 1880 to 1914, with some aspects remaining until the Bretton Woods breakdown in 1971. The gold standard was a commitment by participating countries to maintain fixed prices of their domestic currencies in terms of a specified amount of gold, and to maintain fixed prices by a willingness to buy and sell gold to anyone at that price. As we saw in Chapter 4, the gold standard broke down during World War I but was briefly reinstated from 1925 to 1931 as the Gold Exchange Standard. Other countries besides the United States and Great Britain would hold gold reserves under the Gold Exchange Standard. However, this system again broke down following Britain's departure from gold in 1931 and was succeeded by "managed money."

The next attempt at a modified gold standard came about under the Bretton Woods system. Hawtrey gives us some background of what was involved in Bretton Woods. He mentions how two projects arose from Bretton Woods in July of 1944: an International Monetary Fund (IMF) to promote international cooperation in monetary and foreign exchange policy, and an international bank to facilitate international loans to aid post-war reconstruction. With the creation of the International Monetary Fund, every country contributed, along with gold, a quota of its own currency. Therefore, there appeared a stock of foreign exchanges containing all the currencies in due proportion. Any participating country could draw upon this reserve, within limits, by buying whatever foreign exchange it might need with its own money.

The Bretton Woods system functioned smoothly in its early years. But the inflation of the late 1960s resulted in large dollar outflows that strained Bretton Woods to the breaking point. The initial breakdown was only partial. The main cause of the breakdown of Bretton Woods was the end of gold convertibility of the dollar in 1973. The IMF is an important survivor from the breakdown, and the convertibility of currencies among each other and the importance of autonomy of national economic policies are the other two legacies of the Bretton Woods system. Williamson adds that another significant reason for the failure of Bretton Woods was the vagueness with which two important aspects of balance-of-payments were addressed. The first was the question of which country had the responsibility to initiate adjustment action and when that action should occur; and second, the question of techniques that should be used to effect adjustment when desired.

However, Bretton Woods implicitly incorporated the expectation that both surplus and deficit countries have a responsibility to seek payment adjustments. The system was equally ambiguous about techniques that were supposed to be employed to effect adjustment. The current account restrictions were frowned upon, but capital account restrictions were permitted, and they could not contribute to current account adjustments.

Holding yet another view, Oppenheimer went so far as stating that the breakdown of the Bretton Woods system had nothing to do with any inadequacies of the system itself. He believes it was entirely attributable to the refusal to revalue gold. Had the United States been prepared to reverse its previous stand and had it urged a decisive increase in the price of gold, it should have been possible to re-establish a smoothly functioning gold exchange standard, at least for a short time. Most economists did not doubt the feasibility of such a strategy, but they questioned its desirability, as opposed to the alternative of developing a fiduciary reserve asset.

Other reasons for the collapse of Bretton Woods were increased productivity of the German, Japanese, and Swiss economies. There was also a greater awareness of the unjust benefits of the United States as perceived by the rest of the world. After the United States closed the gold window in 1973 and announced that it believed the currencies of other industrial countries should be revalued relative to the dollar, the participating countries had little choice but to float their currencies vis-a-vis each others' currencies. The immediate effect of this widespread floating was the breakdown of the gold standard. Along with the U.S. decision to press for the revaluation of other currencies, there was a mass incentive created to shift funds out of the dollar into the revaluation candidates that only the most dedicated countries could contemplate facing.

Cooper believes Bretton Woods would have broken down sooner or later even without the inflation of the late 1960s. The convertibility of gold and the dollar was bound to become increasingly doubtful as dollar liabilities rose over time relative to the U.S. gold stock.

All of these dynamics set the stage for a new monetary system on the international level. In the aftermath, a few things were very clear. The formation of the

European Monetary System (hereinafter "EMS") was an indication that countries favored stable rates. The recent catastrophes in Argentina, Brazil, Mexico, and Israel are strong reasons for order and discipline in international monetary transactions. As late as 1985, the increase in the value of the dollar created the fears of a trade war between the United States and Japan, necessitating a coordination of the whole system in general and among industrialized countries in particular. In the next section, we concentrate on some of the suggestions made by economists in dealing with the modern problems of international monetary disorder. A complex problem does not have an easy solution. Even if there are several views about the future of the international monetary system, the chance of any one being implemented in full is very small. All views stand a chance, which makes this topic an interesting one to pursue.

Evolution of the Euro 19.3

One of the major developments in the international monetary system since 1990 is the introduction of the euro as the currency of prime importance. The "euro" is the name of the proposed single currency of the European Community. Essentially, the euro is simply the European Currency Unit (ECU) renamed, because ECUs will be exchangeable one-for-one for new euros. The ECU was the basis for the European Monetary System.

ECU is pronounced "EK-you," after the name of an old French coin with an equivalent spelling. The ECU is defined in terms of pieces of European currencies, making it a composite, or basket currency, in origination. Since its creation, the euro has become a currency of denomination for euro bonds and bank certificates of deposit, among many other uses.

When the European Monetary System was launched on March 13, 1979, the system was based on the average behavior of the participant countries of the European Community. If the Community average was five percent inflation, then a country with either zero percent inflation or ten percent inflation would cause strains in the system. All this economic coordination took place through a country's exchange rate. A country was on track just as long as its exchange rate with respect to the ECU did not depart too much from a fixed value—the ECU central rate. The Maastricht Treaty added additional criteria other than exchange rates.

The Maastricht Treaty was finally approved (through a subterfuge) by the remaining holdout, Denmark, in May of 1993. The Treaty set out three stages of further transition to a monetary union between participant countries of the European Community. The first stage was to have been completed by January 1, 1994, and involved the elimination of "all restrictions on the movement of capital between Member States, and between Member States and third countries." This goal was not actually achieved.

The second stage began on January 1, 1994, with the creation of the European Monetary Institute (EMI) in Frankfurt, Germany. The EMI was a precursor to a proposed European Central Bank, which in the future is supposed to implement a common European monetary policy, conduct foreign exchange operations, hold reserves of member countries, and promote smooth payment mechanisms. The goals of the EMI itself were more modest. The EMI was supposed to hold the gold and foreign exchange reserves, and oversee the operation of the European Monetary System and promote the use of the ECU and an ECU clearing system.

The euro is the sole currency in fifteen countries which constitute the "Eurozone" or "Euroland." There are some other areas and small countries that use euro as their currency as well. As of 2008, nine European Union member countries have currencies other than euro, but they all are required to join the euro in the future. An "optimum currency area" is a geographical region in which it would maximize economic efficiency to have the entire region share a single currency. While the exchange rate risk is eliminated with such an arrangement, the cost of exchanging the currencies is also reduced and that translates to big savings for firms and businesses. Financial markets on the continent are expected to be far more liquid. The reduction in cross-border transaction costs will allow larger banking firms to provide a wider array of banking services that can compete across Eurozone.

A currency is attractive for international transaction when it demonstrates stability in value and acceptability to others. While the euro has made substantial progress, a few challenges undermine it serving as the major reserve currency. Persistent excessive large budget deficits of some member nations, some economically weak members, conservatism of some financial markets, and inertia amongst some members are main stumbling blocks in its future. Nonetheless, the performance of the euro in recent years compared with such currencies as the U.S. dollar is very impressive. In 1999, one euro was traded at 1.18 U.S. dollars, by October 26, 2000, it had fallen to 82 cents, but it recovered remarkably to parity of one U.S. dollar by July 15, 2002. From then on it has picked up value tremendously to reach $1.59 on July 15, 2008. While this was partly due to hardships in the U.S. economy, other factors involved an efficient working of European Monetary Policy. There seems to be a bright future for euro as the major currency of the modern world.

International Monetary System: What's Ahead? 19.4

How can the standards and benefits of the International Monetary System be improved? Meier (1982) says, "The design of an international monetary system is a very difficult task. It involves policy choices that take international monetary affairs into the political limelight, affecting the benefits and costs among nations and often requiring the resolution of conflicting interests."

Southward gives the list of what he thinks are the main objectives of an International Monetary System. The system must be capable of achieving monetary stability, restoring acceptable levels of employment and sustainable growth, and checking the present strong inflationary and stagflationary policies. It must be supportive of a process of global development, especially for Third World countries. The interests of the majority of the world must be reflected. All countries should participate in the institutional arrangements for international monetary management. There should be the establishment of an international currency unit as an international means of exchange and primary reserve asset. A certain degree of automatic procedures are needed in the transfer of resources through reserve asset creation by the international community.

Some lessons from the European Monetary System can be easily learned. Connolly explains some of the pointers that may be taken from the EMS. All of the main currencies of the European Economic Community (EEC) participate in the EMS, except the British pound sterling. The system aims to enforce a fixed exchange rate among participating countries, at least within a band, whereas exchange rates are floating in relation with outside currencies (although there is dirty floating). The internal fixity of exchange rates implies central bank interventions, and a complex system of indicators has been designed to help in the determination of respective responsibilities of central banks.

Two systems have been given particular consideration by the EMS:

1. A snake-type system, as seen in the early 1970s, where there is a need for intervention when the bilateral exchange rate between two currencies reaches its upper or lower limits, and
2. A basket-type system, where the need for intervention is determined by the fact that one currency reaches its upper or lower limits in relation to the basket of currencies (European Currency Unit, for instance).

In actuality, a mixed system was adopted. The intervention of central banks is not obligatory until a currency fluctuates at least 2.25 percent above or below its parity in terms of another currency in the system. This is the same as the old snake system, but a new concept has been added: the "divergence indicator." The divergence indicator is not the same for each of the currencies that make up the European Currency Unit (ECU). This is because the probability of reaching a given limit of fluctuation is not as great for a currency weighted lightly in the ECU as for one that is weighted heavily. The indicator acts as a signal; it does not trigger automatic action. The country concerned can then intervene in exchange markets, alter its monetary or fiscal policies, or make an adjustment in the currency's parity.

The advantage of central banks over the market in stabilizing the exchange rate is smaller, the shorter the period under consideration, even when central banks kept information on their monetary policies to themselves. EMS arrangements are in no way optimal since the central banks claim that they defend fixed rates within banks in the short run, but do not make any firm commitment for the long run. Putting aside the solution of a truly competitive system in the production of money, a second-best solution would imply perfect flexibility of the exchange rate without intervention in the short run. Where some information would be given to the market for the long-run value of the exchange rate, either because all central banks would use a policy of monetary targets or because they would be committed to the attainment of predetermined values of the exchange rate in the long run and would be able to hold to their commitment. Unfortunately, the EMS arrangement is just the opposite.

Predetermined exchange rates in the long run are not necessarily "fixed rates." Fixity of exchange rates is an irrelevant problem, because if information on the future course of exchange rates was perfect, there would not be any reason to prefer fixed rates. Fixity would mean only that there is a link to national inflation rates, which has no justification especially if the "common" inflation rate is high. In fact, social welfare can be increased by central banks in two different ways: by giving good information on the future of exchange rates and/or monetary policies, and by following monetary policies to minimize the inflation rate. Exchange rate fixity does not imply that any of these functions correctly maintain the fixity of exchange rates.

There is much discomfort concerning the present international monetary system. One of the important reasons for this distress is the large external debt that has been accumulated around the world, more specifically with developing economies. Due to the uncertainty inherent in the system, the international monetary arrangements are not stable. Dissatisfaction with very short-run and year-to-year movements in real exchange rates, combined with technological developments, will sooner or later force a desirable change in existing arrangements. Cooper has some additional suggestions: the creation of a common currency for all industrial democracies and a common monetary policy. In this arrangement, the individual countries could determine their fiscal policy actions, but those policies would be constrained by the need to borrow in the international market.

Presently, we have exchange rate flexibility that has helped retain an open trading and financial system. These flexible exchange rates have generally corrected for differences in national inflation rates. However, two features of the present exchange rate system will not be satisfactory over the long run:

1. Movements in real exchange rates have a major unwelcome effect on national economies. But movements in real exchange rates cannot be easily controlled by the usual instruments of national economic policy. This is because determinants of exchange rates are diverse and complex. Nonetheless, sometimes policies have worked sufficiently because it is the other country's responsibility to recognize the effects of disequilibrium adjustment in the balance of payments of its partners.
2. The present arrangements of creation of reserves are not sustainable over the long run. The dollar as the principal reserve medium has been accepted, but not without some uneasiness. In recent years, the productivity in U.S. manufacturing has not kept up with other developed economies. This has already created problems. Several other weaknesses of reliance on the U.S. dollar will become more apparent as the rest of the world starts having doubts about U.S. dominance.

With greater sensitivity to changes in real exchange rates, governments must reduce arbitrary movements in real exchange rates in order to maintain an open trading system. An adjustable peg system of exchange rates that requires occasional discretionary movements in market exchange rates is not likely tenable. Cooper believes these variables lead to the conclusion that we will need a system of credibly fixed exchange rates if we are to preserve an open trading and financial system. Exchange rates can be fixed if international transactions take place with a single currency. He maintains that this is possible only if there is a single monetary policy and a single authority issuing the currency and directing the policy.

Korteweg argues that exchange rates should be government-determined, not market-determined, and should be used as an instrument of economic policy. For a macroeconomic view, a country's competitive position may be thought of as being determined by the value of its currency in terms of a trade-weighted basket of its competitor's currencies, as well as by the country's tradable-goods price level relative to prices. In this system there would be less uncertainty compared to the present flexible exchange rates, if carried out over-ambitiously.

In another view, Southward proposes an idea as a solution for the world monetary problem and makes a case for a world central bank. The purpose of a world central bank would be to provide a uniform and universally acceptable currency with stable purchasing power, and to exercise systematic control over the total supply of currency reserves. If the central bank was organized as a better version of the IMF, no changes in voting arrangements would be necessary. The system would separate the reserve currency function from the function performed by national currencies on the international exchange market. This could be accomplished by creating a new unit of international currency. This would avoid the complex dilemma faced by U.S. authorities in the Bretton Woods system.

The uniform currency would be defined as equal to a basket of currencies, similar to Special Drawing Rights (SDRs), with each currency valued at its exchange rate and weighted in proportion to the country's share of world trade or according to some other appropriate economic measure. The central banks could deposit national currency holdings in a substitution account, receiving the new currency in return. The world central bank would issue any additional reserves needed for adequate growth of the world economy. The national currencies would constitute a steadily declining portion of the world's currency reserves. It is doubtful that the idea for a world central bank will be implemented because many nations, especially developing ones, fear loss of sovereignty over their monetary affairs. And yet, national monetary authorities are far from being free to act independently. Southward's proposed system certainly does not completely shelter nations from the international consequences of ill-considered domestic economic policies.

There is one strong argument for supporting a world central bank: no alternative has satisfactorily worked. Each system without a central bank has generated instabilities in the world economy. Unless some link of international unity can be created in money matters, the probability of instability remains high. Hence, we support the concept of having a sole governing body so that irresponsible domestic policies would not be tolerated.

Bernstein outlines some steps that could be taken to give foreign monetary authorities greater confidence in the dollar. One solution proposed is the establishment of a *substitution account* in the IMF in which countries could place some or all of their dollar reserves. A participating country would transfer to the account any dollar assets it does not wish to hold and would receive a credit balance denominated in SDRs.

This substitution account would provide participation members with an automatic diversification of their foreign exchange reserves in the sixteen currencies that comprise a unit of SDR in proportion to their importance in that unit. The purpose of the substitution account is to avoid large changes in the currency composition or reserves. Participating countries must be able to use their SDR-denominated reserve assets in balance of payments settlements in the same way they now use their dollar reserves. Most countries would likely want dollars when converting their assets. If the U.S. Treasury were to buy assets held in the substitution account, it could either become a holder of such assets itself or retire them in exchange for an equivalent amount of U.S. securities held by the account. The establishment of a substitution account could contribute to greater stability in the international monetary system, but only if the United States were to take responsibility for the SDR value of the assets in the account. Also, one has doubts about the overall cooperation from European economies and developing countries for this establishment, as they are disturbed even by the recent phenomenon of an overvalued dollar.

Morse describes an alternate way in which the international monetary system might be organized, namely, a tiered system where governments of the industrialized world would institutionalize their relations with each other by coordinating their action so as to reduce the ability of each to harm the others and to buffer as far as possible their own network of interactions from outside pressure (i.e., least developed country). Governments in less-developed countries would want to attach themselves to international institutional arrangements that would preserve a structure of economic stability and order, and also guarantee them some participation in the formulation of rules, but not on an equal basis as the governments of the industrialized economies would have to abandon the traditional liberal norm of universality. The system would be global in scope, so different rules would have to be applied to different types of activities and relationships. Any international codes that emerge should embody what government does with respect to the exchange rate regime, adjustment mechanism, and mode of handling convertibility.

Five or six governments would assume major responsibility for "managing" international financial relationships. There would be formal arrangements governing the determination of exchange rates and supporting mechanisms. There would be informal agreements concerning targets for domestic economic goals and national sovereignty.

Morse further believes that his system could serve to enhance the major objectives associated with the liberal international monetary system: price stability, full employment, free trade, economic growth, and a defused adjustment process. This system is geared more toward pluralistic international order in which no single society plays such a predominant role that it can abuse the autonomy and freedom of others. This system would depend partly on the willingness of the members of the club to work out an economic truce with one another. This in itself is doubtful.

Suggested Further Reading

Bernstein, E. M. 1982. Outlook for the dollar and other international assets. *The International Monetary System: A Time of Turbulence:* 410-29.

Connelly, M. B. 1982. The European monetary system. *The International Monetary System: Choices for the Future:* 180-97.

Cooper, R. N. 1982. A monetary system for the future. *Journal of Economic Issues,* Vol. XVII: 168-84.

Hawtrey, R. C. 1946. *Bretton Woods for Better or Worse,* pp. 1-55.

Korteweg, P. 1980. Exchange-rate policy, monetary policy, and exchange rate variability. *Essays in International Finance,* No. 140: 1-28.

Meier, G. M. 1982. *Problems of a World Monetary Order,* No. XIV: 242.

Morse, E. L. 1976. *Alternatives of Monetary Disorder,* No. XIV: 28-29.

Oppenheimer, P. M. 1974. World monetary developments and the committee of twenty. *Aussenwirtschaft:* 46.

Rivera-Batiz, F. and L. A. Rivera-Batiz. 1994. *International Finance and Open Economy Macroeconomics,* 2nd ed. New York: Macmillan.

Southward, F. A. 1979. The evolution of the IMF. *Essays in International Finance,* No. 135: 1-65.

Williamson, J. 1977. Why Bretton Woods collapsed. *The Failure of World Monetary:* 8-29.

Chapter 20

Fiscal and Monetary Policy-Making in the United States

A Historical Review

SUMMARY

Our study of macro-monetary theory culminates with an investigation of how its principles have influenced policy-making in the United States. Appropriately, the final chapter paints a broad historical overview of fiscal and monetary policies in the United States and evaluates their performance with theory as a guiding light.

At the beginning of the 20th century, economic thinking was dominated by the Classical economists. Their advocacy of Laissez-faire doctrine prompted an inactive U.S. fiscal policy response to the Great Depression. Nonetheless, as the late 1930s ushered in the Keynesian revolution and World War II, government expenditure naturally increased. The New Deal policies, in particular, personified Keynesian ideas, and the introduction of the Phillips Curve hypothesis in the 1960s provided strong theoretical support for the adoption of expansionary fiscal policy. After all, the unprecedented growth of the 1960s increased tax revenue. Yet, the 1973 oil price spikes led to recession in 1975, and expansionary policies were adopted in response with the intention of lowering unemployment. Counter-intuitively, price levels and the unemployment rate rose further, creating stagflation. Moreover, increased competition from abroad meant that both trade and budget deficits started to slowly increase in the late 1970s. Again, the official response to this inflationary force was to adopt even more activist policies, since Neo-Keynesians believed the Phillips curve in the 1970s had merely shifted to the right.

The early 1980s witnessed severe economic hardships, and the Reagan administration reacted by implementing serious tax reductions in 1986. Interest rates declined dramatically, investment started to pick up, and real GDP nearly doubled from 1980 to 1987. However, this economic turnaround was in fact accomplished via a quadrupling of the budget deficit from 1980 to 1988. Even more noticeable in these years was the ever-increasing trade deficit. Yet, inflation was absent in these days and interest rates and the unemployment rate declined. In the 1990s, fiscal policy continued to be expansionary, as government expenditure actually came to equal the share of private domestic investment in national GDP. Importantly, this increased government expenditure was accompanied by technological revolution, which boosted production and income and gave the government a moderate budget surplus in 1999 and 2000. Nonetheless, the big shock of September 11, 2001, shifted the pattern of government expenditure toward national security outlays. Moreover, uncertainty and risk became so vast that business investment declined, the housing market stagnated, and real GDP growth witnessed a major setback. Ominously, the U.S. technological growth rate slowed considerably in the years after 2001.

Monetary policy, like fiscal policy, was dormant in the early years of the 20th century. The Federal Reserve System was established in 1913, but its initial objectives were not inclined toward policy activism. Rather, the primary job of the Federal Reserve System was to control bank failure and to act as a lender of last resort to the banking system. By the 1960s, the Keynesian notion that interest rate targeting should be of utmost concern had gained popularity, and changes in money supply were seen as the instrument to achieve this objective. This gave way to a severe debate in the early 1970s between Keynesians and Monetarists regarding the proper path for monetary policy. Keynesians believed that solving the unemployment problem required an expansionary monetary policy, while Monetarists perceived all inflation as a monetary phenomenon caused by excessive money supply growth in the economy.

Finally, the Federal Reserve System shifted its aims in 1979, vowing to keep money supply growth in check irrespective of the interest rate level. This "monetarist experiment" was not very successful initially, but it eventually achieved its main purpose of lowering the inflation rate, from 13.5 percent in 1980 to 3.2 percent in 1983. In the 1990s, American dominance in total factor productivity, technological innovation, and industrial output was entrenched. Monetary policy in these years was prudent, pragmatic, and carefully carved. Nonetheless, the tragic events of September 11, 2001, were financially devastating to the U.S. economy. The overall response of monetary policy to these events was to lower the interest rate to very low levels, which fostered adventurism in the country's mortgage industry. As housing prices declined in 2007, the economy went through a severe housing crisis. Lower technological growth, lower willingness of producers to take risk, and the onset of the Iraq War in 2003 have combined to infuse sluggish economic growth. While the economic prospects of the United States are in doubt, we are certain that theory accurately describes past and present U.S. fiscal and monetary policies. Likewise, the principles of macro-monetary theory are useful tools to help us ponder the prospects of the future.

20.1 Introduction

Earlier chapters have given us the flavor of macroeconomic theory; in this chapter we analyze economic growth in the United States. We will evaluate the performance of fiscal policy (section 20.2) and follow it with the performance evaluation of monetary policy (section 20.3). Our main objective here, therefore, is to mesh theory with practice and show that theoretical principles have in fact mattered in policymaking in the United States.

20.2 Fiscal Policymaking in the United States

As we saw in Chapter 5, the Classical economists offered very little help for policy activism. In fact, their advocacy of laissez-faire policy made quite an impact on the inactivity of U.S. fiscal policy in the Great Depression era. In 1930, for example, the government expenditure of less than $1 billion was merely 5 percent of the GDP. The GDP in 1929 was roughly $19 billion. This clearly was an indication that the government sector's role in the economy was at a very low level. The tremendous unemployment of that period made little impact on the thinking of economic policy. However, as the Keynesian revolution was set in the late 1930s and as World War II broke out, government expenditures naturally increased, either by design or by the need of the day. Fiscal policy became quite active in terms of raising the GDP (of course, for defense-oriented production in early years) in the early 1940s. In the immediate post-World War II period, however, there was increasing faith in government activity as many more programs were started and added to existing ones. The New Deal policies, the advent of the Social Security system, the increased expenditure on highway systems and national parks, and the unemployment benefits program are classic examples of Keynesian policies in action in these decades. In general, the GDP started picking up due to these programs, the Great Depression-like phenomena became a distant memory, and the positive effects of Keynesian advice were widely seen. This gave policymakers even more reason to adopt more expansionary fiscal policies. By the 1950s, government involvement in the U.S. economy gathered more momentum.

In the 1960s, the introduction of the Phillips Curve Hypothesis and the strong theoretical proof for government activism, aided by a cadre of Keynesians working in U.S. government offices, made it easy to adopt expansionary fiscal policy. While the Johnson administration's income tax rebates of 1966 were the biggest tax break so far, there were some attempts to increase government expenditure with such programs as "putting man on the moon before the end of this decade," as President John F. Kennedy had declared. Even a small increase in the unemployment rate was seen as an opportunity to increase the government's expenditures. The unprecedented growth of the 1960s (recall that the 1960s was the most prosperous decade in the history of U.S. economic growth) increased tax revenues and therefore, in initial years, the effect of increased government expenditures on the budget deficit was negligible. U.S. imports were increasing without much cost to the government, as the dollar was made the key (and reserve) currency in the Bretton Woods system. The major economic dominance of the United States in the 1960s was so significant that other countries, including the U.S.S.R., were producing GDPs that were of miniscule importance. Clearly, the 1960s was the decade of supremacy for the U.S. economy, which barely diminished after that period until the year 2000 onward. So, the Keynesian policies were showing great positive effects until, of course, the major setback arrived in 1973. While the Vietnam War channeled resources to somewhat non-productive areas, the oil dependence of the U.S. economy was vividly experienced when the Organization of Petroleum Exporting Countries (OPEC) determined to come up with the first oil shock in 1973.

In many different ways, the 1970s were turbulent years for the U.S. economy. While there was a significant increase in oil prices in 1973 (30 percent in one shot), there were other hardships as well. The recession of 1975 created lower aggregate supply (shift of the aggregate supply curve to the left) simultaneous to increased aggregate demand (shift of the aggregate demand curve to the right), as more expansionary policies were adopted with the intention of lowering unemployment. However, all these forces combined to raise both prices and unemployment, creating the problem of stagflation. The U.S. labor productivity growth slowed down, and countries like Japan and Germany started catching up with the U.S. economic growth rate. The increased competition from abroad made U.S. exports less attractive, and the trade and budget deficits started slowly increasing in the late 1970s. The response of policymakers to the inflationary forces, interestingly enough, was to adopt even more expansionary policies. As mentioned before, this was partly because of the Neo-Keynesian idea that more expansionary fiscal policy was needed to solve unemployment and to respond to the Phillips Curve shifting to the right in the 1970s. This probably made matters worse, as inflation reached 15 percent in 1979 and unemployment approached 8 percent. In 1980, Republican presidential candidate Ronald Reagan introduced the idea of the "misery index" (addition of the inflation rate and the unemployment rate) and very successfully showed that it was at its highest level during the Carter administration from 1976 to 1980. While the economic hardships were quite visible, the theoretical challenges by monetarists to traditional Keynesian ideas were at a peak, too.

Milton Friedman (recipient of the Nobel Prize in Economics in 1976) was successful in showing that expansionary policies are not only undesirable, but that they also harmed the economy. A "great debate" of the 1970s for adopting fiscal policy was popular for two completely opposite views of macroeconomists. In these chaotic times, a new OPEC price increase of 1979 raised questions about wage and price controls. There were gasoline quotas, a Greyhound bus drivers' strike, an air traffic controllers' strike, a renewed energy for protectionism, a call for energy conservation, and, to top it all, the Iran hostage crisis. Table 20.1 shows the relevant data of the U.S. economy for the 1970s. As can be observed, there was a consistent increase in the rate of growth of government expenditures, especially in the late 1970s when the economic hardships were the most severe. The government expenditure of $233 billion in 1970 was allowed to go up to $566.2 billion in 1980, an increase of more than 150 percent in ten years. Tax revenues, however, did not keep up with this growth in government expenditures, partly due to the severe recession in 1975. By 1976, the budget deficit of the U.S. government had increased to $40 billion; it further increased to $70 billion by 1980. This expansionary fiscal policy was criticized by monetarists (and Republicans), who put

TABLE 20.1

	GDP	G	Tx	Federal Funds Rate	CPI	CPI Inflation Rate	M1	M2	Unemployment
1970	1,038.5	233.8	84.1	7.2	38.8	5.7	209.1	601.5	4.9
1971	1,127.1	246.5	85.9	4.7	40.5	4.4	223.1	674.4	5.9
1972	1,238.3	263.5	94.4	4.4	41.8	3.2	239.0	758.2	5.6
1973	1,382.7	281.7	109.4	8.7	44.4	6.2	256.3	831.8	4.9
1974	1,500.0	317.9	125.1	10.5	49.3	11.0	269.1	880.6	5.6
1975	1,638.3	357.7	127.4	5.8	53.8	9.1	281.3	963.5	8.5
1976	1,825.3	383.0	144.2	5.0	56.9	5.8	288.8	1,086.5	7.7
1977	2,030.9	414.1	162.6	5.5	60.6	6.5	319.9	1,221.2	7.1
1978	2,294.7	453.6	193.6	7.9	65.2	0.6	346.2	1,322.2	6.1
1979	2,563.3	500.8	220.1	11.2	72.6	11.3	372.6	1,425.7	5.8
1980	2,789.5	566.2	256.3	13.4	82.4	13.5	395.7	1,540.2	7.1
1981	3,128.4	627.5	209.2	16.4	90.9	10.3	425.0	1,679.3	7.6
1982	3,255.0	680.5	283.3	12.3	96.5	6.2	453.0	1,833.0	9.7
1983	3,536.7	733.5	279.8	9.1	99.6	3.2	503.2	2,057.5	9.0
1984	3,933.2	797.0	306.7	10.2	103.9	4.3	538.6	2,222.1	7.5
1985	4,220.3	879.0	332.2	8.1	107.6	3.6	587.0	2,419.9	7.2
1986	4,462.8	949.3	367.6	6.8	109.6	1.9	666.3	2,616.4	7.0
1987	4,739.5	999.5	373.9	6.7	113.6	3.6	743.6	2,786.5	6.2

forward the complete "crowding out" hypothesis in the 1970s. Thus, the 1970s became an interesting decade for government activism and fiscal policy. However, the following decade witnessed a totally different scenario. In 1982, the U.S. economy went through a severe recession, with very high interest rates (20.5 percent prime rate of some major banks in January 1981, which was the highest in the history of the U.S. banking system) and very low investment level; the real GDP stagnated in 1982 and the unemployment rate reached 9.7 percent. The economic hardship was clearly evident everywhere. By this time, the "supply side economics" that was aided by the Laffer curve (Figure 20.1) and adopted by the Reagan administration was running into theoretical problems. But apparently persistence paid off. The main argument of the Laffer curve, made popular by Professor Arthur Laffer, was that if the economy is operating on the declining portion of the Laffer curve, then a reduction in tax rates can increase tax revenues.

The Reagan administration announced and implemented some serious tax reductions in 1986, with income tax filing simplification to reduce the loopholes that encouraged tax evasion. Added to this was the overall optimism exhibited by the President and his supporters, which had a positive effect on the expectations of the public. The economy recovered in an impressive fashion from 1984 onward. Interest rates dramatically declined (from 20.5 percent in 1981 to 9 percent in

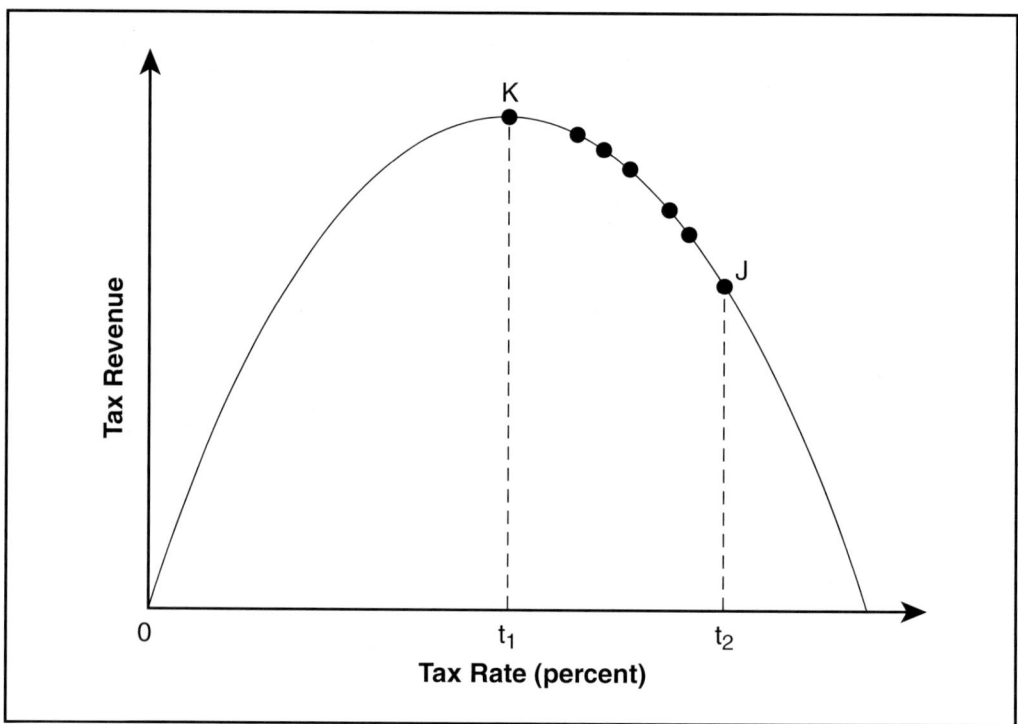

FIGURE 20.1 ■ The Laffer Curve

1986), investment started picking up, and the real GDP nearly doubled from 1980 to 1987. The big turnaround of the economy was considered (especially by Republicans) to be a major tribute to the Reagan administration.

However, this outstanding turnaround of the economy was accomplished by allowing the budget deficit to quadruple from 1980 ($70 billion) to 1988 ($240 billion). In fact, in 1986, 1987, and 1988, the budget deficit figures broke the earlier year's record. The expansionary fiscal policy was also the result of lower tax revenues resulting from the recession in the early 1980s and the slower recovery of tax revenue after the turnaround. What is even more noticeable was the ever-increasing trade deficit in these years. While it is easy to prove the twin deficit phenomenon, the 1980s were the years of its greatest evidence. A simple theoretical argument can help prove the twin deficit possibility.

Consider that basic GDP (Y) = aggregate demand or total expenditures equation, by using our usual notations C (consumption expenditures), I (investment expenditures), G (government expenditures), X (export), M (import). Therefore,

$$Y = C + I + G + X - M \qquad (1)$$

Consider further that total income (Y) can be distributed as C (consumption) + S (saving) + Tx (taxes), so that the left hand side of Equation (1) can be C + S + Tx.

Hence,

$$C + S + Tx = C + I + G + X - M \qquad (2)$$

Canceling consumption C, from both sides and defining M - X as the trade deficit, we get

$$(S - I) + (Tx - G) + \text{Trade deficit} = 0$$

Recognizing that (G - Tx) is the budget deficit, we know that if the Saving and Investment difference is stable, then

$$\text{Trade deficit} = \text{Budget deficit}.$$

Thus, these two deficits act as identical twins; if one increases, the other increases, too. This theory had its predominant evidence in the U.S. economy in the 1980s when the Reagan administration saw record breaking levels for both (especially from 1986 to 1989). While these twin deficits were increasing, the money supply (that we shall visit in the next section) was also increasing and demand management policies were truly expansionary. However, the inflation rate declined in this period from 10.3 percent in 1981 to 1.9 percent in 1986 and to 3.6 percent in 1987. Hence, the increased money supply led to a reduction in the inflation rate! (Interestingly, this was quite contrary to what strong monetarists were proposing.) The unemployment rate declined, the economy prospered, and the policies were totally expansionary despite the political rhetoric of reducing the role of the government sector in private enterprise. So, macroeconomists were baffled by this performance, prompting some authors to write books with titles such as Mystery of the 1980s. The only meaningful explanation for this scenario is the one offered by the "expectations hypothesis," especially the rational expectations hypothesis.

The main message of rational expectations theory was that, if policy effectiveness has to be significant, then giving the economic agents (those who make economic decisions) complete and correct information is disastrous. To put it in the opposite way, if the information is incomplete (and incorrect), and if economic agents are not allowed to expect future inflation for whatever reasons, then the policy effectiveness is the highest, no matter what type of policy change is activated. Thus, a budget deficit which was record breaking did not create inflationary expectations because (maybe) complete and correct information was provided to the decision makers. In many ways, this message was not clear in any time but in the 1980s. In fact, as some economists argued in those days, there could also be a "credibility hypothesis" at work, which puts an automatic limit to the policy effectiveness if government tries to repeat the same misinformation (or limited information) strategy for a long time. In any case, the success of the 1980s was inexplicable by traditional macroeconomic terms. There was an absence of inflation in those days, despite the record breaking expansionary demand management policies. As interest rates dramatically declined, the unemployment rate came down and real GDP increased.

In the 1990s, fiscal policy continued to be expansionary as the government role in the U.S. economy kept increasing. With a higher percentage of GDP in terms of government expenditure, the share of government expenditure came close to the share of private domestic investment. However, this increased government expenditure was accompanied by technological revolution. This boosted production and income to the point that tax revenues increased, and, by the years 1999 and 2000, the U.S. government realized a moderate budget surplus. Thus, the 1990s were characterized by unprecedented growth rates and the decade became the most prosperous in terms of economic gains. The fiscal policy was somewhat dormant, and the issue of a huge national debt made some rounds in the early 1990s. The national debt reached a self-imposed limit of $5.5 trillion, and Congress refused to allow any more government expenditure in light of the limit. The federal government shut down for twelve days for non-emergency services, and a big political debate erupted. In due time, however, the limit was lifted and the government resumed work. In 2008, the national debt has reached roughly $9 trillion.

While fiscal policy performance was impressive in the 1990s, the big shock of September 11, 2001, changed the whole pattern of government expenditure, as well as taxes. From 2001 onward, government expenditures increased in a big way, partly due to national security issues. Moreover, the uncertainty and risk became so overwhelming that business investment declined, the housing market started stagnating, and the real GDP growth rate received a major setback. The rate of technological growth slowed down considerably in the years after 2001. If economic growth is mainly driven by technological growth, as some new models of economic growth argue (such as the one by Romer), then one of the prime reasons for the economic slowdown after 2001 has been the lack of it in the United States following the September 11 tragedy. Added to these economic hardships were two other events that slowed economic growth. The first event was the tremendous success of the euro as the common currency in major member countries of the European Union (EU). As the dollar started losing value with all major currencies of the world, partly due to the record-breaking trade deficits of the U.S. economy from 2001 to 2007, the relative importance of the euro grew significantly. This not only put pressure on the U.S. economic growth rate, but it also made U.S. imports more expensive in relative terms. Second, oil price increases after 2007 made the U.S. economy vulnerable to stagflation-like phenomena. No other nation is more dependent upon oil than the Unites States, as it consumes 33 percent of all oil produced in the world. Of course, the increase in oil prices hurts the U.S. economy the most. Clearly, U.S. fiscal policymakers have faced challenges in recent years due to all of these developments.

20.3 Historical Review of Monetary Policy-making in the United States

While the performance of fiscal policy has had some ups and downs in recent years, monetary policy, at least in the last few years, has been successful in avoiding any major inflation episodes. So, if inflation targeting is the new trend in monetary policy objectives, there has been remarkable success on this front. The most controversial behavior of monetary policy was in the Great Depression, however. There are several reasons why monetary policy was not very active in the early twentieth century.

First of all, the majority of the world was under the gold standard system, and the United States was an active member of this system, where changes in the money supply were not easy to make, as we learned in a previous chapter. Unless there was a change in the gold production of a country, any increase in the money supply was not possible. Second, the monetary theory that prevailed (namely, the old quantity theory of money) in those days proposed that any increase in the money supply is not necessary nor desirable, as it only leads to higher prices, and therefore inflation. Hence, any active monetary policy was not seen to be a good policy choice. Third, the Federal Reserve System, which has been examined in earlier chapters, was established only in 1913, and did not have a clear purpose of changing the money supply. It was believed that the main job of the Federal Reserve System was to control bank failures and act as a last resort in providing loans to the banking system. Hence, any discretionary increase in the money supply, even in the full brunt of depressionary forces (circa 1933), was not seen to be a viable option. For these reasons, the Federal Reserve did not serve as an active weapon to overcome the Great Depression, and that became a topic of great debate between Keynesians and Neo-Classical economists.

Keynesians argue that in the Great Depression the U.S. economy was already in a liquidity trap, and even if monetary policy had tried to do something about the Depression it could not have been successful. The interest rate had already reached a very low level, and monetary policy could not have been effective in those circumstances. Monetarists (especially Milton Friedman) argue that monetary policy and the Federal Reserve System did not do enough in those days. If there were some special actions, such as offering a free loan to the banking system or a purposeful substantial increase in the money supply, the situation could have been better controlled. The Great Depression was a problem of special magnitude and therefore it warranted a special policy step. According to monetarists, therefore, monetary policy did not take that special action, and therefore it is partially responsible for prolonging the Great Depression era. Several economists have tried to find a compromise for the behavior of the Federal Reserve during the Great Depression, but it remains an unsettled issue.

Just after the Great Depression, the major test of the Federal Reserve and monetary policy came with the advent of World War II. As one would expect, money supply was allowed to grow at a very high rate to finance war expenditures and to channel the resources into defense-oriented production. Of course, all bets are off when survival is at stake, and World War II was no exception to this general belief. In the post-1945 period, however, monetary policy became quite active, with deliberate changes in money supply to either lower the interest rate or to increase the aggregate demand, as was the case in the Korean War.

By 1950, the Keynesian argument which implied that "pegging the interest rate" should be the objective of monetary policy was getting popular and open market operation (OMO) was seen as an acceptable way to change the domestic money supply. In the 1960s the "bills only" policy of conducting monetary change became a popular tool. It essentially meant that short term Treasury bills (say a 91 day or less maturity period) were used in the open market to activate the change in money supply. The Keynesian philosophy was the dominant force in theoretical underpinnings of the Federal Reserve in the 1960s. The Federal Reserve Board was chaired by an eminent economist, William McChesney Martin, Jr., who had strong Keynesian leanings. Hence, the 1960s were characterized by interest rates as the main policy target and money supply change to effect the lowest possible interest was seen as the instrument to achieve desired objectives. In fact, conventional wisdom was that monetary policy can do several things at the same time, namely, increasing GDP, lowering inflation, reducing the interest rate, and achieving low unemployment. Major changes in money supply, as well as in interest rates, were commonplace, and the objectives of monetary policy were varied and complex. The experience of the late 1960s was somewhat disappointing, however. While the tremendous increase in the money supply led to high inflation, the targets of lowering unemployment and increasing GDP were not fulfilled. Therefore, monetarists started recognizing that besides controlling inflation, monetary policy should have no other objective. In their opinion, it was wrong that money supply was used to achieve so many things that its excessive increase gets nothing done. So, as we saw in earlier chapters, the recommendation of the "monetary rule" as the guide for monetary policy was seen as a significantly different, but an absolutely necessary, step.

While the controversy between monetarists and Neo-Keynesians started to get heated in the late 1960s, it reached its peak in the early 1970s. There were two separate groups of macroeconomists who advocated totally different paths for monetary policy conduct. As we have reviewed in earlier chapters, the arguments for and against the monetary rule, and the controversy between rules vs. discretion, seemed to be unending, with two completely opposite views of macroeconomists.

A stage of further confusion and controversy was set in the early 1970s, when outside shocks became more serious with high inflation, low GDP, stagflation, and high unemployment gripping the U.S. economy. The recession of 1975 was the most serious one after the Great Depression and, curiously enough, it was accompanied by high inflation. The monetary policy response to this clumsy and unprecedented situation was purely Keynesian. In fact, as Neo-Keynesians advocated that the stability of the Phillips Curve was still intact, and that there is only a rightward shift in the Phillips Curve, it was believed that to solve the same problem of unemployment, monetary policy had to be even more expansionary to raise the aggregate demand. It seems that the policymakers believed that the cure for unemployment was more important than the threat of further inflation. Hence, as Table 20.2 shows, the money supply (M1) was allowed to grow by roughly 25 percent from 1976 to 1980, while M2 grew by roughly 60 percent in the same period. This was done despite the inflationary forces already at work,

TABLE 20.2

	GDP	G	Tx	Federal Funds Rate	CPI	CPI Inflation Rate	M1	M2	Unemployment
1988	5,103.8	1,039.0	418.9	7.6	118.3	0.1	774.8	2,936.6	5.5
1989	5,484.4	1,099.1	438.2	9.2	124.0	4.8	782.2	3,060.0	5.3
1990	5,803.1	1,180.2	453.1	8.1	130.7	5.4	810.6	3,228.0	5.6
1991	5,995.9	1,234.4	454.5	5.7	136.2	4.2	859.0	3,348.0	6.8
1992	6,337.7	1,271.0	482.6	3.5			965.9	3,410.3	
1993	6,657.4	1,291.2	508.9	3.0	144.5	3.0	1,078.4	3,446.7	6.9
1994	7,072.2	1,325.5	541.6	4.2	148.2	2.6	1,145.2	3,494.2	6.1
1995	7,397.7	1,369.2	596.2	5.8	152.4	2.8	1,143.0	3,566.3	5.6
1996	7,816.9	1,416.0	666.7	5.3	156.9	3.0	1,106.8	3,738.0	5.4
1997	8,304.3	1,468.7	739.5	5.5	160.5	2.3	1,070.2	3,924.3	4.9
1998	8,747.0	1,518.3	813.6	5.4	163.0	1.6	1,080.7	4,207.5	4.5
1999	9,268.4	1,620.8	906.8	5.0	166.6	2.2	1,101.4	4,518.0	4.2
2000	9,817.0	1,721.6	1,018.2	6.2	172.2	3.4	1,103.6	4,785.4	4.0
2001	10,128.0	1,825.6	933.6	3.9	177.1	2.8	1,140.2	5,203.4	4.7
2002	10,469.6	1,961.1	836.8	1.7	179.9	1.6	1,196.2	5,592.9	5.8
2003	10,960.8	2,092.5	790.0	1.1	184.0	2.3	1,273.5	5,983.8	6.0
2004	11,712.5	2,226.2	884.3	1.4	188.9	2.7	1,344.4	6,266.3	5.5
2005	12,455.8	2,372.8	990.2	3.2	195.3	3.4	1,371.8	6,553.4	5.1
2006	13,246.6	2,527.7		5.0			1,374.4	6,858.7	4.6
2007				5.0			1,369.2	7,263.0	4.6

and reached the level of 13.5 percent in 1980. Additionally, the nominal interest rate reached a historical high of 16.4 percent in 1981. While the economic difficulties mounted in 1978 and got worse in 1979, the energy crisis also precipitated matters, as OPEC announced another price increase in 1979. There were strikes and lock-outs called by several labor unions, such as Greyhound bus drivers, the United Auto Workers, and the United Steel Workers. President Carter's administration needed to do something drastic to solve the problem of stagflation, so in July of 1979 the Chairman of the Federal Reserve Board, Arthur Burns, was replaced by a strong monetarist, Paul Volcker.

As soon as Paul Volcker took office, his new direction and influence on monetary policy were visible. On October 7, 1979, the Federal Open Market Committee called an emergency meeting, and a dramatic announcement was made with the following basic conclusion: The Federal Reserve would keep money supply growth under check, irrespective of the interest rate level, and the target of the monetary policy would be to keep money supply growth within a restrictive band, while the interest rate would be allowed to move in a larger band of fluctuation. With an announcement of this kind, the financial community realized that cash was not easy to come by, so the stock market on the next day retracted and the interest rate started moving up. By July 1981, recessionary forces were quite underway, and during 1982 and 1983, the GDP became quite sluggish with a full-blown severe recession. With high interest rates, private domestic investment declined, but foreign financial investment increased, creating an upward pressure on the value of the U.S. dollar in the international market. By 1982, another change in monetary policy was visible, but a formal announcement about it was meticulously absent. From 1983, both M1 and M2 show a drastic increase without any formal acceptance by monetary policy to have made an official change in the stable money supply as its target. In fact, in macroeconomic literature, the change in money supply from 1979 to 1983 is considered to be a "monetarist experiment" of the Federal Reserve.

Unfortunately the monetarist experiment was not very successful; in fact, it only raised the interest rate and lowered GDP growth, but it achieved its main purpose of lowering the inflation rate from 13.5 percent in 1980 to 6.2 percent in 1982 and to 3.2 percent in 1983 (see Table 20.1). In 1983, the unannounced (unanticipated by economic agents) increase in money supply also worked as a wonder. While the interest rate started declining in 1984, investment and GDP picked up and the Reagan administration became one of the most successful administrations in making an economic turnaround in such a short period. (As President Reagan put it several times, the economy was "bottoming up," and economic turnaround was the most important of his administration's achievements in his opinion). The Volcker years, from 1979 to 1987, were somewhat turbulent, but mostly very successful in achieving remarkable economic growth. From 1987 to 1990, the U.S. economy further increased its productivity and growth, so that the 1980s broke the record of the 1960s and became the most prosperous decade in the history of the United States. While this economic turnaround was being achieved, the money supply was increasing at a very high rate but inflation was declining! Specifically, from 1983 to 1989, this inverse relationship between money supply and inflation rate is quite visible. While this would put monetarism in a big quandary, it does not have great support from traditional macroeconomic principles, except through the expectations hypothesis. As we learned before, policy effectiveness is the highest when a money supply increase is "unanticipated or unexpected." No other administration can claim the success of the Reagan administration, partly because correct and complete information was not provided to the economic decision makers in those years. (Maybe President Reagan was a great actor, after all!) When economic forces were in negative territory, he provided confidence by discarding the existence of the energy crisis, boasting about the greatness of American society, labor productivity, optimism, and putting his public zeal to work. All of these things appeared to be more crucial for policy effectiveness than the policy actions themselves.

In July 1987, as Paul Volcker finished his second term, Alan Greenspan was chosen by President Reagan as the chairman of the Federal Reserve Board, and as we now know, he served the longest term of any chairman, until 2006. During his leadership, economic changes occurred in such a wonderful way that the inflation rate rarely went above 7 percent (in fact, in some years it even reached 2 to 3 percent, as can be seen in Table 20.2). The real GDP grew substantially, interest rates stayed moderately low, and real domestic private investment was high. The stock market saw some of its most glorious days in the history of the United States, and growth in all macroeconomic sectors was at enviable levels. The American dominance in total factory productivity, technological innovation, and industrial output was spreading all over. In fact, as mentioned before, the 1990s were the most prosperous years of any time. As Table 20.2 shows, all macroeconomic variables were in unprecedented territory. The monetary policy in these years was prudent, pragmatic, and was in general carefully carved.

However, the biggest challenge to the management skills of Alan Greenspan and his team came after September 11, 2001. The tremendous loss in the tragic events of that day was financially devastating to the U.S. economy. The overall response of the monetary policy to these events was to lower the interest rate further; in fact, the discount rate went as low as 1.25 percent in 2002. This made some adventurous mortgage bankers lend money at sub-prime rates and at very high amounts (for example, 120 percent of the value of the house). As housing prices declined in 2007 and onward, the economy went through a severe housing crisis. The money supply growth rates from 2003 forward were not exceedingly high, but lower technological growth, overall uncertainty, the lower willingness of producers to take risks, and the onset of the Iraq War combined to result in sluggish economic growth. The future of monetary policy will be decided by how accurate policy changes are and how they are anticipated. Therefore, in general, the effect of monetary policy from 1983 onward has been remarkably successful, leading to greater importance of the Federal Reserve System

This chapter has connected all the theories discussed in earlier chapters regarding the U.S. economy. In essence, the ability of any theory to describe realistic events in accordance to its prescription defines its success. It is, therefore, fascinating to see that most of the theories that we have discussed have amazing value and great application. No wonder that the economic profession is valued so highly, as it is quite evident that few understand it so clearly.

Suggested Further Reading

Barro, R. 2008. *Macroeconomics: A Modern Approach,* Chapters 12, 13, 15, and 16. Thomson/Southwestern Publications.

Blanchard, O. 2008. *Macroeconomics,* 5 ed., Chapters 24–27. Pearson.

Froyen, R. T. 2006. *Macroeconomics: Theories and Policies,* 7 ed., Chapters 17 and 18. Prentice Hall.

Kulkarni, K. *Simplified Macro-Monetary Theory,* Chapters 7–9. New Delhi: Serials Publications.

Index

A

accelerationist theory, 212, 217–218
accelerator, 205
accelerator-multiplier theory, 200, 205
adaptive expectation theory, 223, 226–227
aggregate demand, 34, 37, 71, 144
    with active government, 92f
    in commodity market, 75
    composition of, 277
    curve, 87, 287f
    excess, 190
    influencing structure of, 92
    raising, 93
    representing, 77
    stable, 180
aggregate demand schedule
    characteristics of, 282–283 derivation of, 279–283, 282f
aggregate demand-aggregate supply framework, 265, 277. *See also* aggregate demand; aggregate supply
    classical economists view on, 268f, 269, 288–290
    Keynesian views on, 268f, 269, 290–292
    monetarists view on, 269–270, 270f
    stagflation and, 271f
    as tool, 279
aggregate supply, 34, 37, 72, 92, 144
    determining, 278
    reduced, 190
aggregate supply curve, 287f
    derivation of, 283–288
agriculture sector, 200
air traffic controllers strike, 311
airfares, 31
Aldrich-Vreeland Act, 129
Alexander, Sidney, 259
Allen, R. G. D., 148

APC. *See* average propensity to consume
APS. *See* average propensity to save
arbitragers, 29
Argentina, 112
assets
    monetarists' definition of, 175
    stock of, 81
ATS. *See* automatic transfer to savings
Austria, 56–57
automatic transfer to savings (ATS), 106
autonomous investment multiplier, 75, 77
autonomous spending multiplier, 90
average propensity to consume (APC), 79
average propensity to save (APS), 83

B

balance of payments (BOP), 236, 251–259, 298
    absorption approach to, 259
    behavior of, 259–262
    deficit in, 251
    elasticity approach to, 259
    measuring, 236
    monetary approach to, 260
bankers' acceptances, 108
banking
    correspondence, 117
    fractional reserve, 123
    free system of, 116
    regulations, 104
banks. *See also specific banks*
    commercial, 116–118
    controlling failure of, 308, 316
    money creation from, 104, 118–121
    mutual saving, 116
    "run on the," 120
Barro, Robert, 266, 273
BB curve, 236, 255, 256f
    general equilibrium using, 257f

Bentham, Jeremy, 141, 143
Bernanke, Ben, 130
"best government is the one that governs least," 63
bimetalism, 111
bimetallic standard, 54
black market, 31
Board of Governors, 127
bond(s), 108
    market, 69
BOP. *See* balance of payments
Brazil, 112
Bretton Woods agreement, 46
Bretton Woods system, 57–59, 297, 310
    as adjustable peg, 58
    breakdown of, 47, 295, 298
Brunner, Karl, 172
business cycles, 201–203
    cause of, 203–206
    governmental actions and, 52
    near monies and, 109
    politics and, 206
    reducing, 180
    stages of, 199
"by keeping all other things constant," 18

C

Cagan, Phillip, 226
Cambridge equation, 148, 149
capital, 1, 4
    account balance, 252
    consumption allowance, 41
    financial, 5
    market, 67
    physical, 5
capitalism, 1, 6
cattle, 110
CCC. *See* Civilian Conservation Corps
certificates of deposits, 105
ceteris paribus, 18
checking deposits, 111–112
    ordinary, 106
    types of, 106
check-less society, 112
circular flow, 1
    types of, 6

Civil War, 55
Civilian Conservation Corps (CCC), 98
coffee, 21
coins, 106, 111–112
    Federal Reserve Banks and, 135
    unfit, 135
COLA. *See* cost of living index
commercial paper, 108
commodity market, 67, 73
    aggregate demand in, 75
commodity market equilibrium, IS curve and, 237–240
communism, 1, 6
consumer price index (CPI), 33, 36, 189
consumer sector, 38, 77
consumers, number of, 21
consumption, 19, 75, 77
    behavior, 78–80
    capital, allowance, 41
    change in, 79
    decline in, 93
    determinants of, 80–81
    determinants of, "non-income," 81
    function, 79*f*
    income and, 78
    near monies changing, 109
Cooper, Richard, 56
copper, 110
cost of living index (COLA), 35, 194
cost-push factors, 190
CPI. *See* consumer price index
Credibility Hypothesis, 232, 314
credit
    cards, 115
    consumer, 81
credit unions (CUs), 116
crowding out hypothesis, 182–184, 312
currency, 54, 111–112, 300. *See also specific currencies*
    Federal Reserve Banks and, 135
    physical, 122
    unfit, 135
current account, balance on, 252
CUs. *See* credit unions

D

debt contracts, 115
debt, national, 182
    2008, 314
deficit
    balance of payments, 251
    financing, 191
    payment, 59
    trade, 308
demand. *See also* aggregate demand; money demand
    bond market, 69
    changes in, 22
    deposits, 105
    excess, 132, 141
    foreign exchange, 254, 255f
    in loanable funds market, 69, 70f, 71f
    management policies, 237
    market, 16
    needs and, difference between, 17
    schedule, 18, 18f
demand curve
    demographic distribution and, 21
    income and, 21
    inverse relationship and, 19f
    for policy decisions, 29–32
    shift in, 12f, 20f, 21
demand, law of, 15, 18
    justification for, 15
    validity of, 19
demand-pull factors, 190
demographic distribution, 21
Denison's law, 183
Denmark, 299
Depository Institutions De-Regulation and Monetary Control Act (DIDMCA), 117
depreciation, 41
depression, 199, 201. *See also* Great Depression
DIDMCA. *See* Depository Institutions De-Regulation and Monetary Control Act
discount rate, 73, 133
    changes, 134, 137
    reduction in, 137
discount window, 134

"discounts and advances," 133
double-entry bookkeeping techniques, 146, 251
Douglas, Paul, 143

E

economic and monetary union (EMU), 60
The Economic Consequences of Peace (Keynes), 96
economic development, 43
economic growth, 9
economic hypothesis, 12
economic stagnation, 53
economic system, 6
economics
    branches of, 4
    defining, completely/correctly, 3
    Keynes description of, 3
    normative, 2, 7
    positive, 2, 7
    Robbins on, 3, 4
    supply-side, 266, 271, 312
    Viner on, 3
economics, classical, 307
    aggregate demand-aggregate supply framework and, 268f, 269, 288–290
    historical background of, 143–144
    Keynes revolution against, 64
    labor market and, 289f
economy
    barter, 113
    closed, 86
    money supply on, effects of, 153
ECU. *See* European Currency Unit
EEC. *See* European Economic Community
Effective Market Classification rule, 209
Elementary Principles of Economics (Fisher), 145
Eltis, Walter, 100, 101
EMI. *See* European Monetary Institute
employment, full, 92, 93
    government role in, 93
    Keynes on, 93
EMS. *See* European Monetary System
EMU. *See* economic and monetary union
energy conservation, 311
enterprise, 1, 4, 5

equation of exchange, 146
    criticisms of, 148
    revision of, 169
EU. *See* European Union
euro
    evolution of, 299–300
    future of, 300
    success of, 315
Eurodollars, 108
Euroland, 300
European Central Bank, 300
European Currency Unit (ECU), 296. *See also* euro
    renaming of, 299
European Economic Community (EEC), 59
European Monetary Institute (EMI), 296
    creation of, 300
European Monetary System (EMS), 46, 59, 296, 299
    lessons from, 301
    success of, 60
European Monetary Union, 296
European Union (EU), 315
    money supply, 125, 126f
Eurozone, 300
exchange rates, 253
    adjustable peg system of, 303
    adjustment policy, 101
    equilibrium, 254
    fixed, 302
    flexible, 303
    government determined, 303
    internal fixity of, 301
    mint, 55
    predetermined, 302
expenditure, 38–39
    consumer class, 78
    curve, 86f
expenditure, government, 39, 75, 77, 93, 247, 308
    increased, 190–191
expenditure line, total, 87
exports, 77
    net, 39, 252

F

federal funds rate, 133
Federal Open Market Committee (FOMC), 127
    decision-making process of, 132
    meetings of, 132
    membership of, 131
    organization of, 131–132
Federal Reserve Banks, 127
    automated clearinghouses, 136
    board of directors, 133–134
    check processing, 135–136
    coins and, 135
    currency and, 135
    depository institution services, 135–136
    government services, 135
    monetary policy role of, 134
    New York, 134, 137
    organization of, 133–134
    regulation, 134–135
    supervision, 134–135
    wire transfers, 136
Federal Reserve Board (FRB), 127
    decisions made by, 131
    functions of, 130–133
    membership to, 130–133
Federal Reserve Communications System, 136
Federal Reserve Note, 129
Federal Reserve System, 103, 316
    authority layers of, 127
    establishment of, 308
    objectives of, initial, 308
    origin of, 129
Fellner, William, 232
financial institutions (FIs), 104
    functions of, 117
FIs. *See* financial institutions
fiscal policy, 93, 237, 309–315
activism on, 181
    announcing, 228
    effectiveness of, 225–226, 225f, 228
    expansionary, 101, 182, 240, 308, 311–312, 314
    foreign trade and, 100–102
    "great debate" for adopting, 311

Great Depression and, 307, 309
IS-LM framework and, 247f
pure, 182
Fisher, Irving, 69, 139, 141, 143
health insurance and, 145
on inflation, 71
life of, 144–146
Fisherian equation, 146, 149
flow concept, 109
FOMC. *See* Federal Open Market Committee
foreign exchange market, 253–254
demand for, 254, 255f
equilibrium of, 254–259
supply for, 254, 255f
foreign trade sector, 39, 77
fiscal policy and, 100–102
FRB. *See* Federal Reserve Board
free information, 228
Friedman, Milton, 169, 172, 207, 217, 311
"luxury goods" thesis of, 179
on money demand, 173
Frisch, Ragnar, 144

G

garbage-in-garbage-out (GIGO), 41
gasoline quotas, 311
GDP. *See* Gross Domestic Product
General Price Level, 37
General Theory of Employment, Interest and Money (Keynes), 73, 77, 95, 149
geometry, 9
Germany, 298
Ghana, 31
GIGO. *See* garbage-in-garbage-out
Glass, Carter, 129
GNP. *See* Gross National Product
gold, 110
excess of, 49
market price, 54
mint price, 48
mint ration of gold to, 54
for non-monetary purposes, 51f
pound sterling and, 55
refusal to revalue, 298
related commodities, 50

scarcity of, 110
stock growth, 56
supply curve, 48
Gold Exchange Standard, 297
gold standard, 45, 295, 297, 315
Austria and, 56–57
benefits of, 45, 52
breakdown, 45, 47, 53
classical, 47, 54–56
contempt for, 53
defecting from, 53
drawbacks to, 53
without gold, 60
Great Britain and, 57
heyday of, 47
historical perspectives, 54–59
inflation and, 46
international, 54
international price equalization and, 52
inter-war years, 56–57
money supply under, 48
pre-World War I, 56
returning back to, 52–53
rules of, 48
stability of, 52
success of, 55
Sweden and, 57
World War I and, 47
goods
complementary, 21
consumer, 36
final, 33, 35
generic, 20
inferior, 20
intermediate, 36
luxury, 179
market, 71, 72f
normal, 20
stock of durable, 81
substitutes of, 21
goods and services account, balance of, 251–252
government activism, 169
government sector, 38, 77, 91–94
full employment and, 93

graphs, drawing, 9–12
Gray, John, 143
Great Britain
    gold standard and, 57
    inflation in early 1800s, 141
Great Depression, 143, 316
    economic situation in, 73, 74t
    fiscal policy in, 309
    fiscal policy response to, 307
    Keynes and, 95
    monetary policy during, 164–165
    United States policies during, 96–97
Greenspan, Alan, 130, 139, 320
    criticism of, 131
Gresham's law, 111
Greyhound bus drivers strike, 311
Gross Domestic Product (GDP), 35
    adjustment for calculation of, 37
    criticism of, 34
    data on, 44
    deflator, 33, 37
    equilibrium level of, 75, 92
    gap, 76
    limitations of, 34, 43
    1929, 309
    nominal, 36
    potential level of, 65
    real, 33, 37
    theoretical definition of, 35
    total income approach to, 40
Gross National Product (GNP), 33, 35

H
Hansen, Alvin, 204
HDI. *See* human development index
health insurance, 98
    Fisher and, 145
health, public, 98
Hicks, John R., 237
Hoover, Herbert, 73
horizontal summation, 27
housing crisis, 308
How to Live (Fisher), 145
human
    behavior, 12
    capital formation, 273–274

human development index (HDI), 44
Hume, David, 139, 143

I
IBT. *See* taxes, indirect business
ID. *See* initial deposit
illegal transaction, 31, 43
    price controls and, 197
illiquid, risk of being, 158
IMF. *See* International Monetary Fund
imports, 39, 77
    function, 253
income
    consumption and, 78
    demand curve and, 21
    distribution, 6
    effect, 18, 170, 177–178
    equilibrium line of, 87
    final national, 33
    high disposable, 191
    money and, 109
    permanent, 174, 176, 207
    personal, 4
    policy, 196
    time interval for receipt of, 157
income, equilibrium
    changes in, 88
    determination, 88f
income, national (NI), 41
income, per capita (PCI), 41
income-expenditure theory, 173
indebtedness, consumer, 81
Index Number Institute, 145
India, 41
    Keynes and, 96
    macro-monetary theory and, 267–274
    monetary theory and, 274–275
    money supply management in, 274–275
Indira Gandhi Institute of Development
    Research, 275
Indonesia, 112
inelasticity, 129
inflation, 52
    balanced budget and, 195
    causes of, 189–192
    consequences of, 188, 192–195

costs of, imaginary, 192–193
costs of, real, 193
cure for, 52, 188, 195–197
in early 1800s Great Britain, 141
expectation of, 71, 86
Fisher on, 71
future, 221, 223
gold standard and, 46
marginal efficiency of capital and, 85
measuring, 189
monetarist model of importation of, 261
rate, 81
run-away, 112, 193
social view of, 194
targeting, 315
tax, 47
types of, 187
unemployment and, 169, 211
world-wide, 53
inflation, cost-push, 182, 187, 265, 270
cause of, 191–192
natural calamities and, 192
unions and, 192
inflation, demand-pull, 182, 187, 288
cause of, 191
initial deposit (ID), 120, 137
innovators, psychology of, 203–204
insurance companies, 117
interest rate, 73, 245
money demand and, inverse relationship between, 161
money substitutes and, 158
mortgage, 10
nominal, 71
normal, 160
pegging, 166, 316
real, 71, 155
saving and, 84
Thomas on, 160
intermediaries, 29
International Financial Statistics, 44
International Monetary Fund (IMF), 44, 252
creation of, 58, 297
substitution account in, 304–305
international monetary system, 57

basket-type, 301
flexibility in, 58
future of, 59–60
improving, 301–305
objectives of, 301
snake-type, 301
international openness, 273–274
international price equalization, 46
gold standard and, 52
interventionists, 201, 208–209. *See also* non-interventionalists
investment, 75, 77
changing, 240
determination, 163f
elasticity of, 240
factors, 84
financial, 84
function, 100
as injection, 87
Keynes on, 86
marginal efficiency of capital and, 85
optimal, 85f
real, 84
responsiveness of, 240
"invisible hand of nature," 17
Iran hostage crisis, 311
Iraq War, 320
iron, 110
IS curve, 235
commodity market equilibrium and, 237–240
derivation of, 237, 239f
IS-LM framework, 235. *See also* IS curve; LM curve
advantages of, 244, 245
disturbances in real sector and, 246–250
fiscal policy and, 247f
general equilibrium and, 244f
monetary disturbances and, 245–246
weaknesses of, 277

J

Japan, 298
jawboning, 139
Jevons, William, 200, 203
Johnson, Harry, 260

K

Kennedy, John F., 310
Keynes, John Maynard, 57, 58, 73, 77, 149
    classical economies, revolution against, 64
    death of, 96
    describing economics, 3
    education of, 95
    on full employment, 93
    Great Depression and analysis of, 95
    health of, 96
    Indian finance and, 96
    influence of, 94–95
    on investment, 86
    life of, 95–96
    main message of, 94
    on monetary policy, 162–166
    policy recommendations by, 171
    popularity of, 76
    Roosevelt and, 97
    on Say's Law of Market, 66
    shortcomings, 99
Keynesian chain, 163, 164, 231
    break down of, 164, 248
Keynesian Cross, 87, 265
    decline in emphasis on, 267
Keynesians, 94
    aggregate demand-aggregate supply framework and, 268f, 269, 290–292
Korean War, 316

L

labor, 1, 4
labor market, 67, 73
    analysis and optimum employment, 284f
    classical economics and, 289f
    equilibrium, 67, 68, 285f
Laffer, Arthur, 271, 312
Laffer Curve, 272, 272f, 312, 312f
laissez faire, 65, 143, 150, 307, 309
land, 1, 4
    reward for, 5
law of changeable returns, 284, 286
LDCs. *See* less-developed countries
legal requirement ratio (LRR), 118–119, 131
    changes in, 138

legal tender, 106, 111, 112
Lerner, Abba, 259
less-developed countries (LDCs), 42
"Let the economy function by itself," 63
Lewis, Arthur, 31, 196
Life Extension Institute, 145
liquidity
    of money, 114–115
    preference, 115, 159
    preference curve, 159–160, 159f
    risk and returns, 115
liquidity effect, 170, 177
liquidity trap, 154, 164, 173, 247, 248, 316
    LM curve and, 249f
    monetary policy and, 165f
    money demand curve and, 248f
liquor, 110
LM curve, 235, 236, 242f
    derivation of, 237
    liquidity trap and, 249f
    money market equilibrium and derivation of, 240–243
    quantity theory of money and, 249
    shifts in, 243
loanable funds market
    demand in, 69, 70f, 71f
    supply in, 69, 70f, 71f
Loanable Funds Theory, 69–73
    criticism of, 70
    modifying conclusion of, 71
LRR. *See* legal requirement ratio
Lucas, Robert, 228

M

Maastricht Treaty of 1993, 296
    approval of, 299
macroeconomics, 1, 4
    general equilibrium of, 243–245
    theory, 65
macro-monetary theory, 153
    India and, 267–274
    in open economy setting, 250
"The Making of Index Numbers" (Fisher), 145
margin requirements, 138

marginal efficiency of capital (MEC), 77, 84, 154
    inflation rate and, 85
    investment and, 85
    production cost and, 85
    value of, 85
marginal efficiency of investment (MEI), 84
    increase in, 192
marginal propensity to consume (MPC)
    instability of, 99
    value of, 90
    value of, estimating, 99
marginal propensity to save (MPS), 83
market. *See also specific markets*
    equilibrium, 28*f*
    mechanism, 17
    value, 33, 35
Marshall, Alfred, 18, 96, 143, 148, 259
Marshall-Lerner condition, 101, 236, 259
Martin, William McChesney, Jr., 131, 317
"Mathematical Investigations in Theory of Value and Prices" (Fisher), 144
measure of economic welfare (MEW), 34, 43
MEC. *See* marginal efficiency of capital
MEI. *See* marginal efficiency of investment
metals. *See also specific metals*
    availability of, 110
    durability of, 110
    stability of, 110
MEW. *See* measure of economic welfare
microeconomics, 1, 4
    Say's Law of Market and, 66
middlemen, 29
Mill, John Stuart, 65, 143
Minford, Patrick, 266, 273
misery index, 310
monetarists, 166, 172
    aggregate demand-aggregate supply framework and, 269–270, 270*f*
    definition of assets, 175
    definition of wealth, 170
    evolution of, 184
    model of importation of inflation, 261
    popularity of, 179

Monetary Control Act of 1980, 134
monetary policy, 122, 127, 237
    announcing, 228
    effectiveness of, 162, 162*f*, 225–226, 225*f*, 228, 231
    in Great Depression, 164–165
    historical review of, 315–320
    IS-LM framework and, 246*f*
    Keynes on, 162–166
    liquidity trap and, 165*f*
    role of Federal Reserve Banks, 134
    transmission mechanism for, 176–182
monetary rule, 195
monetary standards, 111
monetary theory, 77, 139, 143
    India and, 274–275
    origins of, 144
    weaknesses of classical, 153
money
    behavioral definition of, 105
    broad, 122
    creation from banks, 104, 118–121
    easy, 165
    evolution of, 110–113
    full-bodied commodity, 111
    functional definition of, 105
    functions of, 103, 113–115
    glamour and, 110
    hoarding, 156
    illusion, 280, 291
    income and, 109
    liquidity of, 114–115
    managed, 297
    as means of transfer payments, 113
    as measure of deferred payment, 115
    as measure of value, 113, 114
    as medium of exchange, 113
    narrow, 122
    paper, 54
    physical definition of, 105
    real output of, 141
    representative commodity, 111
    small denominations, 106
    as store of value, 113, 114, 149

money (continued)
    substitutes and interest rate, 158
    as total debt of government and commercial banks, 105
    understanding meaning of, 105
    velocity of, 141, 169, 173
    wealth and, 110
money creation model
    assumption 1, 118
    assumption 2, 118–119
    assumption 3, 119–120
money demand, 156–157, 241
    determining, 160–161, 170, 174–175
    Friedman on, 173
    functions of, 175
    interest rate and, inverse relationship between, 161
    interpretations of, 176f
    liquidity trap and, 248f
    precautionary, 153, 158
    speculative, 153, 158–160, 164
    stability of, 173
    transactionary, 153, 156–158, 156f
    types of, 153
"money does not matter," 164, 173
money flow, 6, 7, 7f
money market, 67, 73
money market equilibrium, 154, 160–161, 161f, 164, 177f, 241, 241f
    derivation of LM curve and, 240–243
money, quantity theory of, 146–150
    criticisms of, 148
    developments in, 172–176
    inconsistencies in, 148
    LM curve and, 249
    revised, 172
    revised, implications of, 179–182
money supply, 103, 240
    around world, 123–126
    data, 107t
    determining, 161
    on economy, 153
    European Union, 125, 126f
    figures, 108t
    under gold standard, 48
    L, 106, 108
    M_0, 122, 124, 125
    M_1, 106, 111–112, 122, 124
    M_2, 106, 122, 124
    M_3, 122, 125
    M_4, 125
    management in India, 274–275
    measures of, 103
    tools for, 136–139
    of United Kingdom, 125
    United States, 123–125, 123f
    value of, 49
mono-metalism, 111
moral suasion, 138
Morgan, J. P., 129
Morgenstern, Oskar, 41
MPC. *See* marginal propensity to consume
MPS. *See* marginal propensity to save
Muth, John, 226

N

National Health Conference in 1938, 98
National Health Program, 98–99
national income accounting, 33, 35
National Institute of Bank Management in Pune, 275
National Monetary Commission, 129
national pride, 58
Natural Rate Hypothesis (NRH), 218, 219
natural resources, 98
The Nature of Capital and Income (Fisher), 146
NDP. *See* net domestic product
near monies, 108
    business cycles and, 109
    changing consumption, 109
    consequences of, 109
negotiable order of withdrawal (NOW), 106
net domestic product (NDP), 33, 41
net economic welfare (NEW), 34, 43
NEW. *See* net economic welfare
New Deal, 95, 97–98, 307, 309
    recovery, 97
    reform, 97
    relief, 97
    second, 98

New Growth Theory, 266, 274
    factors, 273
NI. *See* income, national
non-interventionalists, 201, 206–208. *See also* interventionists
non-market transactions, 41
    examples of, 42
Nordhaus, William, 43
normal goods, 20
NOW. *See* negotiable order of withdrawal
NRH. *See* Natural Rate Hypothesis
nuclear radiation, 42

O

official reserve settlement balance, 252–253
offset coefficient, 261
offset effect, 261
OMO. *See* Open Market Operations
OPEC. *See* Organization of Petroleum Exporting Countries
Open Market Operations (OMO), 136–137, 316
opportunity cost, 5, 6
optimal currency area, 300
Organization of Petroleum Exporting Countries (OPEC), 270, 310
Owen, Robert L., 129

P

Paper Credit (Thornton), 144
paradox of flexibility, 28, 72, 161
Patinkin, Don, 172
Paul, Ron, 125
PCI. *See* income, per capita
Phelps, Edmond, 217
Phillips, Arthur William Housego, 210, 213
Phillips Curve, Expectation Augmented, 212, 220–221
Phillips Curve Hypothesis, 193, 211, 309, 317
    accelerationists, 219*f*
    doubts about, 217
    introduction of, 307
    modern, 216*f*
    non-accelerationists, 220*f*
    original, 214*f*
    popularity of, 212, 215

pianos, 145
Pigou, A. C., 148
portfolio decision, 115
postponement of payments, 115
potential money multiplier, 120
pound sterling, 301
    gold and, 55
    overvalued, 57
PPC. *See* production possibilities curve
PPF. *See* production possibilities frontier
PPI. *See* producer price index
price, 114
    bubble-effect on, 196
    ceiling policy, 30
    as dependent variable, 18
    effect, 170, 178
    expected, 81
    floor policy, 31, 32*f*
    future, 21
    of gold, 54
    index, 33, 36
    law of one, 46, 52
    level, 176
    market-determined, 30
    stability, 56
    votes, 17
price controls, 29–30, 196, 197
    economic consequences of, 30
    illegal transactions and, 197
    Lewis on, 31
price, mint, 45, 295
    gold, 48
prime rate, 133
producer price index (PPI), 33, 37
producer sector, 38, 77
producer surplus, 26–27, 26*f*
product market, 77
production
    cost of, 25
    diseconomies of, 42
    distribution, 6, 43
    factors of, 1, 4
    of Germany, 298
    of Japan, 298
    joint, 25

production *(continued)*
    marginal efficiency of capital and, 85
    negative externalities of, 42
    of Switzerland, 298
    technology of, 25
production possibilities curve (PPC), 2, 8, 8f
    shape of, 8
production possibilities frontier (PPF), 8
profitability effect, 24
profit-seeking research/development, 273–274
property, 110
prosperity, 199, 202
protectionism, 311
Pujo, Arsène P., 129
Pujo Commission, 129
The Purchasing Power of Money (Fisher), 146
purchasing power parity theory, 262

Q
quadrants, 2
quality controls, 197
quantity controls, 197
quantity theory equation, 147
    modification of, 148

R
rational expectation theory, 223, 224, 227–230, 314
RBI. *See* Reserve Bank of India
Reagan, Ronald, 310
Reaganomics. *See* supply-side economics
real flow, 6, 7f
recession, 199, 203, 319
    1975, 310
recovery, 199, 202
related products, 21
rent, 5
Reserve Bank of India (RBI), 266
    controlled expansion of, 275
    Economic Analysis Wing, 275
    functions of, 274
Reserve Bank of India Act, 274
resource allocation effect, 196
resource cost, 25

reward for land, 5
Ricardo, David, 65, 143
Robbins, Lionel, 1
    on economics, 3, 4
Robertson, Dennis, 70
Romer, Paul, 273
Roosevelt, Franklin, 95
    Keynes and, 97

S
Samuelson, Paul, 42, 100, 200, 205
Sargent, Thomas, 227–228
saving
    determinants of, non-income, 84
    function, 82–84
    interest rate and, 84
    as leakage, 87
    line, 11
saving and loan associations (S&Ls), 116
Say, John Baptiste, 63, 65, 143
Say's Law of Market, 63, 66
    Keynes on, 66
    on microeconomic level, 66
Schumpeter, Joseph, 200, 203
SDRs. *See* Special Drawing Rights
secular stagnation hypothesis, 200, 204
seigniorage, 112
Senate Banking Committee, 139
September 11, 2001, 308, 314–315, 320
silver, 50, 110
    mint ratio of gold to, 54
simplified money multiplier, 120
Skidelsky, Robert, 97
slope, 2, 11
    defining, 10
S&Ls. *See* saving and loan associations
Smith, Adam, 17, 65
social programs, 93
Social Security, 309
socialism, 6
Southeast Asian crisis, 112
Special Drawing Rights (SDRs), 108, 252, 304
specialization, 113
stabilization policies, 201, 237

stagflation, 102, 169, 171, 194, 212, 288
    aggregate demand-aggregate supply framework and, 271f
    peak of, 268
Stein, Herbert, 251
stock, 108
    concept, 109
    of durable goods, 81
    gold, growth of, 56
substitution effect, 18, 24
    on consumption side, 19
Summer, William Graham, 144
sunspots theory, 200, 203
supply. *See also* aggregate supply
    bond market, 69
    excess, 141, 143
    foreign exchange, 254, 255f
    in loanable funds market, 69, 70f, 71f
    schedule, 24, 24t
"supply creates its own demand," 63, 66
supply curve, 24
    of gold, 48
    individual, 27-29, 27f
    market, 27-29, 27f
    for policy decisions, 29-32
    shift in, 26
supply, law of, 15, 23-26
    justification for, 15
    validity of, 24
supply-side economics, 266, 271, 312
surplus, consumer, 22-23
Sweden, 57
Switzerland, 298
symmetalism, 111
System Open Market Account, 132

T

target zone proposal, 60
taxes, 40, 81
    business, 25
    decreased, 191
    direct, 91
    evading, 44, 312
    gift, 91
    indirect, 91
    inflation, 47
    as leakages, 91
    multiplier, 94
    property, 91
    Reagan administration cut in, 272
    responsibility for, 91
taxes, income, 91
    filing simplification, 312
    lump-sum, 91
    raising, 93
    rebates of 1966, 309
    structure of, 22
taxes, indirect business (IBT), 41
Taylor, John, 272-273
Taylor's rule, 266, 272-273
tea, 110
technology
    distribution, 6
    revolution, 308
Tennes*See* Valley Authority, 98
Thatcher, Margaret, 271
The Theory of Interest Rates (Fisher), 145
"there is no such thing as a free lunch," 1, 5
Thomas, Lloyd, Jr., 110, 111
    on interest rate, 160
Thornton, Henry, 143, 144
Three Mile Island Nuclear Generating Station, 42
time deposits, 105
time lag
    data, 230
    impact, 224, 230
    implementation, 207, 224, 230
    inside, 207, 224, 230
    non-interventionists and, 225
    outside, 207, 224, 230, 231
    recognition, 207, 230
    transmission, 224, 230
    types of, 230
tobacco, 110
Tobin, James, 43
trade
    deficit, 308

trade *(continued)*
    liberalization, 273–274
    war, 299
traveler's checks, 112
Treasury securities, 136
Treatise on Probability (Keynes), 96
trough, 201

U

unemployment, 98
    inflation and, 169, 211
    as surplus of labor, 214
    voluntary, 65
United States Coinage Act of 1792, 54
United States Coinage Act of 1834, 54

V

value of marginal product of labor (VMPL), 285
variables, 9
    examples of, 9
    independent, 2, 9–10
    relationships of, 9
    relationships of, direct, 10
    relationships of, inverse, 10
    relationships of, negative, 10
    relationships of, positive, 10
variables, dependent, 2, 9
    price as, 18
Versailles Peace Conference, 96
Vietnam War, 59, 310
Viner, Jacob, 3
VMPL. *See* value of marginal product of labor
Volcker, Paul, 131, 318, 320

W

wage rate, 67, 285
    equilibrium, 286
    quantity of labor v., 68f
    sticky, 188
wage-price spiral, 196
Wallace, Neil, 228
Walras Law, 67, 236, 256–257
wants
    collective, 3, 4
    double coincidence of, 113
    individual, 3–4
    social, 4
war. *See specific wars*
wealth, 173–174
    monetarist definition of, 170
    money and, 110
Wealth of Nations (Smith), 17
White, Harry, 58
Wholesale Price Index, 37
Wickstead, P., 105
wire transfers, 136
world central bank, 303–304
    argument for, 304
World War I
    gold standard and, 47
    outbreak of, 56
World War II, 309, 316
    United States policies during, 96–97

Z

"zone of monetary stability," 59